Indigenous Research of Land, Self, and Spirit

Robin Throne
University of the Cumberlands, USA

IGI Global
PUBLISHER of TIMELY KNOWLEDGE

A volume in the Advances in Religious and Cultural Studies (ARCS) Book Series

Published in the United States of America by
IGI Global
Information Science Reference (an imprint of IGI Global)
701 E. Chocolate Avenue
Hershey PA, USA 17033
Tel: 717-533-8845
Fax: 717-533-8661
E-mail: cust@igi-global.com
Web site: http://www.igi-global.com

Library of Congress Cataloging-in-Publication Data

Names: Throne, Robin, 1960- editor.
Title: Indigenous research of land, self, and spirit / Robin Throne, editor.
Description: Hershey, PA : Information Science Reference, 2020. | Includes bibliographical references and index. | Summary: “This book explores recurrent generational implications and ongoing challenges with land dispossession, relocation, reacquisition, governmental influences, and economic impacts to contemporary indigenous land cultures”-- Provided by publisher.
Identifiers: LCCN 2019058357 (print) | LCCN 2019058358 (ebook) | ISBN 9781799837299 (hardcover) | ISBN 9781799837305 (paperback) | ISBN 9781799837312 (ebook)
Subjects: LCSH: Indigenous peoples--Social conditions--Case studies. | Indigenous peoples--Land tenure--Case studies. | Indigenous peoples--Education--Case studies. | Indigenous peoples--Ethnic identity--Case studies.
Classification: LCC GN380 .I33 2020 (print) | LCC GN380 (ebook) | DDC 305.8--dc23
LC record available at https://lccn.loc.gov/2019058357
LC ebook record available at https://lccn.loc.gov/2019058358

This book is published in the IGI Global book series Advances in Religious and Cultural Studies (ARCS) (ISSN: 2475-675X; eISSN: 2475-6768)

British Cataloguing in Publication Data
A Cataloguing in Publication record for this book is available from the British Library.

All work contributed to this book is new, previously-unpublished material. The views expressed in this book are those of the authors, but not necessarily of the publisher.

For electronic access to this publication, please contact: eresources@igi-global.com.

Advances in Religious and Cultural Studies (ARCS) Book Series

Nancy Erbe
California State University-Dominguez Hills, USA

ISSN:2475-675X
EISSN:2475-6768

Mission

In the era of globalization, the diversity of the world and various cultures becomes apparent as cross-cultural interactions turn into a daily occurrence for individuals in all professions. Understanding these differences is necessary in order to promote effective partnerships and interactions between those from different religious and cultural backgrounds.

The **Advances in Religious and Cultural Studies (ARCS)** book series brings together a collection of scholarly publications on topics pertaining to religious beliefs, culture, population studies, and sociology. Books published within this series are ideal for professionals, theorists, researchers, and students seeking the latest research on collective human behavior in terms of religion, social structure, and cultural identity and practice.

Coverage

- Globalization and Culture
- Sociology
- Politics and Religion
- Cultural Identity
- Human Rights and Ethics
- Stereotypes and Racism
- Impact of Religion on Society
- Gender
- Social Stratification and Classes
- Group Behavior

IGI Global is currently accepting manuscripts for publication within this series. To submit a proposal for a volume in this series, please contact our Acquisition Editors at Acquisitions@igi-global.com or visit: http://www.igi-global.com/publish/.

The Advances in Religious and Cultural Studies (ARCS) Book Series (ISSN 2475-675X) is published by IGI Global, 701 E. Chocolate Avenue, Hershey, PA 17033-1240, USA, www.igi-global.com. This series is composed of titles available for purchase individually; each title is edited to be contextually exclusive from any other title within the series. For pricing and ordering information please visit http://www.igi-global.com/book-series/advances-religious-cultural-studies/84269. Postmaster: Send all address changes to above address.

Titles in this Series

For a list of additional titles in this series, please visit:
http://www.igi-global.com/book-series/advances-religious-cultural-studies/84269

Social, Educational, and Cultural Perspectives of Disabilities in the Global South
Sibonokuhle Ndlovu (University of Johannesburg, South Africa) and Phefumula Nyoni (University of Johannesburg, South Africa)
Information Science Reference • © 2021 • 306pp • H/C (ISBN: 9781799848677) • US $185.00

Immigrant Women's Voices and Integrating Feminism Into Migration Theory
Florence Nyemba (University of Cincinnati, USA) and Rufaro Chitiyo (Tennessee Technological University, USA)
Information Science Reference • © 2021 • 281pp • H/C (ISBN: 9781799846642) • US $195.00

Impact of Immigration and Xenophobia on Development in Africa
Mavhungu Abel Mafukata (Department of Development Studies, University of South Africa, South Africa)
Information Science Reference • © 2021 • 323pp • H/C (ISBN: 9781799870999) • US $185.00

Handbook of Research on Using Global Collective Intelligence and Creativity to Solve Wicked Problems
Ziska Fields (University of Johannesburg, South Africa)
Information Science Reference • © 2021 • 537pp • H/C (ISBN: 9781799823858) • US $235.00

Handbook of Research on Cultural Heritage and Its Impact on Territory Innovation and Development
Lídia Oliveira (University of Aveiro, Portugal) Ana Carla Amaro (University of Aveiro, Portugal) and Ana Melro (University of Aveiro, Portugal)
Information Science Reference • © 2021 • 447pp • H/C (ISBN: 9781799867012) • US $245.00

Women Empowerment and Well-Being for Inclusive Economic Growth
Shailja Dixit (Amity University, India) and Sana Moid (Amity University, India)
Information Science Reference • © 2021 • 259pp • H/C (ISBN: 9781799837374) • US $195.00

Dialectical Perspectives on Media, Health, and Culture in Modern Africa
Alfred O. Akwala (Technical University of Kenya, Kenya) Joel K. Ngetich (Kabianga University, Kenya) and Agnes Wanjiku Muchura Theuri (National Youth Service School of Business Studies, Kenya)
Information Science Reference • © 2021 • 275pp • H/C (ISBN: 9781522580911) • US $185.00

Handbook of Research on Business, Socioeconomic, and Educational Challenges for Women
Alice S. Etim (Winston-Salem State University, USA) and James Etim (Winston-Salem State University, USA)
Information Science Reference • © 2021 • 400pp • H/C (ISBN: 9781799857631) • US $245.00

IGI Global
PUBLISHER of TIMELY KNOWLEDGE

701 East Chocolate Avenue, Hershey, PA 17033, USA
Tel: 717-533-8845 x100 • Fax: 717-533-8661
E-Mail: cust@igi-global.com • www.igi-global.com

Editorial Advisory Board

Table of Contents

Editorial Advisory Board

Table of Contents

Detailed Table of Contents

The chapter presents a review of the literature on Native American education and the use of culturally responsive instruction to guide the implementation of a computer-based reading program to increase engagement and reading levels for Native American secondary students for a quantitative single-case study on the effects of using Achieve3000 while using a culturally responsive model for selecting reading samples. Study findings noted though student reading levels increased and reading engagement improved in some key areas, no significant difference was found between groups. The implications of these findings are that use of a culturally responsive pedagogy to select self-relevant materials for a computer-based reading program may help Native American students to increase their reading levels and reading engagement scores, but not at a significant rate. Future research should consider whether these pedagogies and other strategies may improve Native American reading literacy.

Chapter 7
Land, Rights, and Tenure Insecurity on Customary Land in Zambia: Protecting "Thyselves".......... 102
Ephraim Kabunda Munshifwa, Copperbelt University, Zambia
Niraj Jain, Copperbelt University, Zambia
Roy Alexander Chileshe, Copperbelt University, Zambia
Anthony Mushinge, Copperbelt University, Zambia

Land is a key asset in the lives of village communities in Zambia. It is thus at the centre of their livelihood strategies as it provides social, economic, and financial benefits to these communities. The paradox though is that despite acknowledging its importance in the lives of village communities, tenure on this land is poorly protected by the state resulting in high insecurity for its occupants. In many instances, there are no clear regulations on its use and alienation while traditional authorities are also ill-equipped for the task of administering this land. The question then that emerges is: In this perceived absence of state protection, how are village communities protecting themselves from threats of dispossession by foreign investors, urban elites, and the state's own actions? This study found that village communities are using various means to protect themselves, including issuance of local land holding certificates.

Chapter 8
Land as Agency: A Critical Autoethnography of Scandinavian Acquisition of Dispossessed Land in the Iowa Territory 118
Robin Throne, University of the Cumberlands, USA

This chapter presents findings from a critical arts-based autoethnographic study of Iowa digital maps and historical archival data of the Iowa territory (1838-1846) for Indigenous Nations with previous land tenure. Researchers have noted land and voice dispossession for these Indigenous Nations resulting from forced removal followed by decades of intentional cultural erosion, forced assimilation, loss of language, and religious discrimination and persecution into the latter 20th century. Current research highlights the resultant damage of these historical losses on living descendants of Indigenous land-based cultures. Agency of self was explored from a socialized perspective of a descendant of Scandinavian immigrants who acquired dispossessed land within the Iowa territory. This was contrasted with a cultural perspective of land as capital wealth vs. the principles and tenets of land-based culture whereby agency may be strengthened via Indigenous knowledge rooted in land-based connections and environmental sensitivities. Data representation involved poetic excerpts of land as agency.

This chapter is a critical review of circle practices. The author first examines the philosophical underpinnings behind similar practices of restorative justice, circles, circle practices, and talking circles. Then, the author explores the description of protocol and procedures of talking circles in the literature by various others. Thirdly, this literature review examines talking circles used in practice in the literature. This chapter synthesizes and critiques existing literature, as well as video resources and oral tradition. Circle practices are a traditional Native American practice of communication and community which has a strong spiritual core as a means for restorative justice. For some Native American people during talking circles, it is believed the person holding the eagle feather or talisman cannot tell a lie.

This chapter presents a study conceptualized to assess the accessibility of land claims records preserved at the Kruger National Park (KNP) of South Africa. The study used a qualitative method through document analysis and interviews. The sample of the study comprised land claimants and archivists based at the KNP archives. The key finding revealed land claimants use their democratic rights through the Promotion of Access to Information Act of 2000 to request land claim records from KNP archives. The findings aid tools were essential to assess records preserved in the archives even though some of the records were not found in the park.

Situated in the Mesoregion of the Acre River, Plácido de Castro is a small municipality in the Brazilian state of Acre. In 2015, with the consent of the authorities, a group of people of Huni Kuin ethnicity occupied an abandoned, state-owned piece of land in the municipal territory, namely, the Parque Ecológico. For two years, the Huni Kuin group has lived in the Parque Ecológico, decontaminating and revalorising the land. Afterwards the Huni Kuin have been gradually dispossessed of the occupied land via various coercive actions, some of which were backed by the authorities. In this paper, the authors draw upon media releases as well as an interview with Hunk Kuin cacique Mapu, in order to signify the events in terms of a violent performance of settler colonialism in the face of the legitimate reclamation of Indigenous sovereignty over Brazilian land. In particular, they look at the ways in which political authorities, police forces, social services, and the broader non-Indigenous society unanimously cooperate towards the total effacement of Indigenous bodies, communities, and subjectivities from the land.

Detailed Table of Contents

Craig Santos Perez, poet and activist from Guam, uses his poetry to call attention to the negative effects of colonialism and militarization on his homeland and the Pacific. He reminds his readers of the mistreatment of his people the Chamorros, the special "unincorporated" status of Guam and the land that is taken over little by little by the US Army. His poems reveal information about the life circumstances of the author's community and respond to, as well as critique, the colonial conditions of Guam. This study looks at everyday objects mentioned in Perez's poetry and seeks to unfold the "mission" of these objects. "Everyday objects" do not only refer to traditional objects, but also, to modern objects (borrowed from western culture) which relate to the everyday life of the Indigenous people of Guam. The argument of this research is that ordinary objects, which have significance in Pacific culture, are deliberately placed in the poems by Perez. They convey the message of resistance, decolonial protest and pursuit of survival and can be considered as representations of activism.

The Gullah Geechee people originally came to the United States as enslaved Africans from the coast of West Africa. Because of harsh conditions along the sea islands, spanning from North Carolina to Florida, the enslaved were often left to work the land while plantation owners retreated to less hostile, inland environments. As a result, many Gullah Geechee cultural, linguistic, and artistic practices remained intact. Today, there is interest in preserving these rich traditions. Because of environmental and cultural threats, preservation efforts must focus on sustainability. This qualitative, critical theory research includes interviews with musical performers from the sea islands and details their perceptions of the role music plays in sustainable heritage tourism. The researchers explored if music performance could be used to promote preservation locally, through tourism to cultural corridor sites, and globally, through touring musical acts. Participants urged caution with traditional tourism models and emphasized the role of younger generations in preserving Gullah Geechee music.

This chapter explores the degree to which Native American culture impacts the resiliency of Native American students earning degrees at three tribal colleges in the southwestern part of the United States. This is a qualitative case study that was based on the following research question: "How does Native American culture contribute to the resiliency of Native American students who are earning a degree at a tribal college?" This chapter focuses on the concerns of Native American students, and the cultural events they may have encountered during their educational journey. The research data were collected from interviews of 18 Native American students who were in their last year of college. Themes surrounding culture, resiliency, tribal colleges, academics, and Native American role models were discovered and used to determine the impact Native American culture has on the resiliency of Native American students.

Land is a promising asset that acts as a stimulus for indigenous people to act and respond within their natural limits. The natives enjoy great kinship with the land. They deem the land as one with the humankind: a living, breathing, and thinking being. They believe that they live under the constant protection of the green produce of the land and they ought to protect it in return as it plays a key role in determining the possibility of survival of the tribal community. Any attempt at enforced displacement, tribal eviction, land encroachment, land diversion, or land alienation leads to disintegration of the tribal community. Trespassers trying to dispossess the aboriginals of their land not only impact the indigenous ethnic formations but also affect the ecological balance. The chapter provides an incisive sociological scrutiny to trace the origin of the pressing crisis of tribal land alienation, by adopting Gopinath Mohanty's Paraja as a case study, to understand its catastrophic repercussions on the forest communities and the natural habitat.

This chapter considers how modernity has affected the livelihood of Paliyar community and how they have been affected by forest dispossession. Whether the weaning away from the forests has been manufactured or part of the systemic exploitation is discernible. The chapter traces the history of the Paliyars, their belief structures, and indigenous knowledge within sacred spaces. The chapter also presents a discussion of the relation between land and spiritual tradition as well as the importance of land to identity, transfer of oral tradition, and indigenous traditional knowledge. Removing the Paliyar from the land continues to erode their tradition, knowledge, and identity.

This chapter examines unique challenges in the way of Native American educational success as well as solutions to overcoming. The chapter addresses why intergenerational trauma matters, the impacts of public policy on Native American people such as the Native American Languages Act of 1990, and the importance of Native American people being connected to the land, protecting traditions, language, and their ancestors. The purpose of this literature review is to shed light on Native American educational barriers and to critique existing literature. Areas analyzed include the trend of low rates of educational attainment among Native Americans, the history of abuse towards Indigenous people and other minorities, the impact on individuals, and solutions for the future. There is a need for Native American students to stay connected to cultural tradition, cultural relevancy in education, role models for Native American people, and an importance of Native American students staying connected to family.

This chapter revolves around the impact of socio-political diaspora to the concept of tribal-ancestral land, which is sacred to the community and the cultural identity of the T'boli, an ethno-linguistic group. A narrative discourse approach is used to illustrate the tribe's struggles to the existing hegemony, particularly with the dynamics between the tribe and other inhabitants, the intrusions of other values and exploitations of their ancestral domains as explored across a changing sociocultural milieu. In an attempt to provide understanding of cultural identity amidst the changing social landscapes, the authors describe, identify, explore, and interpret the subject. Hence, the chapter provides the worldview of T'boli people and offers a narrative juxtaposition of the three opuses from three different fields. Further research is needed to ensure protection and preservation of the T'boli culture and its identity and indigenous significance within Southeast Asia and, specifically, the Philippines to better understand this land-based culture.

This autoethnographic research presents personal stories from the author, connecting family, land, and music. He recounts stories his Ojibwe grandmother shared about her time in Franz, a small railroad village in northeastern Ontario that is now a ghost town. The connection to Franz is established through memories from his grandmother. Inspired to write a song, the author aimed to reconnect to Franz itself. The study follows the author's personal journey to visit his grandmother's land for the first time, making new connections and stories along the way. The research utilizes Indigenous autoethnography, Indigenous storytelling, and arts-based methods, such as a/r/tography, to link his stories to those of his grandmother, resulting in a reflection of storytelling, community history, and (re)connection to land, woven together by stories from the family matriarch.

Foreword

I have known the editor of this book through my connection to the topic of land, particularly through her previous works on the dispossession of land cultures, voice dispossession, and women's land rights. When she wrote me to ask if I would "at all consider writing a brief Foreword" for this book, I quickly indicated that "I will do it." How could I not take up the task? The main reason for my rather quick response to the editors's request for a Foreword was twofold. First, a Foreword would give me unhindered insight into emerging knowledge on land and property tenure from the lens of the dispossessed populations. Being empathic to land injustice herself, *Robin Throne* has in this book put together a structured knowledge base on the intersection of land injustices from various social justice perspectives. Second, I quickly sensed that it would give me the opportunity to also give a voice to those who suffer from the ills of land dispossession all over the world. When you live in a country like Namibia, like I do, you will come face-to-face with the evil consequences of land dispossession in its most gruesome form. Namibia is a country where the *joy* earned from dispossession lives side by side with the *sufferings* of the dispossessed. Living in such a country, and belonging to the dispossessed, emboldens one's spirit to speak or write against land injustices.

Land (including its associated natural resources) in most societies is central to the delivery of socio-economic activities. It is a source to individual livelihoods options, communal identities, and the basis for environmental health. Investigations into historical dispossessions of land allow scholars to understand resource-related dehumanization experiences people have faced in the past, and still face today. These investigations underscore two things. First, the criticality of finding ways to address the historical traumas of marginalized populations. This helps to further inform developmental theories of land injustices, the wellbeing of the marginalized populations, and the tools necessary to ensure that the marginalized attain improved wellbeing. Second, it opens the lid of atypicality in the minds of the perpetrators of land injustices. Understanding the *whys* and *hows* of their atypical acts can, perhaps, enable activist scholars to develop a wedge capable of holding back history from unguarded repetitions. None of these are possible without understanding of the connotation of land (as a gift of nature), self (as identity and belonging to land) and spirit (as the quest for survival from land). Addressing this complex connectivity of land, self and spirit is a unique contribution of this book to both contemporary and future literatures. It also makes this book both a literary and experiential journey.

Land colonization, whenever and wherever they happened, have always killed resilience—i.e., the amount of stress a human-environment system can absorb and still build and increase its capacity for livability better than before. When a community loses its resilience, it is more susceptible to generational failure as it cannot absorb instabilities as it previously could over a long period. Tackling the situation—in terms of both theorizing and practicalizing how to disburden land colonization consequences—requires the understanding of the indigenous, the awareness of the self and the spirit to engage in change.

There is a vast body of research on land dispossession, but a compendium of research on the plight of Indigenous Nations from around the world and the retinue of traumas they go through due to land dispossession are not available. Understanding indigenous land related challenges requires self-awareness, as well as a spiritual or non-material aspect of understanding land issues beyond its everyday manifestations. This book, *Indigenous Research of Land, Self, and Spirit,* provides readers with insights into the various land related struggles people face around the world. It gives readers access to multiple perspectives of land injustices from five continents. It features interesting case studies from Africa, Asia, Europe, North America, and South America. The volume is organized into 16 main chapters. The first chapter objectivizes land and uses poetry to communicate land decolonization in pursuit of survival. The second chapter delves into the sustainability of cultural practices for people under environmental and cultural threats. The third chapter, viewing knowledge as a natural resource, unpacks the nativity and sustainability nexus of Native American higher education, with concerns on its impact on resiliency. The fourth chapter promotes the socioenvironmental ideology of living off the land "for the land and by the land." This mantra calls for respect to the people-livelihood-land relationship. The strategies promoted in this chapter provide bases for discouraging enforced displacement, tribal eviction, land encroachment, and land diversion or land alienation. The fifth chapter deconstructs land as a spiritual medium and presents how people have been affected by forest dispossession. It evokes renewed discourse concerning the relationship between land and spiritual traditions, and the importance of land to identity, transfer of oral tradition, and indigenous traditional knowledge. The sixth chapter reflects on knowledge and learning for Native Americans in the context of cultural responsiveness through online instructions. The seventh chapter deals with the challenges of land rights and tenure insecurity in customary communities. It emphasizes a fit-for-purpose way to govern customary land. The eighth chapter links land dispossession to disempowerment. It shows how land dispossession is linked with voice dispossession for Indigenous Nations due to "forced removal followed by decades of intentional cultural erosion, forced assimilation, loss of language, and religious discrimination and persecution."

The ninth chapter reflects on the power of learning as part of Indigenous Peoples' tradition of circle practices. The tenth chapter tackles the relevance of land documentation and record-keeping as a tool for the accessibility of land. The eleventh chapter looks at how the non-Indigenous society (e.g., police forces, political authorities, and social services) collaborate in the effacement of Indigenous communities from their land. The twelfth chapter unravels the unique challenges in the path of successful Indigenous education. The thirteenth chapter revolves from the socio-political diaspora to the concept of ancestral land interlinkages with the cultural identity in tribal groups. The fourteenth chapter hinges on memory as an element of land tenure regimes. It depicts art forms—such as songs and stories—as a means of connecting to land. The fifteenth chapter explores the link between physical dispossession and historical trauma. The chapter evocatively states that "historical trauma has been established as a by-product of cultural and physical suppression" and supports it with evidence.

This volume unties the knots of unfreedoms holding back societies suffering from historical land injustices on their paths to sustainability while aspiring for a better quality of life. It also deconstructs the land or resource fantasies of the historically marginalized within their governance isolations or exclusivities in the countries where they are situated. The communication tools used by the authors embrace both the arts and sciences.

Put simply, this book provides an uncondensed study of global indigenous research of land and detailed accounts of land dispossession experiences and processes going forward. The authors' approaches to explaining these issues are simple and direct, and yet diverse. Most importantly, the book discusses meaningful solutions to these challenges in diverse ways. The volume is a merger of scientific narratives and activist voices locked to educate and teach solution-led indigenous research on land and related issues. It draws together these scientific narratives and activist voices from an inspiring group of contributors offering awareness into the world of Indigenous Peoples and marginalized populations suffering from historical and contemporary land injustices.

The book raises specific questions on the impact of land colonization to people around the world and ignites new ideas for tackling the consequences of historical land injustices in various aspects of development policies—e.g., policies on the environment, land and natural resources, education, forestry, and sociocultural development. By reading this book, policymakers will become more informed about development strategies and options for tackling the challenges encountered in societies suffering from the traumas of historical injustices. They would also gain access to important elements of knowledge for making informed decisions in Indigenous societies.

In broad terms, the many topics covered in this book include environmental studies, property sciences, indigenous natural resource governance and women's land rights issues, to mention a few. I encourage all scholars (including students) and activists interested in the historical aspects of land to read this book. As a reading material, the book will be a valuable scholarly resource to scholars of land and natural resource governance, history of resource dispossession, land colonization and restorative studies geared towards sustainability or resilience. To those looking for specific information on the historical injustices or solutions to it (e.g., activists and researchers), the book provides information on relevant techniques towards healing the wounds of the past. What I have done in this Foreword is to alert readers about why this book is worth reading. That aside, there is a rare knowledge in store for readers who flip over to the next chapter of this book.

Uchendu Eugene Chigbu
Department of Land and Property Sciences, Namibia University of Science and Technology, Windhoek, Namibia

Uchendu Eugene Chigbu *is Associate Professor in Land Administration at the Department of Land and Property Science, the Namibia University of Science and Technology (NUST), in Windhoek. His works fall within the interface between Social Sciences and Geodesy (or Social Geodesy). He has more than 10 years of experience in the formulation of land methods for addressing societal challenges. His most impactful work in the field of land administration and management is the Tenure Responsive Land Use Planning: A Guide for Country Level Implementation, which has been adopted by the UN-Habitat for piloting in the Global South. The concepts and practices from this document are currently being piloted in Uganda, the Philippines, Laos, and Zambia. He is the Co-Chair of the International Training and Research Cluster of the Global Land Tool Network (in the UN-Habitat). He is also the Co-Chair of the Urban-Rural Dependency Working Group in Commission-8 of the International Federation of Surveyors (FIG). He is highly published on land issues. He sits on the Editorial Boards of the journals, Land Use Policy (Elsevier) and Local Development & Society (Routledge).*

Preface

To pray you open your whole self

To sky, to earth, to sun, to moon

To one whole voice that is you.

...

We see you, see ourselves and know

That we must take the utmost care

And kindness in all things.

~Joy Harjo, Eagle Poem[1]

Indigenous scholars have long noted the importance of land and the natural environment as a source of sustenance for self and spirit as well as central to Indigenous ways of knowing. It has been said that when the connection to land is restored, this connection can foster agency for the individual and a deeper insight into life purpose among this Earth. It may be no coincidence the tenets and principles of land-based cultures continue to be revisited as we live in a time when natural resources are threatened and understanding of the importance of our role as land curators versus landowners is deconstructed and decolonized. Much is also to be gained from Indigenous ways of knowing and culturally responsive education to ensure our youth embrace their essential identities, gain solace and strength from the land, and protect their cultural heritage to carry forward the intergenerational knowledge for the future.

The advocation for ongoing land-based research continues across disciplines and examinations continue in the environmental natural sciences while transdisciplinary views of sustainability, environmental protection, and land-based cultures diffuse such borders as they impact all areas of research in business, education, health sciences, the social and behavioral sciences, and of course, history. The application of land-based research findings continues to improve practice across these disciplines and are necessary to a 21st century view and understanding of past atrocities, inequities, and dispossession among many peoples and cultures. A land-based orientation may aid those to better understand language, social connections, gender, culture, property, possession and dispossession, proprietorship, economy, and individual agency from a vital perspective. A reorientation to the land may bring, for some, a renewed perspective for plants, animals, waterways, air, health, and wellbeing whereby a changed introspective relationship to the land and others may also occur.

The chapters included here ring the globe from North and South America to Africa to Asia and call to action the need for cognizant awareness of our personal and collective connection to land as community, wherewithal, nourishment, strength, and for many of these communities, resilience and persistence for continuity of life and wellbeing. Results starkly highlight the similarities between land-based cultures regardless of continent. We can learn much from the research efforts, activism, reclamation, education, art, music, poetry, historiography, photography, and distinct voices of these chapter authors. I am honored to serve as editor of this collection by Indigenous and non-Indigenous scholars who encompass these global analyses of the diverse aspects of land-based cultures, the impact on the self and spirit, as well as the need for healing from the individual and generational trauma experienced by land dispossession and oppression.

Robin Throne
University of the Cumberlands, USA

ENDNOTE

1 Harjo, J. (1990). Eagle poem. In *Mad Love and war*. Wesleyan University Press. Joy Harjo is the first Native American U.S. Poet Laureate and only the second Laureate to hold three consecutive terms.

Chapter 1
Decolonizing Guam With Poetry:
"Everyday Objects With Mission" in Craig Santos Perez's Poetry

Anna Erzsebet Szucs
National Sun Yat-sen University, Taiwan

ABSTRACT

Craig Santos Perez, poet and activist from Guam, uses his poetry to call attention to the negative effects of colonialism and militarization on his homeland and the Pacific. He reminds his readers of the mistreatment of his people the Chamorros, the special "unincorporated" status of Guam and the land that is taken over little by little by the US Army. His poems reveal information about the life circumstances of the author's community and respond to, as well as critique, the colonial conditions of Guam. This study looks at everyday objects mentioned in Perez's poetry and seeks to unfold the "mission" of these objects. "Everyday objects" do not only refer to traditional objects, but also, to modern objects (borrowed from western culture) which relate to the everyday life of the Indigenous people of Guam. The argument of this research is that ordinary objects, which have significance in Pacific culture, are deliberately placed in the poems by Perez. They convey the message of resistance, decolonial protest and pursuit of survival and can be considered as representations of activism.

INTRODUCTION

Literature is an important platform for speaking up against injustice. Activism and Indigenous literature are often connected and Indigenous authors write as a political act. Craig Santos Perez, poet and activist from Guam, uses his poetry to call attention to the negative effects of colonialism and militarization on his homeland and throughout the Pacific. In his poetry, he constantly reminds his readers of the mistreatment of his people the Chamorros, the special status of his home country (an "unincorporated territory" of the United States of America) and the disappearing land that is taken over little by little by the US Army. Guam is a strategically important place for the US Navy due to its central location in the Pacific Ocean. However, it is rarely talked about in the media and generally presented as a holiday

DOI: 10.4018/978-1-7998-3729-9.ch001

paradise, and not as an important military base it is. It is invisible to the public. Perez, living in diaspora and looking at his original home from afar, wants to show the reader the reality of the colonized Guam through poetry. "I started writing poetry after my family migrated from our home(is)land of Guahan (Guam) to the state of California. Poetry became a way for me to stay connected – to remember where I come from." This connectedness to the land is clearly represented in his poetry. Perez criticizes the US Army that occupies increasingly larger areas of the island of Guam and mistreats the Natives on their own land. His poems can be read as activist texts because they reveal important information about the life circumstances of the author's community and respond to, as well as critique, colonial and post-colonial conditions of the Pacific and Guam. This study looks at everyday objects mentioned in Perez's poetry and seeks to unfold their "mission." "Everyday objects" do not only refer to traditional objects of the Chamorro culture, but also, they can be examples of modern objects (borrowed from western culture) that relate to the everyday life of the Indigenous people of Guam. The research analyzes poetry from the poet's ongoing multi-book series titled *from unincorporated territory*, which currently stands at four books; *[hacha]*, *[saina]*, *[guma'] and [lukao]*.

BACKGROUND

The Power of the Colonized Guam

Ferdinand Magellan was the first European to reach Guam in 1521 and the following three and a half centuries Guam was under Spanish colonization. In 1898, after signing the Treaty of Paris as the end of the Spanish-American War, Guam was transferred to the United States and remained under the US Army's control until 1941 when the Japanese army occupied and renamed it to Omiya-Jima (Holy Shrine Island). After three years of occupation by the Japanese army, the US Armed Forces "liberated" Guam on July 21st of 1944. Guam's special status; "unincorporated territory," was given in 1950, when US President Harry Truman signed the Organic Act. It stated that Guam could stay a self-governing country, but in the same time it would be dependent on the absolute power of the US Congress, as well as the US armed forces would continue to exercise extensive control (Woodward, 2013, p. 69-70). With the Organic Act, a civilian government was established, however citizens of Guam are under the control of the Department of Interior and thus, they are not given the full rights of US citizenship (Heim, 2018, p. 134). The Office of Insular Affairs defines an unincorporated territory as a "United States insular area in which the United States Congress has determined that only selected parts of the United States Constitution apply" (qtd. in Lai, 2011, p. 4). On the contrary, the "incorporated" states are all parts of the United States and enjoy the benefits of the US Constitution (p. 4). Many criticize the status of being "unincorporated," since, in it, Guam is caught in an enforced colonial bond (Na'puti & Bevacqua, 2015, p. 840). In an infamous interview, Lieutenant Colonel Douglas from the US Air Force said; "People on Guam seem to forget that they are a possession, and not an equal partner." Furthermore, he added, directly addressing the people of Guam: "you belong to me and I can do with you as best I please" (Lieutenant Colonel Douglas qtd. in Na'puti & Bevacqua, 2015, p. 839-840).

Hillary Clinton called the twenty-first century "America's Pacific Century" (Clinton qtd. in Perez, 2015b, p. 621) as the Pacific region is strategically crucial for the US military. The US brought considerable changes to the Pacific and Guam since World War II. Guam is home to a large US military base that occupies one-third of the island today (Heim, 2018, p. 135). Along with the US military came the

Trans-Pacific Partnership (TPP) that has an immense influence on international trade and the increasing business transactions on Guam and the neighboring countries (Perez, 2015b, p. 621). Guam's economy is strongly dependent on tourism, the army, and jobs from the service industry that are related to the military (Hsu, 2012, p. 286). Teresia Teaiwa calls the interweaving between militarism and tourism "militourism," where the military establishes the tourist industry which later conceals the source that controls it (Teaiwa qtd. in DeLisle, 2016, p. 563). US territoriality and colonialism have transformed the Pacific and it has affected all aspects of the everyday lives of the citizens, such as their language, dining, architecture, sport, clothing, literature and so on (Perez, 2015b, p. 622). The military has also been exploiting the island to dispose of environmentally hazardous waste material and uses a nearby island to its military firing practices (Hsu, 2012, p. 286). Moreover, thousands of US Marines are planned to relocate from Okinawa to Guam, which gives justification to new build-ups on the island. However, constructions are delayed due to lawsuits disputing environmental protections of the building sites and because historical and cultural artifacts have been discovered during the excavation (South, 2019).

Resurrected Connection With Chamorro Land

The land tells the history of the colonial times, as the consequences of the US militarism and colonialism all over the Pacific are palpable in the landscapes and the forced dislocations, write Na'puti and Bevacqua (2015) (p. 841). Military bases, new ports, countless hotels and their facilities made Guam's landscape visibly different. Historically, colonization by the Spanish and later the Americans fundamentally shaped the lives of Chamorros (the Native people of Guam) through religious conversions, the institution of new education systems and cohabitation practices. The cumulative effect was the disconnection of the Chamorros from their land. These influences together lessened their desire to preserve and take care of nature and what nature could provide (p. 852). However, when the US military discovered and disrespected historical and cultural artifacts at the new live firing range complex's construction site, which is neighboring the ancient Pågat village, locals finally felt obligated to defend their homeland with its cultural legacy and reconnected with their old values (p. 853). The mistreatment of these valuable cultural artifacts was important in reawakening their connection to the land. After reviving newly found old values, people protested and spoke up against the military development as they were fed up with the colonizers and with not being heard. Soon, Pågat became the leading symbol for people of Guam who wanted to take part in the decision making on their island (p. 853). Pågat is considered a highly endangered historic site in the area. It preserves the remains of the lattes; the stone foundations of buildings and houses from prehistorical times, as well as subterranean freshwater resources, remedial plants, clay pots and dishes, and work tools of the ancient Chamorro people (p. 846). Social movements and local activism arose as a reaction to the military build-ups, endangered ecology, disappearing culture and the forgetting of one's history (p. 847).

Pacific Islanders have an ingrained awareness of place, Vicente Diaz and Kehaulani Kauanui explain (2001), and identifying with their islands is common in every Pacific community. The land and the sea are not only part of their genealogies, but also, they are the foundations of every sovereignty movement, just like the one in Guam over Pågat, to rebuild Native identity (p. 318-319). Na'puti and Bevacqua (2015) argue that Indigenous sacred spaces are often marginalized in the Pacific. Hence, an assertion of the identity based on Indigenous knowledge and sacred sites is extremely important in order to understand that colonialism is a forced relationship upon them, recover balance, and empower the community to make a connection and start a conversation with each other as well as with other Indigenous communities that are already involved with decolonizing their land and resisting colonial powers in the Pacific (p. 838).

Guam is considered one of the most crucial military bases in the globe, but at the same time, strategically, the most invisible, too (p. 843). It rarely appears in scholarly or popular discussions and it is presented to Americans as an imaginary place, a paradise for tourists with welcoming and congenial indigenes (Perez, 2015b, p. 623). The image that comes to one's mind about Guam and the Pacific, in general, is a romantic holiday destination. The general public is not well-informed about the military actions that take place in the area every day. Likewise, Elizabeth M. DeLoughrey (2019) warns that militarizing the ocean and its islands is often unnoticed and not represented in scholarly discussions and literature in the humanities (p. 22). However, she also suggests, it appears that scholars and activists are awakened as they are demanding "critical ocean studies" and starting to understand that the ocean is not an "aqua nullius" (a blank space) like the colonial powers imagined, but instead it is full of life filled with boundless of marine species and diverse Indigenous cultures (p. 22). The task of these knowledgeable activists and scholars is to pass on the information and worries, and alert others about the injustice encountered by the Indigenous people.

As a consequence, numerous local and regional movements speak up against US military bases. They vocalize their resistance and highlight the negative impacts on their land and their daily lives caused by military actions (Na'puti & Bevacqua, 2015, p. 844) Even though many Chamorros join the US Army, they still recognize the depressing truth that the military inhabits their native land. Activists show resistance through reaching back and emphasizing the importance of culture, caring for the environment that surrounds them, and getting in touch with their history (p. 848). Craig Santos Perez argues that Pacific Islanders are ready to claim back "*real* and *symbolic territories* through acts of survival, agency, adaptation, and resilience" (Perez, 2015b, p. 622 emphases added). Activists do not only reveal the problems surrounding physical dislocations in their demands but also, blame the US military for mentally separating indigenes from their cultures. Chamorros are physically removed from their homes to help the expansion of the military base, but at the same time, they are excluded from decision-making about their land (Na'puti & Bevacqua, 2015, p. 842).

Literature as Resistance

Literature is an important platform for speaking against injustice and inequality. Activism and Indigenous literature are oftentimes linked together. Literary and scholarly works are frequently charged with political messages and connected to civil rights movements among the island countries of the Pacific (Rowe, 2015, p. 259). In his influential essay "The Ocean in Us," Tongan-Fijian writer and environmental activist Epeli Hau'ofa, urges the people of the Pacific region to develop a "common identity" that could guide them act collectively. He claims that they do not stand a chance if acting alone, individually opposing the colonial forces, but in unison, as a community of nations, they would have a better opportunity to survive the predicaments that the colonial past has brought upon them (p. 33). Hau'ofa is not the only writer who uses a literary platform to try to better the conditions of the environment and the people. Other Pacific Island writers, such as poet Brandy Nālani McDougall, insist that Indigenous people should restore the connection with the basic elements, "salt-water" and the ancient customs of their culture in order to fight against colonialism and ecological devastation and improve the conditions of their community (McDougall qtd. in Peek, 2013, p. 80).

Environmental and social activism can be examined side-by-side since they seem to exhibit strong connections. As Amilcar Cabral (1993) explains, the productive force of people in every society can be seen in their attitude towards and treatment of nature (p. 55). The relationship between man and nature, and man and society, is a way to relate to history and culture, which plays an important role in activist movements. The source of resistance can be found in a culture that later develops movement and activism against domination, says Cabral (p. 55-56). Activism is always based on cultural knowledge that is important for the specific community that starts the movement. Candice Elanna Steiner (2015) suggests that to the Indigenous people of the Pacific these islands are not only living spaces but also maintainers of culture and identity. She quotes Reverend Tafue Lusama, a church and community leader from Tuvalu, who mentioned the same idea; "Land is equivalent to life in our culture" (p. 149). Since land, identity, social interactions, culture and Indigenous knowledge of Pacific Island societies intertwine, we must study them simultaneously.

Indigenous writers and poets write as a political act. The activism is not simply in the content of the text but also in the act of writing itself. These texts are filled with cultural and historical references that are passed on to the reader. Craig Santos Perez (2019) explained it precisely in an interview:

Poetry has always been important parts of political movements, and political movements have always inspired poetry. Poetry can help us articulate our own politics and interrogate oppressive structures and the language(s) of power. Poetry is a form of empowerment and inspiration. Poetry is a creative act amidst acts of destructive violence. Poetry is an expression of dignity, humanity, resilience, and hope

Perez plays an active role in activism through his writing. In his poetry, he displays the negative effects that colonialism, militarism and tourism have had on his home country. He is from Mongmong, Guam, but currently lives in Hawai'i where he teaches at the University of Hawai'i, Manoa. He received numerous prestigious fellowships and awards for his work, including the prominent American Book Award, which has never been won by a Native Pacific Islander before. He is the co-founder of Ala Press, together with Brandy Nālani McDougall, the only US-based publisher that focuses exclusively on Indigenous Pacific Islander literature. His poetry project, an ongoing multi-book series titled *from unincorporated territory*, currently has four published books; *[hacha]*, *[saina]*, *[guma']* and *[lukao]*. The themes of these poetry collections are political and cover a range of topics including, history, translation, environmentalism, colonialism, tourism, Indigenous myths and more. The texts often incorporate maps and quotations from original documents to underscore how colonialism operates through language, explained Perez (2019) in an interview. He also pointed out that the family stories are included and paralleled with historical events in order to address the bigger political-historical picture and show the human side of history and how it has affected his immediate family. His poems reveal, he continued, "the politics of survival, resistance, and resurgence" and for that, he wants to articulate "decolonial politics through poems of protest, critique, and witness".

Native American Anishinabe writer Gerald Vizenor (2008) finds "survivance," a term coined by him, in Native stories. He claims that "the nature of *survivance* is unmistakable in native stories, natural reason, remembrance, traditions, and customs. The character of survivance creates a sense of native presence over absence, nihility, and victimry" (p. 1 emphasis added). In other words, Native people have to be present and must not act as victims. Indigenous communities can only survive, he explains, if they resist and reject dominance by adopting and incorporating old traditions and tribal wisdom into their daily lives (p. 11). Vizenor argues that the recollection and continuation of Native stories, traditions and customs are crucial for survival. In other words, if Indigenous communities carry on telling and re-telling stories, and myths, they will live on. As long as the younger generation learns the old stories, the history of their people will be remembered and continued. Including myths and old stories in printed literature can be seen as modern ways of resisting domination, and of persistence to pass on Indigenous knowledge and tools of literary activism to the younger generation. There is strength and survivance in everyday objects, too. Just like Native stories, they carry on cultural meaning and instigate continuance. Similar to stories, objects carry important cultural knowledge, too. Objects that originally appeared in ancient myths and stories are now revived in contemporary literature, including Perez's, to carry messages of activism. They pass on activist ideas of the peoet's as they perpetuate and claim "survivance" for the Chamorro culture.

EVERYDAY OBJECTS WITH MISSION IN CRAIG SANTOS PEREZ'S POETRY

What does "everyday object" mean in the context of *this* paper? Merriam-Webster Dictionary gives a sufficient interpretation which is more applicable to answer this question. An object is "something material that may be perceived by the senses" and "something that when viewed stirs a particular emotion" (Object, n.d.). This paper analyzes ordinary objects from literary texts by Perez to demonstrate that they carry cultural meanings and "stir" other emotions than the ones generally known and accepted. It focuses on the connotative, cultural and historical meanings of the objects and investigates Perez's reasons for incorporating them into his writings. Due to the attached cultural significance, stories, histories and traditions attributed to particular objects, this research does not limit the examination solely to the objects, but expands its scope to the everyday life practices that accompany them.

There is no discernible distinction between culture and nature in Pacific Islander principles, therefore, it is argued that they can be, and must be, studied together. In nature, on the land and in the ocean, there are natural objects which are regularly depicted to carry cultural significance. Similar to man-made objects, they are often presented in Pacific Islanders' literature, including Perez's works, and since they convey cultural importance, too, they are included in the examination of everyday objects of this paper. When "everyday objects" are mentioned both man-made and natural objects are implicated. Objects in Pacific Islanders' literature have never been purely ordinary—they are heavily charged with cultural and historical significance and the use of objects in the examined texts of Perez takes a step further to activism. The additional meanings come from history, traditions, stories, myths and legends. The objects are representations as they stand in for activism. Representations convey cultural meaning and often the meanings are constructed by Perez who consciously chooses historically and culturally important objects from his respective society. The readings of the texts containing ordinary objects as representations are interpreted to have a "mission." The "mission" that is proposed in this study is political and rooted in Chamorro traditions, cultures, histories, present day struggles and the foreseeable future of Guam. It will be disclosed how literary activism is carried out in Perez's poetry through objects and how everyday objects can act as agency to deliver this mission.

Everyday objects can be traditional objects that relate to Chamorro culture. In this instance, the object's importance comes from the cultural, historical or mythological references. They are connected to local everyday life practices that are still often being enacted by the community. Some objects are in danger to be forgotten or become extinct. In these cases, it is the poet's responsibility to immortalize the object, and the stories and traditions embedded in them, for the future generation. Objects mentioned in Perez's works can be modern, too. Their presence in Chamorro culture is the result of colonization. These objects are usually depicted in negative tone and are added to the text to call attention to the consequences of colonialism and the problems Chamorro people face. Objects, whether they are traditional or modern, man-made or natural, are a big part of who Chamorro people are as a community. They carry stories that shaped the history and are shaping the future of Guam.

OBJECTS FROM AN UNINCORPORATED TERRITORY

Perez's cultural identity is connected to more than one culture and language. He openly says that the aim of the *from unincorporated territory* project is to "re-territorialize" his mother language, his physical self, and, in addition, his Native identity (Woodward, 2013, p. 68). To accomplish this goal, he utilizes different writing techniques as well as multiple languages, such as Chamorro, English, Spanish and Japanese. Chamorro is the native language of Guam and the other three are the languages of the colonizers, historically and in the present day. By using more than one language, Perez acknowledges the importance (whether positive or negative experience) of the shared past and enhances the significance of the Native language. He incorporates other languages to signal the colonial past and the colonizers' culture to show how together these foreign influences are integrated into Chamorro culture and everyday life (Lai, 2011, p. 2).

Many authors use code-switching between English and their native language, Michelle Keown (2007) discusses. Quoting Gilles Deleuze and Félix Guattari, she points out that when a "minor" author uses a "major" language, the language of the controlling group, in their writings, he or she "deterritorializes" the language of the dominant group by permitting the "minor" language to enter the "major" language's system (p. 164). Therefore, the "minor" language "occupies the dominant language," weakens its absolute power and "shifting the parameters of meaning" to the cultural realm of the "minor" writer (p. 164). For Perez, the "minor," oppressed, and occupied group of Guam is his own people, the Chamorros. He uses the Native language to dominate the other three. Chamorro readers will feel pride, connectedness and kinship reading Chamorro texts and foreign readers will have to consult outside sources, such as a dictionary, if they want to understand the text entirely. Perez, obtaining the knowledge of the language, takes back the power from the non-native speaking reader. Chamorro language is particularly significant as, in the past, to help "culturally assimilate" children to western culture, it was banned in schools and even the Chamorro-English dictionaries were taken and burned (Hsu, 2012, p. 285). Nowadays the language is taught again in public schools and there is a growing common interest in traditional customs and values (p. 287). The later part of this chapter will analyze plenty of examples of ordinary objects mentioned in the Chamorro language. Besides representing material culture and performing traditions, these objects mentioned in the Indigenous language, carry extra, significant connotations to the literal ones, such as Indigenous concepts and worldviews.

Perez often plays with translation in his works, however, these translations are inconsistent. English versions of the Chamorro words are sometimes translated directly after each word, sometimes a few pages later, and sometimes are not translated at all. Due to the unpredictability of the translations, readers must turn the pages back and forth in order to find the link and translations among particular poems, explains Paul Lai (p. 11). This makes reading complicated but also engaging as it requires much attention which is ideal if the author wants to remind his readers to a particular argument.

Perez suggestively practices translation in his work. For example, he translates Guåhan, the original Native name of Guam, as "*[we] have*" and makes an effort to give numerous examples of the use of the term, similar to a dictionary article, by defining what they, as a people, still have and are after the colonization (Perez, 2017, p. 27-28). "As in *[we] have* deep water and the U.S. expects [us] to home port 60% of the Pacific Fleet. … As in *[we] have* resources for the taking. … As in *[we] have* been tricked out and targeted," and so on (p. 27). At last he defines Guåhan: "As in *[we] have* serious identity issues because our original meaning has been translated as "lost"" (p. 28). He admits that he and his people have lost the real meaning of Guam and are unable to find it because of the identity problems they encounter due to the before mentioned foreign powers. They have been defined, named and "translated" by the colonizers.

In the long poem titled "*ginen* tidelands," in *from unincorporated territory [guma']*, Perez (2014) lists sea animals; different type of fish, shark, and sea turtles in Chamorro language; "toninos / tanguisson / atuhong / halu'u / haggan bed'di / haggan karai" (p. 42), and tells the history of the colonizers, the constructions and their devastating aftermaths on Guam in English. Through this list, he visibly shows how the land, its natural environment and its living beings were colonized by crossing out *only* Chamorro words in the poem. Moreover, one can understand that not only land and its creatures can be colonized, but also the language itself by giving each object, place, and creature a new name. During the building of the new infrastructure and changing the landscape with forts, ports, naval coaling station, artificial reef, laying pipes across the ocean and creating wharves (p. 41-43), the Spanish, Japanese and Americans named the "unknown" animals, plants and landscapes. By doing so, they colonized the language, too. Throughout the four books, Perez frequently uses strikethrough font to imply Guam's ambiguous status as an "unincorporated territory" with limited rights and without representation in the United Nations" (Hsu, 2012, p. 297).

He crosses out not only Chamorro words, but other important texts as well. For instance, the footnotes in the poem "*from* tidelands" in *from unincorporated territory [saina]* are crossed out. They contain Perez's (2010) testimony in front of the United Nations Special Political and Decolonization Committee (Fourth Committee) in New York City addressing the topic of Guam's continued colonization. Another text crossed out and must be mentioned is the list of the Chamorro soldiers who lost their lives around the world while serving the US Army in the poem "ginen ta(la)ya" in *from unincorporated territory [guma']* (2014): "[U.S. Army 1st Lt. Michael Aguon Vega, 42, a Guam native, died after he sustained injuries from a roadside blast in Iraq]" (p. 32) is one example and the list of names continues for pages. Only the name of the soldier is not crossed out. Therefore, it can be postulated that Perez uses strikethroughs to call the readers' special attention. Things that are silenced by the colonizers are the ones in strikethrough. It is either the Chamorro words related to culture or, in the case of the list of the dead soldiers, the fact that they are dying because of the US Army. Using this technique, Perez gives voice to the silenced, by visualizing them with the strikethrough font.

Perez admits that, like so many of his kin, he is not fluent in Chamorro. After moving to the United States as a child, he "lost [his] first language" and he apologizes for it: "so many of [us] have left / guåhan / for military and school, / jobs and hospitals \\ / forgive me, i lost / our fino' haya: *first / language* in transit, ghost / words // who'll translate / me to you \\ i clutched / my passport aboard / I batkon aire: *the air / boat* to san francisco" (Perez, 2017, p. 16). He translates words and expressions between Chamorro and English and undermines the authority and importance of English by using the language and framework of his cultural background instead of the colonizers' (Keown, 2017, p. 164). Chamorro words are more important and seem to be more expressive to him than they would be in English and thus Chamorro becomes the dominant language in the text.

An example of translating traditional Chamorro objects, names of food, animals and heavenly bodies appears in a poem titled "*from* tidelands." The poem is divided into ten sections and spread out through the book, requiring the reader to turn the pages back and forth in order to follow the sense of the poem. Two parts of the mentioned poem are entirely in Chamorro language first, and thirteen pages later in multiple languages; English, Spanish, Japanese, and Chamorro, blended together (Perez, 2010, p. 67, 83). In the first version of the text, twenty-three Chamorro words can be read, while in the second variant contains only six, seven English, six Japanese and four Spanish words. The first, Chamorro version of the poem reads: "puti'on / plåtu / guihan dångkolo / rusåt / kulepbla / katupat / paluman / haggan / higai / guagua' kuadråo / gue'ha / kuronan potta / tuhong / guagua' antigu / bålas / saligao / hugeten månglo' / henton ulu / guihan dikike' / apåcha / uhang / piña / sinangan'ta" (p. 67 star, plate, large fish, rose, snake, traditional rice dish cooked inside a woven pouch made of coconut-leaves, bird, green sea turtle, woven palm leaves, square basket to carry fish, fan made from coconut fronds, door wreath, hat, old fashioned basket, bamboo whip, centipede, windmill, headband woven from coconut leaves, small fish, grasshopper, shrimp, pineapple, our spoken words). All objects and creatures that are referred to in the poem are related to Chamorro traditions or Guam's natural environment. They can be read as representations of activism since they display additional meaning, especially because they appear in both Chamorro and in colonial languages. As the readers turn the pages back and forth to read the two parts together, they recognize that while time and history progressed, the Chamorro object and language were colonized and lost their original meanings and disappeared. In this poem, Perez calls attention to the disappearing culture and traditions while replacing Native words with foreign ones. However, he also encourages perseverance with the six untranslatable Chamorro words. The words or phrases that were not changed into other languages are puti'on (star), katupat (rice pouch), higai (woven palm leaves), guagua' antigu (basket), henton ulu (headband) and sinangan'ta (our spoken words) (p. 83). They represent ancient knowledge (navigation by stars), traditional customs (rice dish, weaving, basket, headband), and Native language (spoken words). In the poem, all of these objects metaphorically survive colonization; by not being translated, Perez helps to ensure they continue to live on in his poetry.

In other parts of the series, Perez explores the meaning of water; evidently one of the most important elements in *from unincorporated territory*. Hanom (or water) is a reoccurring word and image in all four books. It is often written three times as hanom hanom hanom, other times only once, sometimes in parentheses, sometimes without, and again other times in italics. Water supports life and it constitutes a large amount of the human body. "[O]ur bodies are sixty percent water" (Perez, 2010, p. 129) is a sentence that appears throughout the series and Perez plays with its variations. He "dismantles" the human body and studies its parts: "*[our] bones are twenty percent of water*" (Perez, 2014, p. 40), "*[our] blood is eighty percent water*" (p. 9), "our tongues are 70% hånom" (Perez, 2017, p. 39), "our hair is 10% hånom" (p. 51), "our skin is 40% hånom" (p. 67). For him, it is important to show how much the human body is connected with the ocean that constitutes most of our Earth, and so we have to take care of it. "[O]ceania is five parts lands to a thousand parts water," writes Perez (Perez, 2010, p. 129), emphasizing the connectedness between water and land, but also showing how small and vulnerable island communities are. He calls attention to the rising water level around these defenseless islands; "i didn't know 'sea level' / would remind me of 'shelter'" (p. 106). Once the sea level reaches a certain point, there will be more and more climate refugees from the Pacific, he warns.

Perez, a father, is concerned about his daughter's future. His child was born in Hawai'i and she met with water at an early age. She was rinsed in the sink, bathed in the tub, and while still a baby, in the ocean. These intimate moments of the infant meeting the purest element are set side by side with the environmental problems caused by militarism and foreign developments. Perez paints a sinister picture of the environment while he and his wife are bathing the baby in the ocean: "pilot whales, deafened / by sonar, are bloated and stranded / ashore," "schools of recently spawned fish, lifeless, / spoil the tidelands," and the parents and the daughter "shiver like generations of coral reef / bleaching" (Perez, 2017, p. 13). Although the setting of the poem seems peaceful, there are problems hidden "under water." He utilizes water as an object to talk about serious issues and uses poetry to call the reader's attention to them.

Water (the ocean) can connect the author to a community; the past, present and future generations on and away from Guam. The opening poem of *from unincorporated territory [saina]*, titled "*from* sourcing", starts with "water:" "*'[hanom] [hanom] [hanom]'* / ~ / what echoes across waters: / taotaomo'na—" (ancestors) (p. 13). Perez, living in diaspora in Hawai'i, still connects with his homeland through water. He can still "hear" the calling of his ancestors. He recalls a happier period of his people "*before* / contact *before* / colonialism *before* / history" and draws strength from the ancestors who remain with him in "histories" and "*in* our bodies." The poem ends on a positive note: "[we] / will continue *after in* / all *afters*" (p. 13). This idea echoes the Native American writer's, Gerald Vizenor's (2008) idea of *survivance*. As long as the ocean connects Chamorros and other indigenes, as long as they remember history, traditions, and their ancestors, as long as they resist foreign domination, they will survive and they will succeed even in colonial circumstances.

An important, traditional object of the Chamorros that was connected to everyday life and carries traditional knowledge, the sakman (canoe), is another recurring topic in Perez's poems. In the past, Chamorros used canoes to discover the islands around, to connect with other Indigenous communities, to fight in wars, to obtain food from the ocean and so on. Below it is the explanation and history of the sakman after colonization by Perez (2010):

> *the sakman—an outrigger canoe—once numerous in the waters of the mariana islands ... sometimes exceeded forty feet in length and were known as the fastest sailing vessels in the world—following the chamorro-spanish wars [1671-1698] the spanish colonists began destroying the sakman and forbade chamorros to sail the ocean ... the sakman was later burned. by the mid 19th century the knowledge of how to build and sail them was lost. ... in 2007 members of tasi [traditions about seafaring island] ... built a 33-foot sakman ... they named [it] 'saina': 'parents elders spirits ancestors'— on 9/20/08 the sakman was blessed and entered the waters—it was the first time in centuries a sakman could be seen in the waters around guam. (p. 14-15)*

Hence, the title of Perez's second book of the series includes the word "saina" and the cover page of the poetry collection juxtaposes two different types of boats: an old black and white drawing of a sakman on the top of the page and a color photograph of five seafarer US Navy ships on the bottom. The sakman, once an everyday object of the Chamorros, has returned to the ocean and it symbolizes resistance and activism. As long as sakmans sail the seas, Chamorros and their culture will survive. In the poem titled "*from* aerial roots" Perez explores the process of "building and launching of the sakman with [his] own memory of canoe paddling as a student at Chief Gadao Academy" (Hsu, 2012, p. 301). The paddling experience as a young boy had left a deep impact on Perez. After moving away from Guam for more than a decade, "[he] can still feel the burn of movement in [his] body from pulling the currents—still the movement rooted in—[his] body still overseas areal" (Perez, 2010, p. 129). Through him and remembrance, traditions of sailing will live on.

The third book of the series, *from unincorporated territory [guma']*, deals with an object, the *latte*, which is symbolic to the foundation of Chamorro culture because it used to give the basic infrastructure to buildings in Guam in the pre-contact times. Perez (2014) describes it in his book. "*Latte*, or *latde*, are stone structures composed of two parts: a haligi (vertical pillar) and a tasa (bowl-shaped capstone) *the fallen latte is the sign*. The haligi—carved from limestones, basalt, or sandstone—ranges in height from three to nine feet and is wide at the base *bullets ricochet* and narrow towards the top. The tasa, made from inverted coral head or carved from limestone, sits atop the haligi *this raised house to sing*. Completed latte structures *gives us their message* were arranged in parallel rows of at least four pairs evenly spaced. They formed the foundation of homes, schools, canoe shelters, food sheds, and communal spaces *momongmong*" (p.18). Archival images of latte structures are shown on the cover page of the book and placed side by side with a photograph of a US military airplane, a tank, and a large selection of bombs. The juxtaposition of the two images is clear: while the Chamorro culture is supported by natural stone pillars, the American values are built on war and violent occupation.

Because of the earlier mentioned military buildup at Pågat, the archeological remains of the latte village are in danger of disappearing forever. Moreover, besides the latte remnants, there are other valuable elements on the land that need to be taken into consideration: "The Department of the Navy prepared the Draft Environmental Impact Statement (DEIS) to access the military buildup *this cage*. … According to the DEIS, the military planned to build their live firing range complex in an area along the northeastern coast of Guåhan *[we] have* known as Pågat, an ancestral latte village *bullets fragment and*. Many people *ricochet* travel to Pågat to fish, hike, and collect medicinal herbs; to learn about Chamorro culture and history *cues to navigate*; and to seek guidance from the ancestral spirits that dwell there *to sing future*. Pågat is also home to Mariana eight-spot butterfly, an endangered native species *is born and fed and grows and"* (p. 60).

If the military firing range is built, traditional customs, local animals and plants, will be lost, and the ancestral spirits, important components of the old religion, will be disturbed. Perez, to emphasize the importance of the issue, visually juxtaposes other texts by italicizing and inserting them into the main text. The italicized texts, since visually distinctive, catch the reader's attention. The placement and the content of these inserted texts are both important. "The fallen latte is the sign" of the ancient spirits "giv[ing] their message" to the living, explains Perez (2014) on another page in the same book (p. 14). Latte used to be the base of "[homes, schools, canoe shelters, food sheds, and communal spaces" and they were the heartbeat (momongmong), the vital force, of the community. The firing range would symbolize quite the opposite. Soldiers would train there day by day and practice how to *take* life. By adding the sound of the heartbeat to the text in Chamorro, the poet accentuates the message that there will be no heartbeat (instead, there will be death) if the firing range was built.

Moreover, it would resemble a "cage," a prison, and the ancestral village would be soon covered with "bullets fragment and ricochet." Chamorros hold great respect for their ancestors and Indigenous culture and they have historically relied on their guidance. If the space of these practices is taken from them, there won't be much left to "navigate" them towards the future. At last, the endangered creatures of Pågat could not reproduce and would go extinct if the ecological conditions are changed.

In another poem titled "*ginen* tidelands" Perez compares the human skeleton to the latte architecture: *[our] bones*: / acho' latte / *removed from*— / to museums (p. 16). If latte is removed from Guam and placed in museums, where only dead objects are preserved, the culture will die the same way as humans could not live without their skeletons. Therefore, by emphasizing the importance of such an object in these poems and throughout the book, Perez's text can be interpreted as an activist statement against the military buildup on Pågat.

Maps of Guam and the Pacific are other recurrent objects in Perez's poetry. He includes actual maps, maps that are made up of texts and poems about his experience with maps in his series. In an interview with Lantern Review (2010) he explained the function of maps in his work:

The "actual maps" in my first book are ... both visual poems and illustrations of the rest of the work. ... [T]hey function in two ways: first, they center "Guam," a locating signifier often omitted from many maps. Secondly, the maps are meant to provide a counterpoint to the actual stories that are told throughout the book. While maps can locate, chart, and represent ... they never show us the human voices of a place. I place this abstract, aerial view of "Guam" alongside the more embodied and rooted portraits of place and people.

In his first poetry book *from unincorporated territory [hacha]*, Perez incorporates four actual maps. The first one (Perez, 2018, p. 28) shows the historical "Spanish Galleon trade route between Acapulco and Manila" on which Guam was a crucial stop (Perez, 2015a). The second one is a World War II Pacific Map that shows the Japanese control over Guam (Perez, 2018, p. 29). It is significant because most history books make no mention of the history of Guam under World War II, even though it was attacked just like Pearl Harbor and occupied by Japan for three years; the only US territory taken over during the war (Perez, 2015a). The third map shows the importance of Guam as an air travel transit center between the United States, Asia and other islands of the Pacific (Perez, 2018, p. 30). The last, fourth, map reveals the US military bases on Guam which occupies one-third of the island (p. 85). These four maps not only show the great significance of Guam in the Pacific, but also the succession of the (ongoing) colonization. First, the Spanish exploited the island's favorable location. Later the Japanese controlled it and last, American militarism and tourism took it over. As Lai (2011) simply puts it; the visual map poems can disclose and (visibly) connect politics, history and culture more precisely than written ones (p. 16). Although Guam always was and still is an important place in the Pacific and beyond, it is not often mentioned in history books and media. "We are invisible," says Perez (Perez, 2015a). In the preface of *from unincorporated territory [hacha]* he (2008) explains what he means by "invisible:"

On maps, Guam doesn't exist: I point to an empty space in the Pacific and say, "I'm from here." On some maps, Guam is a small, unnamed island; I say, "I'm from this unnamed place." On some maps, Guam is named "Guam, U.S.A." I say, "I'm from a territory of the United States." On some maps, Guam is named, simply, "Guam"; I say, "I am from Guam." (p. 7)

Before European travels, Chamorros relied on different kinds of navigation tools, such as song maps. "After journeys were completed, a song would be created that would weave geographic, biological, and sensory elements together to form a map. These songs would take on features such as the stars, the color of the water, the features of shorelines, changes in clouds, the songs of birds. So long as these songs were remembered and passed on, a return journey was always possible" (Bevacqua, 2015, p. 84). After the arrival of the European explorers, who treated the Pacific Ocean as an empty space, cartographic representations of it were developed, where the area typically separated Asia and the American continent (Iris, 2010). Since then, Chamorros, as well as other Pacific communities, have been forced to look at the world in another way. Instead of song maps and remembrance, they had to learn to "read" and understand visual maps which were created by and for Western navigators (Lai, 2011, p. 15). The same way, Perez cannot help, but search for his homeland on the vast western world map and try to find it through the different names that foreign powers attached to it.

In his fourth book, *from unincorporated territory [lukao]*, Perez (2017) returns to map poems again and includes four of them. The first one is the "Telegeography cable network" that connects countries in and on the two sides of the Pacific Ocean. Here again, Guam plays a central role in distributing the cables among communities. In a note below the picture, Perez states that "more cables have landed on Guam than in either Hawai'i or California" (p. 9). The second map is an illustration and combination of three other maps and shows the "Key US Bases in Pacific Pivot Buildup" (p. 25). By combining three maps ("Mariana Island Training Area EIS," "NOAA IOOS: Pacific Ocean States, territories, etc." and "DITC: Acoustic Effects on Marine Mammals"), Perez shows the overlapping effects the military buildup causes in the area. The third map is of Guam titled "Toxic Chemicals of Guam," and it reveals the locations of the more than a hundred dumpsites of the island (p. 41). The fourth map is the plan of Fire Training Airforce field and the text below describes how the build-up will negatively affect wildlife (p. 57). While the first book and its four map poems took us through historical points and showed the importance of Guam in the region as well as opposed it with its invisibility, the last book and its maps reflect on the negative consequences of colonization. They show the present, but also, predict a pessimistic future for Guam.

Perez, like other Chamorros, locally and abroad, tries to make sense of and find his identity in the colonial context. As Paul Lai (2011) argues, maps are important approaches to determine one's roots of origin and also to establish how one will be perceived by others (p. 15). The fact that Perez cannot find his homeland on the map because it is absent or it is there, but constantly named differently by various powers and for diverse political reasons, is of course symbolic. His experience is shared by many Chamorros who try to grab on to maps and names, hoping they will guide them to answers regarding their origin. Instead of looking for Guam on the world map, Perez provides us with *his* collection of maps. This time, *he* chooses what to show us —— the different definitions of Guam: as a center of trade and later of air travel, occupied nation throughout post-contact history, militarized island and the effects of militarization on people and environment. This definition is not only one or the other or nothing at all, presented by foreign powers, but a mixture of various definitions; the truth told by a man who is both a Native Chamorro and an American and whose binary identity is tied to more than one land. In this sense, maps are representations of guidance for one's spiritual journey. We can look at these maps as important objects that display activist messages. Through them, the reader can see the problems indigenes on Guam encounter: social and environmental issues brought by modernization and militarization. Perez places these maps strategically and sometimes adds a few notes or explanations. However, he does not comment on them, instead, he lets the pictures and numbers speak for themselves. This way these map poems can act as activist texts that signal resistance without stating it directly.

The stone is the final object with the mission discussed in this chapter. It is argued that the stone carries more than its literal meaning and demonstrates the importance of connection to the land. The significance of the stone derives from an old Chamorro myth, "How the Women Saved Guåhan from a Giant Fish," that emerges again and again in Perez's poetry. It tells the story of a large fish that attacks Guam every night and slowly eats away the island, stone by stone. The men try to thwart the fish by chasing it on canoes but all their efforts are unsuccessful. Finally, the women use their hair to weave a large net and manage to capture the fish and save Guam from the giant fish. However, Perez's "version" is not the first modern emergence of the old story. In the past years, Chamorro activists reached back to such "traditional wonder histories," as Bevacqua and Bowman (2016) call them, because they incorporate the old values and teachings of the ancestors which can be applied and used to inspire Indigenous movements and activism (p. 70). The giant fish, of course, symbolizes the American army that takes away the land little by little. The well-known story helps to pass on the vision of activist groups, such as Nasion Chamoru (Chamorro Nation) and others, and speaks against colonialism and militarism. At the same time, it encourages environmental sovereignty and political and cultural independence of the Chamorros (p. 72). This tale became essential in activist rhetoric because it shows the possible destruction of the land due to military developments and the feasibilities to speak up against it and confront it (p. 79).

Interestingly, Perez (2010) includes two different versions of the myth in *from unincorporated territory [saina]*. The first one is told by the poet's grandmother:

once / in days of / our / before time / ancestors / in days / when chaifi (god of the underworld) / virgin mary / not yet come … / a huge fish / lived underground / tunnel between / pago and agana bays / each night ate / stone until / hole / [we] afraid / be no earth / after many generations passed / to days of spanish / mary came / she / knew how to help [us] / she / takes a long silken hair / from / her head makes a loop / she throws it over the fish's head / captive / she / ties the fish / of reach / of earth / so today / if you stand / over tunnel / listen / you can hear / angry beating / tail against / walls / forever / trying to escape from / her hair. (p. 26-28)

This version clearly shows the Christian influences on the ancient tale. Many Chamorro tales, that once had great cultural relevance, have been replaced by stories that served the building of a powerful empire of the westerners. Even though Chamorro stories did survive the colonization of the tales, they were changed and contorted to accommodate the Eurocentric, Christian colonial ideology (Bevacqua and Bowman, 2016, p. 73). Undoubtedly, this happened to this myth, too. Virgin Mary came to Guam to save the Chamorros from their unchristian lifestyle. Although the beast is captured and locked under the earth, perhaps to hell, it is still trying to come back to corrupt the people of Guam, and they are only safe as long as their belief in Virgin Mary is strong.

The second "version of the story of i guihan dångkolo (big fish) [as told before]" appears in a later part of the book (Perez, 2010, p. 55): "*once / the center / of [our] island / eaten away both sides / land between agaña bay and pago bay / becoming more narrow / "if this keeps on [guam] will be cut into two / we must do something to stop it / as [we] talked s messenger brought word / a giant fish had been seen in pago bay / nibbling nibling / deeper / deeper*" (p. 55). Later the men go "*looking / for the giant fish / [we] didn't find it / for it [is] hiding*" (p. 71). At last, the women of Guam "*cut /off some of their long / beautiful / hair / and wove / it into a net / spread out in every direction / then they / began to sing / the fish heard the sound / it swam in to the / underland waters / to hear more clearly*" (p. 97). After it swam close enough, lured by the women's singing, "*[we] dived into the water / spreading net / great fish became tangled / […] / save [our] island / with the magic / of [your] hair / singing*" (p. 122). The original version is not infiltrated with western culture yet and it shows how community working together can maintain security of the land and continuation of the culture. By setting the stories next to each other, Perez shows that it is not only the military might that endangers Chamorros. Foreign ideas, values, lifestyle and religion can be just as dominant as tangible ones. The island that disappears stone by stone refers not only to the land but also to Chamorro culture. The texts are therefore a call for resistance.

The literal meaning of losing the land is shown in another poem as parts of the official documents of the Organic Act are contrasted with the myth. A short passage of the story ("'each night ate / stone until / hole / [we] afraid / be no earth'" (p. 33) is inserted into a three pages long text from the Organic Act that includes the lengthy list of the areas that were seized by the US government (p. 31-33). Perez also shows the magnitude of the portion of the land that was taken through signing the Act by inserting such a limited passage of the traditional story. One can sense how little the Chamorro voices had been taken into account when dividing the land simply by *looking* at this poem. While the text of the Organic Act is italicized, the lines from the myth are normal and stand out clearly from the official document. The poet plays with visuals to show the small, remaining voice of his people. Despite colonization, they are still present and their voices can still be heard.

CONCLUSION

Indigenous people in Guam and elsewhere in the Pacific struggle for sovereignty and decolonization. Local activists often express resistance through displaying cultural identity, such as connecting to their history, traditions, local customs, everyday objects from their culture and stories (Na'puti & Bevacqua, 2015, p. 848). Besides giving the joy of reading, literature can also be a medium to pass on activist messages. As Perez said it in an interview, poetry is empowering and it has always been a powerful tool in political movements and the other way around; authors were always inspired to create by these movements (Perez, 2019). In his work, he addresses cultural, historical, ecological issues that his people have to endure every day due to the centuries-long colonization and militarization of Guam. Often, he does not state his opinion directly but instead uses different techniques to get through his messages. He gives clues to his readers, plays with numbers, percentages and visuals by adding pictures and maps, or arranging texts in an impactful manner. He translates Chamorro words only pages later to force his readers to re-read previous passages and search for meaning throughout the books very consciously. Sometimes he sends his readers to websites where one can get more information and understand the activist message more precisely. His clues often include everyday objects that convey deep meaning in Chamorro culture. The few of them, such as traditionally made objects and food from Guam, the sakman (canoe), latte building structures, different kinds of maps, and slowly disappearing stones as metaphors of the land, were analyzed in this chapter. It was argued that by mentioning these ordinary objects and placing them strategically in his poems, Perez wants to reveal the consequences of colonialism and militarism on Guam. The survival of the traditional objects and activities that surround them symbolizes the survival of Chamorro culture and it depends on the Indigenous community. Perez assists the continuation by including these objects and acts in his poetry, emphasizing their importance, and addressing the urgent issue of their (objects and culture) approaching possible disappearance. "Our native voices are political expressions," says Perez, and as long as Indigenous activists "express the politics of survival, resistance, and resurgence" for example "through poems of protest, critique, and witness," the culture and the people of Guam will live on and thrive in the future.

REFERENCES

Bevacqua, M. L. (2015). The song maps of Craig Santos Perez. *Transmotion*, *1*(1), 84–88.

Bevacqua, M. L., & Bowman, I. K. (2016). Histories of wonder, futures of wonder: Chamorro activist identity, community, and leadership in "The Legend of Gadao" and "The Women Who Saved Guåhan from a Giant Fish.". *Marvels & Tales*, *30*(1), 70–89. doi:10.13110/marvelstales.30.1.0070

Cabral, A. (1993). National liberation and culture. In P. Williams & L. Chrisman (Eds.), Colonial discourse and postcolonial theory: A reader (pp. 53-65). Hertfordshire, UK: Harvester Wheatsheaf.

DeLisle, C. T. (2016). Destination Chamorro culture: Notes on realignment, rebranding, and post-9/11 militourism in Guam. *American Quarterly*, *68*(3), 563–572. doi:10.1353/aq.2016.0052

DeLoughrey, E. M. (2019). Toward a critical ocean studies for the anthropocene. *English Language Notes*, *57*(1), 21–36. doi:10.1215/00138282-7309655

Diaz, V. M., & Kauanui, J. K. (2001). Native Pacific cultural studies on the edge. *The Contemporary Pacific*, *13*(2), 315–342. doi:10.1353/cp.2001.0049

Diaz, V. M., & Kauanui, J. K. (2001). Native Pacific Cultural Studies on the Edge. *The Contemporary Pacific*, *13*(2), 315–342.

Hau'ofa, E. (2005). The ocean in us. In A. Hooper (Ed.), *Culture and Sustainable Development in the Pacific* (pp. 32–43). ANU Press.

Heim, O. (2018). How (not) to globalize Oceania: Ecology and politics in contemporary Pacific island performance arts. *Commonwealth Essays and Studies*, *41*(1), 131–145. doi:10.4000/ces.402

Hsu, H. L. (2012). Guåhan (Guam), literary emergence, and the American Pacific in *Homebase* and *from unincorporated territory*. *American Literary History*, *24*(2), 281–307. doi:10.1093/alh/ajs021

Iris. (2010). The page transformed: A conversation with Craig Santos Perez. *Lanternreview*, 2. Retrieved from http://www.lanternreview.com/blog/2010/03/12/the-page-transformed-a-conversation-with-craig-santos-perez/

Keown, M. (2007). *Pacific islands writing: The postcolonial literatures of Aotearoa/New Zealand and Oceania*. Oxford University Press.

Lai, P. (2011). Discontiguous States of America: The paradox of unincorporation in Craig Santos Perez's poetics of Chamorro Guam. *Journal of Transnational American Studies*, *3*(2), 1–28.

Na'puti, T. R., & Bevacqua, M. L. (2015). Militarization and resistance from Guåhan: Protecting and defending Pågat. *American Quarterly*, *67*(3), 837–858.

Object. (n.d.). In *Merriam-Webster Dictionary*. www.merriam-webster.com/dictionary/object

Peek, M. (2013). Kinship flows in Brandy Nālani McDougall's *The Salt-Wind/Ka Makani Pa'akai*. *Feminist Review*, *103*, 80–98.

Perez, C. S. (2008). *From unincorporated territory* [Hacha]. Kaneohe, HI: Tin Fish Press.

Perez, C. S. (2010). *From unincorporated territory* [Saina]. Richmond, VA: Omnidawn Publishing.

Perez, C. S. (2014). *From unincorporated territory* [guma']. Richmond, VA: Omnidawn Publishing.

Perez, C. S. (2015). *The poetics of mapping diaspora, navigating culture, and being from (Part 1)*. Doveglion Press. Retrieved July 20, 2019, from http://www.doveglion.com/page/2/?s=Craig+Santos+Perez%3A+The+Poetics+of+Mapping+Diaspora%2C+Navigating+Culture%2C+and+Being+From+&submit=Search...#038;submit=Search

Perez, C. S. (2015). Transterritorial currents and the imperial terripelago. *American Quarterly*, *67*(3), 619–624.

Perez, C. S. (2017). *From unincorporated territory* [lukao]. Richmond, VA: Omnidawn Publishing.

Perez, C. S. (2019). Poet to poet interview: Rajiv Mohabir and Craig Santos Perez. *Kenyon Review*. Retrieved from https://www.kenyonreview.org/2019/02/poet-to-poet-interview-rajiv-mohabir-and-craig-santos-perez/

Rowe, J. C. (2015). Transpacific studies and the cultures of US imperialism. In Y. Shu & D. E. Pease (Eds.), *American studies as transnational practice: Turning toward the transpacific* (pp. 259–275). Hanover, NH: Dartmouth College Press.

South, T. (2019). Marine corps plan to relocate from Okinawa to Guam needs a review, Commandant says. *Marine Corps Times*, 3. Retrieved from https://www.marinecorpstimes.com/news/your-marine-corps/2019/05/03/marine-corps-relocation-from-okinawa-to-guam-worthy-of-review-commandant-says/

Steiner, C. E. (2015). A sea of warriors: Performing an identity of resilience and empowerment in the face of climate change in the Pacific. *The Contemporary Pacific*, *27*(1), 147–180.

Vizenor, G. (2008). *Survivance: Narratives of native presence*. Lincoln, NE: University of Nebraska Press.

Woodward, V. S. (2013). "I guess they didn't want us asking too many questions": Reading American empire in Guam. *The Contemporary Pacific*, *25*(1), 67–91.

KEY TERMS AND DEFINITIONS

Chamorro: The Native people of Guam. Also, the native language of Guam.

Guam: A small island country in the Pacific Ocean. Guam is an unincorporated territory of the United States of America.

Guam Organic Act (48 U.S.C. § 1421 et seq.): The Organic Act is a federal law that named Guam an unincorporated territory of the United States of America in 1950.

Latte: Large stone foundations of Chamorro buildings and houses from prehistorical times.

Militourism: It is a term coined by scholar and poet Teresia Teaiwa by combining militarism and tourism. It refers to a phenomenon when the military establishes the tourist industry which later conceals the original source that controls it.

Survivance: It is a term coined by a Native American scholar and writer Gerald Vizenor. He claims that Indigenous communities can only survive if they resist and reject western dominance, and by adopting and incorporating old traditions and tribal wisdom into their daily lives.

Unincorporated Territory: An unincorporated territory of the United States is a self-governing country which is, however, dependent on the absolute power of the US Congress, as well as the US armed forces exercise extensive control over it. The citizens of an unincorporated territory are under the control of the Department of Interior and thus, they are not given the full rights of US citizenship.

Chapter 2
Sustainable Heritage Tourism Through Gullah Geechee Musical Performance

Melanie Shaw
Colorado State University Global, USA

Paul A. Shaw III
Union Institute and University, USA

ABSTRACT

The Gullah Geechee people originally came to the United States as enslaved Africans from the coast of West Africa. Because of harsh conditions along the sea islands, spanning from North Carolina to Florida, the enslaved were often left to work the land while plantation owners retreated to less hostile, inland environments. As a result, many Gullah Geechee cultural, linguistic, and artistic practices remained intact. Today, there is interest in preserving these rich traditions. Because of environmental and cultural threats, preservation efforts must focus on sustainability. This qualitative, critical theory research includes interviews with musical performers from the sea islands and details their perceptions of the role music plays in sustainable heritage tourism. The researchers explored if music performance could be used to promote preservation locally, through tourism to cultural corridor sites, and globally, through touring musical acts. Participants urged caution with traditional tourism models and emphasized the role of younger generations in preserving Gullah Geechee music.

INTRODUCTION

Throughout history, researchers, performers, and audiences have been interested in the musical traditions of the Gullah Geechee people. During the *Civil War*, Gullah spirituals including *Michael Row the Boat Ashore* (Allen, Ware, & Garrison, 1867), and *Kumbaya* (National Public Radio, 2012) were identified and catalogued. During this same period, the *Ring Shout* emerged from this same region, as a unique tradition of singing, dancing, percussive clapping, and stick banging (Library of Congress, 2010). As

DOI: 10.4018/978-1-7998-3729-9.ch002

early as 1922, the *Society for the Preservation of Spirituals* began collecting, recordings, and transcribing the songs from the sea islands where the Gullah Geechee flourished (Reed, 2016). In the 1930s, the Gershwin's, DuBose, and Heyward debuted the opera, *Porgy and Bess,* which was influenced by their exposure to Gullah music (National Public Radio, 2000). Then, in the 1990s, children were introduced to Gullah Geechee music through the popular television show, *Gullah Gullah Island* (IMBD, 2019). Today, groups like *Ranky Tanky* and percussionist David Pleasant tour the globe, sharing the music of this region and preserving the sounds of the Gullah Geechee culture (David Pleasant, n.d.; National Public Radio, 2017).

While there are robust musical examples from the region spanning the past 150 years, it is unknown how to leverage performance of these musical offerings to effectively cultivate, represent, and preserve Gullah Geechee music. Moreover, with a growing interest in conservation and sustainable tourism practices, there is a need for research to identify how local musical performance and musical touring can support these efforts. The purpose of this qualitative study was to apply cultural studies and critical theory research to explore the complex relationships between inbound tourist exploration, performance exportation, and musical conservation, as a means of sustainable, cultural preservation.

This cultural study was designed to be anti-oppressive, to allow the researchers to look beyond what is taught and learned, to expose assumptions that underlie accepted, but oppressive ideas maintained by tradition (Gall, Gall, & Borg, 2007). The researchers explored the findings with caution relative to the assumptions of cultural studies, including these tenets: Every society gives privileges to some while oppressing others; Nonprivileged identities result in oppression; Cultural texts are a powerful means of maintaining privilege imbalances; Music can be interpreted in relation to the cultural content of capitalist consumption and production; Power relations mediate thought; Facts are derived from prevailing assumptions and values; and research practices reproduce oppression based on cultural and demographic categories (Gall, Gall, & Borg).

The focus of this research was to explore Gullah Geechee musical performances and their implications for sustainable heritage tourism. UNESCO (2006) noted links between musical and economic diversity. The researchers found that music is a tool to alleviate conditions contributing to poverty in the following ways: music is a source of funds, is a tool for advocacy, is a lure to involve individuals in development programs, and is a way to build tourism. Musical performances attract visitors to the region through attendance at local events and through cultural awareness via exposure to Gullah Geechee touring acts. Thus, music draws interest to heritage and culture, which can support the perpetuation of longstanding musical traditions developed by the Gullah Geechee people.

A qualitative, critical-theory approach was identified as the optimal methodology to evaluate the perceptions of musicians within Gullah Geechee culture regarding the possibility of sustainable heritage tourism through musical performance. Cultural studies and critical-theory research allow researchers to explore social structures of power as a lens to evaluate lived experience (Gall, Gall, & Borg, 2007). To capture qualitative data around the topic, a semi-structured interview guide (Appendix A) was created and field tested using a panel of experts to ensure trustworthiness. The instrument was created to capture the experiences of Gullah Geechee musicians. The researchers used critical theory as an interpretive lens to address social structures and issues of power relative to the findings. In order to ensure alignment, interview questions were mapped to the following overarching research questions:

Research Question One: What strategies can be used to promote Gullah Geechee musical conservation?
Research Question Two: What role can music play in supporting sustainable heritage tourism?

The researchers received IRB permission to conduct the study from Colorado State University Global. After permission was granted, the researchers identified contact information for Gullah Geechee musical performers and scholars. Those identified were emailed invitations to participate in the study. When a participant indicated an interest, an informed consent form was emailed for review, and an interview was scheduled. The researchers met with musical performers and conducted semi-structured interviews lasting approximately 45 minutes. Interviews were audio-recorded and transcribed using Transcribe Pro software. Transcriptions were sent to interviews for member checking. Then, transcripts were loaded into NVivo12 qualitative software and an analysis was conducted to identify themes pertaining to each research question.

BACKGROUND

The World Bank Group (2018) recognized that preservation of cultural heritage and sustainable tourism promotes local economic development. In addition, these approaches advance social integration and reduce poverty. Dragouni (2017) noted cultural heritage sites often suffer from neglect and degradation in economically disenfranchised areas. As such, any efforts to promote sustainable tourism practices must involve those with a vested interest in the community. Convincing current power holders to share control with nonexpert stakeholders is one of the biggest challenges in sustainable tourism management (Dragouni). For example, the City of Savannah (2018) created a plan for tourism management, with partners including the Downtown Neighborhood Association, Historic Savannah Foundation, National Trust for Historic Preservation, Tourism Leadership Council, and Visit Savannah. The goal of the commissioned work was to balance resident needs, preserve culture and heritage, and promote a positive visitor experience. Nowhere in the 68 pages of the report is there mention of the Gullah Geechee community. This is but one example of how the Gullah Geechee community is often left out of critical conversations that inform policy, directly impacting their lives.

Carlsen and Butler (2011) noted there are problems inherent in current tourism practices that result in a magnitude of barriers, problems, and impacts to local communities. These problems must be confronted in an active move toward greater sustainability. As such, a process of change is needed to move away from traditional tourism practices toward those that can result in respectful and intentional preservation. There are no simple solutions to sustainability (Carlsen & Butler).

Heritage tourism has traditionally centered on sharing inherited assets from infrastructure to arts. Sustainable tourism development requires meeting the needs of the local community, satisfying tourist demands, and protecting cultural and natural resources (Omar, 2013). Sustainable heritage tourism is defined as activities in the local community designed to promote cultural, environmental, and economic preservation (European Union, n.d). Researchers have shown that if tourism is overseen with intentionality, it adds to the development of the local community and the preservation of historic sites. In addition, tourism can increase financial support for conservation from governmental and nongovernmental agencies, visitors, local community members, and the private sector (Atsbha & Satinder, 2019). Du Cros (2001) demonstrated a link between the sustainability of local culture and arts in his research on heritage tourism. Further, Du Cros noted a link between tourism and cultural heritage management; yet, Garrod and Fyall (2000) noted that most academics have focused on cultural, educational, and practical aspects of heritage tourism without addressing sustainability. Sustainability is key as the National Trust for Historic Preservation placed the Gullah Geechee homesites on the list of most threatened places because of development, rising costs, and an influx of residents drawn to coastal living opportunities (National Geographic, 2014). As Pearce and Atkinson (n.d.) noted, sustainability requires that individuals pass on existing cultural assets to the next generation. Thus, those concerned with conservation of both culture and land must ensure intentionality around heritage tourism and sustainability. As Garrod and Fyall concluded, new tourism management philosophies and practices are needed to ensure conservation goals are met.

The Gullah Geechee have struggled to maintain their cultural heritage. From enslavement and land dispossession to disenfranchisement, now more than ever, strategies are needed to ensure heritage preservation through economic development. Tourism is one way to promote cultural awareness and investment. Atsbha and Satinder (2019) noted the importance of providing significant cultural exchanges between tourists and the local community. Such exchanges ensure tourist satisfaction and promote sustainable tourism practices. Because musical performance provides interactions between the audience and artist, it is a logical medium to promote cultural awareness. Gullah Geechee musical performers attract tourists to the Cultural Heritage Corridor and serve as ambassadors outside of their communities by exposing global audiences to historic and contemporary music from the region.

Music generates money for artists and the recording industry. Attali (2017) noted, in many countries more money is spent on music than other forms of leisure. Music is a commodity and its performers receive financial gains through concerts, record and merchandise sales, and publication of music.

SUSTAINABLE HERITAGE TOURISM THROUGH MUSICAL PERFORMANCE

In this study, the researchers were interested in exploring how music might play a role in cultural preservation. They were specifically interested in the idea that musical imports (i.e. tourists traveling to the Sea Islands to attend Gullah Geechee musical performances) and exports (i.e. Gullah Geechee musical performers touring nationally and internationally) might promote sustainable heritage tourism. In order to investigate this topic, interviews were held with five Gullah Geechee musical experts. An interview guide was developed and matched to the two research questions, and then the instrument was field tested by a panel of research experts to ensure trustworthiness. Suggestions were integrated into the instrument based on expert feedback. The interviews were recorded, transcribed, and member checked to ensure accuracy. Following member checking, the interviews were loaded into Nvivo 12 and coded for emergent themes. Below is the outcome of the data analysis, as organized by research question.

Research Question 1

For research question 1, the researchers asked: What strategies can be used to promote Gullah Geechee musical conservation? Interviewees were asked how they viewed their role in music and to define Gullah Geechee music. They were also asked how the music has been preserved throughout history. Interviews revealed several salient themes. These themes captured a myriad of ways that Gullah Geechee music can and has been preserved. Participants noted how the music emerged from enslaved Africans brought to the United States who were able to practice some of their native musical traditions. Despite persistent racism, many of the artistic traditions were preserved and passed down from generation to generation. As such, the rich musical traditions of spirituals, ring shouts, lined hymn singing, and rhythmic expression continue and can be traced even to contemporary popular music. Participants also discussed cultural and linguistic preservation as part of the Gullah Geechee musical tradition.

Enslaved Africans and Persistent Racism

Several of the interviewees noted the longstanding origins of Gullah Geechee music, which emerged when enslaved Africans were brought over to the Sea Islands spanning from North Carolina to Florida. Because of harsh conditions, plantation owners were absent much the year, which allowed for cultural preservation among the remaining enslaved community. Yet, preservation is a loaded concept because of the history of slavery and the persistence of racism. For example, one participant noted that legalized racism and chattel slavery are some of the horrors that must not be overlooked in any exploration of the Gullah Geechee. He noted:

You are talking chattel slavery, lynching, land dispossession, Jim Crow, hyper-incarceration, rebellion – there are similarities between this culture and Native American culture as you can see – there is a certain complexity in this that hasn't been resolved in regular entertainment... It's life. That is, for Gullah Geechee or any African Based music - it is a "life in all its aspects" principle. That is a foundational principle of African-based expression.

He noted that any preservation attempts may be problematic because of the troublesome history of racism that persists in the Gullah Geechee community. He noted:

Even a term like preservation becomes problematic, too. Now I am talking about a Savannah thing... a Good Old Days dialogue, nostalgia, or way-back-then-when focus, which covers other meaningful content. With proper respect we would be coming out of the Native influence. Seven generations – African concepts like Sankofa principles are not nostalgia or heritage brands. We have to watch nostalgia, and heritage projects. We need not preserve—but do something else.

Another participant noted that many of the Gullah Geechee songs have not been widely attributed or heralded as part of this rich musical tradition. He pondered:

The question is why – We still associate plantation life and slavery here – so the appreciation and tribute has not been as readily acknowledged, like it has been with the blues in the Delta. Blacks didn't want to hear about this music that was traced back to slavery. But, with some of the recent work – it has opened up their eyes to show this culture is important. Even well beyond that.

One musical expert stated that Gullah culture involves careful consideration of many influences. She stated:

It's one thing talking about Gullah, but sometimes we have this perpetual cycle of having the image of all about slavery...There is more to being black in America then talking about the Civil Rights Movement, so to speak-or the Civil War. Gullah is much bigger than that. That image of plantation singers, that's one thing, but you do have to show the mathematician, the scientist, the farmer, the educator. You have to show all aspects of the Gullah culture, and not just focusing on people dressing up in plantation garments.

One participant noted that the isolation of the Sea Islands allowed for preservation of many of the elements and traditions found in Gullah Geechee music. He noted that same isolation prevented his family from encountering some of the racism faced by other African American communities. He stated:

All of the teachers that we had were black teachers, all of the people that we interacted with, like family, were black people. So, we did not - I did not - have to deal with racism… So, when you have one family living in one area-don't have anyone other than family and the community-racism may not be a big factor. I asked my great-great-grandmother to speak to me because I wanted to interview her because the church that I went to -or that I attended - did moments in black history. So, I asked her "Did you ever have to deal with racism growing up?" She stopped and she thought about it and she said, "honestly and truthfully, no I didn't, because there was no one here, but black folk."

Rich Musical Tradition

Gullah Geechee music is a rich, expressive tradition that encompasses many genres including spirituals, church music, lined hymn singing, ring shouts, and even spans todays contemporary music. When asked to define Gullah Geechee music, participants often struggled to categorize or limit the types of songs belonging to the community. Participants spoke of dances, rhythms, instruments, song forms, and geographic influences in the music throughout the interview process. One participant discussed how the church influenced the performance. He defined the ring shout and discussed how the White church limited and, consequently, changed its trajectory. He stated:

The Shout that most people would think of when they think of the black church would be catching the Holy Ghost in church, which, honestly and truthfully, if we were to talk about how church was now and compared to church then, a lot of what happens when people catch the Holy Ghost now would have actually caused them to be banished from the church. There were religious rules against dancing in church. That's where the African Americans had to kind of conform to what church was for White people. They did not do the high-energy expression of the Holy Spirit coming down. So, what the Gullah Geechee did was their interpretation of the Christianity that was given to them. The movements of the Ring Shout you still find done in Africa today, you still find done in Jamaica today, you still find done in Cuba, Brazil, Trinidad. The only difference is the rhythms are different, because the drum was outlawed in the United States. So, it was their interpretation of bringing in what was familiar to them and making it fit the situation and the circumstances that they were in.

When an African American person says they shout in church, they're referring to catching the Holy Ghost, the Holy Spirit coming down in church. However, when we refer to the shout or when you may hear someone within my family refer to the shout, we're referring to the Ring shout, which is the dance-like movement within the ring. So, the Shout within the African American church has completely changed and transformed from the Ring shout that we've become, you know, so popular for. The Ring Shout would be the shuffling, dance-like movement - performed in a ring. Along with the percussion of the wood floor - the large stick on a wood floor - that would be the definition of a ring shout - and that is done in a ring.

Another participant noted:

All of the major pieces to what it is to present black, African American music were present; the dancing, the ability to improvise, it was all there. And, of course, the spiritual side of it. Let yourself go and just feel the music and communicate with the other parishioners through song and shout.

One interviewee stated that the music can even be traced to today's popular genres. He affirmed:

The rhythm of the Shout, you'll find it in Hip-Hop, you'll find it in Blues, or find it in Soul.

Another stated:

The Ring shout is the root, the core, the foundation of American music.

And another added:

The Ring shout can be looked at as spirituals with the African rhythm. A spiritual is nothing more than a Shout song without music. A Gospel is nothing more than a Shout song with a piano, a tambourine, a drum. Then you have R&B. R&B is Gospel with a more upbeat tempo. Jazz, the same thing. So, it all starts from one area and it just evolves and takes on another life of its own. At the end of the day, when it's all said and done, it's still the same thing, but different instruments being used.

Participants noted the myriad geographical and musical influences in and from Gullah Geechee song forms, stating:

Honestly, when it comes to music, it's literally something that is constantly going, always evolving.

People want to try to put Gullah Geechee Music in a box and you can't.

Gullah Geechee music is basically in so many ways, the root, the core, and the foundation of a lot of the popular music we hear today.

You might focus on the way that the voice cracks and in the inflections of the voice when we sing a specific song, you'll hear those things within the gospel.

The closest connection America has to the Caribbean and that America had to Africa - that's how I would define Gullah Geechee music.

It's the same exact thing when it comes to Gullah Geechee music. You have these various schools from various different places all coming together. You have these various different pools from various cultures that came and dominated specific areas and that's what brought that music or that way of music to those specific areas. So, it may vary and may differ depending on the community.

Things have to be parsed out if you are talking about Gullah Geechee, African or Indigenous inspired expression – there are rules of play and interplay that don't allow them to fit into either music or art categories.

Music is universal. Whether you speak the same language or not, melodies of sorrow and joy and happiness are the same throughout the world.

You'll see the ring shout movement among dances of Cuba and Jamaica. So, it's kind of weird and kind of meshing together

A lot of the communities are the bearers of the Ring Shout; however, a lot of the communities where the ring shout once existed, have died out such as South Carolina and various other communities in Georgia. Those communities had a lot of contact with white people. They wanted to conform to their white counterparts. So, in South Carolina from my understanding - You'll find that they sing the songs, but they don't do the movement.

The clave of New Orleans music is the same - the funeral march – procession. One of the foundational observances is a ring shout. In New Orleans, those processions – they are like straightened out ring shouts. They are dancing and part of the celebration of life. It was more of a communal support for surviving another day.

The characteristics of Gullah Geechee music - you hear them in spirituals. Dvorak noticed this – this is our legacy. These are our spirituals. And so, going beyond to blues, jazz, hip hop, rapping, - come on. Those back beats are here and then connected to the Caribbean music- which is similar.

Participants mentioned the tradition of lined hymn singing as a major aspect of Gullah Geechee music: Three participants noted:

My church is one of the few that has actually kept line hymn singing alive. In fact, when other churches have their deacons learn line hymn singing, they actually send them to our church, because there's so many different hymns. A lot of the younger ones in the congregation, they feel that lined hymn singing is dull and boring, and no one understands the words. A lot of churches are taken with the idea of replacing lined hymn singing with a praise and worship team. Unfortunately, those churches are losing out on a very fun and important source of music within the black church. There's something within the emotion, and the energy, within that atmosphere, that happens with line hymn singing that does not happen when you have a praise and worship team. The energy, the feeling, the emotions are different. As funny as line hymn singing can be, because you're looking at someone who stands up there, says some words - half the time you might catch the word - you might not - and then you have to go behind them and slowly drag out what it was that they just got finished saying. Half the time, nobody really knew what they were saying. Nobody was really paying attention to what they were saying - but then, you realize the congregation started paying attention. I started listening - I started to pay very, very, very close attention to the words that were being lined. And that's when I started to really appreciate lined hymn singing. The same can be said for the ring shout.

Lining a hymn – They would go to church and be presented with a biblical text but the slaves couldn't read. A deacon who could read or had memorized the line would speak all of the versus out. He would then give them a meter. Long meter was very common on all tunes and was very ornate. He would go through all of the verses and sing two lines. Those would be repeated. Sing, repeat, sing, repeat. And then do the melody. The words would be given to them. And to hear these – the tunes have just been forgotten. Now what has happened. Some of those hymn line tunes took over the spiritual tunes. Sometimes they would just sing tunes from hymn lines interchangeably with spiritual tunes.

Lining is the Gullah Geechee interpretation of a hymn, because you hear the congregation start off singing and then slowly, the hymn quickly builds. As it builds, they'll start doing the rhythm for the ring shout and they'll start clapping that rhythm for the ring shout. You won't find that live in the churches in South Carolina.

Language

During interviews, language was commonly mentioned. Participants found it easy to define the cultural identity factors within the Gullah Geechee community, and discussed the primary role of the creole language spoken even today. Interviewees discussed how diverse accents are often associated with the Gullah Geechee language. Participants contributed these ideas:

The dialect of Gullah that we speak is very different from what you may hear in South Carolina or Savannah. The people here in Savannah think that I'm from the Caribbean, when I'm actually speaking Gullah. People in South Carolina understand it, but they even think that I'm from the Caribbean. Gullah Geechee people are just like any other African ethnicity. You may have a specific group within a specific area, like the Mandinka for instance. You may have the Mandinka in Mali but, the way that they speak will sound completely different from Village to Village, from country to country. And then you have those subgroups within those groups. It is the same way within the Gullah Geechee people. Each sea island has its own distinct sound.

Gullah Geechee people in South Carolina, a large majority or a large population of their ancestors came from the Bahamas. So, what you would hear would sound very similar to Bahamian English and while you may have some people who sound, you know, very similar to those in Trinidad and those who came from other areas like my ancestors. A lot of my ancestors came from the Bahamas, Jamaica, and Haiti. So, the older generation, due to education over the years, the dialect that you would hear from my great-grandmother differs from my grandma and it is different than you hear from my mother and when you get to me, I put my great grandmother, mother, and grandmother all together.

If you hear a Gullah speaker, you would declare they were from Barbados or the Bahamas.

There are very few people who speak the Gullah language today. It's more of a dialect. But still, that's a start. We were taught to straighten the tongue out all the time, because it was important for everybody to speak the King's language.

They didn't tell Scottish immigrants to speak differently. They didn't tell British immigrants or Russian immigrants to speak differently, with their dialects…Even when I was growing up, we were taught to speak properly. But now, I tell my students, it's whatever is appropriate at that moment; the way you speak at home-that's fine; the way you speak with your friends-that's fine. Now, when you are out in public or in my class, then this is how you speak (grammatically correct). But you still do not deny who you are as a person, or what your culture is-trying to find that delicate balance.

Today, everyone wants to make their connections all the way back to Africa, but yet the thing that connects them to Africa is right here in the United States. And that's weird for me. It's like it made me appreciate my own culture, Gullah Geechee culture. That is the closest connection to Africa that I have.

Research Question 2

The second research question was: What role can music play in supporting sustainable heritage tourism? The researchers were interested in understanding how musicians and scholars viewed the ability of music to sustain and bring awareness to Gullah Geechee culture through musical touring acts and also through individuals traveling to the coastal islands to watch live musical performances. Interviewees were asked how music might be a tool for the Gullah Geechee community to promote cultural, environmental, and economic preservation. They were also asked about their role in sustainable heritage tourism. Two primary themes emerged from interviews – tourism caution and heritage preservation.

Tourism Caution

The researchers approached this topic with excitement about the role that music might play as a tool for sustainable heritage tourism, but one of the biggest surprises in the study was how negatively participants viewed tourism. Many expressed deep concern for practices surrounding tourism and they urged caution in using that word in a positive way. One participant wondered why more Gullah Geechee artists are not well known. Another participant remembered how touring helped her find her musical *self.* Interviewees noted:

What sells is comforting, has entertainment value, keeps the regular flow of money, so that it might be turned into a show thing or tour…but...this is disrespectful to me. So – it's not music at all.

It's life…Suffering, pain, spiritual vitality, self-determination, escape, rebellion, freedom – as opposed to happiness such as in escapism, eudemonism, entertainment, gratification, making a buck– etc.

With the music industry at its best, it might be greatly challenged to respectfully absorb this…We need to watch these effects of commodification…We have to watch nostalgia, and heritage projects. We need not preserve—but do something else. Something different needs to happen that is not tourism or preservation. You don't tour or preserve segregation, counter-democracy, lynching, and slavery.

Tourism is explicitly a part of the problem. The dividends go to serve a particularly empowered group. Their desires are valued over what democratic or community development would be. For example, Savannah is a black city, an African American and Indigenous people's repository—but structured tourism does not support this fact. Savannah is trying to sanitize itself.

The controlling powers are fully resistant – it is not only race resistant – but resistant in terms of participation as a whole. This is a problem of leadership. Not the people. Something unique has to happen here—and given the great repository of African and Native culture and history in this region, it should happen here.

When people come here, the culture itself disappears. So, it's important to take it out, so that the people who live here, can then learn the respect of their own culture.

With other artists like Ron Daise, Anita Prather – it is surprising how many people have never heard of them. You wonder why that is so? I believe one of the roles I can play is to help make this music known – and these people a household name. Expanding that is going to be pivotal. Media, documentaries, grants, traveling around.

I grew up in a Christian home with hymns and my mother was a master musician and so she opened the world of music to us. My first hearing of a concert choir would be Mormon Tabernacle Choir. Mom thought there was not a better choir in the world. However, growing up like that, I sort of lost my voice. My first major tour going abroad, I didn't know whether I was black or white. In the black church I was too white, and I was concerned about being too black in the white church. But when I went abroad, I found my voice. Europe only wanted me to sing from the belly of my soul. So, once arriving to South Carolina, that's what I heard. The music spoke to my soul. It just said, this is who you are. Embrace it.

Heritage Preservation

Participants were passionate about the roles community and connection with family and ancestral roots play in sustaining the traditions embodying Gullah Geechee music. All participants noted the importance of fostering a vested interest among younger generations of Gullah Geechee as a key sustainability factor. Education was mentioned as playing a critical role in teaching children about this music and in creating relevance by linking the characteristics of more traditional musical song forms to modern applications like Hip-Hop and Rap. Other participants cited the critical role of ancestors in the Gullah Geechee musical tradition. Participants stated:

I think too often we view it as not as important as it is. Rice is important, the coast is important, language is important, but music is the easiest way to connect. It is simple – immediate. Music connects – here is a song – boom. To me, it is easy. Our books were written by historians and anthropologists, and so music was just thrown in the background. Many of our leaders are not musicians, so it is just thought of as an afterthought, you know? But I think it is much more central than that, as I have been doing – just trying to show this is language, history, all involved in this one piece. When you realize the drum was banned, you have a stick and hands to pound. Such polyrhythm – coordination. And for the past few years – I have been clapping wrong. For years, I was doing the women's rhythm. So, there are roles to play and each has his part.

When I perform, it is not me. My ancestors who taught me the music come through me into the song. I can hear the person who taught me the song – the one I first heard perform it – in my voice. I become my ancestors in the performance.

I realized as I got older the music was nothing more than the story. Those stories are really about what happened during slavery. On those rare occasions, my great-grandmother would call me and my cousin into the living room and she'd grab the broom from out of the corner and ring shout in the living room. Or, she would sit with us and tell us, you know stories, you know stories about her mother or stories about how the shout stayed within our family for so many years and it wasn't until they actually put it in a script that I really began to pay attention. And that made me have a love to learn it - because it looks cool. So, looking at it, it was the entire Community coming together and it wasn't just - you know- a few people left in the group shouting. It was literally members from our entire Community coming together - family members from California, New York, Colorado, Florida, Washington State – wherever. They were coming together, spilling out of our church to do the shout. There would be even more people when my grandmother was little.

One thing that we have done is trying to connect communities together more. There are people where you still wonder why it hasn't spread.

You know Beaufort is focused on reconstruction and the mayor has been really behind this project. A traveling tour – a musical that will travel throughout involving high school and middle school kids is going to be an important part of this. The children will tell the history through music. But that is exciting. It is a great way to hook the younger kids through hip hop, rap, jazz – so – if I can pull it off, it will be great. I would also love to bring one or two older singers to connect with the younger – and make that ancestral link. Intergenerational connection.

At Sandy Island – we have an app where kids can listen on their phones to the music to try to build relevance. Finally, we must look to the future to see how it will last and adapt. That is key. Will it still be here 30-40 years from now? St. Helena is fine – other islands are more in jeopardy. I think the risk is that one thing will be consumed by another. Resorts, development, Wal-Mart- it scares me.

That connection remains – we need to fully embrace that to overcome any stigma. Sometimes how they speak results in judgement – and that is a shame. In some schools – they were trying to teach Gullah to the teachers so that these kids can get the support they need – to reduce the stigma.

Not just African Americans, but all Americans didn't know anything about the Gullah contribution- especially the contribution when it comes to music.

My mother was one of the spearhead movements into bringing Gullah to the forefront so all of us was, basically, thrust into this movement. From the educational side of it, teachers are always concerned about 'the standards, the standards.' The standards and the objectives are always the same. They are never going to change. For me, it's more so giving teachers the creativity of thinking about other aspects of music as opposed to just doing those classical pieces that students study every year. The average person does not realize that the piano and the banjo are African. So, when we talk about what can we do with Gullah, there is no area in a textbook where the Gullah should not be included.

It's all about educating teachers how to recognize your student population, whether its local, international, or immigrants - education in Gullah culture, period. And, making students more self-aware. A lot of the time, whether African American or white, students are not self-aware of who they are - where their family comes from. We get nationality, race, and culture mixed up all the time. They're not mutually exclusive.

SOLUTIONS AND RECOMMENDATIONS

The findings must be evaluated with caution relative to the assumptions of cultural studies. As Gall, Gall, and Borg (2007) noted, issues of power and social structures must be addressed in critical-theory research. As such, the researchers considered the implication of the findings through the central tenets of critical theory and identified solutions and recommendations through this theoretical lens.

Every Society Gives Privileges to Some While Oppressing Others, Power Mediates Thought, and Facts Are Derived From Prevailing Assumptions and Values

Participants were cautious of words like preservation and tourism. These terms tend to be defined, and subsequent plans for them implemented, by those in power. The result in Savannah, Georgia was continued marginalization of Gullah Geechee communities. Participants noted how they have been excluded from discussions around tourism. In Savannah, there is no mention of the Gullah Geechee in the city's tourism management plan. It seems that the power structures in place are controlling the facts, and thus, the narrative of prevailing assumptions and values around touristic draw. This narrative excludes the rich, historical tradition of the Gullah Geechee in many parts of the heritage corridor. The Gullah Geechee have been oppressed throughout time – not only as enslaved Africans and enslaved African Americans, but also during the periods of land dispossession at the conclusion of the Port Royal Experiment (Ochiai, 2001), Jim Crow, and today, when extinction of this rich culture is a legitimate threat due to rising land costs, lack of funding, and deaths of elders, who have long promoted the traditional music of the Gullah Geechee.

Nonprivileged Identities Result in Oppression and Research Practices Reproduce Oppression Based on Cultural and Demographic Categories

Because the researchers of this study are White, we felt a strong responsibility to not only disclose our own race, but to take steps to avoid any cultural appropriation or oppression throughout the research process. As privileged academics, we felt the enormity of checking our privilege and understanding the experiences of our participants – to allow them each to tell their stories of this music and how best it can be preserved. One of our participants gifted us with a wonderful parting comment. She stated, "God does not care who carries the banner. He doesn't care what we look like. He just wants us to do it. Had it not been for my White brothers and sisters, I wouldn't have been able to do it, because Blacks were not appreciative of this cultural tradition. They were embarrassed by it. It took our White brothers and sisters to lift me up, to encourage me, to financially back me – they saw the good in it. That is why my music is out there today. It is the same mindset that helped Harriet Tubman, Sojourner Truth – along those same lines – be mindful, we cannot make this journey by ourselves. It takes all of us – every last one of us."

Cultural Texts Are a Powerful Means of Maintaining Privilege Imbalances and Music Can Be Interpreted in Relation to the Cultural Content of Capitalist Consumption and Production

Several years ago, *The New York Times* ran a story entitled, *A Black Cultural Tradition and its Unlikely Keepers*. In this article, Freedman (2011) journaled how the Society for the Preservation of Spirituals, which was founded in 1922, has been largely responsible for curating, recording, transcribing, and performing Gullah spirituals that otherwise would have been lost. Scholars, folklorists, and preservationists have been working to save and record in written, video, and audio formats much of the Gullah Geechee musical tradition. Yet, often, those entrusted to archive these artifacts are outgroup, and also have privilege because of race, occupation, or social status. Thus, the very practices of preservation may maintain privilege imbalance. In fact, even the members of the most well-known Gullah Geechee musical act, Ron and Natalie Daise, who starred on the Nick Jr. television show, Gullah Gullah Island, have not reaped the financial gains others have from preservation of African American artifacts. Grimshaw (2017) interviewed the Daises and captured these words:

After the show was over, there was this perception that we were rich, laughed Ron, which wasn't the case. We were typecast and pigeonholed as only doing Gullah programming and only doing children's programming, so few offers followed. I had to find work, and I really didn't like teaching. I was never meant to be in a classroom. After Natalie and I helped dedicate the Lowcountry Center at Brookgreen Gardens during Gullah Days, it eventually led to a job offer, and here I am. (para. 15)

Several of the participants expressed concerns about consumerism, music industry practices, and the potential to perpetuate harms against Gullah Geechee performers in an effort to preserve the culture. As such, any preservation attempts must be carefully integrated with efforts to ensure further harms are not enacted.

FUTURE RESEARCH DIRECTIONS

The researchers provided a cursory exploration of strategies to promote musical and cultural awareness; yet, were not able to conclusively find value in a model of tourism supported by interviewees. Because of the caution many participants felt about the words - preservation and tourism, further exploration is needed to develop a model that would allow for cultural perpetuation and musical awareness without the consequences of current tourism or archival practices. Current practices have resulted in disenfranchisement, oppression, and power imbalances. Future trends must ensure cultural preservation that includes the Gullah Geechee community as drivers of the plan and vision. Moreover, participants urged involvement of younger generations as a pathway to healthy, nonharmful preservation. Ingroup cultural awareness – as modeled in ancestral sharing throughout the history of the Gullah Geechee, seems to hold the most significant promise to protect and continue the rich musical traditions described and embodied by research participants.

Future research might be conducted with non-musicians, familiar with sustainable heritage tourism and cultural fragility to determine formalized processes that can be enlisted effectively to support the Gullah Geechee heritage corridor. In addition, research with other visual and performance artists would extend the ideas presented herein and allow for greater transferability. Finally, as noted by several interviewees, grant money is greatly needed to support cultural preservation among sea islanders. Providing funding for projects that would financially benefit the heritage corridor would be a great boon for the Gullah Geechee.

CONCLUSION

In this qualitative study, the researchers explored the possibility that music could be a powerful cultural asset for sustainable heritage tourism in Gullah Geechee communities throughout the Cultural Heritage Corridor. Musicians and scholars of Gullah Geechee culture shared their experiences and ideas regarding how best to conserve Gullah Geechee music. The time-honored tradition of learning from elders in the community emerged as a critical element of musical preservation. Passing the music on to younger generations proved key to securing its future vitality and relevance. Participants also discussed the role of music within the broader context of sustainable heritage tourism. While consensus around exporting Gullah Geechee music through musical touring acts emerged as a positive strategy, musicians' feelings surrounding heritage tourism at the local level were inextricably tied to impressions of commercial tourism and negative examples of the latter's effects within the cultural corridor. The prevailing sentiment was that a new model for creating a sustainable heritage is needed. Members of the Gullah Geechee community must have an equal stake in its vision. Such a model needs to account for the musicians, community members, environment, and visiting tourists. None of these groups are exclusive from any other. They must be considered as a whole-from the outset of planning.

ACKNOWLEDGMENT

The researchers wish to acknowledge the music professionals who shared their time with us to provide perspectives on the important role music plays as a pathway to sustainable heritage tourism.

We wish to extend our gratitude to David Pleasant for sharing his insights and samples of his musical offerings with us during the early research stages.

Thank you to our field testers who provided valuable suggestions on our semi-structured interview guide.

This research received no specific grant from any funding agency in the public, commercial, or not-for-profit sectors.

REFERENCES

Allen, W. F., Ware, C. P., & Garrison, L. M. (1867). *Slave songs of the United States*. A. Simpson & Co. doi:10.5479il.78680.39088002074508

Atsbha, G. A., & Satinder, K. (2019). The structural relationship between tourist satisfaction and sustainable heritage tourism development in Tigrai, Ethiopia. *Heliyon*, *5*(3), e01335. Advance online publication. doi:10.1016/j.heliyon.2019.e01335 PMID:30957037

Attali, J. (2017). *Noise: The political economy of music*. University of Minnesota Press.

Carlsen, J., & Butler, R. (Eds.). (2011). Island tourism: Towards a sustainable perspective. Oxforshire: UK: CABI. doi:10.1079/9781845936792.0000

City of Savannah. (2018). *Framework for Savannah's tourism management plan*. Retrieved from https://www.savannahga.gov/DocumentCenter/View/14245/Tourism-Management-Plan?bidId=

Dragouni, M. (2017). *Sustainable heritage tourism: Towards a community-led approach*. Retrieved from https://discovery.ucl.ac.uk/10025949/1/E-thesis.pdf

Du Cros, H. (2001). A new model to assist in planning for sustainable cultural heritage tourism. *International Journal of Tourism Research, 3*(2), 165–170. doi:10.1002/jtr.297

European Union. (n.d.). *Sustainable heritage tourism*. Retrieved from https://europa.eu/cultural-heritage/sites/eych/files/sustainable-cultural-tourism-recommendations_en.pdf?token=PsePI9T4

Freedman, S. G. (2011, June 16). *A black cultural tradition and its unlikely keepers*. Retrieved from https://www.nytimes.com/2011/06/18/us/18religion.html

Gall, M. D., Gall, J. P., & Borg, W. R. (2007). *Educational research* (8th ed.). Pearson.

Garrod, B., & Fyall, A. (2000). Managing heritage tourism. *Annals of Tourism Research, 27*(3), 682–708. doi:10.1016/S0160-7383(99)00094-8

Grimshaw, P. (2017). *A Gullah family: Ron and Natalie Daise*. Retrieved from https://grandstrandmag.com/feature/a_gullah_family_ron_and_natalie_daise

IMBD. (2019). *Gullah Gullah island*. Retrieved from https://www.imdb.com/title/tt0177444/

Library of Congress. (2010). *Ring shout*. Retrieved from https://www.loc.gov/item/webcast-5109

Lim, C. C., & Bendle, L. J. (2012). Arts tourism in Seoul: Tourist-orientated performing arts as a sustainable niche market. *Journal of Sustainable Tourism, 20*(5), 667–682. doi:10.1080/09669582.2011.636817

National Geographic. (2014). *Being Gullah or Geechee, once looked down upon, now a treasured heritage*. Retrieved from https://news.nationalgeographic.com/news/2014/10/141017-gullah-geechee-heritage-corridor-lowcountry-coast-sea-islands-sweetgrass/

National Public Radio. (2000). *Porgy and Bess*. Retrieved from https://www.npr.org/2000/10/08/1112186/porgy-and-bess

National Public Radio. (2012). *When did kumbaya become such a bad thing?* Retrieved from https://www.npr.org/2012/01/13/145059502/when-did-kumbaya-become-such-a-bad-thing

National Public Radio. (2017). *Ranky Tanky builds on the music and culture of slave descendants*. Retrieved from https://www.npr.org/2019/07/26/745583378/ranky-tanky-builds-on-the-music-and-culture-of-slave-descendants

Ochiai, A. (2001). The Port Royal Experiment revisited: Northern visions of Reconstruction and the land question. *The New England Quarterly, 74*(1), 94–117. doi:10.2307/3185461

Omar, H. (2013). *The development of sustainable cultural heritage tourism in Malaysia: Implication for planning and management.* Retrieved from http://etd.uum.edu.my/3595/

Pearce, D., & Atkinson, G. (n.d.). *The concept of sustainable development: An evaluation of its usefulness ten years after Brundtland.* Retrieved from https://pdfs.semanticscholar.org/a986/23c43d6de44735ec6232b1fa208ec7281d50.pdf

PleasantD. (n.d.). *David Pleasant.* Retrieved from http://www.davidpleasant1.com/

Reed, D. V. (2016, October 26). *Society for the preservation of spirituals.* Retrieved from https://www.scencyclopedia.org/sce/entries/society-for-the-preservation-of-spirituals/

World Bank Group. (2018). *Cultural heritage, sustainable tourism and urban regeneration: Capturing lessons and experience from Japan with a focus on Kyoto.* Retrieved from https://documents.worldbank.org/curated/en/938741531140109250/pdf/128058-WP-Kyoto-CHSTUR-postTDD-final-PUBLIC.pdf

ADDITIONAL READING

Alcoff, L. (1992, Winter). The problem of speaking for others. *Cultural Critique, 20*, 5–32.

Bhandaru, D. (2013, April). Is White normativity racist? Michel Foucault and Post-Civil Rights racism. *Polity, 45*(2), 223–244. doi:10.1057/pol.2013.6

Delgado, R., & Stefancic, J. (2017). *Critical race theory: An introduction.* New York University Press.

Dewey, J. (2005). *Art as experience.* Penguin.

Downs, J. (2006). *Why we write: The politics and practice of writing for social change.* Taylor and Francis.

Jones-Jackson, P. (1987). *When roots die: Endangered traditions on the sea islands.* University of Georgia Press.

Parrish, L. (1965). *Slave songs of the Georgia sea islands.* Folklore Associates, Inc.

Pyatt, T. (2006). *Gullah history along the Carolina lowcountry.* Author.

Rice, M. (2009). *Music education through Gullah: The legacy of a forgotten genre.* Author.

KEY TERMS AND DEFINITIONS

Cultural Heritage Corridor: The Gullah Geechee Cultural Heritage Corridor is a federal national heritage area designated to promote the conservation of these historic communities.

Geechee: Referring to people from the Sea Islands of Georgia, who were originally brought to the United States involuntarily during slavery.

Gullah: Referring to people from the Sea Islands spanning from North Carolina to Florida, who were originally brought to the United States involuntarily during slavery.

Lining a Hymn: A song leader sings the lines of a hymn and the congregation repeats them. This type of singing is still practiced in some Gullah Geechee churches. The practice likely began as a result of low literacy rates among parishioners who could not read the hymnal.

Ring Shout: A type of musical performance involving dancing, shouting, and percussive rhythms common in Gullah Geechee communities.

Spiritual: A spiritual is based on psalms and hymns merged with African musical styles.

Sustainable Heritage Tourism: Referring to activities in the local community designed to promote cultural, environmental, and economic preservation.

Touring: Referring to musical performances given outside of an artist's local community.

APPENDIX 1: INTERVIEW QUESTIONS MAPPED TO RESEARCH QUESTIONS

1. We identified you as an expert who could inform our research about Gullah Geechee (GG) music. How do you see your role in this art form? (RQ1)
2. How would you define GG music? (RQ1)
3. How has GG music been preserved throughout history? (RQ1)
4. What preservation strategies are needed to ensure the vitality of GG music in the future? (RQ1)
5. How might music be a tool for the GG community to promote cultural, environmental, and economic preservation? (RQ2)
6. What role might GG musical touring acts or tourist visiting the Cultural Heritage Corridor to attend GG musical performances play in sustainable heritage tourism? (RQ2)
7. How do you see your own role in sustainable heritage tourism? (RQ2)
8. Is there anything else you would like to share with us regarding GG music and our research study? (RQ1, RQ2)

Chapter 3
A Qualitative Study of Native American Higher Education and Student Resiliency

Elizabeth Peralez
Colorado Technical University, USA

ABSTRACT

This chapter explores the degree to which Native American culture impacts the resiliency of Native American students earning degrees at three tribal colleges in the southwestern part of the United States. This is a qualitative case study that was based on the following research question: "How does Native American culture contribute to the resiliency of Native American students who are earning a degree at a tribal college?" This chapter focuses on the concerns of Native American students, and the cultural events they may have encountered during their educational journey. The research data were collected from interviews of 18 Native American students who were in their last year of college. Themes surrounding culture, resiliency, tribal colleges, academics, and Native American role models were discovered and used to determine the impact Native American culture has on the resiliency of Native American students.

INTRODUCTION

Native Americans who navigate American systems of higher education "must absorb a great deal of factual content, and they must also place that knowledge into the context of their own tribal and community traditions" (Deloria, 1994, p. 7). As a Native American educator, Vine Deloria, Jr. went on to add that "the thing that has always been missing in Indian education and is still missing today, is Indians" (p. 62). He also acknowledged that Native Americans who serve on various educational committees easily conform to non-Indian educational vocabulary and concepts. Deloria asserted that these Native Americans leave their native heritage behind and do not attempt to incorporate Native heritage into the educational tasks they perform. He argued that Native Americans involved in education should work to address three main issues: a) recognize the cultural differences Native American students face in the classroom, b) find ways to involve family in educating Native American students, and c) seek more

DOI: 10.4018/978-1-7998-3729-9.ch003

academic funding for textbooks, curriculum, and teacher training. Native American educators can use educational research as a way to address these continual issues even today.

Their native culture surrounds native American students who live on the reservation, but when they leave the reservation, they must live in mainstream America's society and culture. Some Native American students chose to attend tribal colleges on or near a reservation. For these Native American students, this chapter explored the impact of their native culture on their success in completing their educational journey. Faircloth and Tippeconnic (2010) researched data from the National Center of Education Statistics and found that 50% of Native American students do not complete their education. They recommend that more research is needed on the emphasis Native American culture has on dropout and graduation rates. This chapter explores the degree to which the integration of Native American culture in the campus environment of three tribal colleges affected student success and resiliency. Three tribal colleges from the southwestern part of the United States were a part of this study. The results of this study did illuminate if native culture helps or does not help Native American students' resiliency to stay in school.

BACKGROUND

Native American education today is very different from how it began with boarding schools, where the focus was to remove the "*Indian*" from the Native American students. Historically, the U.S. government had four goals in providing academic education for all Native American students who were sent to boarding schools. The first was to civilize them by teaching them "to read, write, and speak the English language" (Adams, 1995, p.21). The next goal was to individualize them by teaching them to work for individual gain of property, money, and to learn American egotism. Also, the U.S. Government sought to Christianize them so they would "embrace an entire ethical code" (p. 23), which would allow them to be responsible for their Christianity. Lastly, the government wanted to train them for citizenship by teaching them to accept that the taking of their land was justifiable, and the only hope for their race was to join in American progress.

Adams (1995) revealed several early struggles that resulted in the resistance of Native Americans students to their education. First, Native American students struggled with being separated from their parents to attend school. Second, older Native American students struggled because they viewed their education as an "assault on their cultural identity" (p. 223). Third, Adams described their struggle in psychological terms; he stated they struggled with cognitive control. Native American culture, like other cultures, has a distinct paradigm of the world that impacts views, decisions, and actions. Adams acknowledged this as cognitive control. Native American students struggled with knowing what to think and how to act because they faced a severe culture clash between their culture and the white culture exhibited in the boarding schools. Though many Native American students struggle with their education, a growing number have persisted and continued to the point of seeking higher education.

In order to understand their resiliency, it is essential to recognize the current challenges experienced by a majority of Native American college students. These challenges include a) the perception that white campuses are hostile toward them, b) inadequate preparation for college in high school, and c) low levels of financial support (Jackson, Hill, & Smith, 2003).

DeVoe and Darling-Churchill (2008) reported "in 2007, some 44 percent of American Indians/Alaska Natives age 25 or older had attended some college or completed an undergraduate or graduate degree" (p.148). They also stated that the number of enrollments for Native American students in colleges and universities more than doubled from 1976 to 2006, from 76,100 in 1976 to 181,000 in 2006. The number of Native Americans in tribally controlled colleges grew from 13,583 in 1976 to 17,255 in 2006. In 2006, there were 32 tribally controlled colleges. Tribal colleges differ from traditional colleges in their focus on Native American culture to preserve and enhance Native American languages and traditions (DeVoe & Darling Churchill, 2008).

As the "self-determination" movement grew during the 1960s, Native American leaders began to consider how higher education could save the tribal culture and strengthen reservations. They initially considered the specific needs of Native American college students. They believed that college-age Native American students needed personal attention to overcome geographic isolation and social barriers, such as suicide and alcohol-related deaths. The Civil Rights movement influenced native American leaders, and they realized the need to control higher education for Native American students (Fann, 2004). In 1968 the Navajo Community College opened as the first Tribal College. The American Indian Higher Education Consortium (AIHEC) reports it was established in Arizona by the Navajo Nation, and in 1997 the Navajo Community College changed its name to Diné College (AIHEC, 2008).

Pember (2008) implied that the Tribally Controlled Community College Assistance Act of 1978, signed by then-President Jimmy Carter, has been the essential legislation since the beginning of tribal colleges because it provided funding for tribal colleges. In the past college, classes were often held in abandoned buildings, barns, or even trailers. As a result of their struggle to just survive, tribal colleges could only offer associate degrees that centered on general education. The mission of tribal colleges today is: (a) to provide, through the curriculum, learning environments that restore traditional Native American cultures, and (b) design and teach courses that can be transferred to American four-your colleges and universities (The American Indian Higher Education Consortium, 2008). As tribal colleges continue to work to achieve their mission, they support various tribal cultures while seeking to preserve an overall Native American culture. "Although there is a great deal of diversity in tribal culture and traditions, valuing spirituality and culture is central to the philosophy of the tribal college movement" (Pember, 2008, p. 1).

History of Native American Education

Papanek (1994) revealed that for early Native American children, the family was their primary source of education. The extended family of grandparents, aunts, uncles, and cousins were all involved in teaching tasks and skills they would need as adults to ensure the continuation of the tribal community. The elders in the family were the ones who taught the native children about their own tribe's values and traditions. Deloria (1994) asserted that tribal elders taught their people in traditional ways before the U.S. Government attempted to take over Native American education. From 1875 to 1928, the goal of formal or mainstream education for Native Americans was assimilation into American culture (Adams, 1995). One of the goals of the U.S. government was to decide the most convenient way to settle ownership of the newfound land. In the minds of the U.S. Government officials, the native culture was unacceptable, and the natives were seen as savages (Adams, 1995). The government believed that educating Native Americans into the culture, values, morals, and habits of American society would allow them to become productive citizens. The idea of educating Native Americans became popular since waging war against the natives would be too costly. According to Adams (1995), the cost of a war with Native Americans could have exceeded \$22 million, whereas only \$1,200 to educate one Native American student for eight years. Therefore, the U.S. military choose assimilation over elimination (Fletcher, 2008). The U.S. government saw education as a quick fix, and in 1850 Congress provided money to a fund called the Civilization fund, which was to be used to transform Native Americans into model citizens that resembled the European colonists (Federal Education Policy and Off-Reservation Schools 1870-1933, 1999).

Adams (1995) revealed that U.S. policymakers created day schools near the edge of reservations where students would go in the mornings to be trained in white civilization but return to their native families and homes at the end of the day. In 1870, Congress provided $100,000 for schools among native tribes that would be run by various religious organizations. A year earlier, the government had given churches and missionaries the authority to act on behalf of the government in hiring all personnel on reservations. Around 1893, the government mandated that Native American children from ages six to sixteen to attend school. Since the schools were on the reservations and the children lived at home with their families, and within their own culture, it did not take long for the U.S. government to realize that assimilation was not working through the Day schools (Adams, 1995; Keohane, 2006).

The next attempt to transform Native Americans was through boarding schools. The first boarding school was established in 1860 on the Yakima Native American Reservation in Washington State. Initially, the school provided an academic education consisting of reading, writing, math, science, history, arts, and learning to speak the English language. The hope was that through this formal education, young Native Americans would become citizens (Southwest Native American Relief Council, 2006). According to Adams (1995), "If the problem with Indians was that they were savages, then what Indian children needed was a civilized education." (p. 21). The Protestant Republicans of the mid-19th century believed that in order to assimilate young Native Americans, they would have to be trained in Christianity (Southwest Native American Relief Council, 2006). The most well-known boarding school was the school started by Richard H. Pratt.

Before Richard Henry Pratt was involved in education, he served in the Indiana cavalry in April 1861. After fighting for the Union in the Civil War, he returned to run a hardware store in Logansport, Indiana. However, Pratt soon realized that he was meant to be in the military and rejoined the Army. After being commissioned as a second lieutenant, he was sent out west and fought Native Americans for eight years. During this time, as he saw Native Americans slaughtered, he started to believe that if Native Americans were to survive, they needed to be immersed in the American culture and American way of life (Adams, 1995). Pratt was able to test his theory when he was given vague orders to supervise the incarceration of 72 Apache prisoners. The prisoners were sent to Ft. Marion, which was near St Augustine, Florida. There Pratt was able to begin his experiment of educating the Native Americans.

Adams (1995) reported that Pratt did not waste time trying to change his Native American prisoners' culture to that of the white man's culture. He started by removing all the leg irons and giving all prisoners uniforms soon after they arrived at Fort Marion. Pratt began to meet with the prisoners and talk to them about what it would take for them to survive in a white man's world and ways they could embrace the white man's civilization. Pratt began to integrate the Native Americans into the community of St. Augustine. He allowed some prisoners to leave the fort and walk around the city. Pratt also began to focus on teaching the Native Americans the English language and Christianity. Soon Pratt was holding two-hour school days where the Native American student prisoners were learning English and the ideals and values of the white man's culture. Some young Native Americans declared their belief in the Bible and no longer practiced their native beliefs and traditions.

Pratt persuaded The Secretary of War to allow him to open a boarding school in Carlisle, Pennsylvania, in an abandoned military post (Federal education policy & off-reservation schools 1870-1933, 1999). The school opened on November 1, 1878. Trafzer, Keller, and Sisquoc (2006) revealed that the school was initially a living experiment on Native American students. Carlisle's founder and first superintendent, from 1879 to 1904, was Captain Richard Henry Pratt. He was confident that his rigorous five-year program of academic, vocational, military, and Christian training would serve Indian children's attachment to family, community, and all aspects of their past and teach them to dress, talk, behave, and think like white Americans. (p. 101) Pratt recognized that the importance of the school's success would come from the validation of white Americans. To get the support of Americans, Pratt created and published a sizeable monthly newsletter, which he considered the voice of the school. It focused on the achievements of the school. A second more modest publication of the school was a paper whose focused readers were to be students who had left the school and returned to their reservations (Trafzer et al., 2006). Once the Carlisle boarding school opened, it became an official part of the national system of Native American education (Marr, n.d.).

Boarding schools were established off the reservations so that the students would have no contact with their families. According to Adams (1995), the Native American students were often in shock the first few days as they were forced into what must have seemed like another world. The Native American children were helpless, defenseless, bewildered, and forced just to try to survive (Federal education policy & off-reservation schools 1870-1933, 1999). As young Native Americans were taken, many times by force, from their families to boarding schools, the first experience for many was the cutting off their long hair. They received new "White" names and were forced to eat food that was very different from what they usually ate. The children had to march and live in dormitories (Southwest Native American Relief Council, 2006). A typical day began early and consisted of specific tasks, which included regular inspections. Bells were used to control the timing and sequence of tasks, such as brushing teeth, washing hands, lining up, exercising, and marching. Students spent half the day in the classroom, and the other half performing work assignments. The academic curriculum consisted of U.S. history, learning the English language, math, reading, spelling, some music, and art (Marr, n.d.). The girls spent half the day doing household tasks (i.e., laundry, sewing, cooking, and cleaning), while the boys learned carpentry, blacksmithing, and other vocational skills (Adams, 1995).

The Superintendent of Native American Education from 1898 to 1910 was Estelle Reel, who believed the curriculum should focus on manual skills since an academic education would not result in Native Americans becoming economically independent (Marr, n.d.). Therefore, in 1901, Reel developed a curriculum that centered on teaching agricultural skills to Native American students. In 1915, after Reel left her position, this trend continued (Federal education policy & off-reservation schools 1870-1933, 1999). During Reel's time, Charles Lummis was beginning to change the direction of Native American education. Lummis was a supporter of the boarding school approach until 1888 when he moved to New Mexico. He saw firsthand the effects on parents of taking children from their homes. By 1892, he was involved in influencing Congress to repeal the policy requiring Native American children to be taken from reservations to distant boarding schools. Through his relationship with President Theodore Roosevelt, he was able to influence government officials' views on Native American policy. In 1928, during the final years of his life, he saw John Collier, an American Indian activist, become commissioner of Native American Affairs (Thompson, 2001). This was the beginning of the end for boarding schools; however, their impact on Native American education did linger.

Though boarding schools victimized Native Americans in an era of acculturation, they also provided a place for cultural persistence (Adams, 1995). Davis (2001) stated that boarding schools caused Native Americans in the late 20th century to seek political and cultural self-determination. Despite the goal to destroy Native American cultures, boarding schools facilitated cultural persistence in unintended ways.

As students from different tribes were forced together, it drove each to hold onto their tribal identities. Those that did graduate from boarding schools returned to their tribal communities and, through their education, often became tribal leaders. Some worked to strengthen local and national level traditional cultures; for instance, in Santa Fe, where the Native American school was used for assimilation, it is now a place that centers on political and cultural self-determination (Davis, 2001).

Tribal Colleges

According to Boyer (2004), there was considerable doubt in the minds of many when the idea of tribal colleges was first announced to the public. At first, mainstream and existing traditional colleges would not accept transfer credits from any tribal college. Nugent (2003) stated that the idea behind the creation of tribal colleges was to provide a learning environment where Native American students could acquire skills that could help them, and their families, seek better jobs in an effort to increase their economic status. Tribal colleges provide education to some of the poorest and least academically skilled students in America. Tribal colleges allow access to education for many Native American students who are the first in their family's history to attend college and seek higher education. Delos (2009) asserted that tribal colleges are growing as a result of reaching out to more high school students. He revealed that as tribal governments seek to revitalize their culture, they are looking to education, and more tribes are considering establishing a tribal college of their own. Delos also stated that the core mission of tribal colleges is to preserve tribal culture and language, which is one of the main differences between them and traditional universities.

Boyer (2004) stated a common goal of all tribal colleges is the desire to create Native American leaders. Since most tribal colleges are located on reservations, a college education is within reach of most Native American students. Williams (2007) found that tribal colleges are centered on the principle that Native American students should not have to abandon their culture while earning a college degree. Tribal colleges also provide a second chance for Native American students who are unsuccessful at a traditional college or university (Boyer, 2004). Nugent (2003) reported that tribal colleges create a Renaissance-like atmosphere for Native American students who often experience a rebirthing of their culture and values. This can lead to Native American students feeling empowered as they claim their own cultural identity (Boyer, 2004; Nugent 2003). Williams (2007) stated young and old Native Americans are starting to see the value of a college education from tribal colleges, which integrates their culture, uses Native American role models, and allows them to stay at home. Reha (2007) revealed that tribal colleges are a way to educate Native American students without them having to leave the reservation for other parts of the country. One tribal college formed a partnership with a traditional university, and the university provides the opportunity for students to take classes at the university through distance education. Reha wrote that educating Native American students at home and on the reservations could positively improve living conditions on reservations.

St. Germaine (1995) revealed how Native American college students who went from schools on reservations, which tend to be like small village schools in Alaska, to predominantly White educational institutions, like major universities, can experience some degree of cultural shock. For example, some schools built on reservations are circular, a native type of architecture for spiritual reasons, while traditional American school buildings are not. Tribal colleges can be a way for Native American students to transition from one culture to another. St. Germaine believes that if educators do not address cultural issues, Native American students will feel the pressure to choose one culture over the other.

The American Indian Higher Education Consortium (AIHEC, 2008), reported in 2007 the total percentages of degree types for all tribal colleges as (a) 0.5% for master's degrees, (b) 6.6% for bachelor's degrees, (c) 68.3% for associate degrees, (d) 23.7% for certificate, and (e) 0.9% for apprenticeships and diplomas. The AIHEC also reported for 2007 the following breakdown of total graduations by disciplines for all tribal colleges: (a) liberal arts were 19.1%, (b) social sciences were 16.4%, (c) vocational/career programs were 14.5%, (d) business were 13.9%, (e) education were 11.7%, (f) nursing and health were 8.7%, and (g) sciences were 5.3%.

Native American College Students

Watts (2003), Assistant Director of the American Indian Research Opportunities at Montana State University, found Native American students did not feel comfortable, and even feel pressured in classroom situations where instructors look to them to speak on American Indian topics as if they were to speak for all Native Americans. Students explained they were more concerned about the current state of racism than what happened to Native Americans in the past. The Native American students wanted their instructors to understand that when Native American students do not speak in class, it does not mean that they are not paying attention. The students pointed out that Native American thought process is different, and that English may not be their first language. The Native American students expressed that they do not seek special treatment; they only want to have an equal opportunity to pursue their educational goals. Native American students also considered themselves family-oriented because they tried to stay involved with family activities back home, while at the same time balancing their academic studies. Lastly, it was stressed that all of the above might not apply to every Native American college student.

Morales (2007) reported on some of the characteristics of Native American college students; for instance, it is difficult for Native Americans to speak in front of classmates because they were taught to be silent as a way of showing respect. Morales also revealed how being around Caucasians was difficult because there is no silence; one student told Morales there are little talking and noise on the reservation. Most tribal college students are described as nontraditional students. The average student is in the late 20s and is a single parent with at least three children. The student is the first in the family to attend college and work full-time (Williams, 2007). Boyer (2004) found that more and more Native American students who are attending tribal colleges are studying online, which allows them to stay at home. However, as of early 2009, Delos revealed that changes are occurring; younger Native American students are attending tribal colleges, with an average age between 16 and 24 years with some coming straight from high school.

Delos (2009) found that it is not uncommon for Native American students to enroll in a traditional university first and then transfer to a tribal college in order to receive the help and support they need to succeed. Delos also found that many Native American students do not want to leave their families. Therefore, without a nearby tribal college, they may never have the opportunity to earn a college education. Deschenie (2004) described how one student stopped drinking while attending college because she wanted to succeed and earn a college degree. Another student used words like learning, struggle, reward, and inspiration to describe her educational journey at a tribal college. According to Rehr (2007), one student, who after six years of struggling at a traditional college, returned home to her reservation and earned a double major in business administration and marketing at the local tribal college. Rehr also found that the key to this student's success at a tribal college was the one-on-one time she needed and received from her instructors. Aragon (2002) stated that Native American students desire learning environments where instructors provide consistent feedback and use various types of media. The American Indian College Fund (2008) and Deschenie (2004) reported that 73% of Native American students seek a college education to help their families. As of 2008, it was reported that 64% of Native American Students seek a college education in order to help their people.

Morales (2007) stated that some universities, which are not tribal colleges, provided tribal or cultural support for Native American students. These institutions invited tribal elders to counsel Native American students while the students are working towards a college degree. The elder served as a mentor, and at times explained to the professor why tribal traditions and ceremonies take Native American students away from their college courses. This is important because Morales observed that Native American students do not hesitate to leave their college life when called to participate in a tribal ceremony. Teicher (2006) revealed how an advanced mentor program at Northern Arizona University (NAU) was designed to improve the retention of Native American students. In 2006, 10% of the NAU student body was Native American, and only about 29% were graduating within six years. University leaders hoped that Native American students would turn to mentors during difficult times while at the university. It was reported that Native Americans face culture shock when they first arrive at a university setting. NAU set up a program for various tribal leaders to become resident elders; they would help students live in two worlds, their native world, and the university world. One task of the elders was to assist professors in understanding their Native American students.

As NAU attempts to bridge the culture gap for Native American students, educators must recognize how they contribute to the issues Native American students encounter. One barrier educator creates for Native American students is when they cannot or choose not to acknowledge their individual cultural biases when teaching these students. Educators must identify their individual biases and recognize how they are open to cultural influences and be better trained to understand the issues Native American students can face in traditional college settings (Wilder, Jackson & Smith, 2001). Another barrier for Native American students is often the lack of relationships that encourage their educational journey. Faculty who became mentors for Native American students and nurtured them found their students were more successful in their transition from high school to a college setting (Wilder, Jackson & Smith, 2001).

St. Germaine (1995), a professor at the University of Wisconsin-Eau Claire who grew up on the Lac Courte Oreilles reservation in Wisconsin, stated that cultural obstacles for Native American students play a role in their educational success. He explained that instructors should use a curriculum that is based on subject matter that directly relates to Native American student's lives. He reported that cultural theorists have implied that educators need to have some form of native culture awareness and be able to structure curriculum around Native American students' cultural needs. However, there needs to be educational research studies to support what cultural theorists are stating. St. Germaine reported that Native American students who experienced academic success in reservation schools failed almost instantly in White educational institutions. He explained that in White schools, the Native American students' encountered racism and isolation, along with teachers expecting little success academically.

Challenges for Native American Educators

Pember (2008) believed that schools controlled by the Bureau of Indian Affairs (BIA) attempted to use Western education on Native American students in boarding schools but failed. The boarding school era was responsible for attempting to eliminate Native American cultural identity. A mistrust of education is still prevalent in many Native American homes. Native American students continue to face numerous challenges and struggles as they work toward completing their education. As a result, many Native Americans drop out of high school and college. Darmon (2006) stated that (a) family, (b) tribal obligations, and (c) ceremonial obligations are often reasons why first- and second-year students drop out of college. Deloria (1994), believed one way to improve resiliency for Native American students was to incorporate a tribal perspective into all areas of their educational experience. However, it is not known if Native American culture, when infused in the educational environment, is a factor in Native American resiliency in higher education. Therefore, the problem to which this chapter was directed was, does Native American culture impact the academic success of Native American students?

The purpose of this study was to explore the degree to which the integration of Native American culture in the campus environment of three tribal colleges affected student success and resiliency. Three tribal colleges from the southwestern part of the United States were a part of this study. The results did illuminate if native culture helps or does not help Native American students' resiliency to stay in school. The question for this study was, "How does Native American culture contribute to the resiliency of Native American students who are earning a degree at a tribal college?" The following questions were used as guiding questions: a) How does the cultural support Native American students receive from their specific tribal colleges contribute to their resiliency? b) What are the aspects of their native culture that impact Native American students' ability to continue and complete their higher educational journey?

Their native culture surrounds native American students who live on the reservation, but when they leave the reservation, they must live in mainstream America's society and culture. Some Native American students chose to attend tribal colleges on or near a reservation. For these Native American students, this study did research the impact of their native culture on their success in completing their educational journey. Faircloth and Tippeconnic (2010) researched data from the National Center of Education Statistics and found that 50% of Native American students do not complete their education. They recommend that more research be conducted on the emphasis Native American culture has on dropout and graduation rates. This research study examined how current students at three tribal colleges in the southwestern United States viewed the influence of their native culture on their academic lives. The data gathered and analyzed did provide information to tribal college educators on what impact, if any, native culture has on student resiliency. The results of this study will help Tribal educators, at tribal colleges, better understand the Native American students' ability to persevere and overcome obstacles they may encounter on their way to completing their educational goals.

SOLUTIONS AND RECOMMENDATIONS

The focus of this chapter was to explore the degree to which native culture influences the resiliency of Native American students through their higher educational journey. Three tribal colleges from the southwestern part of the United States were a part of this study. The central research question was, "How does Native American culture contribute to the resiliency of Native American students who are earning a degree at a tribal college?" To answer the research question, data was collected from students attending three tribal colleges in the southwest. Five to seven students, who were in their last year of college, were interviewed using a field-tested set of interview questions. Various sub-themes were found within each of the following themes: (a) culture, (b) resiliency, (c) tribal colleges, (d) academics, and (e) Native American role models.

Within the topic of culture, Native American students defined their native culture as who they are as a person. Native American students stated that their native culture had influenced their daily life decisions. The students also indicated that their native culture included their family and all traditional teachings. Papanek (1994) stated that elders in the family were the ones who taught the native children about their tribal values and traditions. The Native American students within this study viewed their family and tribal past as their blood memory. Strong and Winkle (1996) reaffirmed that Indian bloodlines are essential to the survival of many individuals. For the Native American students in this study, their culture is tied to who they are, their family and tribe, and their history. The students also expressed a connection between their culture and their resiliency to complete their college degrees.

Within the topic of resiliency, Native American students revealed that their native culture, like stories and prayers, helped them overcome struggles and stay in school. They also expressed the need for more support from tribal elders in the areas of traditional practices. The Native American students seek ways to grow culturally since they stated they turn to their native culture on how to live and for decisions they make in their lives. Jackson et al. (2003) described the need for Native American students to draw on cultural traditions. Guillory and Wolverton (2008) pointed out the need American students have for a Native American student center on campuses, and they recommended collaborative programs with local and regional tribes.

Within the topic of tribal colleges, Native American students shared how tribal colleges are places where they can be themselves and learn from Native American instructors. Coleman (2009) claimed that Native American students had an easier time learning when concepts were inserted into tribal language, history, and culture. Coleman also stated that Native American students trusted Native American instructors more than non-Native instructors. The Native American students also expressed the need for courses on Native American topics to help them grow culturally. St. Germaine (1995) explained that instructors should use a curriculum that is based on subject matter that directly relates to Native American student's lives. Lastly, the Native American students in this study also viewed tribal colleges as a place where they could learn about leadership from the Native Americans who lead the tribal colleges. Within the topic of academics, Native American students revealed that they worked hard academically to make their families proud. Guillory and Wolverton (2008) found that Native American students, at times, felt extreme pressure not to disappoint their families. Jackson et al. (2003) revealed that Native American students need family support. The Native American students also shared that curriculum centered on traditional roots provides an environment where they can express themselves freely. For the students of this study, academic success was not just earning a college degree and getting a good-paying job. It also included applying what they learned during their education journey to their lives going forward.

Within the topic of Native American role models, Native American students expressed a need for Native American role model to have the following characteristics: a) ability to motivate and encourage, b) ability to communicate to both young and college-age natives, c) be resilient in leadership d) live a true native lifestyle, e) ability to teach Native American students in native ways, and f) help Native American students live a good life. Native American students need role models who can relate to their culture, understand their struggles, been through some of their struggles, and succeeded in life. Jackson et al. (2003) found that Native American students who lived with someone who completed college viewed the experience as beneficial. The students believed that this type of role model could mentor them and help them overcome their educational struggles. Jackson et al. (2003) recommended that Native American students develop personal relationships from mentors to receive support and encouragement to complete their degree programs when faced with challenges.

These were the finding of this study; however, other findings were revealed. An interesting finding in this study was how the family could hinder their educational journeys. As stated earlier, the Native American students of this study stated that their family does positively influence their academic success. However, Native American students also revealed that the family could draw them away from school since their family comes first. When a family member back home is ill or needs help in any away, Native American students feel torn between staying at school or returning home to their reservation to help their families in any way they can. Another interesting find was how Native American students feel some of their struggles are because they are Native American. When away from home or off the reservation, it can be difficult for them to find their identity or place in society.

The results of this study provide some insights for Native American educators, especially at tribal colleges, and educators at higher education institutions regarding: a) culture, b) resiliency, c) tribal colleges, d) academics, and e) Native American role models. Regarding culture, Cleary and Peacock (1998) acknowledged that native culture does influence the learning of Native American students. The Native American students in this study revealed how they turn to aspects of their native culture to help them during their educational journey. They also provide insight regarding resiliency. Strand and Peacock (2003) defined resiliency in terms of Native American students' ability to stay strong in the face of adversity and that Native American students who can overcome stress and challenges exemplify resiliency. Native students shared that the following aspects of their native culture help them with school: a) stories told by their grandfathers, b) prayers, c) native beliefs and spirituality, and d) native value system. Tribal colleges can also be a place where their native culture can influence native American students.

Surrounding insight on tribal colleges, Nugent (2003) asserted that tribal colleges create a Renaissance-like atmosphere for Native American students who often experience a rebirthing of their culture and values. This can lead to Native American students feeling empowered as they claim their own cultural identity (Boyer, 2004; Nugent 2003). For the Native American students in this study, being around other Native Americans was comfortable, and they felt free to express themselves and be themselves without the pressure from the dominant culture. Coleman (2009) reported that Native American students have an easier time learning when concepts are explained in terms of their tribal language, history, and culture. The Native American students in this study shared how they can do better academically when school is part of their community and culture. The students also revealed how they desire Native American role models.

Teicher (2006) reported that when Northern Arizona University (NAU) sought to increase their Native American retention and graduation rates, they looked to including native role models. Teicher reported that when NAU started having various elders on campus, they helped Native American students with various cultural issues. Native American students at NAU acknowledged that the elders were welcoming and there when they needed someone to talk to who had possibly experienced the problems they were currently facing. The Native American students in this study expressed the desire to have Native American role models to provide an example of someone who has struggled in their way and succeeded. In addition to these insights, it is recommended that more research be conducted in the areas of higher education for Native American students.

FUTURE RESEARCH DIRECTIONS

The following future research is recommended for the field of education. Since this study focused on Native American students who were in their last year of completing a degree at a tribal college, it is recommended interviewing Native American students who are in all phases of completing their degree at a tribal college. This future research could provide an understanding of whether or not native culture impacts the resiliency of Native American students earlier in their educational journey. It is also recommended to expand this research to a more representative sample of tribal colleges. There is also a need to research Native American students who attend public and private two-year and four-year colleges and major universities in the United States. It would also be interesting to explore Native American students seeking degrees from an online university. This future research could reveal how a Native American student's resiliency is impacted by attending a college or university where there is no primary emphasis on Native American culture. Some of the Native American students interviewed in this study expressed an interest in additional courses on Native culture that focuses on herbal medicines, storytelling, and traditional teachings. These students believed these courses could help them grow culturally. Future research is needed to see if additional courses on Native culture would help Native American students grow culturally.

The Native American students in this study shared that if tribal elders visited, counseled, and mentored Native American students, it would help them grow culturally. There is a need for future research to see if this would be true. It is recommended that a phenomenological study be conducted to research the lived experiences of both native and non-native faculty within a tribal college setting. In reviewing the literature, there is research on the impact of teaching styles of native and non-native faculty. However, no research could be found on the lived experiences of native and non-native faculty and what it means to them to teach at a tribal college. More research could focus on the differences between how native and non-native professors view the influence of native culture on the resiliency and academic success of Native American students during their educational journey. Swisher and Tippeconnic III (1999), endorsed the belief that an excellent instructor can enhance the learning experience of all Native American students. This study interviewed both men and women. Reyes and Shotton (2019) found that Indigenous men are entering college at a lower rate than Indigenous men. Therefore, they believe more research is needed to explore issues that Indigenous men face in seeking a college degree. Native American education has changed, and more change is needed through future research.

CONCLUSION

This research study examined how current students at three tribal colleges in the southwestern United States viewed the influence of their native culture on their academic lives. The data gathered and analyzed provided information on the impact native culture has on student resiliency. The results of this study concluded that Native American students believe their native culture impacts every aspect of their lives and the decisions they make in their lives. It is this self-connection to their native culture that impacts their resiliency to earn a college degree. If Native American students are provided the opportunity and environment to grow culturally within their educational environments, these students could be successful in their higher educational journey. With more educational success, Native American students could seek higher educational degrees from bachelors, masters, and finally, onto doctorates.

REFERENCES

Adams, D. W. (1995). *Education for extinction*. University Press of Kansas.

American Indian College Fund. (2008). Retrieved from https://www.collegefund.org/downloads/Fact-Sheet_2007.pdf

American Indian Higher Education Consortium. (2008). *Sustaining tribal colleges and universities and the tribal college movement: Highlights and profiles*. Systemic Research Inc.

Aragon, S. R. (2002). An investigation of factors influencing classroom motivation for Postsecondary American Indian/Alaska students. *Journal of American Indian Education, 41*(1).

Boyer, P. (2004, November/December). Tribal colleges: Building native communities. *Native Peoples, 17*(7), 24–28.

Cleary, L. M., & Peacock, T. D. (1998). *Collected wisdom: American Indian education*. Allyn and Bacon.

Coleman, T. (2009). *Putting tribal culture in school lessons*. Retrieved from http://www.reznetnews.org/article/putting-tribal-culture-school-lessons-27310

Damron, A. D. (2006). *Tribal colleges look for ways to retain students*. Retrieved from http://www.iaiachronicle.org/archives/ RetainStudents.htm

Darling-Churchill, K. E., DeVoe, J. F., & Snyder, T. D. (2008). *Status and trends in the education of American Indians and Alaska Native: 2008*. Retrieved from https://nces.ed.gov/pubs2008/2008084.pdf

Davis, J. (Winter 2001). American Native American boarding school experiences: Recent studies from native perspectives. *Organization of American Historians, 15*. Retrieved from https://www.oah.org/pubs/magazine/deseg/davis.html

Deloria, V. Jr. (1994). *Indian education in American*. American Native American Science & Engineering Society.

Delos, R. C. (2009). *Tribal colleges' top priority for Obama: 'Full and forward funding'*. Retrieved from http://www.diverseeducation.com/artman/publish/article_12160.shtml

Deschenie, T. (2004, November/December). Following the Dakota Way: Sisseton Wahpeton College. *Native Peoples, 17*(7), 30.

DeVoe, J. F., & Darling-Churchill, K. E. (2008). *Status and trends in the education of American Indians and Alaska natives* (NCES 2008-084). Retrieved from https://nces.ed.gov/pubs2008/2008084.pdf

Faircloth, S. C., & Tippeconnic, J. W. III. (2010). *The dropout/graduation rate crisis among American Indian and Alaska native students: Failure to respond places the future of native peoples at risk*. The Civil Rights Project/Proyecto Derechos Civiles at UCLA. Retrieved from https://www.civilrightsproject.ucla.edu/research/dropouts/faircloth-tippeconnic-native-american-dropouts-2010.pdf

Fann, A. (2004). *Tribal colleges: An overview*. Retrieved from https://www.ericdigests.org/2003-2/tribal.html

Federal education policy & off-reservation schools 1870-1933. (1999). Retrieved from http://clarke.cmich.edu/NativeAmerican/treatyeducation.htm#nas

Fletcher, M. L. M. (2008). *American Native American education: Counternarratives in racism,struggle, and the law*. Routledge.

Guillory, R. M., & Wolverton, M. (2008). It's about family: Native American student ppersistence in higher education. *The Journal of Higher Education, 79*(1), 58–84. doi:10.1353/jhe.2008.0001

Jackson, A. P., Smith, S. A., & Hill, C. L. (2003). Academic persistence among Native America college students. *Journal of College Student Development, 44*(4), 548–565. doi:10.1353/csd.2003.0039

Keohane, S. K. (2006). *The reservation boarding school system in the United States, 1870-1928.* Retrieved from http://www.twofrog.com/rezsch.html#excerpt

Marr, C. J. (n.d.). *Assimilation through education: Boarding schools in the northwest.* Retrieved from https://content.lib.washington.edu/aipnw/marr.html

Morales, L. (2007). *A Navajo student feels the tug of home.* Retrieved from http://www.npr.org/templates/story/story.php?storyId=6845552

Nugent, T. (2003, January 25). Tribal colleges a study in success. *Canku Ota, 79*, Article 6. Retrieved from http://www.turtletrack.org/Issues03/Co01252003/CO_01252003_New.htm

Papanek, J. L. (Ed.). (1994). *Cycles of life*. Time-Life Inc.

Pember, M. A. (2008). *Tribal colleges stay true to mission*. Retrieved from http://diverseeducation.com/article/11509/tribal-colleges-stay-true-to-mission.html

Reha, B. (2007). *Tribal colleges offer specialized education.* Retrieved from https://minnesota.publicradio.org/display/web/2006/12/01/tribalcolleges/

Reyes, N., & Shotton, H. (2019). *Association for the study of higher education. Retrieved from Southwest Native American Relief Council.* History & Culture.

St. Germaine, R. (1995). *Drop-out rates among American Indian and Alaska native students: Beyond cultural discounted.* Academic Press.

Strand, J. A., & Peacock, T. D. (2003). Nurturing resilience and schools success in American Indian and Alaska Native students. *The International Child and Youth Care Network.* Retrieved from http://www.cyc-net.org/cyc-online/cycol-1203-resilience.html

Strong, P. T., & Van Winkle, B. (1996). "Indian Blood": Reflections on the Reckoning and Refiguring of Native North American Identity. *Cultural Anthropology, 6*(4), 547–557. doi:10.1525/can.1996.11.4.02a00050

Swisher, K. G., & Tippeconic, J. W., III. (Eds.). (1999). *Next Steps, Research and Practice to Advance Indian Education.* Charleston, WV: ERIC.

Teicher, S. A. (2006). *Nurturing Native Americans on campus.* Retrieved from https://www.csmonitor.com/2006/0222/p14s01-legn.html

Thompson, M. (2001). *Charles Lummis: Native American Rights Crusader*. Retrieved from http://www.charleslummis.com/Native Americanrights.htm

Trafzer, C. E., Keller, J. A., & Sisquoc, L. (Eds.). (2006). *Boarding school blues: Revisiting American Indian educational experience*. University of Nebraska Press.

Watts, J. (2003). *Native American students*. Retrieved from http://www.montana.edu/teachlearn/Papers/Native%20American.pdf

Wilder, L., Jackson, A., & Smith, T. (2001). Secondary transition of multicultural learners: Lessons from the Navajo Native American Experience. *Preventing School Failure*, *45*(3), 119–124. doi:10.1080/10459880109603326

Williams, R. B. (2007). Tribal colleges: The model for cultural- and Community-based Education Reform. *Diversity*. Retrieved from http://www.diverseeducation.com/artman/publish/article_10287.shtml

ADDITIONAL READING

Ashford, E. (2019). Survey supports success of tribal colleges. *Community College Daily*. Retrieved from http://www.ccdaily.com/2019/09/survey-supports-success-tribal-colleges/

Bull, C. C., & Lindquist, C. (2018). In the spirit of our ancestors. *Tribal College Journal of American Indian Higher Education*, *30*(2), 18–37.

Caswell, K. (2009). *In The Sun's House: My Year Teaching on the Navajo Reservation*. Trinity University Press.

Child, B. J. (2000). *Boarding School Seasons: American Indian Families, 1900-1940*. University of Nebraska Press.

Lamb, C. (2016). Struggles and success: The state of teacher education at Tribal colleges and universities. *Tribal College Journal of American Indian Higher Education*, *27*(3), 20–24.

Lomawaima, K. T., & McCarty, T. L. (2006). *To Remain an Indian: Lessons in Democracy From a Century of Native American Education*. Teachers College Press.

KEY TERMS AND DEFINITIONS

Native American: Native American heritage can be traced back to the indigenous peoples of North America.

Native American Culture: Native American culture involves the beliefs, values, and traditions of Native Americans in today's world, especially concerning family, elders, respect for the earth and living in balance with one's self and others.

Resilience: Resilience is the ability to overcome any personal, family, or social challenges that keep a person from continuing to work toward a particular goal.

Tribal College: Tribal colleges are federally recognized colleges or universities with the goal to preserve native languages and native culture.

Chapter 4
Of the Land, for the Land, and by the Land:
A Study of a South Asian Indigenous Tribe, Paraja

Sheelpa Mishra
Nilgiri Degree College, Fakir Mohan University, India

ABSTRACT

Land is a promising asset that acts as a stimulus for indigenous people to act and respond within their natural limits. The natives enjoy great kinship with the land. They deem the land as one with the human-kind: a living, breathing, and thinking being. They believe that they live under the constant protection of the green produce of the land and they ought to protect it in return as it plays a key role in determining the possibility of survival of the tribal community. Any attempt at enforced displacement, tribal eviction, land encroachment, land diversion, or land alienation leads to disintegration of the tribal community. Trespassers trying to dispossess the aboriginals of their land not only impact the indigenous ethnic formations but also affect the ecological balance. The chapter provides an incisive sociological scrutiny to trace the origin of the pressing crisis of tribal land alienation, by adopting Gopinath Mohanty's Paraja as a case study, to understand its catastrophic repercussions on the forest communities and the natural habitat.

INTRODUCTION

Land is a promising asset that acts as a stimulus for indigenous people to act and respond within their natural limits. Indigenous peoples enjoy great kinship with the land. They deem the land as one with the humankind: a living, breathing and thinking being. They believe they live under the constant protection of the green produce of the land and they ought to protect it in return as it plays a key role in determining the possibility of survival of the tribal community. Any attempt at enforced displacement, tribal eviction, land encroachment, land diversion or land alienation leads to disintegration of the tribal community.

DOI: 10.4018/978-1-7998-3729-9.ch004

Trespassers who attempt to dispossess the aboriginals of their land not only impact the indigenous ethnic formations but also affect the ecological balance.

This chapter provides an incisive historical, literary, and sociological critique to trace the origin of the pressing crisis of tribal land alienation by adopting Gopinath Mohanty's *Paraja* as a case study to understand the catastrophic repercussions on the forest communities and the natural habitat. Further, the chapter presents a literary sociological critique for how the Paraja family respond to the atrocities of the power-brokers in the wake of the colonial impact in India. The chapter entails the tragic events and the ensuing changes owing to internal colonialism leading to land encroachment and land alienation in the life of Sukru Jani who valued a spirit of optimism. The chapter author argues the disintegration and displacement of the tribe and the virtual dispossession of the land as a component of the environment are interrelated and brought to effect by the dystopic force of internal colonialism.

BACKGROUND

Land plays a vital role in the life of the indigenous communities. It has social, cultural, economic importance for the natives. It is the food and fodder of the natives. It adds more than just a utilitarian value to the life of the forest communities. It has multiple facets. As a metaphor, it blurs the interconnections between human and non-human objects. As a symbol, it compresses the temporal and spatial distances. As a being, it is both masculine and feminine in character. As the Mother Earth, it is a giver, nourisher and protector of all beings while as a father, it takes care of the economic concerns of the individual. As an invisible spirit, it is full of wonder and mystery. As a metaphysical transcendent, it spiritually elevates the soul and fills the mind with romantic visions. It endows the indigenous group with a feeling of belongingness so much so that the forest dwellers sense of self is not separate from the land (Chopra, 2016).

Behura (1982) rightly opines that "land is the base for apprehending tribal people's identity, culture, religious ethos and personhood, because the peculiarity and uniqueness of native culture and tradition lies in the centrality of land to which natives are emotionally and culturally attached" (p. 1). It is the perpetual dependency on the land that enable the natives to live life as autonomous beings. Given the fact that the people of the hills and the jungles attachment to the land forms an axis of their collective identity forging an ethno-historical and ethno- cultural significance, it becomes imperative to explore the question of human agency generated by colonial intervention, exploitation and inequality. To advance the research, the critical review shall utilize Blauner's (1969) theory of internal colonialism to understand its impact on the Paraja, a south Asian indigenous tribe of Orissa.

The concept of internal colonialism is also reported to have roots in the Eurocentric practice of colonialism. It is experienced in nations that have formerly been a part of the colonialist regime. Marquard was the first to use the terminology of internal colonialism As a Mexican sociologist, Pablo Gonzalez Casanova, observes "with the disappearance of the direct domination of foreigners over natives, the notion of domination and exploitation of natives by natives emerged" (as cited in Chaloult & Chaloult, 1979, p. 85). It highlights the subordination "of rural populations by the urban elites where Anglicized India exploits rural Bharat. The Anglicized urban elites act as 'clientele classes' of the colonial state" (Dey, 2019, p. 249). These are constant reminders of the gap between the rich and the poor, the oppressor and the oppressed. They resist decolonialization. They try all means and ways to suppress the voice of the margins. They work in the guise of the custodians and protectors of law and order. They dehumanize the voiceless and the powerless to establish their rule within. The colony is not only established geographically but also established socially, politically and economically. The colonizers primarily desire to colonize the body, human body be it of men, women or territorial body.

Thus, internal colonialism helps to understand the dynamics of the relationship between the capital class and the labour class, between the bourgeois and the proletariat (Blauner, 1969; Chaloult & Chaloult, 1979). It also brings to the fore the undercurrents of politics, power and resistance. Sergio Salvi (1993), a poet, essayist, and historian of minority languages, used the term" internal colonies "in the cultural sense in *Le nazioni proibite:Guida a dieci colonie interne dell 'Europa occidentale* ('The forbidden nations:Guide to ten internal colonies of western Europe"), which included Catalonia, Scotland, Brittany and Occitania. *Land Alienation and Politics of Tribal Exploitation in India* by Malik (2020) entails a special emphasis on the tribal movement in Koraput district of Orissa. It describes the dual narratives that describe the indigenous population during the British colonial administration, i.e. "identity based isolation" and "development through integration" (p. 1). But the natives deem such assimilation unwelcoming. They consider the word "development" as a neo-colonialist agenda that would only trample their hopes and aspirations. They only prioritize a slow and steady life with no change of lifestyle. S.C Dube in his *Approaches to Tribal Problems in India* adopts four main approaches to the study of tribal problems, political, administrative, political and religious. Although, there is a wealth of literature available on the topic, it reflects the grim nature of humanity and its widespread prevalence. The writers have been able to bring out the glaring tales of exploitation experienced by the native dwellers that trespasses all limits of human tolerance. The review of literature clearly showcases how the indigenous community have suffered generations of irreparable loss in the hands of the bureaucrats, British administrators and state officials, but there is a dearth of research to study the trials and tribulations of the Parajas of Koraput district.

INTERNAL COLONIALISM AND THE PARAJA TRIBE

The chapter presents the study of the Paraja tribe, the trials and tribulations of the community, when faced with the machinations of the colonial forces in Pre-Independent India. The fiction exhibits the conflicting relationship existing not only between the indigenous community and the non-natives but also between the natives and the native collaborators appointed by the British colonial administration. The racial, caste and class differences were often used by the colonial administrators and various policies were also introduced in the territory of the *adivasis* on the pretext of imparting protection and security. But, as the sociologist Devalle (1990) remarks, "In the background of these policies stood a history of military repression and economic exploitation of adivasi land and labour" (p. 80). The capitalist forces were always "seeking to encroach upon and engulf a primordial and elemental way of life" (Mohanty, 1987, p. vi). Mohanty's *Paraja* is a fictional tale but the sociological, philosophical, and anthropological concerns remain contemporary. The Paraja community is not an imaginary group of settlers created by the author for the purpose of a narrative. They are a South Asian tribe settled in the undivided Koraput district of Orissa. Mohanty, formerly an Odisha Administrative Service officer had a chance to spend a significant part of his career with the tribals living both in the plains and the hills of the Eastern Ghats. In fact, his career and posting at Koraput district endowed him with material for his writing and as the citation of the Jnanpith Award received by the author in 1974 duly acknowledges, "in Mohanty's hands, the social is lifted to the level of the metaphysical" (as cited in Mohanty, 1987, p. vi). His narrative tells the tale of Sukru Jani, a Paraja, representing the labour class pitted against the tyranny of the *Sahukar* (money lender), the Forest Guard (a non-native), the Revenue Inspector otherwise known as the Ribini and other local authorities representing the pre-capitalist force.

Unlike the non-indigenous, the Paraja appreciate nature and its bounties. The traditional art forms, folk songs, carnivals, religious ceremonies all represent the indigenous culture of the land. They seldom consider land as a commodity. They believe that they are the children of the land, will toil for the land and shall be duly provided and rewarded by the land. As Behura (1982) opines, "it is the land that owns people and gives them an identity and is the temple through which the tribal people become one with the Supreme Being, the spirits, their ancestors and other segments of the creation" (p. 2). The indigenous community treasure autonomy and economic independence. But with the advent of the colonial rule, the tribal communities were looked down upon as primitive and underdeveloped. Roy Burman (1960), the veteran anthropologist, remarks that in the scale of civilization, "the adivasis sense of history and their culture are declared to be retrograde, a negation of progress, a perpetuation of backwardness" (p. 19). Legitimizing the colonial legacy and dominance over the indigenous groups, the colonialists also subsequently impressed upon the tribals that they had no legal right over the land and the forest resources thereby manipulating the legal records and documents and even the government officials in and around the tribal belts of Orissa causing disharmony among the tribal folks.

Living amidst the woods, he seldom felt alienated. In fact, the land was the opium of the tribal folk. It motivated them and gave them an opportunity to grow. It instilled in them a sense of being and also gave them hopes of becoming the imagined self of their dreams. Sukru Jani led a plain, ordinary life living with his two daughters and his two sons. After the demise of his wife, he has guided his children with his wisdom. His romantic musings have therapeutic effect on him. During his lonely moments, he would gaze upon the hills, the valleys and the dense forest and contemplated the profound control of an inanimate presence responsible for the earthly creation. It takes away his moment of nostalgic retreat induced by the loss of his wife and makes him full again. The nostalgic feeling is also triggered by the memory of a low hillock that was once "densely wooded" but is left bare in its current form, "patches of cultivation having replaced the forest" (Mohanty, 1987, p. 4). In his fancy, he envisions luxurious growth of cultivated lands all around. For a tribal, luxury lay in the greenery and not in the material assets. He looks around to survey his lands and dreams of a future when his village have been completely cleared of forest [---] cut into terraced fields where crops grows [---] and they are all his" (p. 5). The contemplation fills Sukru Jani with unbound happiness. "A sense of peace and repose emanates from the quiet evening and the open hills and fills his being as he inhales" (p. 7). But the conspicuous presence of the men in authority was a constant reminder of the race, caste and class differences that existed between the tribals and the pre-capitalist society.

The periodical encounter between them gradually induced in the mind of the tribals, a feeling of being inferior to the outsiders. Furthermore, the innocent folks had no understanding of the law and order of the system. They would seldom question or doubt the integrity of the man in uniform. A few men of rank were appointed by the local authority in lieu of the colonial administration to collect tax and impose fine on them. The colonial practices and policies were extended by these men who mediated between the colonial authority and the local inhabitants of the tribal belt. They were the Naika, the local headman, a Paraja and the Barik who had submitted to the shared interest of the Revenue Inspector, the Forest Guard and the Raja not only to secure their rank in the community but also to earn their trust so to ward off facing troubles. Barik was appointed to act as the village watchman. The Forest Guard mainly visited on the pretext of safeguarding the hills and the forests and drew money from the tribals by occasionally granting favours and collecting taxes basking in their ignorance of the law of what was due and what was considered undue in the eyes of the colonial administration. Their ignorance was largely pursued, preserved and celebrated by both the local authority and the non tribals to continue thriving in the prospect of generating revenue from them. And so, "he roamed the jungle, searching for offenders" (p. 9).

The Forest Guard made occasional visits to survey the forest resources. He was "in the eyes of the hill folk," "a person in high authority," although his position was insignificant in the official hierarchy. When the Forest Guard was around, tax collection, fine imposition, and prosecution of the tribals became the order of the day. The tribals could only listlessly wonder at what human law should keep them away from fulfilling their daily needs and provisions. Failing to comprehend the rhetoric of the civilization, they could either surrender to the law or seek money from the officials and in either way settling the account by paying either in cash or kind the alleged sum decided by the interrogating official, a token of it often shared by a chain of others of inferior rank, waiting to profit from the incident. The Forest Guard was "the only arm of the law in a stretch of vast forest [---] and the hill folk held him in mortal fear" (p. 11). Besides "those who put him there expected him to do his duty" (p. 9), but he not only misappropriated the funds raised through taxes and fines but also exploited the locals for his benefit.

Sukru Jani led a peaceful life, but his growing age and obligation towards his children raised concerns regarding their future. Sukru Jani "needed more land because his was a growing family" and also had to build a house as according to the tribal custom the married sons were supposed to have a house of their own. Being a man of the hills, he was unfamiliar with the conspiracies, intrigues and maligned motives of the materialistic world. He approached the Forest Guard seeking his permission to clear a patch of land to gather wood for construction. The Forest Guard granted his wish to clear a patch of land in the Mali Damaka Hill. During his next visit to the hill, the Forest Guard cunningly solicited a promise of a favour from Sukru Jani in return for his favour. Sukru Jani obliged: "You have to command and I obey" (p. 21). Little did Sukru Jani knew that the Forest Guard was prying on his elder daughter, Jili. Felling trees in the forest, Sukru Jani was momentarily lost in his thoughts trying to rationalize the legitimate role of the Forest Guard or any official intruding in matters of the land. He exclaims with mixed emotions,

What beautiful lands they are! And all these forest lands can be reclaimed and crops raised on them! Why should there be forests, when they mean nothing to us, and not crops? After all no one can own the forest. Land can be owned by anyone and the owner can grow crops there. God created all these lands for human beings- what a shame that man prevent his fellow men from putting them to their proper use!

However, he also knew that with his little knowledge of the socio-political affairs of the world, he could neither question the colonial system nor do anything significant to put an end to it. He continued his act of felling and cutting the trees. Sukru Jani had just reached home when he receives the messenger of the Forest Guard demanding Jili, Sukru Jani's elder daughter, to be sent to him. The infuriated father attacks the messenger and drives him away with abuses and blows. The messenger tries to pacify his anger and cajoles him to surrender but a true Paraja was "not for sale" (p. 30). Sukru Jani was worried as he had acted emotionally and not rationally. The fear of a "foreboding of tragedy" (p. 32) continued to haunt him. The next day, the news of the Forest Guard's exit from the village cured the anxiety of Sukru Jani. The sons and the father continued felling and clearing the trees with great vigour. In their innocence, "they never felt that the timber which they were cutting down and burning was the Raja's property" (p. 33) and that they were committing a punishable offence. "Their heads were like stone, into which such arguments and considerations could scarcely enter" as they believed that "everything they grew on the hills was theirs to use."

Sukru Jani had attained a newfound happiness to satisfy his need of more land to serve the needs of his growing family. On the contrary, his misery had only begun. Soon, the Forest Guard returned with two other officials who caught Sukru Jani red-handed felling the forest reserves. Upon interrogation, Sukru Jani claimed to have sought the permission of the Forest Guard. But having returned to seek revenge for the humiliation, he feigned ignorance of the latter's offence and poured abuses on Sukru Jani. He also alleged that Sukru Jani was responsible for clearing another patch of land that was instead used by other tribals in exchange of undue favours extended to the Forest Guard. Sukru Jani was a man of integrity and honesty but false allegations were stamped on his character addressing him as "rascal", "desperate rogue." Sukru Jani failed to understand that, "no existence in the jungle is possible unless one learns to play hide and seek with the law" (p. 35). He was declared guilty and a heavy fine was imposed on him amounting to four score of rupees. The situation only worsened when the headman, using his diplomatic ways, tries to persuade him to arrange the fine by becoming a *goti*, a debt bound labourer.

The thought of serving as a *goti* was initially met with resistance followed by reassessment, helplessness, hopelessness but finally succumbing to the arrangement. Land, that was a source of life, has suddenly turned to become a source of deprivation. Thus, land proves to be an agent of change, of fate in the life of a tribal. In his misery, he imagines the spirit of his long dead wife, Sombari, impersonating all life on earth, sobbing and weeping and drenching the earth hinting at the "advancing wave of destruction" (p.45). Sukru Jani is not only consciously threatened by the detachment from his land but also unconsciously disturbed by the saddened fate of events. When he is asleep, he dreams of his "land and the lands of others around it." He imagines the neighbouring lands grown full of crops that lay secured from the prying eyes of the strangers in contrast to his own that yielded only flowers and lay unprotected from the cattle class. He suddenly woke up with a grim realization that his dream might soon be a reality. Instead of whining and crying upon his doomed state any further, he and Tikra, his younger son, approach the moneylender and exchange their labour for a sum of fifty rupees.

Their dependency on land forces them to acquiesce to the demands of the Sahukar; yet, Sukru Jani remains optimistic even in adverse conditions. The thought of becoming a *goti* ought not to be as saddening as it seemed. Sukru Jani justifies his plight against the backdrop of cultural determinism, "Everyman is some other man's *goti* and the master for whom he works is himself driven by some unseen spirit, which rides always on his back and commands him" (p. 47). But the Sahukar did not run a fair trade. He resorted to foul ways to betray the tribals and become wealthy and powerful. Dire need and evil conspiracies against them, landed them to seek help from the moneylender and in the name of proposing a fair deal he "would become master of their lands and of their money and of their bodies and their souls. It was only a question of time" (p. 49). Thus, the Sahukar never freed the *goti* but bound him to his contract till their death and the family of Sukru Jani had undesirably fallen a victim. Not only the Sahukar, but the local negotiators also duped Sukru Jani into believing that the Forest Guard had indeed demanded a fine of fifty rupees to resolve the matter when in fact he was given only fifteen rupees to close the matter. The rest was divided among the corrupt locals.

Land had different implications for different individuals living in a class and caste based community. For the privileged, land implied an addition to their wealth and assets but for the poor tribal land reflected their existence. Whereas the wealthy treasured the physical value of the land, the tribal treasured the metaphysical value of the land. Sukru Jani believed that "Man does not possess the soil; he is possessed by it. He can grip the soil in his fist, but it laughs, and waits; and one day he drops down, and the soil is enriched" (Mohanty, 1987, p. 368). Thus, The tribal believed as being the children of the mother earth, the hills or the land as opposed to the privileged who held the conviction that "the whole earth belonged to them, the men with the gold" (p. 57). Time and again, Sukru Jani was drawn into occasional reverie driven by his love for his land. He was reminded of his own land that would require his labour to yield the best of the produce only if he could attend to it anymore. In fact, in the family of Sukru Jani, if there was one thing that bound them all it was their dreams attached to the land. Meaning and significance of land differed from person to person in the family. Sukru Jani viewed land as spectre, as agent of change. To Paraja women, Jili, Bili, and Kajodi, land is food and a promise of eternal security to a household. To Mandia, land is a memoir, a legacy. Mandia believes "it was no mere piece of land, but a record of the history of those past generations, of their bygone tales of sorrow and rejoicing and of tradition and change (p. 62). The Paraja men also believed that the land represented their capacity to provide for their family. It is a physical manifestation of their strength, vigour, their capacity to yield and endure. No sooner does the harvest season arrives, the "the people of the village were on their lands." Mandia also associated his love for the land with his love for his beloved. In his playfulness, he failed to separate his primal emotions for the land and his beloved. In other words, "his house overflowing with rice and his heart overflowing with Kajodi, became one and inseparable in his consciousness" (p. 63). Thus, land had an instrumental role in accomplishment of all their hopes and dreams and unfulfilled desires. It was a piece of solace and connected them with their past, present and future.

Life as a *goti* began for both Sukru Jani and Tikra on a positive note with a hope of soon reclaiming their good old times. They served as debt-bound labourers of the master, Ramachandra Bisoi, whose only purpose was to search "constantly for new lands to annex, new *gotis* to enslave, new kingdoms to add to his empire" (p. 64). Loomba (2015) defines "colonialism as the forcible takeover of land and economy" (p. 23). The internal colonizers like the European colonizers also harboured the belief that the control of man over nature is the path towards progress. Hence, Ramachandra Bisoi, resorted to exploitative means to extract maximum benefit from the land he annexed.

Hegemony is achieved through conditions set forth in the contract that forever bound them to remain *goti*. Bisoi as master, also enjoyed the privilege of modifying the terms of the agreement when there was a faintest possibility of losing his aid. The process of establishing a colonial regime began with the means of forming a combination of repressive structures and institutions represented by the Revenue Inspector, Forest Guard and Ramachandra Bisoi along with an ideological structure represented by the community of local head members such as the Naika, the Barik and the Chalan. In the weekly fair, Mandia was caught brewing liquor illegally and was imposed with a fine of fifty rupees. The habit of arresting a tribal red-handed and then imposing him with a heavy fine, that was way beyond his earning capacity, was a traditional way of dominating the poor tribals. The accused could either pay the fine or be imprisoned for violating the law. The tribals felt it worthwhile to accept the life of a debt bound labourer than the life of a convict. Mandia pledged to become a *goti* by borrowing the fine from Sahukar and started his new life in the company of his father and brother. The trio were optimistic that sooner or later they will find a way out of the chaos little realizing the evil motives of the Sahukar.

As the troubles of Sukru Jani continue to intensify with each passing day, the wealth and power of the Sahukar continues to grow. The Sahukar's tale of splendour and riches was built on a heap of lies, deceit, dishonesty, and trickery. He used treacherous means to seize the land that he wishes to acquire. He has no pity or mercy for the poor tribal peasants who have no other means but to live on the cultivated crops of their land. Sahukar's empire stood flanked by two small villages inhabited by Kondhs. In order to unethically grab their land, Sahukar set up a liquor shop and urged the Kondh tribe to buy liquor to their heart's content and kept them indebted to him. Later he would warn them saying' "Are you going to pay up or give me your land?" (Mohanty, 1987, p. 120). Thus, the moneylender kept on using foul means to acquire their land and the tribal peasants eventually losing their source of living fell at his feet for loan and become his slaves forever. "They had watched the moneylender's power grow and new houses rise up on the land which was now his" (p. 121). They fear to rebel against the moneylender as the moneylender "had many friends in officialdom" who lend indirect support to exploit the tribesmen and benefitted from it. Land encroachment and land dispossession was often a regular practice among the internal colonizers to assert their rule and dominance. Their words became law for the tribesman who had a "natural horror of the law" and they were afraid of "doing anything which might be unlawful" (p. 122). Unable to comprehend the evil plot of these men and understand the law of the land, they would often fall into their trap and lose their most cherished asset, the land. The Sahukar's unjust treatment to Sania Paraja, is an account of the unlawful way of manipulating the law to one's own advantage. Unlawfully dispossessing Sania Paraja, a tribal of his land, Sahukar even tries his best to give the tribals a lesson by subjecting him to rigorous imprisonment for four months. "The Sahukar was not content with suppressing possible mutinies; like all successful tyrants he knew the importance of sustained terror. Whenever a touring official came to the village, the Sahukar would meet him with a long list of grievances" (p.124-125) and the officials "who loved nothing better than to parade their authority" would hurl abuses at his *gotis*. Only on rare occasions, does the Sahukar face any resistance from the government officials. Even then, he continues to engage in his schemes to do much worse than what he did. On one occasion, when the land acquired by Sahukar was rightly deemed invalid by a government official for being a tribal land, the latter approached his mentor, Garaja Sundari, Ribini or the Revenue Inspector. The Revenue Inspector planned a way for Sahukar to reclaim his rights over the land and subsequently the "revenue records were doctored to show that the lands in question really belonged to the Sahukar and not to the Kondhs, since it was he who paid the rents" (p. 197). The Kondhs wailed and pleaded as the land was their only means of livelihood but the Sahukar made victory out of their misery and wretchedness.

Land is nothing but an emotional extension of their body. To Sukru Jani "those two rice fields were like the ribs in his chest" (p. 191). He has often brooded over his wish to go back to them but in vain. Although he has experienced starvation; yet, he had never mortgaged his land no matter how tragic his circumstances amounted to. He had learned to live and sustain himself and his family even in odd times and his land had always been his strength. But the thought of his helpless daughters, being exposed to the harsh realities of life and having been left with no food left, haunted him evermore. Caught in a dilemma, Mandia could part with anything for his independence but Sukru Jani found it very difficult to think and act. Unlike his sons,

[...] for Sukru Jani it was different: the land to him was not merely a patch of earth – it was part of his body. He knew every contour and depression in the land; every thorn, every ant-hill had a history. He had watered the land with his sweat and nursed the seedings with the warmth of his own body (p.193)

He worshipped his land as the Earth Goddess prior to the harvest. The land has always been a part of his self. It is as natural as breathing is to him. His labour has never gone into waste. The land has always repaid him the amount of toil, hardship that he has put into it in plentiful. He believed that human life is transient but the land is a permanent marker of their existence and that it will always reflect the footprints of time even after human beings perish because like crops, even human life will end and fall into ashes to be one with the soil. Sukru Jani believed in the simple philosophy that men, whether alive or dead, belong to the land, the soil, the Earth Goddess. Besides one's duty and obligation towards one's land is the greatest duty and "he knows nothing of what lies beyond his fields; he is indifferent to the rise and fall of kings" (p. 199). The worldly affairs have never much affected the rustic lifestyle of Sukru Jani. He continued to live a very satisfied and carefree life under the protection of the forest and the soil until circumstances forced him to become a *goti.*

Sukru Jani loved his lands as much as he loved his children. He had never bothered to gauge his emotions for his children against his emotions for his land. He could not sacrifice one for the other. He did not consider land as external to him. It was his body, his soul. It carried the spirit of Sombari, his wife. Like death, land gave him an opportunity to unify his corporeal frame with both the living and the dead, with the visible and the invisible world, with the physical and the metaphysical world. But his greater responsibility towards his daughters, who were left to starve of hunger, prompted him to mortgage his rice fields so as to buy his independence. Sukru Jani pleaded the Sahukar to accept his land and release him from his services. Sahukar liked his rich land, "which he felt would be ideal for his gardens and orchards" (p. 289) but he feigned disregard and indifference to Sukru Jani's heedings only to trade his land with the least possible amount and mortgaged it. Sukru Jani felt defeated yet the deal was necessary to look after his daughters. He returned to his village and found his daughters working as daily wage labourers to sustain themselves. He persuaded them to quit the work and they returned home. Having mortgaged his land, he was now left with no option but to work incessantly and buy another. After much difficulty, he acquired a patch of land and gave his best to repay Sahukar's debt and provide for his family. But he desperately needed his lands back from Sahukar. Often as he walked past his lands, "he gazed at his lands, he felt like a brother to the forest and the crops [...] he was born of the earth and belonged to it" (p. 275). Although he had acquired a piece of land, yet he could not resist his need to get his lands back. This time his importance for the land had changed. Land now stood as the symbol of his ancestry.

Sukru Jani felt responsible, accountable and answerable not only to himself but also to his forefathers who had left it to him to take care of and felt "he would never find peace, living or dead unless he recovered his land from the Sahukar" (p. 347). He felt ashamed of himself for having to part with it. "He could not help hearing sounds from another, distant world which threatened to snatch him away. Against this other influence he struggled hard, clutching at all the beauty around him unwilling to let it go" (p. 279). To further add to his misery, the Sahukar had planned to dig into his most cherished asset and plant orange trees to which Sukru Jani resisted and protested. He was sent off with the remark, "Paraja dog" and a warning to repay the debt so as to claim his right over his land. Sukru Jani realized that he was but an outsider and his land was now the property of the Sahukar. Sukru Jani could not help feeling overprotective for his land. He throbbed with fear every time he was doubtful about the use that the Sahukar would put his land to. The Sahukar was no more than an inflictor of pain and agony. He imagined "the Sahukar, tearing at his land with his talons while he stood by and watched. The Sahukar's plough seemed to be carving up his own flesh (p. 280).

Sukru Jani had no way out to stop the Sahukar. The orange trees would extract all juice from his land and leave it infertile. The thought of it haunted him so much so that he decided to arrange money to repay his debt to release his land and his sons at once from the clutches of the moneylender. With great difficulty, he managed to sell his land, borrowed money from his friends and accepted the bride price of Bili from Nandibali, his future son-in-law to arrange the debt amount. He went and gave it to the moneylender but the moneylender refused out rightly to release his land on the pretext of having spent an ample amount of money to plough and plan for the plantation of the orange orchard. Sukru Jani was shocked and shattered. He had known that "there is no ladder to help you climb up to heaven, and there are no words to criticize those who are rich and powerful" (p. 301), but Sukru Jani was reluctant to give up. He decided to fight his land back from him by the help of the law. He had little knowledge of the financial burden that it would amount to and was equally ignorant of the treacherous ways of dealings between the custodians of the law and the rich and the powerful. He believed that his only reason of his living still was to get back his land and "he must live until the land was recovered" (p. 361). He fought fairly. He fought with courage and conviction. But the corrupted middlemen misguided Sukru Jani. They asked him to appear for a week later than the date decided for the hearing and consequently made him to believe that he had lost the case as he could not appear on the proposed day. Hearing about his loss, he said, "We are peasants and we've only one way of keeping ourselves alive-by tilling the soil. The case may be dead but the land is not dead; nor are we" (p. 368). His sons cried with anxiety, "the land was our bowl of rice, father. What shall we eat now?" (p. 371). Sukru Jani mustered great courage and conviction to face the Sahukar and decided to plead before him.

The three set out to meet the Sahukar. As the Sahukar entered, they flung at his feet and begged for mercy to him. But the Sahukar was cruel and ruthless. Instead of taking pity on them, the Sahukar verbally abused and kicked and threatened to inflict insufferable torture and pain on the family of Sukru Jani. He continued to rudely offend and criticize them till he was hit with a blow by Mandia and the other two joined him. Mandia shouted finally, "You didn't enjoy the land! You didn't enjoy the land" (p. 373). The three wailed and cried but were to some extent gratified for having sought the revenge that they so long bore in their heart. The act of killing was an act of raising the voice of the margins and leading it onto to the centre. The amount of injustice, ill-treatment, betrayal meted out to them had been paid off. It was the justice of the land. No law is above the law of the land. The law of the land is not man made. It is as natural as all life on earth and it provides equally to all beings on earth. The hierarchy only amounts to have a destructive effect on earth and eventually leads to an ecological imbalance. The Mother Earth nourishes her beings with care, but materialism affects the unifying feature of the soil. Thus, the children of the land need to wake up and recognize the fact that it is the land that possess us and we owe a responsibility to protect it and treat it as our own. Land has been a source of conflict since the evolution of the human species. The brain which is the seat of all intelligence is also the seed of insatiable desires for more. We created the beautiful world with all its grandeur but the evils of class, colour and creed maligned its pristine nature. The differential distribution of power solely on basis of so called –higher birth-has tipped the balance of the nature irreparably. When the land should just have been the source of sustenance, it has in fact become the means to amass more wealth than an individual will ever need to live a fulfilled, productive and healthy life. The lust has shrouded our conscience and leads us to invent nefarious channels to dupe and deceive the less fortunate class of people who look up to us for help and counsel.

Financial tyranny meted out since ages on basis of racial diversity has widened the difference in socioeconomic status that had already been sadly omnipresent (Kumar, 2018; Kumari, 2019). The adivasis have always been looked down upon by the higher order because of their ignorance, their acceptance of undue dominance of caste, their willingness to barter labour for menial wages and most of all their unwitting trust on the authority. India was able to shake off the binding shackles of the British Empire, but the taste of power lingered in certain authoritarian figures which led to the sustained slavery hidden from the outside world. When the world saw a free nation, the truth of the actual colonialism remained in the folds. The oppression, exploitation and discrimination found its way into every vulnerable family and leeched off every means of their existence. The exploitation was not limited to money and labour but sometimes extended sexual favours too.

The blatant disrespect for the protection of primary human rights is appalling. Not only is the exploitation unjust from the jurisdictional point of view but also from the perspective of the just human approach towards fellow men (Kumar, 2018). The exploited class is driven to such extreme extent that the simple, non-conspiring peasants finally resort to murderous means to ultimately find respite from the continuous injustice they had to bear owing to lack of deception in their blood. The simpletons were so ruthlessly hurled with deceit, disrespect and undue debt that they were converted to convicts (Kumari, 2019). The peasants who ploughed the lands to provide for themselves were driven to such desperation that they became perpetuators of a heinous crime. They resorted to all legal means, to all negotiations involving trading labour for land, yet all efforts fail because those understandings were not meant as a means to an end but rather as an extension of the inhuman victimization of the unsuspecting simpletons (Kumari, 2019).

FUTURE RESEARCH DIRECTIONS

The critical review of literature clearly highlighted how the indigenous population have been deprived of their identity through land alienation and land dispossession. Instead of being displaced, they ought to have been assimilated through a humanitarian approach. Instead of alienating them, they ought to be regarded as sacred beings on earth for preserving the earliest cultures (Chopra, 2016). Developmental models ought to be devised to accommodate the hopes and aspirations of the indigenous communities. Research is to be undertaken to study the categories of tribal population in different parts of India: their culture, behaviour, food, clothing, medicinal skills and also how the policies of the government have impacted the lifestyle of the tribal community in the pre-independent India. Further study is also needed and overdue to understand the agricultural changes and food culture owing to the implementation of policies to restrict access to forest resources.

CONCLUSION

Mohanty's (1987) story is not just a tale of a family oppressed, suppressed, and dispossessed of land, but a subtle message to society to awake from a deep slumber and raise voices and awareness against the oppressors on behalf of the mute, uninformed oppressed. Failing to do so will create criminals of people who were otherwise simple farmers: reaping food, ploughing lands, cleaning homes, and sanitising sewage. Land is sustenance and it is a collective responsibility that it merely remains so. The tribe at last may merge with the land so much cherished that it serves as a bed of equality where everyone may rest in peace.

REFERENCES

Behura, N. K. (1982). Forest and tribal world view. *Journal of Social Research*, *25*(1).

Blauner, R. (1969). Internal colonialism and ghetto revolt. *Social Problems*, *16*(4), 393–408. doi:10.2307/799949

Chaloult, N., & Chaloult, Y. (1979). The internal colonialism concept: Methodological considerations. *Social and Economic Studies*, *28*(4), 85–99.

Chopra, S. S. (2016). Tribal identity concerns in literature: A critical study of Gopinath Mohanty's The Ancestor. *International Journal of Research, 3*(5).

Devalle, S. (1990). Tribe in India: The fallacy of a colonial category. In D. Lorenzen (Ed.), *Studies on Asia and Africa from Latin America* (pp. 71–116). El Colegio de Mexico. doi:10.2307/j.ctv3f8qc7.8

Dey, D. (2019). India: The context of its current internal colonialism. In D. Schorkowitz, J. Chávez, & I. Schröder (Eds.), *Shifting forms of continental colonialism*. doi:10.1007/978-981-13-9817-9_10

Kumar, R. (2018). Gopinath Mohanty's Paraja. *Studies in Humanities and Social Sciences, 24*(2), 1–17.

Kumari, S. (2019). Sukru Jani: A legendary protagonist in Gopinath Mohanty's Paraja. *International Journal of English, Language, &. Humanities (Washington), 7*(12).

Loomba, A. (2015). *Colonialism/Postcolonialism* (3rd ed.). Routledge. doi:10.4324/9781315751245

Malik, S. (2020). Land alienation and the politics of tribal exploitation in Odisha. In *Land alienation and politics of tribal exploitation in India*. Springer. doi:10.1007/978-981-15-5382-0_4

Mohanty, G. (1987). *Paraja* (B. K. Das, Trans.). Oxford University Press.

Roy Burman, B. K. (1960). Basic concepts of tribal welfare and tribal integration. In L. P. Vidyarthi (Ed.), *Indian anthropology in action*. Ranchi University.

ADDITIONAL READING

Dube, S. C. (1960). Approaches to the tribal problem in India. In L. P. Vidyarthi (Ed.), *Indian anthropology in action*. Ranchi University.

Elwin, V. (1943). *The aboriginals*. Oxford University Press.

Ganguly, D. C. (1958). *Select documents of the British period of Indian history*. Secretariat Press.

Gupta, D., & Singh, P. K. (2018). The hidden cost of development—A review of mental health issues of displaced tribal populations in India. *Journal of Public Health, 26*(6), 717–723. doi:10.100710389-018-0913-9

Mathur, K. S. (1972). Tribe in India: A problem of identification and integration. In K. S. Singh (Ed.), *Tribal situation in India*. Indian Institute of Advanced Studies.

Mishra, M. K. (2009). Sacred worldview in tribal memory: Sustaining nature through cultural actions. *Language & Ecology, 2*(4), 1–7.

Mohanty, H. (1988). A novel on tribal life: In empathy with tribal ethos: Gopinath Mohanty's Oriya Novel, 'Paraja'. *Indian Literature, 31*(1/123), 133-140.

Mukhia, H. (1981). Was there feudalism in Indian history? *The Journal of Peasant Studies, 8*(3), 273–310. doi:10.1080/03066158108438139

Patnaik, S. M. (1996). *Displacement, rehabilitation, and social change: The case of the Paraja highlanders* (Vol. 177). Inter-India Publications.

Sharma, R. S. (1965). *Indian feudalism: c. 300-1200*. Calcutta University.

Spear, P. (1958). *The Oxford history of India*. Clarendon Press.

KEY TERMS AND DEFINITIONS

Adivasis: A collective group representing the aboriginal tribal population.
Displacement: A way of removing a person or a group from their authorized place.
Dispossession: An act of robbing someone of their land and property.
Eurocentric: A practice of imposing a worldview of the western civilization.
Financial Tyranny: Implies misuse of power for personal gain.
Forest Guard: Appointed personnel to guard forest reserves.
Goti: A debt bound labourer.
Money Lender: A person who lends money on purpose and charges interest.
Mortgage: An asset that can be leased in lieu of another asset.
Paraja: A community of indigenous people belonging to eastern Koraput.

Chapter 5
Receding Dependence on Forests:
A Study of the Paliyar Tribes in India

T. Anantha Vijayah
Gandhigram Rural Institute (Deemed), India

ABSTRACT

This chapter considers how modernity has affected the livelihood of Paliyar community and how they have been affected by forest dispossession. Whether the weaning away from the forests has been manufactured or part of the systemic exploitation is discernible. The chapter traces the history of the Paliyars, their belief structures, and indigenous knowledge within sacred spaces. The chapter also presents a discussion of the relation between land and spiritual tradition as well as the importance of land to identity, transfer of oral tradition, and indigenous traditional knowledge. Removing the Paliyar from the land continues to erode their tradition, knowledge, and identity.

INTRODUCTION

The Paliyar tribes are lesser known and thinly populated tribe existing from time immemorial on the hill tracts of southern part of India. The oral traditions of the Paliyars, trace their antiquity to that of the Hindu pantheon, the Tamil Lord Murugan. Paliyars claim that Lord Murugan's wife Valli was from their tribe. These oral traditions not only establish their antiquity but also their locale to the hill tracts of Palani Hills. Though they live within the Tamil speaking region of southern part of India from time immemorial, there are hardly any references about Paliyars in classical Tamil literature. However, the first documentary evidences were created in a series of volumes on the *Castes and tribes of Southern India* (Thurston, 1909) with extensive description of Paliyar tribes of Tamil Nadu. The description provided evidence and observations of British missionaries as to how the culture had lived prior to colonization and how they were perceived by the British missionaries who reported to the mainland. It is pertinent to note the text was written almost 300 hundred years after the British first colonized the Indian subcontinent and used in this chapter to illustrate the indigenous origins of the Paliyar tribes.

DOI: 10.4018/978-1-7998-3729-9.ch005

BACKGROUND

Every name has a reason, or reason would be attributed to the use of the name. Either way, there are two hypotheses for the reason of their names: They were seen as people from whom others should not receive a curse, hence the name Paliyar. The meaning for the Tamil word *Paliyar* would be those who would curse you and therefore one should not be recipient of their curse. It may be also that the name must have been a derivative from the name of their goddess Palichiamman—those who worship the goddess Palichiamman.

In order to establish the fact whether they belong to indigenous communities a quick look at the definition by the United Nations Permanent Forum on Indigenous Issues would illustrate the issue. The indigenes are identified with certain parameters. Juxtaposing those parameters with the Paliyars would enable us to ascertain the fact that they are without any doubt belong to indigenous communities. Paliyars are accepted by their own people and at their community level as belonging to a specific tribe. They do have a historical continuity with pre-colonial and pre-settler societies. Paliyars do have a strong link to territories and surrounding natural resources. They do have a distinct social, economic or political systems, culture and beliefs and are non-dominant groups of the society and they attempt to maintain their ancestral environments and systems as distinctive peoples. The Government of India has also notified them as Scheduled Tribes in the Gazette of India, and they are identified as people spread over the southern states of Tamil Nadu, Kerala and Karnataka with names Palliyar / Pallegan / Palligan / Palliyar / Paliyan.

As a deeply rooted and settled indigenous people (LaRocque, 2011), Paliyars are also close to their natural habitat and the locale is spread across the western ghats of southern part of India (see Figure 1). And it is this rooting to the geographical locale that makes them indigenous and they believe as other indigenous tribes around the world that they are 'inextricability linked with the earth and everything on it (Ruffo, 2009). Tracing the Paliyar history is to trace the history of humankind. The mid ranges of Palani Hills has nestled within itself prehistoric Dolmen's caves currently discovered in over 20 locations. This suggests that the early man had once roamed the hills and had created a space for themselves on rocky terrains at higher grounds close to water bodies. These archaeological sites project the development of human population from time immemorial. Extrapolating from this scenario is that some human communities must have moved away from the hills to that of the plains. Some communities must have decided to stay put in those hill tracts. Paliyar are said to be one such community that continued to be in the forests from time immemorial. Until recent times they were living in caves and crevices. These hunter gatherer quasi nomadic people had been throughout the forest ranges mostly in the lower Palani Hills and along the Western Ghats at an altitude between 1000 to 1200 meters above sea level. Apart from Palani Hills they are also located in Tirumala hills in the southern state of Tamil Nadu, India. However, in the Madura Manual, it was recorded that Paliyars are the aborigines of the Palani hills. (Thurston) According to another account, Paliyans resided in the jungles near the base of the mountains, in small isolated communities separated from each other by a distance of several miles in southern most part of Tamil Nadu in North Tinnevelly (Thurston, 1909).

Thurston (1909) further recorded the dry season when the Paliyar lived in natural caves and crevices in rocks, but, when leaks occurred during the rains, they erected a rough shed with the floor raised on poles off the ground, and sloping grass roof, beneath which a fire was kept burning at night, not only for warmth, but also to ward off wild beasts. They were experts at making rapidly improvised shelters at the base of hollow trees by cutting away the wood on one side with a bill-hook. Thus protected, they

Figure 1. A Paliyar temple inside the forest.

were quite content during a heavy shower, while Thurston (1909) noted the observers were miserable amid the drippings from an umbrella and a mango tree. The need to trace the past and reflect on contemporary scenarios of the Paliyar tribe arose to establish the current circumstances and sense of receding dependency on the forests for the Paliyar tribes. The choice of the term receding is deliberate by the chapter author and incorporated to establish illustrations for how Paliyar communities are moving away from their dependency on the forests. The consequences of the transformation are far reaching in the sense that it is not only the Paliyar tribes, but also humanity at large risks a disadvantageous position by dislodging the Paliyar community from their traditional homeland.

The choice of the term homeland demands a definition. For the Paliyars, the forests are their homeland. Their relationship with the forest and the land they have been once occupying is so interwoven that a Paliyar cannot be extricated from his land. About their living conditions Tracy had recorded that they built huts entirely of grass consisting of only one room and open at the ends. They had fire to keep them warm and keep animals away from them. They live in small groups in the jungles in Upper Palni hills and the Varushanād valley. They sometimes build themselves grass huts, but often they live on platforms up trees, in caves, or under rocks(Thurston, 1909). Yet, now with the changing environment and newer policies and practices, the Paliyars are forced to move away from their original homeland to the fringes of the forests closer to the mainstream villages. At present they spread over 40 settlements around Palani hills and their foothills close to the forests, mostly adjacent to mainstream villages and hamlets. Most of the original names of the Paliyar settlements were renamed in the existing government records. The change in the names represents a change in their identity and a mental construct of delinking their relations with the forest lands.

PALIYARS RELATION TO THE LAND

Indigenous knowledge systems are based on relationships with the world and people around (Wilson, 2001). For the Paliyars, as like other Indigenous communities, they do not consider themselves as independent entity, but they look at plants, animals, and other humans as a part of their relations and their existence. Their beliefs stem from such an understanding. The Paliyar community believes that every place has its own presiding spirit just like the Romans (Weiner, 2017). These spaces are distinct and a Paliyar would instill certain stone structures for worship in those sacred spaces (see Figure 2). Though certain spaces are earmarked in the forests as sacred which will include water springs, the sacredness is not exclusive to those spaces but extends beyond the confines to that of the forests, trees, and animals. The relation between the Paliyar tribe and the forests is an organic one, an integrated living off the forest which is non exploitative and symbiotic existence though they live off the forests. The Indigenous knowledge systems are based on relationships with the world and people around (Wilson, 2001) and Paliyars are no different. They do not think that they are independent of the nature around them and then the plants, animals and other humans are all part of their relations.

Figure 2. Paliyars invoke their gods in sacred forest spaces.

Thurston (1909) records that the Paliyars had no specific place of worship and believe in demons in the forests around them which they fear besides the Forest Department. However, with regard to their religion and superstitions of the Paliyans, as noted by the Reverend . F. Dahmen, "The principal religious ceremony takes place about the beginning of March. Mayāndi (the god) is usually represented by a stone, preferably one to which nature has given some curious shape, the serpent form being especially valued." Dahmen further added for the Paliyans:

... the stone itself is not the god, who is supposed to live somewhere, they do not exactly know where. The stone that represents him has its shrine at the foot of a tree or is simply sheltered by a small thatched covering. There, on the appointed day, the Paliyans gather before sunrise. Fire is made in a hole in front of the sacred stone, a fine cock brought in, decapitated amidst the music of horn and drum and the blood made to drip on the fire. The head of the fowl ought to be severed at one blow, as this is a sign of the satisfaction of the god for the past, and of further protection for the future. Should the head still

hang, this would be held a bad omen, foreboding calamities for the year ensuing. The instrument used in this sacred operation is the aruvāl, but the sacrificial aruvāl cannot be used but for this holy purpose.

Powers of witchcraft and magic are attributed to the Paliyans by other castes, and probably believed in by themselves. The following device adopted by them to protect themselves from the attacks of wild animals, the panther in particular, may be given as an illustration. Four jackals' tails are planted in four different spots, chosen so as to include the area within which they wish to be safe from the claws of the brute. This is deemed protection enough: though panthers should enter the magic square, they could do the Paliyans no harm; their mouths are locked."

Thurston (1909) further noted the Paliyars regard sylvan deities with great veneration. Kurupuswāmi is the tribe's tutelary god, and, when a great haul of wild honey is made, offerings are given at some shrine. They pretend to be followers of Siva, and always attend the Adi Amavasai ceremonies at Courtallum. As they carry no pollution, they are sometimes employed, in return for food, as night watchmen at the Vaishnavite temple known as Azhagar Koil at the base of the hills. The staple food of Paliyars *thinai* (foxtail millet) and honey are preferred offering for Lord Subramaniya. However, some of the gods and goddess who guard the forests are exclusive to the Paliyars. Their names and figurines were also exclusive to their beliefs. But with the movement of the Paliyars from the interiors of the forests to the fringes of the 'civilized' world, they have renamed their gods in tune with the mainstream pantheon.

Rituals and Cultural Events

As a matrilineal society, rituals for women takes predominance in the community. Primary celebration of the community is that of puberty rites. Puberty rites are celebrated with great fanfare with all their relations around. When a girl attains age, she is taken to the nearby forest stream which is considered sacred (for that matter all water bodies are considered sacred) and is given a ritual bath, and then she is carried by her maternal uncle to the house. She is not allowed to walk or if she walks, cloth is spread on the ground so that she does not hurt the mother earth. Marriage ceremonies are consecrated with wildflowers that are collected from the forests. The dead are buried in the forests in specific locations.

Further, Thurston (1909) recorded these indigenous peoples as wholly illiterate and only a few can count up to 10. A woman had been known to forget her own name, and at a marriage, the father took the hand of the bride, and placed it into that of the bridegroom said, "I give this girl to you. Give her roots and leaves and protect her." The value of a bride or bridegroom depended much on the quantity of roots and other commodities which he or she could collect. Their marriage ceremony consisted merely of a declaration of consent made by both parties at a feast, to which all their relatives are invited. Weddings were conducted without ceremonies, the understanding being that the man would collect food and the woman cooked. When one of them died, the rest leave the body as it was, and avoided the spot for some months. However, with the influence of mainstream culture, many traditions have eroded and instead incorporated mainstream practices within their customs. Though they retain certain traditional rituals, the use of loudspeakers, banners, and elaborate paraphernalia to mirror the mainstream for marriage functions.

Spiritual Link With the Forests

While ethics within the western thought is based on oppositions between culture and nature and human and non-human (Zapf, 2008), the indigenous peoples of the world perceive a continuum in their relation between culture and nature and human and non-human. According to Paliyars, their ancestors are in the forests and that they communicate to them through natural events like strong winds, songs of birds, thunder, etc. It is not just the land, but the memory of the people, of events, places, source of food and herbs everything is linked in the songs and beliefs. Before they venture into the forests for gathering honey, they have rituals that are meant for cleansing themselves and pray. They would desist from sexual contact the day before honey gathering and cleanse themselves for the ritual of honey gathering as it is a very delicate and dangerous maneuver over rock cliffs and deep crevices. As they risk a lot to gather honey, they take at most care to work in groups and offer prayers to the gods.

Their goddess Palichiamman is revered and worshiped at every given opportunity even while going to the forest for honey gathering. Land and forest are considered as Mother and they request their mother for herbs, food and game and at the same time pray that they also leave behind abundant food and herbs for the generations to come. This thought of sustainability is due to the worldview of the community. They do not like to milk their Mother dry. It is interesting to note that the Paliyar tribal community of the South Western Ghats uses the flowering periodicity of this plant to calculate their age.(Sundararaju)

According to Rev. F. Dahmen, the Paliyars are nomadic people living in Upper Palani hills, they sustain with roots, leaves and wild fruits. They live upon roots yams and honey as well. They cook the roots by putting them into a pit in the ground, heaping wood upon them, and lighting it. The fire is usually kept burning all night as a protection against wild beasts, and it is often the only sign of the presence of the Paliyans in a jungle, for they are shy folk, who avoid other people. They make fire with quartz and steel, using the floss of the silk-cotton tree as tinder(Thurston, 1909).

In addition, Thurston (1909) recorded the Paliyars collected for the Forest Department minor produce in the form of root-bark of Ventilago madraspatana and Anisochilus carnosus, the fruit of Terminalia Chebula (myrabolams), honey, bees-wax, and other products, which were handed over to a contractor in exchange for rice, tobacco, betel leaves and nuts, chilies, tamarinds, and salt. The food thus earned as wages was supplemented by yams (tubers of Dioscorea) and roots, which were harvested by digging-stick, and also forest fruits. Thurston recorded the Paliyars were not known to cultivate anything or keep animals except perhaps dogs. Implements were said to be an axe or a knife and a few pots, and Thurston recognized the Paliyars as expert honey gatherers who risked their lives climbing lofty precipices or precipitous cliffs to harvest this honey.

They also sometimes grew wild grains and millets by slash and burn techniques apart from hunting small animals (Thurston, 1909) until a few decades ago. Though they were practicing 'slash and burn' technique for modest agriculture, they remained dependent on seasonal fruits, roots, and honey. They were then fully dependent on the forests, and the hunting-gathering was their only source of food. This practice over generations had ensured a thorough knowledge of forests which is being transferred to the successive generations (Thurston).

Yet, as the Paliyars were forced to stay in settlements their food habits have drastically changed in the past 60 years, resulting in the Paliyars to become sellers of their forest collections to any buyer and more aligned with the market economy. Their dependence on forest for their daily food has been reduced drastically. Contemporary Paliyars depend mostly on the mainstream diet and are dependent on the government for rations. The traditional roots and wild berries have become a delicacy as they are either not available or inaccessible due to various conditions. Thus, the land that was once forest is now being transformed into commercial estates growing vegetables and fruits for mainstream consumption. Apart from the deforestation cleared for tourism, large scale destruction of forests for timber is also a reality. Hence, the source of the traditional Paliyar food has become rare, and as hunting is also restricted, the staple food for the Paliyars remains at stake.

Rev. F. Dahmen writes that for their existence in the forests they were forced to find 'their own remedies: in fact, some Paliyans have made a name for themselves by their knowledge of the medicinal properties of herbs and roots. Thus, for instance, they make from certain roots (periya uri katti vēr) a white powder known as a very effective purgative. Against snake-bite they always carry with them certain leaves (naru valli vēr), which they hold to be a very efficient antidote. As soon as one of them is bitten, he chews these, and also applies them to the wound. (Thurston)

Kattu Raja, a Paliyan in Sirumalai hills was asked to bring a medicinal plant from the forest. He brought part of the plant. It was intrigue for us, as to why he is bringing a part of the plant and not the whole. It was to his understanding that he has located the plant, and he can access the plant at point of time in the future. He had also left a part of the plant to rejuvenate to ensure that it made available for the future. The location and availability for the future is ensured. This they follow for honey gathering, roots extraction and even while hunting. They hunt only the male of a species. They are knowledgeable about male and female trees and act accordingly. Their relation to nature is non-exploitative and ensures sustainability of the forests and its resources. This is what the Paliyar is looking for – a future and availability of nature for his ways of life. Loss of land and access to forest resources is an epistemic violence on the continuation of his liberty to live in harmony with nature.

While Tracy records that Paliyars had 'no idea of hunting, any more than they had of agriculture' General Burton describes them as 'good trackers' and expert hunters of small game which they trap and ambush with native patience for hog, deer, or pea-fowl. However, Rev. F. Dahmen describes in detail their hunting methods thus:

Patience and cunning above all are required in their hunting-methods. One of their devices, used for big game, e.g., against the sambar (deer), or against the boar, consists in digging pitfalls, carefully covered up with twigs and leaves. On the animal being entrapped, it is dispatched with clubs or the aruvāl (sickle). Another means consists in arranging a heap of big stones on a kind of platform, one end of which is made to rest on higher ground, the other skillfully equipoise by a stick resting on a fork, where it remains fixed by means of strong twine so disposed that the least movement makes the lever-like stick on the fork fly off, while the platform and the stones come rapidly down with a crash. The string which secures the lever is so arranged as to unloose itself at the least touch, and the intended victim can hardly taste the food that serves for bait without bringing the platform with all its weight down upon itself. Similar traps, but on a smaller scale, are used to catch smaller animals: hares, wild fowl, etc. Flying squirrels are smoked out of the hollows of trees, and porcupines out of their burrows, and then captured or clubbed to death on their coming out. The first drops of blood of any animal the Paliyans kill are offered to their god. A good catch is a great boon for the famished Paliyan. The meat obtained there from must be divided between all the families of the settlement.

When Paliyars come across carcass of a goat or deer in the forest, they will roast and eat it. They smoke outfield rats from their holes to catch them. Crabs are caught for eating by children, by letting a string with a piece of cloth tied to the end down the hole and lifting it out thereof when the crab seizes hold of the cloth with its claws. Of wild beasts they are not afraid, and often scare them away by screaming, clapping the hands, and rolling down stones into the valleys.

For fishing, the Paliyars use a kind of bark of a tree called karungakodi to numb the fishes in water, and then they collect the floating fishes. Sometimes they were seen using hooks. However, with the current policies of the government hunting is strictly prohibited and the Paliyars are deprived of the traditional hunting practices. The coming generations of the Paliyars would not know how to hunt. The Paliyans spend their time fabricating bird cages and weaving mat, basket or small knickknacks for barter in the local markets. Being a matrilineal society, they have great reverence for women and their deity is a female goddess. They are predominantly community oriented and were in groups who shared the bounty of nature and did not know anything about private property or ownership either of space or property. They were wholly dependent on forests and for them forest and land are Mother Nature and their worldviews are constructed based on this belief.

Oral Traditions

Though they speak the mainstream language, Tamil with a slight dialectic variation, they do not have any written records. Their songs, stories and music are transferred to successive generations. Oral traditions are the modus operandi with which these intangible cultural heritages are transmitted to the successive generations. Children listen to them and practice the music and songs and women dance around. Children are imitated into the system by way of participation in the events, rituals both as participants and observers. Music is considered as a form of communication with their ancestors. They take to music with élan as they create music with any available materials, from broken pans and sticks, bamboo, hides of animals. Music and dance are part of their affair that they sing during rituals, lullaby, puberty ceremonies, marriage and death. Whenever they are not working, music and songs could be heard from their settlements. Whenever they are not working, they would indulge in music just for the sake of it. Prayers sung before going for honey gathering stands testimony to their worldviews that seeks sustainable use of forest resources. The prayers include appeal to the Forests which are seen as mother and requests are made to provide them and the next generations with food and herbs.

PALIYAR IDENTITY AND WHITE SETTLERS

Rev. J. E. Tracy acknowledged the forest had been home for the Paliyar tribes from time immemorial, but Tracy was judgmental in recording that "… the forest seemed to have taught them nothing more than it might have been supposed to have taught the prowling jackal or the laughing hyena" (Thurston, 1909). Paliyars were viewed as ignorant and filthy and were "the most abject, hopeless, and unpromising specimens of humanity" that he had ever seen. Their settlements consisted of about 40 members in a little settlement in a lovely spot by a stream of pure water. Tracy considered Paliyars as "foul and filthy … as if they were animals … unclean ones"(Thurston, 1909). The perpetuation of the idea Paliyars were ignorant communities complicated false perceptions by subsequent generations who considered them as such, resulting in marginalization and identification as the other rather than their due for the wealth of knowledge and expertise in their fields of specialisation.

Tracy further remarked though the Paliyars occupied rich lands which were abundantly irrigated, they lived entirely on nuts and roots, gum gathered from forests (Thurston, 1909). This concept of rich lands by the European missionary and their evaluation of lands based on its commercial value was a part of exploitative mentality of the European settlers. But by extending this line of argument, Tracy revealed Paliyars were not keen on agriculture or exploiting the land (Thurston).This stereotyping of the Paliyars by the colonial enterprise has continued to hold sway over the mainstream today; however, facts remains otherwise. They are privy to immense wealth of bio-intelligence on the flora and fauna of the wild. The process of internalizing the inherent inability was forced on the Paliyars who do not now see themselves as keepers of knowledge but feel that they are losers in the modern world. This has led to large scale alcohol abuse, which has eroded the culture's immense wealth of knowledge and led to feelings of devaluation for the privilege of their indigenous knowledge systems. This may be one of the reasons they need to transform themselves into a modern' community as the need for transformation dovetails traditional knowledge and modernity for a better dignified living and economic prosperity is needed for a driving force in such transition (see Figure 3).

Figure 3. Members of the traditional Paliyar community in their hamlet.

PALIYARS' TRANSITION

In a note written in 1817, Mr. T. Turnbull states that the Madura Pulliers "are never seen unless when they come down to travellers to crave a piece of tobacco or a rag of cloth, for which they have a great predilection. The women are said to lay their infants on warm ashes after delivery, as a substitute for warm clothing and beds."

With the advent of colonialism and rampant exploitation of natural resources, forays into forest for timber had taken the British population to the upper reaches of the Palani hills. Along with them the mainstream people who went as labourers from the plains had also ventured to settle in the forest tracts which resulted in land grab and reducing prime forest areas. This encroachment into the forest lands had an irreparable damage on the Paliyar tribes, their identity, culture and being. Paliyars who were once roaming the forests for hunting, slash and burn agriculture continued to do so till sometime after independence. But slowly they were forced to settle with housing facilities extended to them in specific locations that prevent them from the practice of slash and burn farming in the forests. The forest department looks at them as hindrance to the wildlife and is seeking methods to remove them from core forests regions. It is pertinent to note that no Paliyar was ever killed by human-animal conflict. However, citing safety reasons, the forest departments are attempting to relocate the indigenous communities outside the forest reserves. The government in order to provide 'basic amenities,' is working on fixing them to a particular space and provides the support that the officials think they need. The government is also providing them with ration to wean the Paliyar community away from the forests. The need for him to depend on the forest for his existence is slowly reduced to a greater degree. While forcing the Paliyars to settle in specific locations, even the names of the locations are altered to the convenience of the mainstream thus attempting to erase the spiritual link to the location. For instance, the location Boothanachi koil is renamed as Bharathi Anna Nagar. This subtle variation though does have a deep impact on the psyche of the Paliyars, the emotional and spiritual link to the land is erased by the change in the name. Yet, current day Paliyars who remain in contact with other communities are influenced by the outside world. They utilize technology such as smart phones but remain exploited as farm labourers and the non-timber forest produce they collect are again bought by middlemen at a considerably lower price.

Contemporary Conditions

Once spread over vast geographical space of more than 2669 square kilometers, in the lower altitudes in 54 settlements, the Paliyars are now reduced to less than 30 colonies in the hilly terrain. They are provided with concrete houses and riveted to a specific space for administrative convenience and now counted in government data under one or other mainstream villages. The once nomadic tribe that practiced slash and burn technique is now confined to specific region due to the housing that was provided to them effectively curtailing their free movement across the entire hill tracts. It is pertinent to note that the political leverage the Paliyar community is almost non-existent as they are spread over a vast area and are settled in niche space on the fringes of the mainstream settlements in the hills. Thus, in every village council they are scantily represented as the mainstream would be dominating the village council. An environmental activist and Chairman NEED Trust India, Michael Marian (personal communication, May 1, 2019) opined from the point of view of the politicians, they are valued voters; yet, for the government, they are beneficiaries. For the educated and the mainstream culture, they are economically poor people. This multiple stereotyping of Paliyars has further complicated their ability to assert an identity of their own or even celebrate themselves (see Figure 4). Even while there are checks and balances in the law against exploitation of the indigenous communities (Abhay Bang), it is sad to note that due to ignorance of their rights they remain economically backward, lack education and malnutrition (Ghai, 2018).

LAND DISPOSSESSION

Native lands are sacred not only because of the historical events that happened therein, but also because of the stories that recall those sites and "continue to guide moral behavior and sustain culture" (Teuton,

Figure 4. A typical modern Paliyar settlement of government-constructed row houses on the fringes of mainstream villages.

2008, p. 49). These places of / for the indigenous communities include places of healing, places where medicinal plants grow or special animals can be found, "places for dreaming, visioning and listening to the land" (Jones 2008, p. 6). As the land bears "the bones and stories" (Owens as cited in Mongibello, 2014) of each indigenous community, it becomes central in the process of people's self-identification because it is the very knowledge of the land as well as the knowledge of the land stories that enforces the sense of who they are. Dwelling the landscape is the measure of being, in line with what the anthropologist Tim Ingold has called the "dwelling perspective." (Mongibello)According to Anvita Abbi, prominent linguist, India has treated its tribes fairly well and is treating its tribes with dignity and left them alone most of the time. However, she raises her apprehension about the intrusion into the tribal lands due to increasing industrialization. However, the saving grace is the Tribals are protected under PESA Act of 1996(Ghai, 2018).

Though Recht (2009) reported indigenous knowledge was in mortal danger and required new forms of intellectual property protection to save it, there is yet another danger of indigenous people land dispossession and forest relations thereby permanently disabling and depriving the successive generations from indigenous traditions. They transfer forest lands into agricultural estates in the name of development and as the forest moves further away from the indigenous settlements, and as trees are cut to be replaced by commercial timber plantations, the intimate knowledge of the forests is lost forever with little point of reference. The weaning away of the indigenous communities away from the forests and the relevance of the forest lands to them would result in a situation which is aptly expressed by indigenous activist Wadaka whose fear is that she would find none suitable to transfer the invaluable knowledge might die with her. It saddens her that her people will lose something that was theirs for generations(Jena, 2017).

Apart from the loss of land and the loss of people to carry forward, there is yet another dimension of loss: the loss of cultural constructs. Fowler (2002), in the author's introduction to subordinated peoples in colonial and neocolonial situations, purported not only does the indigenous communities contend with social institutions of dominance, they also face symbolic dominance of ideologies that reflect cultural constructions of the dominant order and rationalize that order. These rationalizations may come to be unconsciously accepted, and in such a scenario, the basic ideologies of the indigenous communities will be lost forever.

Even while the indigenous communities "… accommodate imposed institutions and absorb them into a reinvented tradition or reconstruct dominant social institutions in ways that are locally meaningful and that serve local ends" (Fowler, 2002), the essence of the indigenous communities' ideologies would be compromised as the mainstream's identification with the forests are more exploitative and commercial. However, for the sake of survival, there is a possibility that as Fowler quoted James Scott,"…subordinated people elsewhere have dealt in practical ways with social institutions of dominance by cooperating or by resisting either overtly or through 'everyday forms of resistance."

Commodification

With the sort of settler mentality that is permeating the indigenous communities, the value for the forest produce which was only for consumption has been altered to that of value as a commodity. The access to forest products like honey and other non-timber forest produce has been transferred from being of utility value to that of a commodity value. This alters the fundamental idea of a forest for the indigenous communities. Gratani et al. (2016) appreciating the man-environment relationship of the indigenous communities conclude that indigenous environmental values support sustainability by promoting reverence towards the environment instead of its commodification. However, they are now being forced to commodify the forest produce and they play a vital role in capitalising their knowledge of the forests to exploit it.

For the traditional knowledge to be maintained and developed, it has to be practiced and made relevant. As the traditional knowledge and Indigenous spirituality hinges on the maintenance and renewal of relationships to the land and that they are not recorded in any other form, transmission of the same to the next generation becomes inevitable. However, with the large scale suppression of indigenous cultural expressions during the process of colonization the policies and perceptions of the mainstream act as obstacles (Robbins, 2011) in the practice and transmission of the worldviews to the next generation.

Having moved away from the traditional activities and as of now living as a settlement the need for dependence on forests had reduced a lot. The food rations from the mainstream that is being distributed through the rations had substituted the roots, tuber and honey which they once collected. The school education that is offered had also decelerated the frequency in which the youth being in touch with nature. Paliyars are now hired as farm labourers and this has weaned them away from their traditional reconnaissance into the forest. The reduced need and dependence on forests had also a severe impact on the need to transmit the knowledge to the next generation. The need to develop a new skill set for survival is that of being a farm labourer, and the fact that the formal education being remote they are now in the liminal space where they are losing the relevance of the oral traditions. All these have compounded to reduce their dependence on forests and make most of the oral traditions obsolete, as they do not see a direct use for their knowledge in their day to day life.

FUTURE RESEARCH DIRECTIONS

The continuation of stories, songs and music has given a ray of hope for the Paliyars. Probably their stories, songs and music might possibly influence the mainstream if it listens to them as writer Leslie

Silko, who hoped indigenous novels and stories offered a more effective way to enact social change as they were capable of reaching readers from a profound emotional level and connect them "through time-back to a time before this person was born" (as cited in Romero, 2002).Silko also said these cross-national spiritual connections had the power to resist injustice and were more effective than secular political and nationalist movements (Romero). Therefore, further research is needed to distinguish the government policies impact on the Paliyar community. Future indigenous research is needed to ensure understanding of the Paliyars to better comprehend their value and cultural traditions to protect them as keepers of traditional knowledge.

CONCLUSION

As the dependence on the forests is reduced drastically, Paliyars are now seen as landless labourers. The current construction of the self by the indigenous community is that of being a poor land less labourer and existing on the fringes of the semi-urban settlements in the hilly tracts of Palani Hills. Dependency on alcohol and other drugs, and by the introduction of smartphone technologies, the Paliyar youth are now drawn away from their traditional vocation of honey gathering and hunting. They see themselves as disenfranchised from the mainstream and cannot see the relevance of their cultural ethos in the ever increasing process of assimilation and acculturation. Caught in the=is liminal space, the Paliyars are in the process of transition through the loss of their indigenous knowledge system, which has become redundant and therefore undervalued in the light of modernity. According to researchers Norman and Dakshinamurthy (2004), Paliyars are now an abandoned and neglected community. As Paliyars work on the basis of need they are not keen on working as the mainstream workers do. Hence, they are considered lazy and undependable by the mainstream and not considered for work or assignments.

This ongoing erosion and leaning away from their ancestors, forests render their oral traditions and knowledge of the forests useless as they are being extricated from the land. However, for fringe benefits, they are used as honey gatherers and fire fighters by the forest officials, which exploits their indigenous knowledge and purpose. The once free Paliyars are now riveted to a specific place and made dependent on the government for its daily rations that made them economically dependent. Alienated from the space which provides a culture with spiritual connection, ancestors, and the traditional wellbeing, the Paliyars are now an emaciated figure of the past unable to move forward and assimilate fully into the contemporary development paradigm. Nor may they return to the freedom of the forests, the Paliyars now exist meekly on the fringes of the forest abetting the mainstream settlement.

Therefore, the Paliyars' relation with the forests both ritually and spiritually is undergoing a seismic change due to the phenomenon of settlement mindset that is making thorough inroads into his daily routine and outlook. The sense of happiness that all needs are met and consumed from the forest has given way to accumulation of food and safeguarding it due to fears of lack. This change in the attitude is altering the cultural outlook found hung between the past and a future and an uncertain present. It is unfortunate that they lack the privilege of education of the mainstream nor access holistically to elevate them within a new paradigm. Both legal and political intervention remain remote; thus, the only alternative is often to celebrate themselves for what they are and not to allow internalization of inability to cope with the future. As internalizing inadequacy instead of recognition of the innate potential is damaging. Their contributions to the sphere of herbs, agricultural practices, and novel food sources as the scope for resilience is dwindling slowly but steadily.

The impact of the dominant culture has been tremendous as the Paliyars alter their systems and values accordingly. Though, it is understood any culture is always in a state of flux, this dramatic shift extricates the Paliyar fully from the forest, which would be detrimental to humanity as they are the keepers of rich knowledge source. There needs a change for shift in the mainstream thought process from what Gratani et al. (2016) opined anthropocentric values to that of eco-centric values in their relationship with the environment as practiced by indigenous cultures around the world. Apart from plundering knowledge from the indigenous communities, they may also be deprived of transferring knowledge to the next Paliyar generation by denying access to the sources of the plants thereby leading to threats of biopiracy (DeGeer, 2003).

REFERENCES

DeGeer, M. E. (2003). Biopiracy: The appropriation of indigenous peoples' cultural knowledge. *New England Journal of International and Comparative Law*, *9*, 179–208.

Fowler, L. (2002). *Tribal sovereignty and the historical imagination: Cheyenne-Arapaho politics*. University of Nebraska Press.

Ghai, R. (2018). Tribal rights in India are a grey picture: experts. *Down To Earth*. Retrieved from https://www.downtoearth.org.in/news/environment/tribal-rights-in-india-are-a-grey-picture-experts-62230

Gratani, M., Sutton, S. G., Butler, J. R., Bohensky, E. L., Foale, S., & Stevenson, M. (2016). Indigenous environmental values as human values. *Cogent Social Sciences*, *2*(1), 1185811. Advance online publication. doi:10.1080/23311886.2016.1185811

Jena, M. (2017). *One Earth: Why the world needs Indigenous communities to steward their lands*. Inter Press Service News Agency. Retrieved from http://www.ipsnews.net/2017/08/one-earth-world-needs-indigenous-communities-steward-lands/

LaRocque, E. (2011). *When the other is me: Native resistance discourse, 1850-1990*. University of Manitoba Press.

Ministry of Law. (2007). *The Constitution of India, 1950*. Retrieved from http://legislative.gov.in/sites/default/files/19_The%20Constitution%20%28ST%29%20Order%201950.pdf

Mongibello, A. (2014). Tracking the land/memory: Healing and reterritorializations in Jeannette Armstrong's breath tracks. In *Indigenous perspectives of North America: A collection of studies*. Cambridge Scholars Publishing.

Norman, T. S. J., & Dakshinamurthy, V. (2004). *A case study of Paliyar Tribe of Sirumalai Hills*. The Gandhigram Rural Institute.

Recht, J. (2009). Hearing indigenous voices, protecting indigenous knowledge. *International Journal of Cultural Property*, *16*(3), 233–254. doi:10.1017/S0940739109990166

Robbins, J. A., & Dewar, J. (2011). Traditional Indigenous approaches to healing and the modern welfare of traditional knowledge, spirituality and lands: A critical reflection on practices and policies taken from the Canadian Indigenous example. *International Indigenous Policy Journal*, *2*(4). Advance online publication. doi:10.18584/iipj.2011.2.4.2

Romero, C. (2002). Envisioning a" network of tribal coalitions": Leslie Marmon Silko's Almanac of the dead. *American Indian Quarterly*, *26*(4), 623–640. doi:10.1353/aiq.2004.0008

Ruffo, A. G. (2009). Exposing the poison, staunching the wound: Applying Aboriginal healing theory to literary analysis. *The Canadian Journal of Native Studies*, *29*(1/2), 91–110.

Sundararaju, V. (2018). Neelakurinji: Blue bloom in a blue moon. *Down To Earth*. Retrieved from https://www.downtoearth.org.in/blog/environment/neelakurinji-blue-bloom-in-a-blue-moon-61295

Teuton, S. K. (2008). *Red Land, Red Power*. Duke University Press.

Thurston, E. (1909). *Castes and tribes of southern India* (Vol. 3). Government Press.

Weiner, E. (2017). How geography shapes our identity. *Transcending Borders*. Retrieved from https://trend.pewtrusts.org/en/archive/trend-summer-2016/foreword-how-geography-shapes-our-identity

Wilson, S. (2001). What is an Indigenous research methodology? *Canadian Journal of Native Education*, *25*(2), 175–179.

Zapf, H. (2008). Literary ecology and the ethics of texts. *New Literary History*, *39*(4), 847–868. doi:10.1353/nlh.0.0066

Chapter 6
Culturally Responsive Instruction as Computer-Based Reading Engagement and Literacy Among Native American Students

Jacob Lauritzen
Eastern Arizona College, USA

ABSTRACT

The chapter presents a review of the literature on Native American education and the use of culturally responsive instruction to guide the implementation of a computer-based reading program to increase engagement and reading levels for Native American secondary students for a quantitative single-case study on the effects of using Achieve3000 while using a culturally responsive model for selecting reading samples. Study findings noted though student reading levels increased and reading engagement improved in some key areas, no significant difference was found between groups. The implications of these findings are that use of a culturally responsive pedagogy to select self-relevant materials for a computer-based reading program may help Native American students to increase their reading levels and reading engagement scores, but not at a significant rate. Future research should consider whether these pedagogies and other strategies may improve Native American reading literacy.

INTRODUCTION

In 1971, American students in grades 4, 8, and 12 began taking the National Assessment of Educational Progress (NAEP) test to measure their growth in reading and math (National Center for Education Statistics [NCES], 2014). Longitudinal studies revealed NAEP reading scores for high school seniors have remained stagnant since NAEP testing began in the 1970s (NCES, 2014). In response to these and other concerns, federal and state governments have passed legislation to reform educational practices

DOI: 10.4018/978-1-7998-3729-9.ch006

(Ametepee et al., 2014; Harris, 2012; Kessinger, 2012). These reforms included the No Child Left Behind Act (NCLB), Race to the Top (RTT), and most recently the adoption of the Common Core State Standards (CCSS) (Ametepee et al., 2014; Harris, 2012; Kessinger, 2012). Despite these many attempts to improve reading and math scores, NAEP results suggested these reforms had no significant impact on improving reading scores (NCES, 2014).

The National Indian Education Study (NIES) used NAEP data to study Alaska Native and American Indian students (hereafter referred to as Native Americans) and the study found Native American students scored lower in reading than other culture groups (NCES, 2012). Native American students in Arizona specifically have graduated high school at a lower rate than other culture groups (Stillwell & Sable, 2013). These findings suggested current educational practices are failing to bridge the gap between Native American students and other culture groups in Arizona. To bridge the performance gap in reading scores between Native American students and other culture groups, it was necessary to identify best practices for improving Native American student reading scores.

In 2014, Arizona introduced Arizona's Measurement of Educational Readiness to Inform Teaching (AzMERIT), a new standardized test for English Language Arts and Mathematics (ADE, 2015c). The purpose of AzMERIT was to create a computer-based test that aligned to the Arizona College and Career Ready Standards (Arizona's branding of the Common Core State Standards) (ADE, 2014). In the first year of testing, 65% of students failed AzMERIT for English Language Arts (ADE, 2015d). Of Native American 9th grade students, 92% of students failed the English Language Arts portion of AzMERIT (ADE, 2015d). These findings further supported the need to find appropriate solutions for improving Native American students' reading scores in Arizona.

Researchers have suggested culturally-responsive instruction (CRI) can be an effective model for teaching diverse racial and cultural groups (Adkins, 2012; Cramer et al., 2014). For example, Lopez et al. (2013) called specifically for qualitative research on culturally-responsive instruction for Native Americans. In addition, Adkins (2012) defined culturally responsive English instruction as the use of students' cultural backgrounds as a foundation to build student literacy. Further, Cramer et al. (2014) proposed even deeper implementation with their Integrated Learning Model (ILM). ILM combines elements from previous models to promote equality and cultural awareness with the intention of correcting systemic bias against minority students. The use of CRI and ILM may include the use of self-relevant texts that depict characteristics of students' backgrounds and the intentional connection of textual elements to students' lives (Adkins, 2012; Covarrubias & Fryberg, 2015). In particular, CRI can be used as a model for reading instruction (Adkins, 2012). One aspect of CRI includes the use of self-relevant subject matter for students. Covarrubias and Fryberg (2015) have called for the development of self-relevant models for Native American students. Because the NIES only evaluated quantitative data from the NAEP test, Lopez, Heilig, and Schram (2013) and Richardson and McLeod (2011) called for large-scale qualitative studies on Native American students. Richardson and McLeod (2011) have called for culturally-responsive e-learning strategies for Native American students.

Computer-based devices can be used to support reading instruction to improve student engagement and motivation (Laverick, 2014). Such programs have been used to provide differentiated reading solutions for students with varying reading levels (Turgut, 2012). One such example is Achieve3000. As a differentiated e-reading solution, Achieve3000 is an e-learning tool designed to adapt informational texts to students' identified reading levels (Erguvan, 2015). Achieve3000 tracks the progression of student reading levels in Lexiles, a measure of text complexity and student comprehension of complex texts (Achieve3000, 2016d; MetaMetrics, 2016). In addition to targeting skills and concepts necessary for passing AzMERIT, Achieve3000 also enables teachers to select the articles students will read. With these two capabilities combined, Achieve3000 appears to be an e-learning solution fit for providing differentiation for student's reading levels while allowing for teachers to pre-select article topics consistent with a CRI model for Native American students. Research shows teachers and students feel positive about Achieve3000's ability to improve students' reading levels (Erguvan, 2014; Erguvan, 2015; Turgut, 2012). No peer-reviewed research appears to have been published on minority groups, such as Native Americans, using Achieve3000.

In the 2014-2015 school year, the Fort Thomas Unified School District slowly began implementing Achieve3000 in a few grades as a reading intervention tool in addition to other previous solutions. Teachers were provided training from Achieve3000, but were free to implement the program as they wished with little to no administrative oversight. In 2015, 94% of Native American students at Fort Thomas High School failed the English Language Arts portion of AzMERIT (ADE, 2015b). These scores suggested significant intervention was needed to help these students to improve their reading levels to prepare them for college and careers after high school graduation. A culturally-responsive instruction model was not used previously to implement Achieve3000.

The objective of this chapter is to provide valuable findings on the use of culturally-responsive instruction for Native American students in the context of a computer-based reading program with the hopes of identifying best practices for serving Native American students while also encouraging additional research on the topic in the future. Beginning in the fall of 2017, a quantitative single-case study was conducted on the effect of pre-selecting self-relevant article topics for Native American students to read under a culturally-responsive instruction model while using the Achieve3000 computer-based differentiated reading program. The study sought to identify whether this pedagogical approach could increase Native American high school student engagement during reading and, by extension, increase their reading levels. This chapter presents the results of a review of the past and current research surrounding the historical factors affecting Native American student reading levels and the study findings.

BACKGROUND

Since colonists from Europe came to America, there has been a history of Europeans educating Native Americans. These efforts have come with differing motivations. Some have attempted to educate Native American students to assimilate them to Anglo-European culture and language (Grayshield et al. 2015; Slivka, 2011; Szasz, 2005; Wanberg, 2013). Others have implemented intervention programs to serve the unique needs of these communities (Demmert & Towner, 2003). With these efforts have also come successes and failures that continue to affect Native American education programs today. Tribal elders have identified historical trauma caused by the misguided efforts of the past (Grayshield et al., 2015). Current reports have identified a long-lasting gap between Native American students and their White counterparts (NCES, 2011, 2012, 2014). Culturally-responsive instruction (CRI) has been used with Native American students and other minority groups with varying degrees of success. Some of these and other efforts are now beginning to utilize computer-based reading programs to promote literacy (Council et al., 2016). The following review will investigate a history of Native American education programs, the current state of education within Native American schools and communities, research-based practices for reading instruction, and ultimately the possibility of utilizing computer-based strategies to implement CRI to provide reading instruction for Native American students.

A History of Native American Education

Szasz (2005) identified three common elements shared by Native American students since the 1700s; namely, being removed from their homes, their families, and their communities. Perhaps the most prominent example of this model was introduced by Richard Henry Pratt. Pratt opened the Carlisle Indian Industrial School in 1879 (Slivka, 2011), which was modeled after the Hampton Normal and Agricultural Institute for African-Americans. Pratt felt that an industrial-based educational program would be the most effective way to assimilate Native American students and also included the cutting of male students' hair, required dressing in Anglo clothing, and preventing Native American students from speaking their Native languages (Slivka, 2011). These practices were encouraged by the 1879 annual report of the Commissioner of Indian Affairs, which stated that boarding schools were more effective than day schools (Fischer & Stoddard, 2013).

In 1928, the U.S. Congress commissioned Meriam and Work (1928) to conduct a study on the current state of life for Native Americans on Indian Reservations, including the state of education. At the time, it was common practice to remove Native American students from their homes and communities and to send them to government operated boarding schools. Meriam and Work (1928) advised against this practice, because the structure of boarding schools did not allow students to develop initiative. They argued, instead, for keeping students close to their families by sending students to local public schools or day schools.

Meriam and Work (1928) proposed a Native American education program should differentiate based on students' "individual abilities, interests, and needs" (p. 32). Rather than using a curriculum developed in Washington, D.C., the authors advised teachers should choose their own culturally-relevant texts. He argued that using standardized texts might use examples with content unfamiliar to Native American students. In addition, Meriam and Work (1928) argued for high standards when hiring teachings at Native American schools. This logic was that higher quality teachers would be better able to adapt their teaching to their students' needs.

In 1969, the U.S. Senate commissioned another report on the current state of the American Indian education entitled, "Indian education: A national tragedy—A national challenge." The report outlined many of the legislative and educational failures which had been made in trying to improve educational conditions for Native American students. The report found that Native Americans at the time were often stereotyped for being lazy and drunk and depictions of Native Americans in history books were hostile and negative. Many administrators and teachers were also negative in their feelings toward their Native American students. These depictions and attitudes distorted Native American culture and negatively affected students' self-concept. The report author found that few Native Americans participated on school boards, which in turn led to feelings of powerlessness as Native Americans had little control over their own education. Few materials were available for teaching students about their culture and language and negative feelings toward Native American students were common especially in white communities. Many districts had policies that automatically retained Native American students or, alternately, automatically passed Native American students despite how they performed on achievement-tests. Among the report's findings was the recommendation to "develop culturally sensitive curriculum materials" (U.S. Senate, 1969, p. 116).

In 2008, the Arizona State Legislature introduced an amendment to SB 1108. The proposed amendment would have revoked public funding for educational programs that promoted political, religious, and cultural beliefs counter to traditional American beliefs (O'Leary & Romero, 2010; Writer, 2008).

Though the amendment may have intended to discourage public schools from promoting what they felt were anti-American ideals, it also had the effect of discouraging the promotion of diverse cultures and lived experiences. It also would have had the effect of reinforcing White privilege and culture as a societal norm (Writer, 2008). Though SB 1108 failed, it represents one of many such bills presented that would have affected Native American students by devaluing their experiences by labeling them as un-American (O-Leary & Romero, 2010; Writer, 2008). Two years later in 2010, the State of Arizona passed HB2281, a law prohibiting schools from offering classes or courses that encourage racism, target instruction for a specific racial group, or promote racial unity above individuality (Wanberg, 2013). Though this law was designed to dissolve Mexican-American Studies programs that were seen as being counter-cultural and disruptive, this law could be applied to courses about Native American culture, language, etc. It could also prevent the implementation of CBE programs that could be perceived as designing instruction for Native American students or by promoting Native American culture above student individuality. Should similar legislation continue to be passed, culturally-based instruction programs designed to help minority students and to help them to bridge the educational gap with their White counterparts would effectively be blocked because they could be perceived to promote racial unity, thus being antinationalistic or anti-American.

In 2011, researchers for the National Indian Education Study (NIES) investigated data from recent National Assessment of Educational Progress (NAEP) scores in comparison to previous years (2005 and 2009) to determine the then current state of math and reading scores of Native American students in 4th and 8th grades (NCES, 2012). The study revealed that 47% of 4th grade and 63% of 8th grade Native American students ranked as basic or above basic reading level (NCES, 2012). These scores were consistently lower than non-Native American students and were not statistically different from previous years, revealing that the gap between Native and non-Native students is holding firm; yet, when compared with other races, Native American students consistently scored lower on the NAEP test than any other group (NCES, 2014). Native American students also graduated from high school at lower rates than all other racial groups (NCES, 2011). Research shows a clear need for educational intervention for Native American students, but little research in this area remains available. Of the available research, much of it has been focused on elementary-aged students and not students in secondary schools. Further, because many educational reforms have been designed to improve reading scores, but have failed to do so, it appears that current and recent educational reforms are not helping Native American students to close the reading level gap between them and their non-Native American peers (NCES, 2014).

The historical trauma caused by the practice of forcing students into boarding schools has had a lasting effect on Native Americans. Grayshield et al. (2015) conducted a phenomenological study of Native American elders to identify how historical trauma has affected individuals, families, and communities in the past and present, and what these elders would propose happen as a result. The authors found many elders felt that Bureau of Indian Affairs (BIA) boarding schools had had lasting negative effects and that the historical trauma on Native American communities contributed to current issues such as substance abuse and mental health (Grayshield et al., 2015). The elders suggested the use of a positive counter-narrative that identified positive examples and qualities of Native Americans. CBE could be used as a pedagogical approach to implement this positive counter-narrative in teaching Native American students. Buckmiller (2015) conducted a case study of Native American principals where one administrator noted seeing the lingering effects of boarding schools nearly a hundred years later.

Another result of BIA schools was in the reinforcement of the concept that Native American students have nothing valuable to provide in the classroom. Freire's (2000) seminal work, *The pedagogy of the oppressed*, explained what he called the "banking" model of education, wherein students are vessels that receive knowledge from teachers—like accounts in a bank receiving a deposit (Wanberg, 2013). By intentionally removing Native American students from their homes, their families, and their communities, BIA schools systemically reinforced the concept that Native American students had nothing of value to bring to the classroom and that only their Anglo teachers held the knowledge necessary to make a deposit in students' hypothetical "bank" accounts (Szasz, 2005). Students who feel they have nothing to offer in the classroom would naturally feel more reserved during classroom discussions as they wait for teachers to tell them what they need to know. As of 2013, there were 183 BIA (now called the Bureau of Indian Education [BIE]) schools. Of these schools, 59 are federally operated and 124 are run locally by tribes (Fischer & Stoddard, 2013).

The Current State of Native American Education

In 2013, American Indian/Alaska Native students made up approximately 1% of all students enrolled in public schools in America (NCES, 2016a). This is slightly lower than the average of 1.1% of students in 2012. In 2013 the adjusted cohort graduation rate (ACGR) of American Indian/Alaska Native students across America was 70% (NCES, 2016b). ACGR represents the number of students to graduate high school within 4 years of starting 9th grade. The average ACGR across America for 2013 was 81%. The ACGR for American Indian/Alaska Native students was slightly lower than black students (71%) and Hispanic students (75%). In Arizona, the ACGR for all students in 2013 was 75%. In 2013, 32% of 18 to 24-year-old American Indian/Alaska Natives were participating in college (NCES, 2016a). In 2014 this rate increased to 35%. This rate was similar to black students (33%) and Hispanic students (35%), but was significantly lower than white students (42%) and Asian students (65%).

In 2015, students in Grades 4, 8, and 12 took the NAEP reading test (NCES, 2015). Of the 12th grade students in America who were tested, 37% of all students passed the test scoring at or above proficient reading levels. This was considered passing the test. The rate of 37% passing was not statistically different from scores when the test was administered in 2013. The two highest scoring racial demographics were white students (46%) and Asian students (49%). All other racial groups scored below average, except for students who identified as two or more races (45%). Black students scored the lowest with only 17% of students scoring at or above proficient reading levels. 25% of Hispanic students passed and 28% of American Indian/Alaska Native students passed. Since 1994, the average number of American Indian/Alaska Native students passing the test has fluctuated, ultimately increasing by only 5 points (274 to 279). All racial demographics average failing grades, but American Indian/Alaska Native students have continued to average reading scores almost 20 points lower than White students.

Richardson and McLeod (2011) conducted a qualitative study to identify whether leaders of BIE) schools meet the National Educational Technology Standards for Administrators (NETS-A). In their interviews with 9 principals, they found that though some administrators met standards, all were lacking in one way or another. The authors argued that additional training in technology was warranted. They also noted that a lack of technology coordinators, the challenges of poverty and living in rural areas also presented unique problems for these administrators. These findings are relevant to the proposed study because of how it frames the influence of technological training for administrators on their Native American students. Since the proposed study is focused on computer-based interventions for Native American students in a high poverty area in a rural district, the technological familiarity of their administrators may be relevant.

In 2016 the Arizona Department of Education replaced the Arizona Instrument for Measuring Standards (AIMS) with AzMERIT, their new end-of-course assessment for English Language Arts and Mathematics courses. In the first year of AzMERIT testing, 38% of 9th grade students in Arizona were categorized as minimally proficient, the lowest possible category (see Figure 1). By comparison, 60% of American Indian/Alaska Native students were categorized as minimally proficient. At Fort Thomas High School, 67% of American Indian/Alaska Native students were categorized as minimally proficient (see Figures 1-6 in Appendix B). Across the state, Native American students scored lower than their peers, but at Fort Thomas High school 7% more 9th grade students ranked in this category. Not only are Native American students scoring lower on average, but students at Fort Thomas High School are struggling more than their peers around the state.

The implementation of European-style education for Native American students extends from the 1700s to the present (Grayshield et al., 2015; Slivka, 2011; Szasz, 2005; Wanberg, 2013). Many of these programs focused on the deliberate assimilation of Native Americans into Anglo-European culture and language (Grayshield et al., 2015; Slivka, 2011; Szasz, 2005; Wanberg, 2013). This culminated with the implementation of federal boarding schools (BIA). The historical trauma caused by BIA schools can still be seen in Native American students and classrooms today (Grayshield et al., 2015). Native American students have consistently scored lower on standardized tests and graduate high school at lower percentages than other racial groups (NCES, 2011, 2012, 2014).

Future intervention programs for Native American students should consider the unique needs of Native American students with respect to their culture and historical traumas (Brayboy, 2005; Grayshield et al., 2015; Richardson, 2015; Writer, 2008). Research on CRI and similar approaches with minority students, including Native American students, have shown promising results (Adkins, 2012; Bird et al., 2013; Buckmiller, 2015; Covarrubias & Fryberg, 2015; Cramer et al., 2014; Demmert & Towner, 2003; Garcia et al., 2012; Gist, 2014; Johnson & Eubanks, 2015; Nam et al., 2013; Quijada Cerecer, 2013). These findings also suggested that a methodological combination of TribalCrit and the pedagogical implementation of CRI could be effective in providing effective intervention for Native American students (Brayboy, 2005; Grayshield et al., 2015; Nam et al., 2013; Quijada Cerecer, 2013; Richardson, 2015; Writer, 2008). This chapter will discuss how using a culturally-responsive pedagogy in conjunction with computer-based readings may help to promote engagement and reading levels for Native American students.

Theoretical Framework

As supported by the prior research, TribalCrit served as a theoretical framework for the study (Brayboy, 2005; Grayshield et al., 2015; Nam et al., 2013; Quijada Cerecer, 2013; Richardson, 2015; Writer, 2008). Brayboy (2005) introduced TribalCrit as an application of Critical Race Theory (CRT). In TribalCrit, Brayboy outlined a methodology for educators to approach educational reform and intervention for Native American students. Because the inherent structures of an outside group (e.g., non-Native researchers, educators, etc.) attempting to improve reading scores for Native American students repeats the structures of colonialism, it is appropriate to adopt a culturally-sensitive methodology, such as TribalCrit or CRT, to avoid the repetition of historically traumatic archetypes. One of the primary purposes for adopting TribalCrit as an initiative-taking methodology is to encourage schools and educational systems to provide a counter-space that validates Native American students' culture. Once validated, students may be more motivated to engage in the educational process (Covarrubias & Fryberg, 2015). When paired with

CRI as a pedagogical structure to implement the TribalCrit methodology, teachers and educators have a vision and a roadmap to instruct students.

Writer (2008) explained how the use of TribalCrit can help educators to appropriately frame Native American education without the negative effects of further colonization and pre-service programs do little to prepare teachers to teach students from diverse backgrounds, especially Native American students. The author further argued that viewing education through CRT or TribalCrit as a lens that educators can normalize minority stories and lived experiences (Writer, 2008). Grayshield et al. (2015) further developed the benefit and practical implications of TribalCrit as a methodology for framing the research studies. In preparing to interview tribal elders, the authors used TribalCrit as a method for approaching their research. They felt the characteristics of TribalCrit were appropriate as they collected Native American stories, the data within the stories, and developed a working praxis for promoting change. Buckmiller (2015) conducted a qualitative case study of four administrators at Native American schools and considered administrator perspectives on the challenges they face serving Native American students and how these administrators manage the demands of American style education and Native American culture and values. These works, among others, offer foundational support for TribalCrit as the study theoretical framework.

CULTURALLY RESPONSIVE INSTRUCTION FOR NATIVE AMERICAN STUDENT READING ENGAGEMENT AND LITERACY

Meriam and Work (1928) recognized systemic problems with how federal boarding schools had approached Native American education and proposed the idea of culturally-based education for Native American students (as cited in Demmert & Towner, 2003). Forty-one years later, the U.S. Senate (1969) commissioned a report on Native American education, entitled, "Indian education: A national tragedy—A national challenge." The report called for a type of culturally-responsive instruction (CRI). CRI is the deliberate use of a culturally-centric curriculum that contextualizes instruction within a student's cultural mores (Demmert & Towner, 2003). Fortunately, CRI was implemented to serve students from many differing racial backgrounds and circumstances.

Richardson (2015) explained indigenous methodologies are indigenous ways of knowing. These ways of knowing may be connected to people's lands, waterways, and other surroundings. They are socially constructed through community and through where their communities are located. He continued, "indigenous methodologies are respectful of the complex way one's body is both a conduit and a container of knowledge" (pp. 39-40). Teaching indigenous peoples using CRI not only requires implementing culturally-responsive texts, but also understanding how indigenous peoples make knowledge and by valuing their collective experiences as individuals and communities (Garcia et al., 2012; Richardson, 2015; Freire, 2000).

Demmert and Towner (2003) proposed several specific attributes of a CRI for Native American students. Their proposal included the use of a student's community, language, art, and spiritual beliefs. Demmert and Towner (2003) proposed that Native American student education should be a community-wide effort that includes community members of all ages and that emphasizes preparation for modern technological needs. In reviewing the literature, Lopez et al. (2013) found CRI as an effective strategy for instructing Native American students. Likewise, Quijada Cerecer (2013) argued CRI promoted positive representations of Native American students' cultures. The competing identities taught in Native

American culture and schools have had the negative impact of teaching students that they were "deficient student learners" (p. 603). In response, Quijada Cerecer argued for professional development on CRI and systemic opportunities for students to participate in policy committees to ensure that their voices are being heard and their identities are validated.

Covarrubias and Fryberg (2015) found Native American students felt more "school belonging" when self-relevant role models were included in reading assignments than assignments where role models' ethnicities were self-irrelevant or unidentified. This finding suggested that Native American students would likely benefit from reading examples relevant to their cultural identity, because they are more likely to experience belonging. In a second study, Covarrubias and Fryberg (2015) also found that most Native American students within their study had difficulty identifying role models they knew who had attended college. Of the students who were able to identify personally knowing 8 or more college educated role models, they found that these students' mothers had higher than average educational backgrounds. They also found that these students had similar levels of school belonging than non-Native American students. These findings suggested that Native American students whose mothers had higher than average educational backgrounds were more likely to relate to role models within their communities and to feel belonging in school. Covarrubias and Fryberg (2015) also proposed the deliberate use of Native American role models in reading samples to promote school belonging for Native American students. These findings support Demmert and Towner's (2003) call for a community-wide effort to educate Native American students and Lopez et al.'s (2013) call for CRI as part of these efforts.

Computers for Reading Instruction

Computers have been used within schools to teach literacy for decades. It has been with the advancement of assessment and adaptive algorithms that computer-based programs have begun to provide differentiated instruction for students. It is with the appropriate combination of differentiated solutions and appropriate pedagogies that teachers and students can benefit from advanced technologies to mediate literacy programs. In developing an appropriate theory for computer-based instruction, educators and researchers looked at established learning theories. Perhaps the most common instructional method is based on an instructivist model. Instructionism is a teacher-centric model where the teacher is the primary source of instruction (Schcolnik et al., 2006). This is consistent with the "banking model" described by Freire (2000), where the teacher is the only one in the classroom with capital to deposit into students' banks. In this model, the teacher focuses on students providing a correct answer during assessment. This one-size-fits-all model also requires students to adapt to how the teacher chooses to present information and provide the teacher with a predetermined correct response. Though a dynamic teacher may effectively employ an instructivist style to teach, it is still largely dependent on the teacher to instruct students directly. By comparison, a constructivist model focuses on students' learning through constructing their own knowledge (Schcolnik et al., 2006). In constructivism, students become more central to the learning process. Because teachers can be removed as the primary resource for knowledge creation, constructivist learning activities can be student-driven. Such a model empowers students to interact directly with resources without employing a teacher as mediator.

Bippert and Harmon (2017) conducted a study to identify how teachers use computer-based reading programs and how these teachers feel about computer-based reading programs. The authors focused on teachers using the Read 180, Istation, and Achieve3000 reading programs. Unlike Read 180, Istation and Achieve3000 can be self-contained instructional programs; whereas, Read 180 requires a teacher-led component. Teachers reported varying strengths for these programs, but the authors could find no clear winner. The authors called for more research on the effectiveness of Achieve3000 as a reading program. They also called for additional training for teachers on how to use these programs.

Achieve3000 is a computer-based differentiated reading program that can act as a platform for educators to employ best practices for culturally-responsive instruction by using self-reflective sample texts for Native American secondary students (Achieve3000, 2016b; Covarrubias & Fryberg, 2015; Demmert & Towner, 2003; Lopez et al., 2013). Achieve3000 utilizes research-based practices to guide students through reading activities they call, "The 5-Step Literacy Routine." Depending on the activity, students will complete between 5 and 9 activities. Activities 1-5 guide students through reading and responding to an assigned text. Activities 6 through 9 extend the lesson further through math questions and "stretch" activities that allow students to read a grade-level version of the text and questions (Achieve3000, 2016a).

Hill et al. (2016) conducted an experiment using a cluster-randomized design to identify the effect of Achieve3000 on students based on their school sites. Using data from two years of scores using Achieve3000, the authors found no significant improvement in student scores. The authors found that during the second year of implementation that scores improved, suggesting that with better implementation students were able to improve faster than during the first year of implementation. The authors suggested schools temper their expectations when first implementing the program and that consistent procedures be implemented to ensure fidelity and consistency over time.

Achieve3000 and Culturally-Responsive Instruction for Native American Students

As noted, the past research suggested Achieve3000 could be an effective platform for increasing student reading scores and student engagement when using a culturally-responsive instruction model to implement self-reflect texts for Native American secondary students as part of a consistent reading intervention program. The system has an inherent pedagogical logic, but can be adapted to meet many different pedagogical approaches including CRI. As such, it would be possible to use Achieve3000 as a means of selecting culturally-responsive texts that are self-reflective of students' cultural identities, using attraction theory and other constructivist theories to build upon students' previously acquired knowledge to build knew learning, while using TribalCrit as a guide for maintaining a culturally sensitive approach to using self-reflective texts as part of a reading intervention program. A summary of each aspect of this proposed framework is as follows.

CRI is an adaptable teaching model that could be incorporated into the framework outlined by Achieve3000. Though Achieve3000 does offer a calendar of rotating topics to capture student interest in reading lessons, a structured approach such as CRI could provide additional relevance to motivate and engage students to read (Covarrubias & Fryberg, 2015). A preliminary search of topics within Achieve3000's catalog of lessons revealed that there are at least 24 lessons self-relevant to Native American high school students, though many more are available if the criteria are broadened. This is a sufficient number to conduct the proposed quasi-experiment for a 12 week period of time.

Researchers have suggested students who were motivated and engaged in learning are more likely to perform better academically (Unrau & Quirk, 2014). Minority students have reported increased motivation when teachers use a CRI pedagogy during instruction (Adkins, 2012; Heineke, 2014; Johnson & Eubanks, 2015). Similarly, teachers have reported increased engagement when students participate in self-reflective topics and activities (Nam et al., 2013). The present study sought to address the call for quantifiable results on the implementation of CRI to minority students, specifically Native American students (Demmert & Towner, 2003).

A Computer-Based Reading Program to Provide Culturally-Responsive Instruction for Native American Students

A quantitative single-case study design was used to test the hypotheses for utilization of a culturally-responsive pedagogical approach to implementing a computer-based reading program for Native American students to determine any differences in student reading scores and reading engagement. A nonequivalent control group design was employed to test two groups of Native American high school students as they read differentiated nonfiction articles and completed activities within the computer-based reading program, Achieve3000. The control group read and completed activities on articles pre-selected by the computer program. The treatment group read and completed activities on articles selected by the primary researcher to ensure that they were self-reflective of Native American topics, consistent with a culturally-responsive instruction pedagogy.

The quantitative research questions of this case study were as follows: Q1: What was the impact of using culturally-responsive instruction on student reading scores for Native American secondary students? Q2: What was the impact of using the Achieve3000 computer-based reading program on student engagement for Native American secondary students? Thus, the study answered the call from Bippert and Harmon (2017) to identify the effectiveness of Achieve3000 as a reading program.

The author found use of a computer-based reading program, such as Achieve3000, with a culturally-responsive instructional model for Native American secondary student literacy instruction did not have a significant statistical impact on student reading scores or student reading engagement. Study results also showed the average student did increase his or her reading scores, measured in Lexile levels, and in some aspects of reading engagement, but not to a significant degree. These findings were consistent with similar findings from Hill et al. (2016) who found Achieve3000 had no significant impact on student reading scores.

Covarrubias and Fryberg (2015) argued that CRI could motivate and engage students to read. Unrau and Quirk (2014) added that motivated and engaged students were more likely to perform better academically. Qualitative research had previously identified minority student reports that using a CRI pedagogical model has helped to increase their motivation to read (Adkins, 2012; Heineke, 2014; Johnson & Eubanks, 2015). As such, the present study sought to quantify the implications of using CRI as a pedagogical model for computer-based reading instruction for Native American students.

In regard to research question 1, the null hypothesis was not rejected as the CRI model had no significant difference for Native American student reading levels. Though students reading levels increased on average, the treatment group did not improve at a significantly higher rate than the control group. This was consistent with findings by Hill et al. (2016) who found that over a two year time period that the use of Achieve3000 did not have a significant impact on student reading scores.

Erguvan (2014) conducted a qualitative study on the perspectives of teachers in Kuwait using Achieve3000 for English language instruction in an English as a Second Language course (ESL). Erguvan (2015) conducted a second qualitative study on the perspectives of undergraduate ESL students in Kuwait using Achieve3000. The author found that both teachers and students felt positively about the use of Achieve3000. Bippert and Harmon (2017) also conducted a qualitative study to identify how teachers used computer-based reading programs, including Achieve3000, and how these teachers felt about these programs. The authors concluded that none of the programs in question (Read 180, Istation, and Achieve3000) were perceived to be superior than the others and that additional research should be conducted on the effectiveness of Achieve3000 as a reading program. The present study provided additional findings to the prior research as to the effectiveness of Achieve3000 when using CRI for Native American students, though the present study did not address the particular effectiveness of Achieve3000, findings did show Native American students from both research groups were successful in improving their reading levels.

For research question 2, the null hypothesis was not rejected as use of a CRI model had no significant impact on Native American student engagement levels. Students in the control group demonstrated observable improvement in reading engagement in reading confidence, use of comprehension strategies, deep thinking, and reading enjoyment. Students in the treatment group also demonstrated observable improvement in reading engagement in the same categories of reading confidence, use of comprehension strategies, deep thinking, and reading comprehension as well as demonstrated reduced engagement in reading effort. Both groups demonstrated reduced engagement in reading independence.

Prior research has suggested that implementing CRI into English and English language classrooms could help increase reading motivation and reading engagement in minority students (Adkins, 2012; Heineke, 2014; Johnson & Eubanks, 2015). It has also been used to prepare pre-service teachers to teach minority students (Gist, 2014; Johnson & Eubanks, 2015). Teachers have also reported observing increased reading engagement when students complete activities with self-relevant topics (Nam et al., 2013). Many of these findings have been through qualitative rather than quantitative studies, such as reported for the present study. Demmert and Towner (2003) called for quantifiable evidence to support the use of CRI for Native American students; yet, the study found no sufficient evidence to support the use of CRI to increase reading engagement in Native American students.

SOLUTIONS AND RECOMMENDATIONS

The study findings and the implications of findings contributed to the study theoretical framework and were consistent with proposals from Brayboy (2005) and others to implement culturally-sensitive methodologies when instructing Native American students (Buckmiller, 2015; Grayshield et al., 2015; Writer, 2008). While the study noted no significant quantitative evidence to support the use of these practices at this or other sites, student reading scores did show measurable improvement in the form of increased Lexile levels. If classroom teachers and other educators are to implement a form of CRI into their classrooms, they must first examine the positive findings of TribalCrit as a methodology for embracing Native American culture respectfully and sensitively (Brayboy, 2005; Covarrubias & Fryberg, 2015; Quijada Cerecer, 2013; Richardson, 2015). Others have added that implementing CRI effectively also requires one to understand how indigenous peoples make knowledge and by valuing their experience as individuals and as members of a community (Freire, 2000; Garcia et al., 2012; Richardson, 2015).

The author asserts PK12 educators should find effective ways to validate their Native American students' experiences, which may include promoting positive discussion and writing about their experiences. Teachers may likewise find it difficult to implement a CRI model with Native American self-relevant content difficult to sustain over a long period of time. Other relevant content may need to be found, though it may not meet the criteria used for this study. Student reading engagement scores showed measurable improvement in the form of observable data, supporting the use of a constructivist model to promote engagement when students complete computer-based reading activities. Because constructivism encourages students to create their own knowledge through engaging activities, the onus is on teachers to find effective ways to engage students in computer-based activities (Schcolnik et al., 2006).

Qualitative analyses have consistently reported positive teacher and student perspectives when using Achieve3000 or other like programs (Bippert & Harmon, 2017; Erguvan, 2014, 2015). However, when not implemented effectively, Achieve3000 may not have a significant impact on student reading levels or reading engagement scores (Hill, Lenard, & Page, 2016). Little et al. (2014) found a computer-based differentiated reading program (SEM-R) could replace direction instruction without any perceivable negative effects. The researcher proposes that teachers implement best practices for reading instruction, computer-based instruction, and where appropriate, for minority students such as Native American students. This may include differentiated content to students culture or reading levels (Erguvan, 2015; Little et al., 2014; Turgut, 2012), implementing a hybrid of computer-based constructivist activities where the teacher acts as facilitator and direction-instruction where the teacher as a source of information (Cuevas et al., 2012; Mishra & Koehler, 2006), as well as valuing students' individual lived experiences and findings ways to reflect who those experiences in what they read and what they do in the classroom (Adkins, 2012; Bird et al., 2013; Buckmiller, 2015, Covarrubias & Fryberg, 2015; Cramer et al., 2014; Demmert & Towner, 2003; Gist, 2014; Garcia et al., 2012; Johnson & Eubanks, 2015; Nam et al., 2013; Quijada Cerecer, 2013).

FUTURE RESEARCH DIRECTIONS

Previous mixed-methods and qualitative studies have found positive results from the use of CRI with minority students and specifically with Native American students. The author proposes that future studies could conduct mixed-methods studies to correlate quantifiable results with student perspectives on the use of CRI as a pedagogical model for computer-based reading programs for Native American students. Qualitative methods validate the perspectives and live experiences of Native American students (Freire, 2000; Garcia et al., 2012; Johnson & Eubanks, 2015; Richardson, 2015). Quantitative methods, in contrast, help to triangulate data and validate the perspectives recorded through quantitative measures. Though a significant amount of qualitative seems to be emerging, there remains little quantifiable data available for these topics (Bippert & Harmon, 2017; Demmert & Towner, 2003).

Uslu Ustten and Pilav (2014) surveyed Turkish secondary students to identify their reading interests and habits. The authors found that in some areas that male and female students agreed and disagreed in reading interests and habits and called for future research on the use of CRI for Native American students may likewise compare reading interests and habits of Native American male and female students to see if they felt differently about self-relevant content (Uslu Ustten & Pilav, 2014). As computer-based reading programs gain popularity, interest in quantifying and qualifying these strategies have also become more popular with a variety of other computer-based reading programs have been studied (Bippert & Harmon, 2017; Chen & Huang, 2014; Cuevas, Russell, & Irving, 2012; Fenty et al., 2015; Russel & Cuevas, 2014). Yet, few studies have been conducted on the effectiveness of Achieve3000 and additional research should be conducted to support the continued use of programs such as this (Bippert & Harmon, 2017; Erguvan, 2014, 2015; Hill, Lenard, & Page, 2016).

Researchers have studied the use of one-to-one laptops in computer-based reading programs (Turgut, 2012), computer-based reading programs as supplements to direct instruction practices (Dina et al.,

2014; Fenty et al., 2015; Lysenko & Abrami, 2014), and even how to use accessible programs such as Microsoft PowerPoint to use slideshows to teach literacy skills (Russell & Cuevas, 2014). In addition, pedagogies and methodologies for implementing computer-based reading programs into hybrid learning environments, synchronous and asynchronous e-learning environments, or other learning environments should also be conducted.

The researcher combined three little research topics to focus on the effectiveness of a specific pedagogy for an underrepresented research group. Culturally-responsive instruction has received attention as a research topic, especially for Black or Hispanic students (Adkins, 2012; Johnson & Eubanks, 2015), but little research has been conducted on CRI for Native American students. Achieve3000 has become a popular program to provide differentiated reading instruction for schools with little resources, but it has been the focus of very few studies whether through qualitative or quantitative measures (Bippert & Harmon, 2017; Erguvan, 2014, 2015; Hill et al., 2016). Even computer-based reading programs, which have received quite a bit more attention than these other two topics, require additional research to identify best practices for implementing and improving these programs. In short, all of the various aspects of this study would benefit from additional research to continue to quantify and qualify these pedagogies, methodologies, and practices.

The study results suggested that implementing a CRI model into a computer-based reading program would not have a statistically significant difference for Native American student reading scores or reading engagement. Despite this, the study provided valuable data and findings to the small body of literature available on the use of CRI with Native American secondary students, CRI with e-learning strategies such as a computer-based reading program, and CRI for Native American students using a computer-based reading program. The researcher focused on the effects of these pedagogies and strategies on student reading scores and student reading engagement. Future studies could effectively employ additional qualitative research to corroborate or add to the present findings, qualitative research to record Native American student perspectives on these or other similar pedagogies and practices, and mixed-methods research to combine these methods to corroborate or contrast quantitative and qualitative data to compare student reading scores and student engagement scores to student perspectives (Huang, 2012; Louick et al., 2016; Newton, 2016; Sumbrunn et al., 2016; Valiandes, 2015). Future studies could also extend the present research questions to investigate whether these pedagogies and strategies could affect student reading motivation as well. Future studies could also focus on the effect of other pedagogies or strategies to improve Native American reading literacy.

REFERENCES

Achieve3000, Inc. (2016a). *The 5-step literacy routine*. http://doc.achieve3000.com/marketing/5stepCard_student/5stepCard_student.pdf

Achieve3000, Inc. (2016b). *Curriculum resources*. https://hub.achieve3000.com/pro-teacher-customize-curriculum/curriculum-resources/

Adkins, T. A. (2012). "Can't nobody sleep" and other characteristics of culturally responsive English instruction. *Multicultural Perspectives*, *14*(2), 73–81. doi:10.1080/15210960.2012.673308

Ametepee, L. K., Tchnisala, Y., & Agbeh, A. O. (2014). The No Child Left Behind Act, the Common Core State Standards, and the school curriculum. *Review of Higher Education and Self-Learning*, *7*(24), 111–119.

Arizona Department of Education. (2014). *The basics*. https://www.azed.gov/assessment/files/2014/11/azmerit-overview_the-basics_final_english.pdf

Arizona Department of Education. (2015a). *2013 Arizona NAEP results by achievement-level Percentage*. https://azreportcards.com/Assessments/NAEP

Arizona Department of Education. (2015b). *Arizona report cards – Accelerating student achievement*. https://azreportcards.com/Assessments/Ela

Arizona Department of Education. (2015c). *AzMERIT*. https://www.azed.gov/assessment/azmerit

Arizona Department of Education. (2015d). *AzMERIT and NCSC 2015*. https://www.azed.gov/research-evaluation/files/2015/11/azmerit_ncsc_2015.xlsx

Arizona Department of Education. (2016). *AzMERIT 2016*. https://www.azed.gov/research-evaluation/files/2016/09/2016-azmerit.xlsx

Arizona Department of Education. (2016). *School year 2015-2016 state report card*. https://www.azed.gov/research-evaluation/files/2017/03/state-of-arizona_022417_final.pdf

Bippert, K., & Harmon, J. (2017). Middle school teacher's perceptions of computer-assisted reading intervention programs. *Reading Psychology*, *38*(2), 203–230. doi:10.1080/02702711.2016.1245691

Brayboy, B. M. J. (2005). Toward a tribal critical race theory in education. *The Urban Review*, *37*(5), 425–446. doi:10.100711256-005-0018-y

Chen, C.-M., & Huang, S.-H. (2014). Web-based reading annotation system with an attention-based self-regulated learning mechanism for promoting reading performance. *British Journal of Educational Technology*, *45*(5), 959–980. doi:10.1111/bjet.12119

Council, M. R. III, Cartledge, G., Green, D., Barber, M., & Gardner, R. III. (2016). Reducing risk through a supplementary reading intervention: A case study of first- and second-grade urban students. *Behavioral Disorders*, *41*(4), 241–257. doi:10.17988/bedi-41-04-241-257.1

Covarrubias, R., & Fryberg, S. A. (2015). The impact of self-relevant representations on school belonging in Native American students. *Cultural Diversity & Ethnic Minority Psychology*, *21*(1), 10–18. doi:10.1037/a0037819 PMID:25181325

Cramer, E. D., Pellegrini-Lafont, C., & Gonzalez, L. (2014). Towards culturally responsive and integrated instruction for all learners: The integrated learning model. *Interdisciplinary Journal of Teaching and Learning*, *4*(2), 110–124.

Cuevas, J. A., Russell, L. R., & Irving, M. (2012). An examination of the effect of customized reading modules on the diverse secondary students' reading comprehension and motivation. *Educational Technology Research and Development*, *60*(3), 445–467. doi:10.100711423-012-9244-7

Demmert, W. G., & Towner, J. C. (2003). *A review of the research literature on the influences of culturally based education on the academic performance of Native America students*. Retrieved from https://educationnorthwest.org/sites/default/files/resources/cbe.pdf

Erguvan, I. D. (2014). Instructor's perceptions towards the use of an online instructional tool in an academic English setting in Kuwait. *The Turkish Online Journal of Educational Technology*, *13*(1), 115–130.

Erguvan, I. D. (2015). Kuwaiti undergraduate students' perceptions of ICT in writing classes. *Arab World English Journal*, *6*(1), 280–297. doi:10.24093/awej/vol6no1.22

Eubanks, J. P. (2014). Potential ramifications of Common Core State Standards adoption on information literacy. *Communications in Information Literacy*, *8*(1), 23–31. doi:10.15760/comminfolit.2014.8.1.162

Fenty, N., Mulcahy, C., & Washburn, E. (2015). Teacher-led fluency instruction on students at risk of reading failure. *Learning Disabilities (Weston, Mass.)*, *13*(2), 141–156.

Freire, P. (2000). *Pedagogy of the oppressed* (30th ed.). Bloomsbury Academic.

Gist, C. D. (2014). The culturally responsive teacher educator. *Teacher Educator*, *49*(4), 265–283. doi:10.1080/08878730.2014.934129

Grayshield, L., Rutherford, J. J., Salazar, S. B., Mihecoby, A. L., & Luna, L. L. (2015). Understanding and healing historical trauma: The perspectives of Native American elders. *Journal of Mental Health Counseling*, *37*(4), 295–307. doi:10.17744/mehc.37.4.02

Guthrie, J. T., & Klauda, S. L. (2014). Effects of classroom practices on reading comprehension, engagement, and motivations for adolescents. *Reading Research Quarterly*, *49*(4), 387–416. doi:10.1002/rrq.81 PMID:25506087

Guthrie, J. T., Klauda, S. L., & Ho, A. N. (2013). Modeling the relationships among reading instruction, motivation, engagement, and achievement for adolescents. *Reading Research Quarterly*, *48*(1), 9–26. doi:10.1002/rrq.035 PMID:26412903

Guthrie, J. T., McRae, A., Coddington, C. S., Klauda, S. L., Wigfield, A., & Barbosa, P. (2009a). Impacts of comprehensive reading instruction on diverse outcomes of low- and high-achieving readers. *Journal of Learning Disabilities*, *42*(3), 195–214. doi:10.1177/0022219408331039 PMID:19264929

Guthrie, J. T., McRae, A., Coddington, C. S., Klauda, S. L., Wigfield, A., & Barbosa, P. (2009b). *Reading Motivation Scale* [Database record]. Retrieved from PsycTESTS. doi:10.1037/t23360-000

Harris, D. M. (2012). Leveraging change via competition: The promise and limitations of Race to the Top. *JEP: eJournal of Education Policy*, 1-7.

Hill, D. V., Lenard, M. A., & Page, L. C. (2016). *The impact of Achieve3000 on elementary literacy outcomes: Evidence from a two-year randomized control trial*. Society for Research on Educational Effectiveness.

Huang, S.-H. (2012). A mixed-methods study of the effectiveness of the accelerated reader program on middle school students' reading achievement and motivation. *Reading Horizons*, *51*(3), 229–246.

Johnson, G. M. (2009). Instructionism and constructivism: Reconciling two very good ideas. *International Journal of Special Education, 24*(3), 90–98.

Kessinger, T. A. (2011). Efforts toward educational reform in the United States since 1958. *American Educational History Journal, 38*(2), 263–276.

Laverick, D. M. (2014). Supporting striving readers through technology-based instruction. *Reading Improvement, 51*(1), 11–19.

Little, C. A., McCoach, D. B., & Reis, S. M. (2014). Effects of differentiated reading instruction on student achievement in middle school. *Journal of Advanced Academics, 25*(4), 384–402. doi:10.1177/1932202X14549250

Lopez, F. A., Heilig, J. V., & Schram, J. (2013). A story within a story: Culturally responsive schooling and American Indian and Alaska Native achievement in the National Indian Education Study. *American Journal of Education, 119*(4), 513–538. doi:10.1086/670965

Louick, R., Leider, C. M., Daley, S. G., Proctor, C. P., & Gardner, G. L. (2016). Motivation for reading among struggling middle school readers: A mixed methods study. *Learning and Individual Differences, 49*, 260–269. doi:10.1016/j.lindif.2016.06.027

Lysenko, L. V., & Abrami, P. C. (2014). Promoting reading comprehension with the use of technology. *Computers & Education, 75*, 162–172. doi:10.1016/j.compedu.2014.01.010

Meriam, L., & Work, H. (1928). The problem of Indian administration. Report of a survey made at the request of the Honorable Hubert Work, Secretary of the Interior, and submitted to him, February 21, 1928 (No. 17). John Hopkins Press.

MetaMetrics. (2016). *Lexile infographic*. https://lexile.com/about-lexile/lexile-overview/lexile-infographic/

MetaMetrics. (2017). *Matching Lexile measures to grade ranges*. https://lexile.com/educators/measuring-growth-with-lexile/lexile-measures-grade-equivalents/

Mishra, P., & Koehler, M. J. (2006). Technological pedagogical content knowledge: A framework for integrating technology in teacher knowledge. *Teachers College Record, 108*(6), 1017–1054. doi:10.1111/j.1467-9620.2006.00684.x

Nam, Y., Roehrig, G., Kern, A., & Reynolds, B. (2013). Perceptions and practices of culturally relevant science teaching in American Indian classrooms. *International Journal of Science and Mathematics Education, 11*(1), 143–167. doi:10.100710763-012-9372-x

National Center for Education Statistics. (2011). *Trends in high school drop out and completion rates in the United States, 1972-2009*. Author.

National Center for Education Statistics. (2012). National Indian Education Study 2011. *National Assessment of Educational Progress, 2012*, 1–64.

National Center for Education Statistics. (2014). *The condition of education 2014*. https://files.eric.ed.gov/fulltext/ED545122.pdf

National Center for Education Statistics. (2015). *NAEP 2015 mathematics & reading at grade 12*. https://www.nationsreportcard.gov/reading_math_g12_2015/#reading

National Center for Education Statistics. (2016a). *The condition of education 2016*. https://nces.ed.gov/pubs2016/2016144_ataglance.pdf

National Center for Education Statistics. (2016b). *Trends in high school dropout and completion rates in the United States: 2013*. https://nces.ed.gov/pubs2016/2016117rev.pdf

Newton, X. A. (2016). Striking a balance: A mixed-methods approach to impact-oriented evaluation. *Studies in Educational Evaluation, 51*, 96–107. doi:10.1016/j.stueduc.2016.10.005

O'Leary, A. O., & Romero, A. J. (2010). *Chicano/o students' engagement with Arizona's "anti-ethnic studies" Bill 1108: Civic engagement, ethnic identity and well-being*. http://arizona.openrepository.com/arizona/bitstream/10150/219215/1/MASWP35.pdf

Quijada Cerecer, P. D. (2013). The policing of Native bodies and minds: Perspectives on schooling from American Indian youth. *American Journal of Education, 119*(4), 591–616. doi:10.1086/670967

Reed, D. K., Sorrells, A. M., Cole, H. A., & Takakawa, N. N. (2013). The ecological and population validity of reading interventions for adolescents: Can effectiveness be generalized? *Learning Disability Quarterly, 36*(3), 131–144. doi:10.1177/0731948712451976

Richardson, J. W., & McLeod, S. (2011). Technology leadership in Native American schools. *Journal of Research in Rural Education, 26*(7), 1–14.

Richardson, T. A. (2015). Indigenous methodologies and educational research for meaningful change: Parsing postpositivist philosophy of science and mixed methods in collaborative research settings. *Journal of American Indian Education, 54*(1), 33–62.

Russell, L. R., & Cuevas, J. (2014). Designing customizable reading modules for a high school literature classroom. *TechTrends, 58*(5), 71–80. doi:10.100711528-014-0788-8

Schcolnik, M., Kol, S., & Abarbanel, J. (2006). Constructivism in theory and in practice. *English Teaching Forum, 44*(4), 12-20.

Slivka, K. (2011). Art, craft, and assimilation: Curriculum for Native students during the boarding school era. *Studies in Art Education: A Journal of Issues and Research, 52*(3), 225-242.

Stillwell, R., & Sable, J. (2013). *Public school graduates and dropouts from the common core of data: School year 2009-10: First look (Provisional data).* https://nces.ed.gov/pubsearch

Szasz, M. C. (2005). "I knew how to be moderate. And I knew how to obey": The commonality of American Indian boarding school experiences, 1750s-1920s. *American Indian Culture and Research Journal, 29*(4), 75–94. doi:10.17953/aicr.29.4.b2220582h05507u2

Turgut, G. (2012). A case study on use of one-to-one laptops in English as second language classrooms. *Turkish Online Journal of Qualitative Inquiry, 3*(4), 32–51.

Unrau, N. J., & Quirk, M. (2014). Reading motivation and reading engagement: Clarifying commingled conceptions. *Reading Psychology, 35*(3), 260–284. doi:10.1080/02702711.2012.684426

U.S. Senate. (1969). *Indian education: A national tragedy—A national challenge*. Special Subcommittee on Indian Education of the Committee on Labor and Public Welfare, Senate Report No. 91-501. Washington, DC: U.S. Government Printing Office.

Uslu Ustten, A., & Pilav, A. (2014). A research on high school students' reading interests and habits. *Journal of Theory and Practice in Education*, *10*(4), 764–782.

Valiandes, S. (2015). Evaluating the impact of differentiated instruction on literacy and reading in mixed ability classrooms: Quality and equity dimensions of education effectiveness. *Studies in Educational Evaluation*, *45*, 17–26. doi:10.1016/j.stueduc.2015.02.005

Wanberg, K. (2013). Pedagogy against the state: The ban on ethnic studies in Arizona. *Journal of Pedagogy*, *4*(1), 15–35. doi:10.2478/jped-2013-0002

Wigfield, A., & Guthrie, J. T. (1997). Relations of children's motivation for reading to the amount and breadth of their reading. *Journal of Educational Psychology*, *89*(3), 420–432. doi:10.1037/0022-0663.89.3.420

Wigfield, A., & Guthrie, J. T. (2008). *Reading instrument index*. http://www.corilearning.com/measures/REI.pdf

Wigfield, A., Guthrie, J. T., Perencevich, K. C., Taboada, A., Klauda, S. L., McRae, A., & Barbosa, P. (2008). Role of reading engagement in mediating effects of reading comprehension instruction on reading outcomes. *Psychology in the Schools*, *45*(5), 432–445. doi:10.1002/pits.20307

Writer, J. H. (2008). Unmasking, exposing, and confronting: Critical race theory, tribal critical race theory and multicultural education. *International Journal of Multicultural Education*, *10*(2), 1–15.

ADDITIONAL READING

Brayboy, B. (2013). Tribal critical race theory: An origin story and future directions. In M. Lynn & A. D. Dixson (Eds.), *Handbook of critical race theory in education* (pp. 88–100). Taylor and Francis.

Castagno, A. E., & Brayboy, B. M. J. (2008). Culturally responsive schooling for Indigenous youth: A review of the literature. *Review of Educational Research*, *78*(4), 941–993. doi:10.3102/0034654308323036

Hammond, Z. (2014). *Culturally responsive teaching and the brain: Promoting authentic engagement and rigor among culturally and linguistically diverse students*. Corwin Press.

Kyei-Blankson, L., Blankson, J., & Ntuli, E. (Eds.). (2019). *Care and culturally responsive pedagogy in online settings*. IGI Global. doi:10.4018/978-1-5225-7802-4

McCardle, P., & Berninger, V. (Eds.). (2014). *Narrowing the achievement gap for native American students: Paying the educational debt*. Routledge. doi:10.4324/9781315855615

Sprott, K., O'Connor, J. R., & Msengi, C. (Eds.). (2021). *Designing culturally competent programming for PK-20 classrooms*. IGI Global. doi:10.4018/978-1-7998-3652-0

Stembridge, A. (2019). *Culturally responsive education in the classroom: An equity framework for pedagogy*. Routledge.

KEY TERMS AND DEFINITIONS

Culturally Responsive Instruction: An instructional model that pre-selects exemplars that are relevant and reflective of the students' culture.

Differentiated Reading Instruction: A reading instruction model that customizes texts to a student's specific needs.

E-Learning: An educational process that utilizes electronic devices (e.g., desktop computers, laptops, tablets, or smartphones) and software to support and to improve learning.

Lexile: A measure of text complexity and student comprehension of complex texts used as a representation of students' reading levels and the complexity of the texts they read.

Self-Relevant: Exemplars or content that are relevant and reflective of a student's self-identification.

Student Engagement: The construct of one's affective, behavioral, and/or cognitive involvement in a task or action.

Chapter 7
Land, Rights, and Tenure Insecurity on Customary Land in Zambia:
Protecting "Thyselves"

Ephraim Kabunda Munshifwa
Copperbelt University, Zambia

Niraj Jain
https://orcid.org/0000-0002-5065-6222
Copperbelt University, Zambia

Roy Alexander Chileshe
Copperbelt University, Zambia

Anthony Mushinge
Copperbelt University, Zambia

ABSTRACT

Land is a key asset in the lives of village communities in Zambia. It is thus at the centre of their livelihood strategies as it provides social, economic, and financial benefits to these communities. The paradox though is that despite acknowledging its importance in the lives of village communities, tenure on this land is poorly protected by the state resulting in high insecurity for its occupants. In many instances, there are no clear regulations on its use and alienation while traditional authorities are also ill-equipped for the task of administering this land. The question then that emerges is: In this perceived absence of state protection, how are village communities protecting themselves from threats of dispossession by foreign investors, urban elites, and the state's own actions? This study found that village communities are using various means to protect themselves, including issuance of local land holding certificates.

DOI: 10.4018/978-1-7998-3729-9.ch007

INTRODUCTION

Customary tenure is under threats of extinction in modern societies. One of the major reasons contributing to this vulnerability is the State's own view of customary land, which is often treated as reserves for statutory tenure (Munshifwa et al., 2020) or simply seen as "permissive occupancy" (Wily, 2011 p. 458). In many instances, there are no clear regulations on its use and alienation while traditional authorities are also ill-equipped for the task of administering the land. However, village communities are fighting back through a number of innovative ways to secure their rights. The objective of this chapter is to examine how village communities protect themselves from dispossession by foreign investors, urban elites and the State's own actions in an environment perceived to lack State protection.

The chapter first discusses the various sources of insecurity on customary tenure in Zambia before reviewing literature on the link between land, rights and tenure insecurity. The chapter then goes further to review various initiatives in Zambia on documenting customary land rights through local "bottom-up" mechanisms. The chapter then concludes by noting the gaps in local initiatives with a recommendation that countries should strive to achieve a working mix between "top-down" Land Administration Domain Model (LADM) and "bottom-up" approaches, such as the Social Tenure Domain Model (STDM), in the governance of customary land.

BACKGROUND

Land is an important asset for rural livelihood strategies in customary areas in Zambia. Like in other developing countries, it provides social, economic and financial benefits to village communities (Hanstad et al., 2004; McAuslan, 2007). It is also a basis for political power in a number of communities (Hanstad et al., 2004). Studies estimate that at least 40% of the Zambian population depend on subsistence farming for their survival, emphasizing the critical role land plays in rural livelihood strategies. Much of this subsistence farming is done under customary tenure which is estimated to cover 51-54% of Zambia's land mass. Despite its importance in the survival of these rural communities, rights on this land is often insecure due to a number of factors, which include a growing cash economy, commoditization of land, increased demand by foreign investors and urban elite, etc (Moyo, 2007). The result has been pressure on customary land to convert or formalise to some western-type property rights system, increasing tenure insecurity and threatening village communities with dispossession and involuntary displacement.

SOURCES OF INSECURITY ON CUSTOMARY TENURE IN ZAMBIA

In order to appreciate the need for increased tenure insecurity on customary land in Zambia, it is important to step back and examine threats to this form of land holding. Literature revealed a number of factors as being responsible for insecurity on customary tenure; however, this chapter isolates four such sources due to their scale and impact, namely large-scale agricultural development, large-scale mining projects, state farm block programmes and multi-facility economic zones. Each of these is discussed in the sections which follow.

Large-scale Agriculture

Large-scale acquisition of land for agricultural purposes is often cited as one of the major threats to customary tenure (Boche & Anseeuw, 2013; Bottazzi et al., 2016; Doss et al., 2013; German et al., 2011; Obidzinski et al., 2013). While the majority of villagers use small pieces of land on subsistence basis, foreign and local (or urban elites) investors often acquire large pieces of land with a promise of mechanising farming in rural areas. This rush for land in rural areas has in recent times been referred to as "land grabbing" with a link to foreign capital (Batterbury & Ndi, 2018; Boche & Anseeuw, 2013; Hall, 2011; Herre, 2013). For instance, Herre (2013) cites acquisition of 30,000 hectares of land in Mumbwa by Amatheon Agri Zambia Ltd, 27,000 hectares in Choma by African Crops Ltd and 150,000 hectares in Mpika by Ferrostaal as examples to justify the perceived link between "land grabbing" and expansion of agribusiness. Evidence (Chu, 2013; Nolte, 2014; Sitko, & Jayne, 2014) further show a number of similar cases across the country, however the point in this chapter is that such acquisitions of large tracks of land for agricultural development are happening mostly on customary land whose occupants have weak rights. The result is dispossession and forced displacements (Chu, 2015; Mushinge & Mwando, 2016; Siachitema, 2016). For instance, Mushinge and Mwando (2016) reported of cases of displacement on customary land in Kaindu Chiefdom in Mumbwa District. The study saw large-scale acquisitions as leading to wide-spread displacements, socio-economic exclusion, land conflicts, tenure insecurity and enclosures of common pool resources (Mushinge & Mwando, 2016). Chu et al. (2015) further cities the displacement of 120 households during the process of acquisition and development of 1,575 hectares by Chiansi Irrigation Project in Kafue District. In a number of cases the acquisition of these huge pieces of land does not lead to the envisaged gains such as the creation of employment in rural areas and reduction in poverty. The result is often reduced land available to local communities and heightened insecurity.

Large-scale Mining

Studies have also linked mining to large scale land acquisition (Chu et al., 2015; Gilberthorpe et al., 2016; Kabinga, 2019; Kesselring, 2018; Negi, 2014). With the opening of the North Western Province of Zambia to copper mining, the link between large-scale land acquisition and mining has become clearer. Lumwana Copper Mines on 8,700 hectares, Kalumbila Mine on 50,000 hectares and Kansanshi Mines on 24,865 hectares (after expansion from 21,655 hectares in 2014) are often given as examples of large scale mining projects with potential to impact customary tenure. In all these cases displacement of indigenous people were reported. For instance, Kabinga (2019) reported of large-scale land acquisition by mining conglomerates, citing Lumwana, Kalumbila and Munali Nickel mine projects, and arguing that most of these mining projects are on customary land with weak tenure. Chu et al. (2015) equally cited cases of displacements due to acquisition of large tracks of land by multinationals involved in mining. The study cites 570 households displaced in the acquisition and development of the mine by Kalumbila Mineral Resources Limited in Solwezi District (Chu et al., 2015). This was also confirmed by the *Lusaka Times* story of May 6, 2015, which reported that government had allocated 500 hectares to resettle 600 households who were displaced by mining activities in Kalumbila (Lusaka Times, 2015). Such instances of dispossession and forced displacements are a source of tenure insecurity on customary land. Although in some cases compensation is given, especially on projects by multinationals with conditions to follow international guidelines on displacement and compensation, this still results in disrupted and displaced livelihoods which contributed to increased poverty.

Multi-Facility Economic Zone

The development of Multi-Facility Economic Zones (MFEZ) is a government initiative to support private sector industrial development. Due to the scale of these developments, large tracks of land are required, often on rural/customary lands. Introduced in 2005 and endorsed by the Zambia Development Act (No. 11 of 2006), MFEZs were conceived as a mechanism for enhancing Zambia's competitiveness and industrialization through fostering an attractive business environment, promote export and enhance domestic trade (Government of the Republic Zambia [GRZ], 2006; Mwansa et al., 2020; Zeng, 2016). Currently, three zones have been declared and at different levels of development: these being, Lusaka South Multi Facility Economic Zone (LS-MFEZ) on 2,100 hectares; Lusaka East Multi Facility Economic Zone (LE-MFEZ) on 570 hectares and Chambeshi Multi Facility Economic Zone (CMFEZ) on 526 hectares. While LS-MFEZ is a public sector led initiative, the LE-MFEZ and CFEZ were established by the Chinese government under the Zambia-China Economic and Trade Cooperation agreement. Recent media reports also revealed a new MFEZ, dubbed Jiangxi Economic Cooperation Zone (JXECZ) with a planned investment of USD600 million, being developed on 2,089 hectares of land in Chibombo District, in a predominantly customary area (Lusaka Times, 2020; Nguni, 2020).

By their nature, economic zones are large areas to accommodate a number of foreign and local manufacturing firms. However, in the realities of limited urban land, a number of these zones are being located in the margins of state-customary areas with potential impacts on customary tenure. A case in point is the development of the LS-MFEZ on Forest 23, formerly public land (Chu et al., 2015). Chu et al. (2015) reported on 247 households (1221 individuals) who were displaced in the development of the Lusaka Multi-Facility Economic Zone. With depleting reserves of urban land, the current development trajectory of economic zones implies sourcing more land from rural areas which are predominantly under customary tenure with concomitant impacts. Thus, development of industrial zones will continue to be another potential cause of insecurity on customary land.

State Farm Block Programme

The farm block programme is another government initiative with similar negative impacts on customary land tenure. Through a Presidential Directive of 2002, the Zambian government identified agriculture as a key sector for fighting poverty, which at the time stood at 70% (GRZ, 2005). The development of a farm block in each Province was then seen as an important strategy towards achieving this goal. Thus in 2005, government identified nine sites for the development of farm blocks. Each farm block was seen as a large agricultural area with all basic infrastructure (feeder roads, electricity, water and communication facilities) in place. The whole programme was spearheaded by a Multi-Sectoral Sub-Committee. Each farm block was estimated to cost K114.1 billion[1]at the time.

Despite its good intentions of growing the agricultural sector, the implementation of the farm block programme has similar negative impacts in relation to customary tenure (Chilombo, 2019; Munshifwa et al., 2020). The implementation plan for the farm block programme focuses on the State acquiring large tracts of land which would then be subdivided into different sizes of farms (large, medium and small) before allocating to villagers, local and foreign investors. The land was to be granted on a 99-year leasehold tenure. The Farm Block Development Plan (2005-2007) identified nine (9) site for the development of farm blocks, namely: Nansanga, Kalumange, Luena, Manshya, Solwezi, Simango, Lufwanyama (now Luswishi), Chongwe and Mwase-Mphangwe; a total of 967,750 hectares (see Table 1).

Table 1. Proposed State farm blocks (2005-2007)

No.	Farm Block	Hectares	District	Province
1	Nansanga	155,000	Serenje	Central
2	Kalumwange	100,000	Kaoma	Western
3	Luena	100,000	Kawambwa	Luapula
4	Manshya	147,750	Mpika	Muchinga
5	Solwezi	100,000	Solwezi	North Western
6	Simango	100,000	Kazungula	Southern
7	Lufwanyama (now Luswishi)	100,000	Lufwanyama	Copperbelt
8	Chongwe	65,000	Chongwe	Lusaka
9	Mwase-Mphangwe	100,000	Lundazi	Eastern

Source: Adapted from GRZ (2005)

Implementation of the farm block programme also depended on support from local people and traditional rulers who were seen as beneficiaries through the new infrastructure such as schools, hospitals and other social amenities. Due to financial constraints, implementation was to be phased, with Nansanga, Kalumwange and Luena, being the first; however of the three, only Nansanga had seen the commencement on implementation. However, recent studies have argued that even Nansanga is in "limbo of development" (Chilombo, 2019, p. 61) with serious impacts on livelihoods and tenure.

Other studies, such as Munshifwa et al (2020), also reported on land allocations which have been done in Luswishi, the farm block in Lufwanyama. The *Strategic Environmental and Social Impact Assessment* (SESA) of 2017 for Luswishi listed potential impacts on land tenure, culture and behavior, increase in competition for resources, increased social tension and conflicts over access to resources (African Development Bank, 2017). Similarly, the draft EIA of 2006 for Nansanga noted changes from customary to state land resulting in serious social impacts; among others, cultural, tribal, religious, and ethnic, resulting in conflicts on land (GRZ, 2006).

Though not a conclusive list, it is clear from the four threats discussed in this chapter that the State is directly or indirectly, the biggest threat to tenure security on customary land through programmes such as farm block and multi-facility economic zone developments or by enabling the acquisition of land by private investors for agriculture or mining projects. Furthermore, failure to provide sufficient protection mechanisms for village communities through their traditional authorities leaves them vulnerable to this increased demand for customary land. The lack of drive by the State to produce practical solutions to protect customary tenure lend support to the view that the State itself treats this form of tenure as "permissive occupancy" with limited rights on land (Wily, 2011). In a way customary land is viewed as "reserve" pending identification of more commercially-profit uses; so once such uses are identified the land is then converted. This perspective is problematic in that customary land is a permanent habitat for the majority of rural dwellers who also deserve assurance on their occupation. The following chapter gives a broad-brush of the literature on the link between land, rights and tenure insecurity.

LAND, RIGHTS AND TENURE INSECURITY IN ZAMBIA

Security of tenure is a topical issue in the literature on customary land administration. Globally there is congruency on the impact of tenure insecurity on various development parameters. Literature also points to three common effects of tenure insecurity on farmland, namely, investment effect, market effect and credit effect (Deininger et al., 2011; Place et al., 2002; Tian et al., 2013). Other studies such as the French Development Cooperation (2009) linked improved tenure security to poverty reduction and equity. Wang et al. (2015) also found possession of land use rights documents enabled land renting to non-family members in six provinces in China. It is for this reason that studies have continued to try and understand the sources of insecurity on rural land. In investigating the impact of property rights integrity on long-term tenure security in Jiangxi Province of China, Zhou et al. (2018) found that it was important to identify sources of local tenure insecurity before formulating any policy on land. This study was based on forest land reallocation and expropriation.

In order to provide guidance on how to integrate customary into formal tenure, Mccallian (2018) cites five ways, namely: (a) formal conversion or codification of customary rights and issuance of property titles; (b) registration of local land rights without conversion; (c) state-sanctioned administrative bodies replacing traditional authorities; (d) continuation of traditional land governance institutions; and, (e) establishment of locally-based hybrid bodies. More recent studies show an inclination toward the establishment of locally-based hybrid bodies with strong emphasis on socially legitimate institutions. Thus rather than simply focusing on the weaknesses of traditional land administration systems, recent literature has also highlighted innovative solutions to the problem of insecurity through local initiatives (Hall et al., 2017; Katungula et al., 2019; Mushinge et al., 2020). This has come about because of appreciation that strengthening land rights in these areas will take both local and state bodies and action (Toulmin, 2009). At the local level, communities have to accept these rights as being legitimate in accordance to local knowledge and traditional values. With increased pressure on customary land, the State needs to recognize these rights for them to stand against outside claimants (Toulmin, 2009). UN HABITAT (2017) noted that although governments' recognition of customary rights varies, most of these focus on legal titles and less on village communities' perception of tenure. This study used examples from Cameroon, Nigeria and Kenya. Hall et al. (2017) also noted due to the focus on formal property titles, traditional authorities often reject proposals from the State which they perceive as being aimed at removing their powers on land. This has certainly been the case in Zambia where traditional leaders have often rejected a number of provisions in the draft National Land Policy; the result being a protracted policy review process which has been going on for the past 18 years. However, Hall et al. (2017), citing the *Rural Agricultural Livelihoods Survey Report* of 2015 by Indaba Agricultural Policy Research Institute (IAPRI), noted that over 100 chiefs in Zambia use some form of land documentation practices (IAPRI, 2015). In addition, a number of recent studies and project reports, such as Manuel (2016) in Chile, Ghebru and Lambrecht (2017) in Ghana, Lund and Rachman (2016) in Indonesia and others, have then focused on documenting local solutions to tenure insecurity on customary (indigenous) land.

However, there is an underlying assumption in literature that once title has been obtained, the rights will then be automatically secured. Evidence though shows the need for more to be done. In fact in a number of cases, even when the system provides for the issuance of legal title, land users are not always in a hurry to obtain such legal documents. For instance, Agyeman-Yeboah (2018) argued despite the provision for obtaining legal title, very few took advantage of this in Ghana; in other words, very few land users had title to their land as they felt it was not necessary. This study focused on exploring the reasons which prevented many people from documenting their land transactions. If viewed another way, it could be argued that very few people perceive it has influence whether they have formal documents to their land or not, pointing to other sources for security, particularly social and cultural legitimacy. Therefore, the solution to overcoming tenure insecurity in rural areas is much more than simply the issuance of legal property titles.

The complexity of customary land tenure patterns in Africa are ably captured by Wily's (2010) classification. Wily (2010) categorizes African countries in classes, starting with those who *most* support customary ownership, at least in law (Tanzania, Uganda, Ghana, Mozambique, Southern Sudan, South Africa); *moderate* support for customary ownership (Botswana, Namibia, Madagascar, Angola, Benin, Cote d'Ivoire, Burkina Faso, Niger, Zambia, Nigeria, Lesotho, Senegal, Congo and Central African Republic); *little* support to customary ownership (Malawi, Kenya, Liberia, Sierra Leone, Somaliland, Ethiopia, Eritrea, Somalia, Rwanda, Burundi and Mauritania); *least* (or no) support to customary ownership (Sudan, Cameroon, Mali, Gambia, Zimbabwe, Chad, DRC, Gabon and Swaziland). As admitted by Wily (2020), while this classification may be useful to a certain degree, the exact configuration on the ground is so complex and dynamic with countries in the same class presenting quite different scenarios. Therefore, despite this wealth of information on the impacts of tenure insecurity on various development parameters, such as investment, markets and credit, studies also accept the fact that these may differ from place to place; meaning these impacts need to be contextualized within different local circumstances.

Unlike in the developed economies, sub Saharan Africa faces an additional threat of multinational investors in what is now commonly referred to as "land grabbing" as discussed earlier. With such a complex tenure landscape, caution is needed even as African governments invite foreign capital into customary areas. Hence, Wily (2010) could argue that most governments in Africa are giving away customary land to foreign investors even when property rights on this land have not been formally extinguished. In other words, governments are giving away land which belongs to village communities. Green and Norberg (2018) also cite an active land market as a threat to customary land and traditional systems.

The review of literature across the African continent provides a view of a bleak future for customary tenure systems. In many countries, customary tenure is being "converted" to various statutory forms often underpinned by the neoliberal understanding of property rights – full, private, cadastrally surveyed and titled. Even where the law is in place, its implementation is often problematic, leaving the intended beneficiaries worse off. This is forcing village communities to protect "thyselves." Solutions in many instances have opted to by-pass the State and produce local mechanisms for documenting and protecting customary land rights as discussed in the next section.

PROTECTING THYSELVES

Solutions to tenure insecurity on customary land have traditionally been managed through land reform programmes in a top-down approach; in what Augustinus and Lemmen (2011) refer to as a Land Administration Domain Model (LADM). This essentially falls in the jurisdiction of the State with power to formulate policy and pass legislation. The ultimate objective is the issuance of property titles based on "codified" rights (Mccallin, 2018). In a number of cases, the State has often opted to move slowly when it comes to reforming customary tenure (Munshifwa, 2018). In an environment of increasing threats from large-scale land acquisitions for agriculture, mining, farm blocks and industrial development and the perceived inertia by the State to provide solutions on customary land, village communities have to start from somewhere to provide protection on their land. The preceding sections showed that the State could itself be a threat to customary tenure, hence explaining its indifference or reluctance to reform. Thus, the aim of this section is to show what happens when the State becomes the "aggressor" and village communities have in a way to "fend for themselves" with regards to protecting themselves.

Current studies and other scholarly reports (Hall et al., 2017; Jain et al., 2016; Katungula et al., 2019; Mushinge et al., 2020) point to initiatives at local level. For instance, a number of these studies and organizations now support what could be referred to as "bottom-up" approaches with regards to protecting customary land rights. These initiatives involve the documenting of land rights, through tools such as the Social Tenure Domain Model (STDM). Through these local initiatives, traditional authorities issue ownership documents ranging from simple letters on the chiefdom letterheads to more structured documents called by various names, such as: Customary or Traditional Land Holding Certificates (TLHCs), Local Ownership Certificates (LOC), Certificates of Land Rights (CLR) or Certificate of Customary Land Occupancy (CCLO) (Hall et al., 2017; Jain et al., 2016; Katungula et al., 2019; Mushinge et al., 2020). Jain et al. (2016), for instance, found Local Ownership Certificates (LOCs) in Western Province while Munshifwa et al. (2020) reported on village permits and similar local documents in Lufwanyama District on the Copperbelt Province. Honig and Mulenga (2015) also showed a lack of tenure security amongst small holder farmers in Zambia has resulted in a variety of documents to support ownership on customary, which include official letters on chiefdom letters or standard certificates of customary land usage (sometimes called chiefs' title).

Many of these initiatives are also supported by international organizations such as United State Agency for International Development (USAID), United Nations Development Programme (UNDP), United Kingdom's Department for International Development (DFID), International Fund for Agricultural Development (IFAD) and others. For instance, USAID and UNDP have supported programmes in Central and Eastern Provinces of Zambia aimed at empowering villages in documenting their rights on land. The demand for certification of customary land is not unique to Zambia and has been done in other countries such as Ethiopia, Tanzania, Botswana and Uganda (Knight, 2010; Green and Norberg, 2018).

Augustinus and Lemmen (2011) showed Land Administration Domain Models (LADMs) rely heavily on cadastral coverage which unfortunately is absent in many parts of the global South. STDM is then viewed as a suitable alternative. STDM is a multi-partner initiative of the UN HABITAT, Global Land Tool Network (GLTN), World Bank (WB), International Federation of Surveyors (FIG) and the International Institute for Geo-Information Science and Earth Observation (ITC) used in a number of projects to document customary land rights. It is argued to covers all types of tenure, conventions and social and informal tenure. STDM has thus been used in Zambia, specifically in Chamuka chiefdom, to issue certificates of customary land occupancy (CCLO). Table 2 below summarizes the content of these certificates.

A detailed scrutiny of the content of the CCLO revealed a number of shortcomings. To start with, the disclaimer on the front page of the certificate and Clause 1 of the terms and conditions captures the key limitation of this certificate; the document has no legal backing, hence merely records *de-facto* use. It is not transferrable nor can it be used for financial benefits such as obtaining a loan, and impliedly, selling. However, Clause 4 also seems to suggest the certificate is transferrable with the express approval of the

Table 2. Main features of a "certificate of customary land occupancy" from Chamuka chiefdom, Chisamba District

<table>
<tr><th>Front Page</th><th>Back Page</th></tr>
<tr><td>• Diagram of parcel of land</td><td>• Coordinates of parcel of land – longitude and latitude</td></tr>
<tr><td>• Photo of occupants</td><td rowspan="6">• Terms and conditions
1. A customary certificate is not a title deed hence cannot be used for financial benefits, e.g. obtaining a loan,
2. The powers of the village headperson and the Chief remain the same as before and the bearer of the certificate is expected to accord maximum respect to the traditional authority.
3. The head person and the Chief reserve the right to grant/deny a subject the customary certificate.
4. The transfer of the land either wholesome or subdivision is subject to approval by the Chief and the village head person.
5. The bearer of the certificate should be a person of good standing in society, i.e.
a. Must not have a criminal record
b. Must not engage in civil disobedience e.g. Gender Based Violence (GBV), abusive language, etc.
6. The certificate shall only be used to the landholder upon full payment of a non-refundable fee of K100 within a period of 6 months.
7. The headperson and Chief retain the power to revoke the certificate on the following grounds:
a. If the bearer willfully, deliberately, disregards and obstructs the powers of village head person and the Chief,
b. If the bearer relocates to another village or area.
c. Does not participate in community development activities e.g. village meetings, Kulamba Kubwalo contributions, etc.
8. In the event of death of the owner of land, a new certificate shall be issued to reflect the new owner(s) details.</td></tr>
<tr><td>• Names of occupants, including gender, tenure type and signature. Type of tenure is broken into individual owner, wife to owner, relative of owner or child of owner.</td></tr>
<tr><td>• Village headperson signature</td></tr>
<tr><td>• Chief's signature</td></tr>
<tr><td>• Date of issue</td></tr>
<tr><td>• Disclaimer: This document is not a title deed. Title deeds are only issued by the President of the Republic of Zambia through the subordinate of the Commissioner of Lands. The rights cannot be transferred from the persons listed in this document. In case of any changes this document will be rendered null and void, and a new certificate will need to be issued in consultation with the Chief and respective village head person.</td></tr>
</table>

Source: Extracted from "Certificate of Customary Land Occupancy," Chamuka Chiefdom

Chief and village head person; thus, the nature of this transfer on clause 4 is not clear. Clause 7 provides for the provocation of these certificates by the Chief on a number of reasons. Some reasons are as flimsy as not contributing to local traditional ceremonies. This consequently weakens the same tenure security these certificates are supposed to provide. This was also confirmed by Green and Norberg (2018), arguing TLHCs issued in Eastern Province were increasing powers of the Chief and not necessarily those of the holders. Clause 7(b) provides for the revocation of the certificate if the holder moves to another village, again emphasizing the non-transferability of the document and its temporariness.

Because of these shortcomings, the efficacy of these documents is still an issue of debate, with both positive and negative views. For instance, Mushinge et al. (2020) argued CCLOs have helped improve tenure security in Chamuka chiefdom. As noted earlier, the Chamuka chiefdom project used the Social Tenure Domain Model to document customary rights on land. Similar initiatives have been supported in Petauke District in Eastern Province where the Petauke District Farmers' Association, working under an agreement with chiefs and religious leaders, issued 300 TLHCs in two model villages in Petauke (Green & Norberg, 2018). Green and Norberg (2018) attributed this demand for certificates to increased commodification of land and to chiefs being beneficiaries from the process. It can be concluded that despite the various negative clauses under the terms and conditions, holders of these certificates still report an increased sense of security to a point where vernacular land markets start emerging on the basis of these documents.

The chapter authors note despite progress made so far in "bottom-up" approaches in protecting village communities, a gap still exists with regards to the legal recognition of these documents and the exact level of tenure protection they provide. Thus, the chapter sees the need for a working mix between the two approaches. The challenge in policy formulation and strategy is to find a mix between statutory and social processes, bearing in mind the level of development, customs and culture of each country. The authors also conclude while the top-down approach using LADM is often too expensive and complicated for most village communities, the STDM and similar local level initiatives also lack the legal clout to incentivise investors in rural areas. Therefore, critical thought is needed in order to find a working mix which supports both the social aspects of customary communities and at the same time providing sufficient legal backing to assure holders of their tenure. It is also clear the attempts being made by village communities to protect themselves are due to the sense of insecurity emanating from the State itself and other outside land seekers. This then points to the need for the establishment of locally-based hybrid bodies comprising central and local governments, traditional authorities and representatives of the community in order to achieve a more socially and culturally legitimate outcome.

FUTURE RESEARCH DIRECTIONS

The chapter authors noted the need to investigate what the "ideal" mix should be between the State's "top-down" approach and local "bottom-up" initiatives. At the moment none of these approaches seem to provide a comprehensive solution for the challenges found in most customary areas. The chapter authors also found there is need to contextualize solutions within local scenarios. This means countries in the global South cannot simply import solutions for their customary tenure problems but need to have their own research agenda on customary land tenure. This was highlighted by Maccalin (2018) who noted five options available for strengthening customary land rights; this means each country must understand its own challenges so solutions must then be location-specific due to differences in local traditional norms and customs.

CONCLUSION

The entry point for this chapter was that access to land and its security is paramount to livelihood strategies for village communities and yet even in the face of increased insecurity most governments are reluctant to formulate clear rules and regulations for its utilization and alienation, resulting in serious threats to customary tenure. In the context of the Zambia environment, the chapter discussed four main threats to customary tenure, namely: large-scale agriculture, large-scale mining, multi-facility economic zones and state farm block programmes. This is compounded by increased demand for land due to urbanization and general population increase.

Current evidence though shows village communities, with the assistance of outsiders, are devising their own mechanisms for securing their rights on land. In a way, village communities are moving into protecting themselves. This can be seen in the proliferation of local documents under various names to support ownership and improve security of tenure. It was however clear that in the absence of a clause on legal recognition within the law governing land administration most of these efforts will remain incomplete. Thus, the chapter highlights the need to looks beyond the legalistic reforms at macro level down to the realistic local level which should include social processes in village communities while at the same time providing sufficient legal support. Therefore, there is need to find a working mix between bottom-up approaches, with emphasis on the needs of village communities and social processes, and the states' top-down approaches which emphasize cadastral surveying and title registration. This may inevitably demand solutions be formulated within the context of local conditions and challenges.

REFERENCES

Agyeman-Yeboah, S. (2018). Land rights documentation in Ghana: Experiences from low-income key workers. *European Journal of Research in Social Sciences*, *6*(1), 13–26.

Augustinus, C., & Lemmen, C. (2011, April). What is required to bring the social element into land administration: moving from the land administration domain model to the social tenure domain model+ powerpoint. In *Annual World Bank Conference on Land and Poverty*. World Bank.

Batterbury, S., & Ndi, F. (2018). Land-grabbing in Africa. In *The Routledge Handbook of African Development. Routledge International Handbooks*. Routledge.

Boche, M., & Anseeuw, W. (2013). *Unraveling" land grabbing"-Different models of large-scale land acquisition in Southern Africa*. LDPI Working Paper 46.

Bottazzi, P., Goguen, A., & Rist, S. (2016). Conflicts of customary land tenure in rural Africa: Is large-scale land acquisition a driver of 'institutional innovation'? *The Journal of Peasant Studies*, *43*(5), 971–988. doi:10.1080/03066150.2015.1119119

Chu, J., Young, K., & Phiri, D. (2015). *Large-scale land acquisitions, displacement and resettlement in Zambia*. Institute for Poverty, Land and Agrarian Studies, University of Western Cape.

Chu, J. M. (2013). *Creating a Zambian breadbasket: 'Land Grabs' and foreign investments in agriculture in Mkushi District, Zambia*. https://www.gov.uk/research-for-development-outputs/ldpi-working-paper-33-creating-a-zambian-breadbasket-land-grabs-and-foreign-investments-in-agriculture-in-mkushi-district-zambia

Deininger, K., Ali, D. A., & Alemu, T. (2011). Impacts of land certification on tenure security, investment, and land market participation: Evidence from Ethiopia. *Land Economics*, *87*(2), 312–334. doi:10.3368/le.87.2.312

Doss, C., Meinzen-Dick, R., & Bomuhangi, A. (2014). Who owns the land? Perspectives from rural Ugandans and implications for large-scale land acquisitions. *Feminist Economics*, *20*(1), 76–100. doi:10.1080/13545701.2013.855320

French Development Cooperation. (2009). *Land governance and security of tenure in developing countries*. White Paper, Technical Committee on "Land Tenure and Development". French Development Cooperation.

German, L., Schoneveld, G., & Mwangi, E. (2011, April). Processes of large-scale land acquisition by investors: case studies from sub-Saharan Africa. In *International Conference on Global Land Grabbing* (pp. 6-8). University of Sussex.

Ghebru, H., & Lambrecht, I. (2017). Drivers of perceived land tenure (in) security: Empirical evidence from Ghana. *Land Use Policy*, *66*, 293–303. doi:10.1016/j.landusepol.2017.04.042

Gilberthorpe, E., Agol, D., & Gegg, T. (2016). 'Sustainable mining'? Corporate social responsibility, migration and livelihood choices in Zambia. *The Journal of Development Studies*, *52*(11), 1517–1532. doi:10.1080/00220388.2016.1189534

Government of the Republic of Zambia. (2006). *Report on the Environmental Impact Assessment Carried Out for Development of Nansanga Farm Block in Serenje District*. Ministry of Agriculture and Cooperatives.

Government of the Republic Zambia. (2005). *Farm Block Development Plan*. Ministry of Finance and National Planning.

Green, E., & Norberg, M. (2018). Traditional Landholding Certificates in Zambia: Preventing or Reinforcing Commodification and Inequality? *Journal of Southern African Studies*, *44*(4), 613–628. doi:10.1080/03057070.2018.1461490

Hall, M., Murombedzi, J., Nkonkomalimba, M., Sambo, P., & Sommerville, M. (2017). *Zambia customary land documentation tenure assessment*. USAID Tenure and Global Climate Change Programme.

Hall, R. (2011). Land grabbing in Southern Africa: The many faces of the investor rush. *Review of African Political Economy*, *38*(128), 193–214. doi:10.1080/03056244.2011.582753

Hanstad, T., Nielsen, R., & Brown, J. (2004). *Land and livelihoods. Making land rights real for India's rural poor.* LSP Working Paper No. 12. FAO.

Herre, R. (2013). *Fast Track Agribusiness: Expansion, Land Grabs and the Role of European Private and Public Financing in Zambia: A Right to Food Perspective*. FIAN FoodFirst Informations- & Aktions-Netzwerk.

Honig, L., & Mulenga, B. P. (2015). *The status of customary land and the future of smallholder farmers under the current land administration system in Zambia* (No. 1093-2016-87977). Academic Press.

Indaba Agricultural Policy Research Institute (IAPRI). (2015). *Rural Agricultural Livelihoods Survey Report*. IAPRI.

Jain, N., Chileshe, R., Muwowo, F., & Lupiya, M. (2016). Perceptions of customary land tenure security in western province of Zambia. *International Journal of Social Science Studies*, *4*(2), 78. doi:10.11114/ijsss.v4i2.1264

Kabinga, M. (2019). Mining developments and land acquisition processes in Zambia. *ASC-TUFS Working Papers 2019 Challenges of Development and Natural Resource Governance in Africa*, 167-182.

Katungula, D., Kumwenda, M., Ncube, N., & Chilanga, M. (2019). Innovative Customary Land Governance in Zambia: Experiences, Lessons Learned and Emerging Impacts. *African Journal on Land Policy and Geospatial Sciences*, *3*, 105–115.

Kesselring, R. (2018). At an extractive pace: Conflicting temporalities in a resettlement process in Solwezi, Zambia. *The Extractive Industries and Society*, *5*(2), 237–244. doi:10.1016/j.exis.2018.02.008

Knight, R. S. (2010). Statutory recognition of customary land rights in Africa: An investigation into best practices for lawmaking and implementation. *FAO Legislative Study*, 105.

Lund, C., & Rachman, N. F. (2016). Occupied! property, citizenship and peasant movements in Rural Java. *Development and Change*, *47*(6), 1316–1337. doi:10.1111/dech.12263

Lusaka Times. (2020). *The newly constructed Multi Facility Economic Zone in Central Province belongs to Chibombo District – Wina*. https://www.lusakatimes.com/2020/07/19/the-newly-constructed-multi-facility-economic-zone-in-central-province-belongs-to-chibombo-district-wina/

Manuel, V. (2016). *Underlying causes, consequences and possible solutions to land tenure insecurity of indigenous peoples and local communities in Southern Chile: The case of the MapucheHuilliche Indigenous communities in the Coastal Range Rainforests of MaruLahual* [Unpublished PhD thesis]. Universidad Austral de Chile/TechnischeUniversitat Dortmund.

McAuslan, P. (2007). *Improving Tenure Security for the Poor in Africa—Synthesis Paper: Deliberations of the Legal Empowerment Workshop—Sub-Saharan Africa*. LEP Working Paper No. 8. FAO.

Mccallin, B. E. M. (2018). Integrating customary tenure into formal systems (No. 129135). The World Bank.

Moyo, S. (2007). Land in the political economy of African development: Alternative strategies for reform. *Africa Development. Afrique et Developpement*, *32*(4), 1–37.

Munshifwa, E. (2018, March). *Customary land governance in Zambia: Inertia, confusion, and corruption* [Paper Presentation]. World Bank 2018 Conference on Land and Poverty, Washington, DC.

Munshifwa, E. K., Chileshe, R. A., & Jain, N. (2020). Evolution of customary land tenure institutions in Zambia: The Case of Lufwanyama District in the Copperbelt Province. *Agrarian South - the Journal of Political Economy*, *9*(2), 117–143.

Mushinge, A., & Mwando, S. (2016). Implications of pro-market land policies on customary land users in Zambia: A case of large-scale land investments in Kaindu chiefdom, Mumbwa district. *International Journal of Social Science Studies*, *4*(8), 9. doi:10.11114/ijsss.v4i8.1585

Mushinge, A., Simposya, A. M., & Chowa, S. (2020). Threats of statutory tenure on customary land in Zambia: Evidence from Chamuka Chiefdom in Chisamba District. *African Journal on Land Policy and Geospatial Sciences*, *3*(1), 41–52.

Mwansa, S., Shaikh, J., & Mubanga, P. (2020). Special Economic Zones: An evaluation of Lusaka South-Multi Facility Economic Zone. *Journal of Social and Political Sciences*, *3*(2), 523–539. doi:10.31014/aior.1991.03.02.188

Negi, R. (2014). 'Solwezi Mabanga': Ambivalent developments on Zambia's new mining frontier. *Journal of Southern African Studies*, *40*(5), 999–1013. doi:10.1080/03057070.2014.946215

Nguni, C. (2020). Chibombo economic zone shaping up. *Zambia Daily Mail*. http://www.daily-mail.co.zm/chibombo-economic-zone-shaping-up/

Nolte, K. (2014). Large-scale agricultural investments under poor land governance in Zambia. *Land Use Policy*, *38*, 698–706. doi:10.1016/j.landusepol.2014.01.014

Obidzinski, K., Takahashi, I., Dermawan, A., Komarudin, H., & Andrianto, A. (2013). Can large scale land acquisition for agro-development in Indonesia be managed sustainably? *Land Use Policy*, *30*(1), 952–965. doi:10.1016/j.landusepol.2012.06.018

Place, F., & Otsuka, K. (2002). Land tenure systems and their impacts on agricultural investments and productivity in Uganda. *The Journal of Development Studies*, *38*(6), 105–128. doi:10.1080/00220380412331322601

Siachitema, B. (2016). *Protecting Rural Zambian Communities from Displacement Resulting from Land-Based Investment*. https://www.southernafricalitigationcentre.org/wp-content/uploads/2017/08/GOAL-16-Book-Siachitema.pdf

Sitko, N. J., & Jayne, T. S. (2014). Structural transformation or elite land capture? The growth of "emergent" farmers in Zambia. *Food Policy*, *48*, 194–202. doi:10.1016/j.foodpol.2014.05.006

Tian, W., Zhou, Z., Ma, X., Heerink, N., van Ierland, E., van den Berg, M., & Shi, X. (2013). Land tenure security and land investments in Northwest China. *China Agricultural Economic Review*, *5*(2), 281–307. doi:10.1108/17561371311331133

Toulmin, C. (2009). Securing land and property rights in sub-Saharan Africa: The role of local institutions. *Land Use Policy*, *26*(1), 10–19. doi:10.1016/j.landusepol.2008.07.006

UNHABITAT. (2017). *Monitoring tenure security, data collection questionnaire modules and manual: Cameroon, Nigeria and Kenya*. GLII Working Paper No. 6 /2017.

Wang, H., Riedinger, J., & Jin, S. (2015). Land documents, tenure security and land rental development: Panel evidence from China. *China Economic Review*, *36*, 220–235. doi:10.1016/j.chieco.2015.09.005

Wily, L. A. (2010, April). Whose land are you giving away, Mr. President. Proc. of the Annual World Bank Land Policy & Administration Conference.

Wily, L. A. (2011). 'The law is to blame': The vulnerable status of common property rights in sub-Saharan Africa. *Development and Change*, *42*(3), 733–757. doi:10.1111/j.1467-7660.2011.01712.x

Zeng, D. Z. (2016). *Multi-Facility Economic Zones in Zambia: Progress, challenges and possible interventions*. Centre of Structural Economics Perking University.

Zhou, Y., Ma, X., Ji, D., Heerink, N., Shi, X., & Liu, H. (2018). Does property rights integrity improve tenure security? Evidence from China's forest reform. *Sustainability*, *10*(6), 1956. doi:10.3390u10061956

ADDITIONAL READING

Chileshe, R. A., Jain, N., & Chiselenga, R. (2017). Customary land tenure disputes and rural livelihoods in Zambia: Case of Ufwenuka Chiefdom in Southern Province. *Greener Journal of Social Sciences, 7*(3).

Chilombo, A., Fisher, J. A., & van Der Horst, D. (2019). A conceptual framework for improving the understanding of large scale land acquisitions. *Land Use Policy*, *88*, 104184. doi:10.1016/j.landusepol.2019.104184

Kumwenda, M., Shumba, F., Ncube, N., Antonio, D., Nyamweru, H., Gitau, J., Sylla, O., Mkumbwa, S., & Chileshe, A. (2018). Innovations for securing tenure rights on customary lands through traditional authorities: experiences from Chamuka Chiefdom, *Zambia. World Bank Conference on Land and Poverty*. Washington DC.

Manda, S., Tallontire, A., & Dougill, A. J. (2019). Large-scale land acquisitions and institutions: Patterns, influence and barriers in Zambia. *The Geographical Journal*, *185*(2), 194–208. doi:10.1111/geoj.12291

Munshifwa, E. K., Jain, N., Kaunda, B. S., Masiba, L., Lungu, J., Chunda-Mwango, N., Mushinge, A., & Ngoma, W. (2016). Variances in rateable values in rating practice in Zambia: The role of mental models in value assessment. *Pacific Rim Property Research Journal*, *22*(2), 181–201. doi:10.1080/14445921.2016.1225151

Munshifwa, E. K., & Mooya, M. M. (2016). Institutions, organisations and the urban built environment: Facilitative interaction as a developmental mechanism in extra-legal settlements in Zambia. *Land Use Policy*, *57*, 479–488. doi:10.1016/j.landusepol.2016.06.012

KEY TERMS AND DEFINITIONS

Codification of Rights: Systematic conversion of customary to formal legal rights such as property titles.

Customary Tenure: Conditions under which land and property is held based on local norms and culture.

Land: Area of land comprising physical space on which various rights are assigned.

Land Administration Domain Model (LADM): Land administration systems based on the State formulating policy and implementing, with emphasis on cadastral surveying and title registration.

Land Rights: Relationship amongst humans on the use of land; can be based on legal statute or traditional norms and culture.

Large-Scale Agriculture: Agricultural activities involving the acquisition of large tracks of land for commercial agriculture; often linked to foreign ownership.

Local Land Holding Certificate: Document issued by traditional authorities granting land rights based on social norms and culture; hence providing *de-facto* property right.

Multi-Facility Economic Zone: Land reserved, often through a legal instrument, for the development of an industrial park.

Social Tenure Domain Model (STDM): Land administration systems emphasising traditional and social processes and less on formal titling, hence facilitating documentation of *de-facto* rights.

Tenure: Conditions under which land and property are held.
Tenure Insecurity: Threat of dispossession.

ENDNOTES

1 This equivalent to ZMW114.1million rebased or equivalent to USD5.69 million at current exchange rate of K20.0380 to 1USD. An advertisement in 2011 by the Zambia Development (ZDA) for the development of Nansanga under a Public Private Partnership (PPP) agreement estimated the development cost at USD27million; a sharp increase from the initial estimate http://www.comesaria.org/opportunities/nansanga-farm-block.57.286.html

Chapter 8
Land as Agency:
A Critical Autoethnography of Scandinavian Acquisition of Dispossessed Land in the Iowa Territory

Robin Throne
https://orcid.org/0000-0002-3015-9587
University of the Cumberlands, USA

ABSTRACT

This chapter presents findings from a critical arts-based autoethnographic study of Iowa digital maps and historical archival data of the Iowa territory (1838-1846) for Indigenous Nations with previous land tenure. Researchers have noted land and voice dispossession for these Indigenous Nations resulting from forced removal followed by decades of intentional cultural erosion, forced assimilation, loss of language, and religious discrimination and persecution into the latter 20th century. Current research highlights the resultant damage of these historical losses on living descendants of Indigenous land-based cultures. Agency of self was explored from a socialized perspective of a descendant of Scandinavian immigrants who acquired dispossessed land within the Iowa territory. This was contrasted with a cultural perspective of land as capital wealth vs. the principles and tenets of land-based culture whereby agency may be strengthened via Indigenous knowledge rooted in land-based connections and environmental sensitivities. Data representation involved poetic excerpts of land as agency.

INTRODUCTION

The Mississippi River serves as the state of Iowa's eastern border. The 1830 Indian Removal Act passed by the United States Congress and signed by President Andrew Jackson required the forced deportation of Indigenous Nations east of the Mississippi River and subsequently accelerated Indigenous land cessions west of the Mississippi River (Anderson, 2016; Martinez, 2018). The Act culminated from the era of President James Monroe who had enacted a voluntary land cession effort that largely benefited the U.S. government and land speculators. Continued cession treaties were used as further strategies to facilitate

DOI: 10.4018/978-1-7998-3729-9.ch008

movement of Indigenous people further west (Rigal, 2009). Over the past decade, much research has focused on the acculturation and trauma of these land treaty and cession betrayals (DeMarni Cromer et al., 2018). Bremer (2017) noted:

By the time Iowa opened to formal white settlement on June 1, 1833, an acre purchased from the federal government cost $1.25. Settlers bought about one-third of Iowa's land directly from the federal government with cash; another 40 percent of the state's land was purchased using land warrants that veterans received for military service (p. 263)

By 1840, fewer than 23,000 white settlers had moved into the Iowa territory. Another approximate 150,000 settled by the time Iowa was officially named a state in the Union (Bremer, 2017).

Since the 1980s, some researchers have described the treatment of Indigenous Nations as genocide and ethnic cleansing (Anderson, 2016; DeMarni Cromer et al., 2018; Ostler, 2016). Others have noted land and voice dispossession for these Indigenous Nations from decades of intentional cultural erosion, forced assimilation, loss of language, and religious discrimination and persecution. This lasted into the latter 20th century with no reparations (Altaha, 2017). Still others have noted the atrocities as cultural terrorism and ethnocentric desires for capitalist incorporation, which persists under hegemonic rationales and other forms of justification (Jalata, 2016). While research remains ongoing into the resultant damage of these historical losses on living descendants of these Indigenous land-based cultures (Altaha & Kraus, 2017; Anderson, 2016; DeMarni Cromer et al., 2018; Whyte, 2017), less research has focused on the intentionality of Scandinavian settler societies across the Iowa territory and subsequent dispossessed land acquisition by European and Scandinavian immigrant groups (Carter & Kruzic, 2017).

This chapter presents findings from an autoethnographic study of the Iowa territory (1838-1846) that resulted from an arts-based autoethnographic analysis of Iowa digital maps and historical archival data for the same period (see Figure 1). Fidelity of researcher positionality was used as a conceptual framework to guide the autoethnography as the researcher-participant was outsider to Indigenous cultures who maintained land tenure prior to forced removal and governmental dispossession to stimulate European and Scandinavian immigration. The results of the autoethnographic study presented here focused on the author as researcher-participant to explore the agency of self as socialized from the perspective of a descendant of Scandinavian immigrants who acquired dispossessed land within the Iowa territory. The researcher-participant was socialized and educated within a sociocultural perspective of land ownership synonymous with capital wealth and dissimilar to the land curation expectations of the dispossessed culture. Findings illustrated the moral injury and diminished agency amidst affinity to the feminist principles and community-centered values of Indigenous knowledge of land-based cultures over perceptions of land as capital wealth, which may contribute to the erosion of agency of self and environmental sensitivities.

BACKGROUND

Scandinavian women immigrants were essential to the settlement of the Iowa territory, dispossessed from Indigenous Nations. However, many literary and other depictions characterized these women as singular pioneers of a new frontier, which often led to narrow representations of these women immigrants. These women were often economically dependent upon a spouse or male family members with

Figure 1. Iowa Indigenous land cessions (1830-1860). University of Northern Iowa.

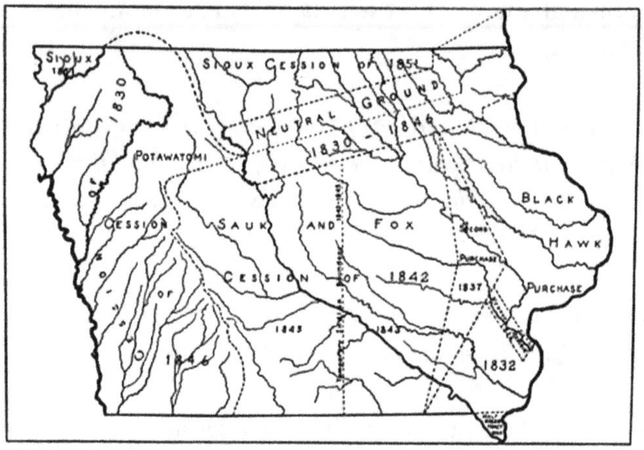

whom they migrated. These male family members sought improved vocational and economic circumstance, religious liberty, or a chance to overcome prior impoverishment in the undeveloped territory, and perchance economic independence. Riley (1977, 1988) disrupted the mythical representations and one-dimensional stereotypes of European and Scandinavian women emigrants who immigrated typically with other family members or spouses to the Iowa territory and the western region.

Riley (1977) divided Western women immigrants into four categories of stereotypical archetypes used widely regardless of race/ethnicity or other individual differences: "(1) the Calamity Jane, (2) the sex object, (3) the frontier suffragist, and (4) the saint in the sunbonnet" (p. 194). The saint was the most prevalent and desired of depictions. Settlement of the Iowa territory opened to resettlement in 1833 following the Black Hawk Purchase Treaty, deemed statehood in 1846, and was counted in the U.S. Census in 1870 (Riley, 1977). This resettlement was induced by U.S. governmental incentives and heavily recruited abroad. Riley (1988) coined the female frontier to deconstruct these mythical representations often perpetuated by Western artists and creative writers who depicted these women immigrants who held sway in spite of the imposing elements of the territory rather than the complex gendered realities of their existence. Conversely, the Indigenous women within the Iowa territory were often depicted as "primitive and crude because they were symbols of the opposition and challenge to Anglo expansion" (Riley, 1992, p. 23). Wives were described as "essential household furniture" (Riley, 1977, p. 196). Likewise, in current self-as-subject research, Carter and Kruzic (2017) noted:

these first white settlers plowed the prairie and drained the wetlands, replacing a rich, diverse ecosystem powered by sun and fire with a pollution-generating agricultural system powered by petroleum-based chemical products (p. 3)

Riley (1988) also noted that the numerous emigrant books and pamphlets used to recruit immigrants from Scandinavia were often targeted to the sentiments of women, advocating for freedom and adventure in the Western migration. By 1870, Scandinavian countries of original comprised with others for eight leading foreign groups by the Iowa Board of Immigration (State Historical Society of Iowa, 1970). These promotional pamphlets were published in various languages. Scandinavian settlers evolved into one of the largest immigrant groups with Norwegians, who often migrated in family units, eventually rising to the third largest ethnicity in what would eventually become the state of Minnesota.

Scandinavian women in the Iowa territory also provided extant writings that highlighted the loneliness of culture women experienced, as well as the transitional adoption of the territory (Riley, 1988). This has been described in the research as the perception of America as a "settler society" (Herlihy, 2011, p. 399), a further dispossession from current society for descendants of these Indigenous Nations and continued cultural proprietorship by the dominant culture to perpetuate a nationalist construction for American identity.

In more current research, Fitzgerald (2015) highlighted how many narratives of Indigenous removal and dispossession focused on men and less on the women's experiences. Although void of gendered examination, they were blended by experience. Further, the author noted that land itself is due a story; the narratives of Indigenous land possession and dispossession are further integrated within the creation narratives (Fitzgerald, 2015). Therefore, discussion of land within a land-based culture is immensely embedded within stories of spirit, origin, and evolution of culture. Likewise, Carter and Kruzic (2017) noted challenges in the decolonization of collaborative between both indigenous and descendants of Iowa's settler-society in the politics of resistance in solidarity with the Standing Rock protests.

The authors further highlighted other researchers who reported how narratives from across the anti-Dakota Access pipeline movement elevated the importance of women's collaboration in the protest efforts (Carter & Kruzic, 2017). The authors, who were self-reported outsiders to the Indigenous Nation, identified with Iowa settler-society culture. Yet they were united in the land-based principles of the standpoint and resistance to the repression of women's voices. In addition, they stood together in moral injury over past dominance and exploitation at the hands of their own ancestry. They said:

Our home—Iowa—presents unique challenges to centering the commons given its long and taken-for-granted history of extraction through industrial agriculture. Yet, from the summer of 2014 to the summer of 2017, women—both indigenous and descendants of Iowa's settler-society—led much of the Dakota Access pipeline resistance in Iowa. The Iowa-based resistance prioritized unlikely alliances and elevated new voices in effort to stop the pipeline and to protect the commons. Participants in the grassroots resistance defined their care for and connections to the commons through diverse, and sometimes divergent, claims-making about landowners' rights, indigenous sovereignty, soil health, corporate control, climate justice, and public health. (Carter & Kruzic, 2017, p. 2)

Like the researcher-participant, these authors utilized autoethnography and researcher positionality as "white, ciswomen and ecofeminist scholar activists who both grew up in rural Iowa" to decolonize an issue within a state established for "settlers' quest for private property and where the agricultural economy privileges settler-society and the extraction and mining of soil through industrial agricultural production" (Carter & Kruzic, 2017, p. 3). Similarly, Datta (2019) found Indigenous enhanced understanding of the relationships between environment and ancestral land and water for both Indigenous participants and nonindigenous participants. Indigenous participants were able to document traditional land-based traditions, which enhanced knowledge and understanding.

New research remains ongoing for restoration of Indigenous knowledge and use of ancestral land to employ meaning and enhance well-being. Freeman (2019) reported the importance of cultural practices, including journeying and place-thought, within ancestral land for Indigenous youth agency. Indigenous knowledge, in connection with the land and natural environment, were intrinsic to self-awareness and formation of identity and agency. Research participants were thereby able to unpack social constructs that were prior barriers to indigenous knowledge and value for land-based practices (Freeman, 2019).

Similarly, Whyte (2017) referred to prior work that has shown that, in spite of the past oppressive structures and traumas of land dispossession, removal and separation, racism, sexism, and discrimination, Indigenous researchers and research participants were able to reclaim indigenous values and reclaim agency via an embodied place-based identity. Finally, Absolon (2016), among others, noted the value of Indigenous knowledge, traditions, and protocols for healing both past and current trauma via land-based connections through Indigenous practices and traditions.

CONCEPTUAL FRAMEWORK

Fidelity of researcher positionality was used as a conceptual framework to guide the autoethnography. The framework was constructed from the author's prior definitions for researcher positionality as relied upon from work by Bourke (2014) and Throne (2012, 2018a, 2018b, 2019) over the past seven years through social justice and indigenous inquiries by a nonindigenous researcher. These positionalities were used to consider an authentic *other* narrative voice. It assessed the fidelity of self as researcher and self-identified researcher positionality throughout the inquiry to dissect another's language to recount narrative voice as remnant of dispossession (Throne, 2018a, 2018b, 2019, 2020). The author also noted that systematic observation of another's experiences with dispossession, especially when outside the land-based cultural experience or from another cultural standpoint, must involve a fidelity of observation and rigorous fidelity of analysis to offer clarity and discovery whereby researcher positionality becomes a necessary lens to inference and interpretation of these observations whether subtle or overt (Hoskins, 2015; Throne, 2018a, 2020). In any case, the rigor of fidelity to positionality remains a necessary standpoint. Reflexivity remained necessary to ensure such viewpoints were continuously examined.

Further, the conceptual framework offered ethical assurances to consider the bounds of one woman's identity and ancestry as researcher-participant to ensure deidentification of all data gathered for the study. This included complex familial relationships that may reference unintended identities other than the researcher-participant (De Silva & Gandhi, 2019; Moravec, 2017). Finally, as De Silva and Gandhi (2019, p. 4) noted, field research findings may also have implications for archival research whereby the gendered perspective of the "daughter" experience may be one unnecessarily protected from self-examination. These gendered politics of the research setting, past or present, living or deceased, may inform knowledge construction due to ancestral and familial complexities that may contrast notions of independent researcher, especially within self-as-subject research.

METHOD

Archival data were gathered in the fall and winter of 2018-2019. The publicly accessible digital collections were analyzed using procedures for self-as-subject autoethnographic analysis and arts-based data representation, including the Iowa Digital Library, Library of Congress/Maps, and GIS Maps from Beacon Schneider. Various individuals gathered the data because the establishment of the Iowa territory and ongoing satellite maps are stored with annual public plat books published in both print and electronic form, including the map of the Iowa district as published in Lea (1836). Data were historical since the establishment of the Iowa territory. They were archived within the online databases listed and publicly available for download access. Iowa territory and state land property records were archived by township and stored in ongoing digital collections. This eased identification for geographic location and subsequent property ownership following the opening of the Iowa frontier to immigration in 1833.

The researcher-participant's archival data and historical manuscript data from prior historical research into women's experiences within the Iowa territory were used for both dispossession and settlement. These were also used as artifacts for autoethnographic generative writing. The generative writing served as an additional vehicle to iterative introspection as founded on the fundamental study assumption that new knowledge can be discovered from deep introspection of the individual lived experience (Moustakas, 1956; Polkinghorne, 1988; Throne, 2019), as well as emergent new knowledge from one researcher-participant's experience constructed from a feminist standpoint (Brooks, 2007; Hoskins, 2015).

Finally, Le Roux's (2017) recommendations for the five criteria to demonstrate rigor within autoethnography were used to guide a rigorous self-as-subject study design: (1) subjectivity; (2) self-reflexivity; (3) resonance; (4) credibility; and (5) contribution. Further, data representation was intentionally arts-based. It consisted of poetic stanzas generated within data analyses to illustrate appropriate narrative representation, narrative impact, and researcher-participant reflexivity. Poetic excerpts were selected via aesthetic merit and Leavy's (2017) concept of aesthetic coherence as aligned with the archival data and the researcher-participant's positionality, as well as for intentional social justice research aims (Brooks, 2007; Le Roux, 2017; Throne, 2019). The excerpts were juxtaposed amidst the relevant map images for data representation (Byrne, 2017).

POETIC REPRESENTATION OF ARCHIVAL DATA

Fifteen maps were gathered from 1833-1846 and analyzed for readability and resonance. Subjectivity and reflexivity were used to iteratively assess open and established boundaries throughout the period. Poetry was used as an introspective device to explore agency via land illustrations and two poem excerpts are presented for pragmatic and literary interpretation from an inside/outsider standpoint.

Hostile

1833

It was not a strength of character

built from the wild-hearted land

these millions and millions of unbending acres

I never measured or counted

solely dependent instead on will

a steely will not found in the lead mines and black sod

Figure 2. Catlin (1840). Outline map of Indian localities in 1833. State Historical Society of Iowa.

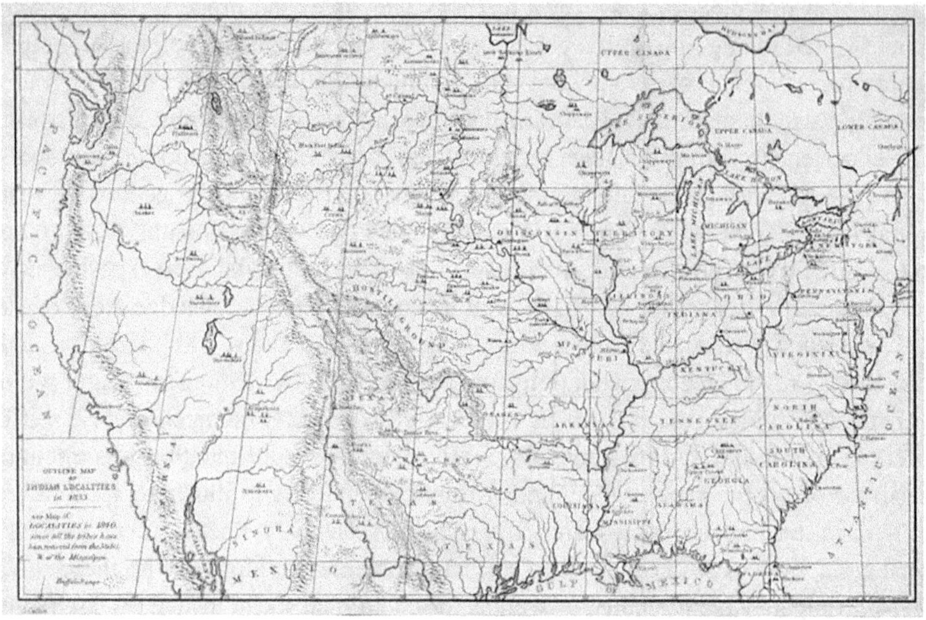

but a hard cold steel ripped from innards of obligation

to this Earth

Land-locked between two rivers

I could not leave

nor would ever abandon my purpose.

I stayed gripped in a time not yet named

labeled and mocked for these places

not what was in me, not what was destined.

I could soar like the generosity of strangers

who shared a circle of faith I found then

not long later

bound me to them forever.

Figure 3. Tanner (1845). Iowa. University of Iowa Digital Library.

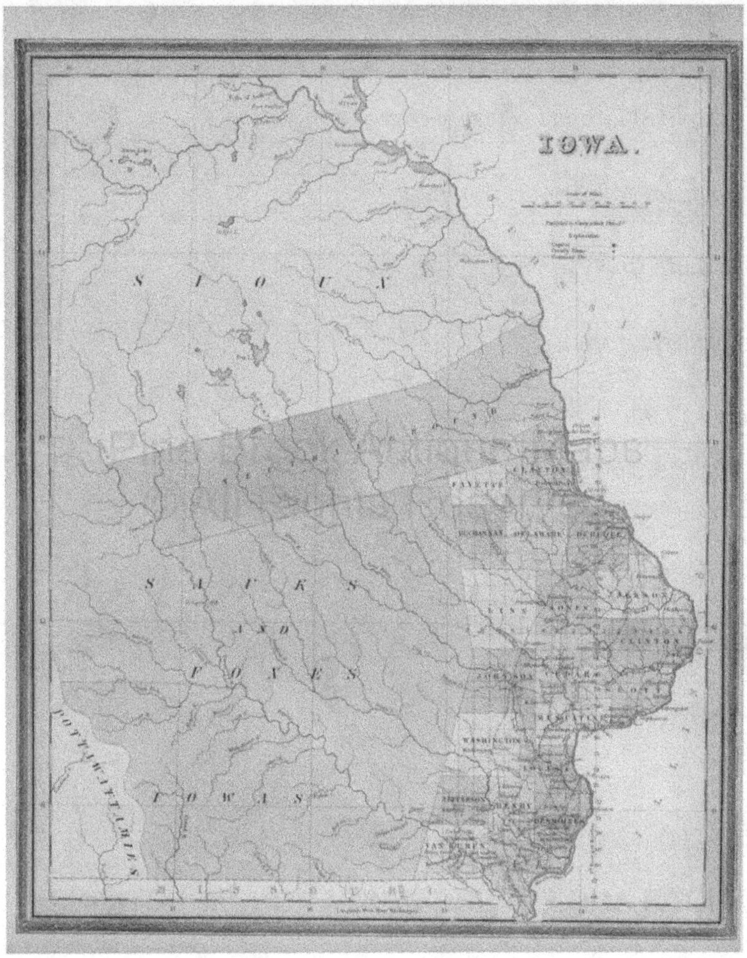

Civilized

1845

The circle soon became a square

squares upon squares emerged

across millions and millions of cultivated acres.

Finely measured with the most efficient precision

an assessment of return, invest, return, invest

Lose. Win. Barter. Take.

Birth order was law and the voice of the others

was dimmed by the seizing breaths of the land

as the squares emerged, tight corners, sharply edged

and when the moon and sun could not reach me

I reached up for them and lost my footing.

I reached for the sky without a stance

forgotten where and why I had been planted

Here.

Higher was better they had always told me

so, I looked up, always up

and I believed them

Until now.

RECOMMENDATIONS AND FUTURE RESEARCH DIRECTIONS

Carter and Kruzic (2017) stressed the importance of continued work to decolonize and dismantle the hierarchies of contested histories. They called for continued research to bring forward new voices and collaborations, including descendants of settler-societies, to continue to disrupt long-held power structures that prevent a collective conversation about Iowa land (Carter & Kruzic, 2017). Similarly, Absolon (2016) noted how colonization creates a fragmented worldview that may prevent holistic view. It was also noted that ethical inclusion and Indigenous cultural frameworks may bring healing for Indigenous and nonindigenous victims of trauma. Numerous other researchers have noted the need to address these historical traumas as they differ widely among individuals, families, tribes, and other collectives (Altaha & Kraus, 2017; DeMarni Cromer et al., 2018; Freeman, 2019).

Freeman (2019) further noted the use of Indigenous knowledge to promote healing and well-being is deeply rooted in reconnections to the land and natural environment. This may offer health solutions for legacy trauma. The chapter author recommends further self-as-subject research by survivors of historical trauma, both inside and outside dispossessed and appropriated cultures. Their work can seek introspective understanding to enhance agency gained by these land reconnections and positionality with land and the local environment and disrupt the settler-American or settler-society notion of belonging to a more collective identity (Carter & Kruzic, 2017; Datta, 2019; Herlihy, 2011).

CONCLUSION

Watts (2013) noted how colonization operationalized the identity of self apart from the natural world, thereby reducing agency. Indigenous place-thought is founded on the premise of a living land that allows human beings to derive agency as only one component of a thinking environment rather than as a centric component (Watts, 2013).

Only if the land decides to stop speaking to us will we enter the world of dislocation where agency is lost and our histories become provocative Indian lore in an ongoing settler mistake (p. 33)

Further, as Riley (1977, 1988, 1992) deconstructed the long-standing stereotypical depictions of frontier women to decompress understanding of these women's experiences, the atrocities specific to women descendants of the historical traumas from the colonization of the Iowa territory deserve further inquiry to potentially inform contemporary issues of human trafficking, immigration, and child removal at issue today. Through iterative introspection and the use of arts-based vehicles to illustrate contemplative insights gained through systematic research may continue to inform not only the researcher-participant about the legacy of trauma and erosion of agency, but also contemporary mechanisms that may prevent and compress agency. Further, the space and time for this research is necessary to continue to orient the self within the period of trauma to better embrace place-thought (Indigenous cosmologies) as an ontological-epistemological (Euro/Western-centric) device to deconstruct stereotypes and misappropriated definitions for self and other long overdue. Perhaps even further, continued contemplative research may bring deeper insights for self to enhance agency in relation to better understanding of environmental resource excavation for capital wealth vs. sustainability amidst historical connections to land and forced removals (Carter & Kruzic, 2017; Datta, 2019; Watts, 2013).

ACKNOWLEDGMENT

With gratitude to the National Archives at Kansas City, Missouri, and Augustana College Special Collections, Rock Island, Illinois, and especially to the archivists for their support of visiting researchers. Additional thanks to the Northcentral University Institutional Review Board for review of the study.

REFERENCES

Absolon, K. E. (2016). Wholistic and ethical: Social inclusion with indigenous peoples. *Social Inclusion (Lisboa)*, *4*(1), 44–56. doi:10.17645i.v4i1.444

Altaha, N., & Kraus, S. (2017). "Kill the Indian, save the man": Native American historical trauma in college students. *Metamorphosis*. Retrieved from http://metamorphosis.coplac.org/index.php/metamorphosis/article/view/67

Anderson, G. C. (2016). The Native peoples of the American West: Genocide or ethnic cleansing? *The Western Historical Quarterly*, *47*(4), 407–433. doi:10.1093/whq/whw126

Bourke, B. (2014). Positionality: Reflecting on the research process. *Qualitative Report, 19*, 1–9. http://nsuworks.nova.edu/cgi/viewcontent.cgi?article=1026&context=tqr

Bremer, J. (2017). Land was the main basis for business: Markets, merchants, and communities in Frontier Iowa. *Annals of Iowa, 76*(3), 261–289. doi:10.17077/0003-4827.12401

Brooks, A. (2007). Feminist standpoint epistemology: Building knowledge and empowerment through women's lived experience. In S. N. Hesse-Biber & P. L. Leavy (Eds.), *Feminist research practice* (pp. 53–82). SAGE. doi:10.4135/9781412984270.n3

Byrne, G. (2017). Narrative inquiry and the problem of representation: "Giving voice", making meaning. *International Journal of Research & Method in Education, 40*(1), 36–52. doi:10.1080/1743727X.2015.1034097

Carter, A., & Kruzic, A. (2017). Centering the Commons, Creating space for the collective: Ecofeminist# NoDAPL praxis in Iowa. *Journal of Social Justice*, 7.

Datta, R. (2019). Clarifying the process of land-based research, and the role of researcher(s) and participants. *Ethics in Science and Environmental Politics, 19*, 1–11. doi:10.3354/esep00187

De Silva, M., & Gandhi, K. (2019). "Daughter" as a positionality and the gendered politics of taking parents into the field. *Area, 51*(4), 662–669. doi:10.1111/area.12525

Dean, J., Furness, P., Verrier, D., Lennon, H., Bennett, C., & Spencer, S. (2017). Desert island data: An investigation into researcher positionality. *Qualitative Research*. Advance online publication. doi:10.1177/1468794117714612

DeMarni Cromer, L., Gray, M. E., Vasquez, L., & Freyd, J. J. (2018). The relationship of acculturation to historical loss awareness, institutional betrayal, and the intergenerational transmission of trauma in the American Indian experience. *Journal of Cross-Cultural Psychology, 49*(1), 99–114. doi:10.1177/0022022117738749

Fitzgerald, S. J. (2015). *Native women and land: Narratives of dispossession and resurgence*. University of New Mexico Press.

Freeman, B. M. (2019). Promoting global health and well-being of Indigenous youth through the connection of land and culture-based activism. *Global Health Promotion, 26*(3, suppl), 17–25. doi:10.1177/1757975919831253 PMID:30964409

Herlihy, J. (2011). Reflections on social engineering and settler-American literature. *European Journal of American Studies, 6*(1), 6–1. doi:10.4000/ejas.8874

Hoskins, K. (2015). Researching female professors: The difficulties of representation, positionality and power in feminist research. *Gender and Education, 27*(4), 393-411. Doi:.2015.1021301 doi:10.1080/09540253

Jalata, A. (2016). The impact of colonial terrorism on indigenous Americans. In *Phases of Terrorism in the Age of Globalization* (pp. 49–71). Palgrave Macmillan. doi:10.1057/9781137552341_4

Le Roux, C. S. (2017). Exploring rigour in autoethnographic research. *International Journal of Social Research Methodology, 20*(2), 195–207. doi:10.1080/13645579.2016.1140965

Lea, A. M. (1836). *Notes on the Wisconsin Territory; particularly with reference to the Iowa District or Black Hawk Purchase*. H.S. Tanner.

Leavy, P. (2017). *Research design: Quantitative, qualitative, mixed methods, arts-based, and community based participatory research approaches*. Guilford.

Martinez, D. (2018). *Documents of American Indian removal*. ABC-CLIO.

Moravec, M. (2017). Feminist research practices and digital archives. *Australian Feminist Studies, 32*(91-92), 186–201. doi:10.1080/08164649.2017.1357006

Moustakas, C. (1956). True experience and the self. In C. Moustakas (Ed.), *The self: Explorations in personal growth* (pp. 3–14). Harper.

Ostler, J. (2016). 'Just and lawful war' as genocidal war in the (United States) Northwest Ordinance and Northwest Territory, 1787-1832. *Journal of Genocide Research, 18*(1), 1–20. doi:10.1080/14623528.2016.1120460

Polkinghorne, D. E. (1988). *Narrative knowing and the human sciences*. SUNY Press.

Rigal, L. (2009). Watershed days on the Treaty Line, 1836-1839. *The Iowa Review*, 202-223.

Riley, G. (1977). Images of the frontierswoman: Iowa as a case study. *The Western Historical Quarterly, 8*(2), 189–202. doi:10.2307/967250

Riley, G. (1988). *The female frontier: A comparative view of women on the prairie and the plains*. University Press of Kansas.

Riley, G. (1992). *A place to grow: Women in the American West*. Harlan Davidson.

State Historical Society of Iowa. (1970). *Studies in Iowa History: Iowa: The home for immigrants*. State Historical Society of Iowa.

Stewart, T., Throne, R., & Evans, L. (2020). A critical review of gender parity and voice dispossession among executive women in higher education leadership. In G. Berg & L. Venis (Eds.), *Accessibility and diversity in the 21st century university*. IGI Global. doi:10.4018/978-1-7998-2783-2.ch005

Throne, R. (2012). Positionality. In *Practitioner research in doctoral education* (pp. 55–77). Kendall Hunt.

Throne, R. (2018a). The letter: Fidelity in researcher positionality to exhume dispossessed voices for Leavy's concept of coherence in feminist narrative research. *Gender and Women's Studies, 2*(1). Retrieved from http://riverapublications.com/journal/gender-womens-studies

Throne, R. (2018b). Hermeneutic archival research & artistic license: Exhuming dispossessed Sauk voices through creative non-fiction. In *14th Annual International Congress of Qualitative Inquiry*. University of Illinois.

Throne, R. (2019). Autoethnography and heuristic inquiry for doctoral-level researchers: Emerging research and opportunities. Hershey, PA: IGI Global.

Throne, R. (2020). Dispossession of land cultures: Women and property tenure among Lowcountry heirs in the Gullah Geechee Corridor. In U. Onyebadi (Ed.), *Multidisciplinary issues surrounding African Diasporas* (pp. 152–174). IGI Global. doi:10.4018/978-1-5225-5079-2.ch007

Watts, V. (2013). Indigenous place-thought and agency amongst humans and non humans (First Woman and Sky Woman go on a European world tour!). *Decolonization*, *2*(1). https://jps.library.utoronto.ca/index.php/des/article/download/19145/16234/

WhyteK. P. (2017). What do Indigenous knowledges do for Indigenous Peoples? Retrieved from https://ssrn.com/abstract=2612715

ADDITIONAL READING

Anthias, P. (2019). Ambivalent cartographies: Exploring the legacies of indigenous land titling through participatory mapping. *Critique of Anthropology*, *39*(2), 222–242. doi:10.1177/0308275X19842920

Barker, A. J., & Pickerill, J. (2019). Doings with the land and sea: Decolonising geographies, Indigeneity, and enacting place-agency. *Progress in Human Geography*. doi:10.1177/0309132519839863

Bataille, G. M., & Mullen Sands, K. (1984). Traditional values in modern context: The narratives to come. In *American Indian women: Telling their lives* (pp. 127–141). University of Nebraska Press.

Gould, R., & Rock, J. (2016). Wakan Tipi and Indian Mounds Park: Reclaiming an Indigenous feminine sacred site. *AlterNative: An International Journal of Indigenous Peoples*, *12*(3), 224–235. doi:10.20507/AlterNative.2016.12.3.2

Gunn Allen, P. (1986). *The sacred hoop: Recovering the feminine in American Indian traditions*. Beacon Press.

Lobo, S., Talbot, S., & Carlston, T. M. (Eds.). (2016). *Native American voices*. Routledge. doi:10.4324/9781315663456

Long Soldier, L. (2017). *Whereas*. Graywolf Press.

Throne, R. (2018). Her kind, a novel (5A ed.). Davenport, IA: 918studio press.

Woodiwiss, J., Smith, K., & Lockwood, K. (2017). *Feminist narrative research: Opportunities and challenges*. Palgrave Macmillan.

KEY TERMS AND DEFINITIONS

Agency: A belief in one's ability to take the initiative necessary to assume an active role in one's own setting, culture, community, content, process, and/or engagement within respective settings.

Iowa Territory: Originally a segment of land within the Louisiana Purchase, from 1838-1846 until it became a state, Iowa was incorporated as a territory with Iowa City as the territory capital. The territory was closed to U.S., European, and Scandinavian settlers until after the Black Hawk Purchase, signed into treaty in 1833.

Land Culture: The terms "land culture" or "land-based culture" are often used in indigenous cultures that view their responsibility as land curators vs. landowners. As such, land is also often connected to the identity and spirituality of individuals within the culture.

Land Dispossession: Land dispossession involves legal and nonlegal means for removal of a person(s) from the possession of land. This often involves displacement and/or penury.

Standpoint: Sometimes synonymous with positionality: standpoint represents the unification of a researcher's complex and layered point of view as informed by the personal and societal influences that form how the researcher sees, experiences, and understands the world.

Voice Dispossession: Voice dispossession involves the filtered, silencing, or reduction of vocality of opinions, ideas, and innovation among specific groups due to oppressive hierarchies, gendered obstacles or barriers, or other societal power domains. Fear or threat of consequences may also impede vocality of individuals amid these societal structures. This can result in decreased well-being, unfair or imbalanced dialogue, repressed innovation, barriers to social justice, and land dispossession.

Chapter 9
A Critical Review of the Native American Tradition of Circle Practices

Thomas Reed
University of San Diego, USA

ABSTRACT

This chapter is a critical review of circle practices. The author first examines the philosophical underpinnings behind similar practices of restorative justice, circles, circle practices, and talking circles. Then, the author explores the description of protocol and procedures of talking circles in the literature by various others. Thirdly, this literature review examines talking circles used in practice in the literature. This chapter synthesizes and critiques existing literature, as well as video resources and oral tradition. Circle practices are a traditional Native American practice of communication and community which has a strong spiritual core as a means for restorative justice. For some Native American people during talking circles, it is believed the person holding the eagle feather or talisman cannot tell a lie.

INTRODUCTION

This chapter presents the results of a critical review of the scholarship surrounding Native American circle practices. This chapter presents results of the review and discusses the existing literature on talking circles as they relate to Native American people. This critical review first examines the philosophical underpinnings behind the similar practices of restorative justice, circles, circle practices, and talking circles. Second, this review explores the explanation of conducting talking circles. Third, this critical review examines the actual practice of talking circles present in literature. The chapter is organized by topic to explore the decolonizing ideologies of talking circles, the Truth and Reconciliation Commission in Canada, the topic of indigenous law versus public policy, protocol for talking circles, discussion of the burden basket, the theme of vulnerability in circles, the oral tradition aspect of circle practices, and an in depth review of a seminal talking circle workshop. This chapter discusses the importance of talk-

DOI: 10.4018/978-1-7998-3729-9.ch009

ing circles for Native American people, as well as the multicultural use of talking circles. The literature surrounding appropriation is also considered.

This review synthesizes and critiques the scholarship, including journal articles, books, films, and interviews, for oral traditions as a valid form of history and knowledge to the Native American community (Vansina, 1985). The chapter also incorporates knowledge from elders, leaders in my Tribal Nation of the Oneida, and family. Family is incorporated because passing down of information between generations is seen as a valid way of transmitting traditional knowledge, also known as the decolonizing practices of testimony, storytelling, reframing, restoring, remembering, revitalizing, regenerating, discovering the beauty of our knowledge, and sharing. Furthermore, learning about the stories and indigenous values help families restore their sense of stability (Native American Rights Fund, 2016). These decolonizing practices are used intentionally in this literature review through indigenizing processes (Smith, 2012) to claim what is predominantly a Euro-American paradigm when viewing indigenous peoples. The purpose of this chapter is to shed light on circle practices and to critique existing literature.

BACKGROUND

As a clarification, the term Native American will be used interchangeably with American Indian, Indian, Indigenous, Aboriginal, First Nations, and native, depending on how researchers in the literature used it. The following are monikers for groups of indigenous people discussed as generally, in academia, the terms Native Americans, American Indian, and Indian refer to people who traditionally, and to this day, occupy North America, referred to as Turtle Island by Native American people (Jervis et al., 2006; Johnston-Goodstar & VeLure Roholt, 2017; Lyons, 1992). In Canada, First Nations people is the term used to describe their original inhabitants (Quinn, 2007). In Australia, the term for their indigenous inhabitants is Aboriginal people (Atkinson, 2002). In New Zealand, the original inhabitants are referred to as Maori (Pihama et al., 2017).

Although it is not standard practice to include a statement of positionality in a literature review, it is my understanding through academics such as Rupert Ross (1996), it is connected and interrelated. Particularly as it pertains to my critiques of literature, I would be remiss if I did not mention my own ethnic identity as an Oneida researcher. This is important to note because my paradigm as an Oneida indigenous researcher is influenced by (a) my ontology, my view of reality; (b) my epistemology, how I think about this reality; (c) my axiology, my morals and ethics; and (d) my methodology, how I go about gaining more knowledge about reality (Wilson, 2008). Research is also seen as ceremony for some indigenous researchers. Shaun Wilson of the Cree Nation puts it best when he states,

Something that has become apparent to me is that for indigenous people, research is a ceremony. In our cultures an integral part of any ceremony is setting the stage properly. When ceremonies take place, everyone who is participating needs to be ready to step beyond the everyday and to accept a raised state of consciousness. You could say that the specific rituals that make up the ceremony are designed to get the participants into a state of mind that will allow for the extraordinary to take place. As one Elder explained it to me: if it is possible to get every single person in a room thinking about the exact thing for only two seconds, then a miracle will happen. It is fitting that we view research in the same way- as a means of raising our consciousness. (Wilson, 2008, p. 69)

It is with this perspective of research as ceremony this literature review is assembled, synthesized, and critiqued.

Philosophical Underpinnings of Circle Practices

This literature review will now explore the philosophical underpinnings of circle practices, one of which is restorative justice. Restorative Justice is a practice which seeks to bring about reconciliation and healing for both the abused and the abuser. Restorative justice also is a key concept when thinking of an indigenous person seeking reconciliation and a connection to their land, self and spirit.

Restorative Justice

In understanding circle practices, it is important to understand the philosophy of other similar practices, such as restorative practices (Sered, 2019). Sered thoroughly described the current criminal justice in America, why it is failing the United States, and why reconciliation is key as a nation and individually. Sered was fair in logic, assessment, and rationale. This author dealt with themes and philosophy at the foundation of restorative justice and the need for reconciliation societally and as human beings.

Sered (2019) made a critical point and lay a philosophical foundation for restorative justice, specifically, circle practices. The literature noted, by sending people to prison, the criminal justice system robs the accused of taking responsibility for their actions. This theme of prison robbing the accused, their accuser, and those in social connections with all parties of proper healing is common (Sered, 2019). This point initially causes a visceral reaction; the idea seemed like an overstatement, and surely, the prison set up could not be effective. However, Sered provided clear evidence for the importance of community connection leading to ideal healing for all parties.

In addition, Sered (2019) articulated prisons fail to offer healing and rob people of taking accountability and not being effective. The criticism here was a blanket statement seemed inaccurate, and I initially thought this could not possibly be true. However, through statistics, facts, anecdotes, and interviews, Sered (2019) made a strong case for reconciliation through genuine conversations in a circle, as opposed to defendants taught to plead not guilty or no-contest. Sered (2019) made a shocking and unsettling point when she stated a grand narrative that jail helps our society or gives people closure not based on data or facts. Again, this statement seemed like it could not be possible. I thought to myself as a researcher, how could this possibly be true. In my graduate program, I perceived our prison system as based on data, analytics, and facts, and could not be a failure. I realized I was going through the stages of loss in dealing with the failure of our current prison system, starting with denial, then anger, bargaining in trying to negotiate the facts, depression, and then anger. However, Sered makes a strong case using data, analytics, and facts to make a case for restorative justice through circle practices.

Furthermore, accountability plays a major role in the healing process. By "doing sorry," as Sered described, in other words putting into action the process of being sorry and seeking reconciliation, people can heal so they do not pass on this pain to others. I think Sered makes a valid point here, and while seeming poetic, the statement is also a valid claim. I do concur with the author; there is a dignified nature of accountability for all parties in a restorative justice healing process.

A particularly powerful point Sered (2019) made was regarding the origins of restorative justice and circle practice. This framework is important for better understanding the framework of restorative justice and how it relates to circle practices by the shared origins in indigenous practices. The author notes restorative justice was used primarily by Plains Indians, the Maori in New Zealand, and a variety of African communities. The point brought up is one of cultural appropriation. Taking and appropriating an indigenous culture has many sides of the argument to consider. For example, an indigenous researcher may perceive academic uses of restorative practice by nonindigenous people as a compliment to indigenous philosophy and genuine recognition of the value of indigenous culture by colonist culture. However, a different indigenous researcher sees the use of restorative justice circles by nonindigenous people as being more of culture vultures and taking culture applicable to them and ignoring a brutal history of abuse, oppression, and genocide. There could further be an indigenous researcher who is a mix of somewhere in between these polar responses, or they may perceive the circumstance completely different. The point Sered (2019) made that transcends ethnicity and deals in the spiritual was an insightful quote where she describes how your mother's dreams for you are like my mother's dream for me.

Sered's (2019) final point concerned the indigenous roots of restorative justice of central significance for circle practices. Sered shared a story of an indigenous person learning the roots of restorative justice are of their culture. Sered stated restorative justice was from traditions of indigenous peoples' own ancestors and culture. This point also recognizes the author's approach and respect toward the origin's and roots of restorative justice, which are also the origins of circle practices. Also, the themes of partnership, collaboration, and interrelatedness are of great importance in circle practices. The points made by the researcher are backed by examples and cited with supportive case study examples.

Desmond Tutu on Philosophical Underpinnings of Restorative Justice

In the philosophical underpinnings of restorative justice, Desmond Tutu is another leader in the field with immense amounts of knowledge. In a presentation, Desmond Tutu noted how we need each other to know how to be human (University of California Television, n.d.). This point was insightful. Tutu articulated how he did not know how to walk, talk, think, or just be human if it were not for other humans. This assertion is one I have not heard articulated elsewhere and it rings true as a reader. The information seems as simple as it is profound. Tutu further details philosophical underpinnings of restorative justice by stating there are no isolated humans (University of California Television, n.d.). This is another point not articulated in the Western description of living. Tutu re-emphasizes a common theme in the literature about gifts (Ross, 1996). Tutu teaches God made us with our gifts and weaknesses so we could complement one another (University of California Television, n.d.). This point again bolsters the idea of community and circles. The Oneida Opening Prayer includes a refrain saying, "Let's put our minds together, so be it in our minds," and this perspective of Tutu seems to align with indigenous philosophy of North America, otherwise known by indigenous people as Turtle Island. A point for healing aligns with Ross, Pranis, Boyes-Watkins, and Tutu: There is no truth without forgiveness and no future without forgiveness. Without forgiveness, Tutu logically articulates people would in a sort of reprisal of revenge, followed by the opposing party with a counter reprisal and so on for infinity (University of California Television, n.d.). Certainly, it brought to mind the adage of "an eye for an eye makes the whole world blind," and the message seems logically sensible. Lastly, in terms of philosophical underpinnings of restorative justice from Desmond Tutu, he reminded people we are not chickens; however, we are eagles, and we are meant to fly. It is remarkable Desmond TuTu would choose the analogy of the eagle, as the eagle has great symbolism and importance spiritually for indigenous people. It is believed to be the bird flying above all other birds and is the liaison to the spirit world. The story TuTu chose to share is powerful as the story allowed the listener to ascribe the meaning as they interpret the story, while also understanding our place in the world.

NATIVE AMERICAN CIRCLE PRACTICES: A REVIEW

In academia, the literature and in practice, talking circles, circle practices, Circles, and restorative justice have a similar structure. However, where the practices delineate is in their origins and how they are used today. Circle practices, which are the focus of this circle, focus primarily on the Native Americans of North America practices. This paper will go further into detail in academic journals, testimony from elders, and resources via online videos which fill in the picture with more detail, the simple as it is elaborate use of circle practices. To understand circle practices, it is still paramount to gain an understanding of other practices such as restorative justice, Circles and talking circles. The core is the same for these different practices; however, they slightly differentiate for their uses. For example, authors describe restorative justice and Circles to be used in criminal justice settings to restore healing (Boyes-Watson et al., 2015; Pranis et al., 2003; Sered, 2019), there are specific Circles for very specific situations such as education, family counseling, sexual abuse to name a few (Boyes-Watson et al., 2015). Circle practices focus on the indigenous roots of the circle (Boyes-Watson et al., 2015, Ross 1996) with certain protocols or guidelines culturally appropriate to indigenous people such as use of smudging by burning of sage and other such details this literature review will go more in depth with later in this paper.

Also, recognition of indigenous people and knowledge to the origins of the practice is a common theme throughout the literature (Pranis et al., 2003). The Yukon and northern Canada region is seen as a place where First Nations Tribes contributed a great deal of knowledge and key components of Circles (Pranis et al., 2003; Ross, 1996). Different author's confirmation of the First Nations people's contribution certainly adds to academic validity.

Circle Practices

A key theme is *conflicts are a part of life.* This is a fundamental truth in my own understanding of the universe. Authors then go on to note people should *use circles to communicate.* Different authors have outlined every minor detail as it pertains to holding a circle for different occasions. Circle practices deal with a Native American spiritual focus; however certain authors such as Pranis note the circle can be amended to fit really whatever situation you feel conflict and communication pertain to. Literature points out a near universal application of circle practices (Pranis et al., 2003). Circle practices have a positive nature to them, are constructive in building one another up, and are designed for healing (Pranis et al., 2003). The community aspect of Circle practices is important in communities taking back the narrative of what is occurring in their communities (Nicolaidis & Raymaker, 2015). I concur with the literature that circle practices can be healing and applied to most situations. An interesting point in the literature is the distinction between act and individual (Pranis et al., 2003; Ross; 1996). This is a reminder I feel is often lost in the Western perspective.

Ross (1996) points out in an interview, often times, community dysfunction in indigenous communities can be a result of colonization and trauma. This point certainly holds relevance in the topic of inherited Post Traumatic Stress Disorder. While not all problems for indigenous peoples can be transcribed to colonists as wars existed between tribes before colonization, many community problems now can be logically ascribed to a desecration of culture by western society and a disconnection from indigenous people's traditional ways.

Interconnectedness

In relation to Ross's explanation on the reverse hierarchy of beings for indigenous people, Pranis, Stuart and Wedge (2003) also concur with this perception. I agree with the way both of these researchers went about acquiring this knowledge, as they did so through the use of elders. In an indigenous, decolonizing framework, this is the correct and appropriate protocol for knowing what is right in a certain culture. For example, take my critiques of this paper: In an indigenous paradigm, a 30-year old with no children would not be considered an elder who is to ascribe how to live or think. For the sake of academia, I continue to walk with a moccasin on one foot and a tennis shoe on the other to navigate the academic terrain and its criticisms. Pranis, Stuart, and Wedge (2003) describe an elder who says "take the horn toad, if you think you are better than them, you will never hear their voice/cry, even if you sit forever in the sun," which to me gives perspective on the importance of the theme of interrelatedness and interconnectedness.

A theme of the literature surrounding circle practices is we are profoundly interconnected (TheDRCA2, 2015). In a training video to Washtenaw County Trial Court and the Dispute Resolution Center on April 22, 2015, Pranis discussed how in the principle of physics, all things are related, and how a principle in physics of the butterfly effect which reveals a butterfly flapping its wings in Brazil will have effects felt in weather in China (TheDRCA2, 2015).

Ross (1996) makes a profound paradigm shifting point in both his book and in a video, where he states the different hierarchies of being for both indigenous culture and colonist culture. Ross recognizes in western culture, the hierarchy is humans on top, followed by animals, then the plants and trees, and lastly the Earth. Ross contends indigenous peoples would assert mother earth is on the top of the hierarchy, for without her we would not be standing on anything. Ross then states the indigenous perspective would then rank plants and trees as second most important, for they are the medicine with which we gain life. Ross states over 70% of western medicine has the root of their medicine from an indigenous plant or organism as well (Hazen, 2012; heartspeak, 2013; Ross, 1996).

While there are countless numbers of stories that could be recounted of Ross on exploring the indigenous philosophy behind circle practices and his work with victims and families of sexual abuse at Hollow Water community in Manitoba, Ross really nails the key difference between western and indigenous culture, which are relationship of things versus characteristic of things and connection versus disconnection. Ross's explanation makes a great deal of sense to myself as a researcher, as I certainly recall being taught the characteristic of things in school growing up as opposed to the relationship between things. In my indigenous education, I have found things to frequently be described in their relation to others. For example, when I introduce myself as an Oneida person, the proper protocol is to explain my tribe in relation to its geographic space, then followed by your families' clan, and then lastly your name. This is done purposefully, as all these things are related and build off of one another. In example, the land is where the tribe comes from in their Creation story, the clan tells a story of the family's place in history and the community and putting yourself last is reflective of the thinking in those communal systems.

In terms of connection versus disconnection, Ross articulates thing strongly in his text when he describes the example of certain Aboriginal people talking to rocks. This rings true in my own indigenous culture, as my people the of the Oneida translate to "People of the Standing Stone" where it is believed a large stone came to our aid in a time of need. The point Ross makes is in a certain indigenous society's, if a person is not talking to rocks, then there believes to be a problem with them because they are believed to be disconnected. However, Ross points out if in a settler society someone decided to talk to rocks, they in turn would be deemed mentally unstable or believed by western medicine there is a problem with him. This paradoxical schism Ross points out between western society beliefs and Aboriginal beliefs is incredibly helpful in naming the divide to therefore recognize ways to better understand one another. I believe this rings true a great deal in my navigation and understanding of academia in juxtaposition with my indigenous lifestyle and education. A supporting example of this would be the concept of time. For many Native American people, time is believed to be a cyclical while Western society view time in a linear Gregorian calendar. All of the above mentioned points relate to circle practices in recognizing the spiritual intention behind different practices (Batley, 2004; Bender & Armour, 2007; Blue & Blue, 2001; Boyes-Watson, 2005; Hadley, 2001; Hazen, 2012; heartspeak, 2013; Huculak, 2001; King, 1997; Mackey, 2000; Melton, 1995; Meyer, 2002).

A seminal point made by Ross is concerning one of the layered meanings of the sacred medicine wheel (Bopp & Bopp, 1989; Coyhis, 2012; Lavallee, 2007; McGabe, 2008; Ross, 1996) which deals with the four colors of the people of the world. This is sacred knowledge and information that I was told by my great uncles on the Oneida Reservation when I was a teenager (F. Cornelius, in personal interview, July 6th, 2010; H. Cornelius, in personal interview, July 6th, 2010). Although, credit to Ross here as I had never had the concept explained to me in such detail. The teaching comes from two different tribal groups, being the Cree and Ojibway. These two different cultural groups having the same teaching also seems to speak to the spiritual nature of circle practices (Batley, 2004; Bender & Armour, 2007; Blue & Blue, 2001; Boyes-Watson, 2005; Hadley, 2001; Hazen, 2012; heartspeak, 2013; Huculak, 2001; King, 1997; Mackey, 2000; Melton, 1995; Meyer, 2002), of perhaps some original truth or original teachings across cultures.

This specific teaching of the sacred medicine wheel is concerning the four different colors of peoples on mother earth, being the black, red, yellow and white-skinned people (Bopp & Bopp, 1989; Ross, 1996). The central point Ross relays here is the four-color groups did not all start at the same time (Ross, 1996). The people of color were thought to be the oldest and were gifted with the "power of sound in Creation." An example is cited of the Aboriginal people of Australia who are thought to have sung into existence what we in a western sense see as the physical landscape. For the people of red-colored skin in what is known as North America by westerners today, these people were given a deep understanding of the relationship between the four orders of the universe. Next came the people of the yellow-colored skin, and they are believed to be gifted an understanding of "the human mind and body" (Ross, 1996, p. 287). Lastly in the teachings of the four colors comes the white-skinned brothers and sisters. These people are thanked by indigenous elders for their gift of the English language, which acts as a bridge for different cultures to better understand one another. As Ross points out, the gift of the English language allows different tribes to learn from one another, "so the Blackfoot could learn from the Mi'kmaq, the Cree from the Navajo, and so on" (Ross, 1996, p. 287). The articulation of the colors being associated with the groups of people was something I was taught by my Great Uncle Frank Cornelius (F. Cornelius, in personal interview, July 6th, 2010), however the origins associated with the regions is a teaching new to me, however, rings true in validity in terms of my indigenous understanding of the universe. The methodology used by the researcher is equally sound, in listening to the teachings of elders from indigenous tribal nations. Native American people across all tribes would consider this form of validity to be the ideal standard.

The Sacred Tree is a book referred and cited across texts for the author's insight into indigenous philosophy and spirituality (Pranis et al., 2003; Ross, 1996). Written with knowledge of approximately 30 elders across Turtle Island, it is written with the combined sacred knowledge of elders across different tribes. The teachings in the book are all teachings that speak to events and spiritual experiences in my own life, often unexplainable. The authors articulate deeply profound spiritual ideas in simple terms. The 12 teachings of The Sacred Tree (p. 290-292) are:

1. Wholeness.
2. Change.
3. Change occurs in cycles or patterns.
4. The seen and the unseen.
5. Human beings are spiritual as well as physical.
6. Human beings can always acquire new gifts, but they must struggle to do so.
7. There are four dimensions of 'true learning.'
8. Spiritual dimension has four related capacities.
9. Human beings must be active participants in the unfolding of their own potentialities.
10. The doorway of the will (volition) must be passed through if someone wishes to become more or different than they are now.
11. Anyone who sets out will be aided.
12. The only source of failure on a journey will be the traveler's own failure to follow the teachings of The Sacred Tree.

These twelve points were originally printed in 1984, and speak completely true to me on a mental, emotional and spiritual level. There is a theme in the literature there will always be another chance (TheDRCA2, 2015) and the path has unlimited patience for those who are willing (Ross, 1996). I believe it is for good reason the book of *The Sacred Tree* is cited from various researchers surrounding circle practices.

Decolonizing Ideology Aspect of Talking Circles

Furthermore, concerning the philosophical underpinnings of talking circles and circle practices is the notion of decolonizing ideologies (Smith, 2013). Linda Tuhiwai Smith lays out 25 foundational ideas of decolonizing ideologies (Smith, 2013, p. 144-162) that overlap with many of the same ideologies of circle practices, whether named or unnamed in previous literature, used by practitioners today. Listed in no particular order of significance, the 25 foundational and seminal projects of decolonization are (Smith, 2013, p. 144-162):

1. Claiming.
2. Testimonies.
3. Storytelling.
4. Celebrating Survival- Survivance.
5. Remembering.
6. Indigenizing and indigenist processes.
7. Intervening.
8. Revitalizing and regenerating.

9. Connecting.
10. Reading.
11. Writing and Theory Making.
12. Representing.
13. Gendering.
14. Envisioning.
15. Reframing.
16. Restoring.
17. Returning.
18. Democratizing and indigenist governance.
19. Networking.
20. Naming.
21. Protecting.
22. Creating.
23. Negotiating.
24. Discovering the beauty of our knowledge.
25. Sharing.

All of the aforementioned listed projects of decolonization have the ability to relate in some way to circle practices. While items number ten and eleven of reading, writing, and theory respectively may not be in the physical circle process, they are being used in the articulation of this literature review as an enactment of those projects.

Truth and Reconciliation Commission

The Truth and Reconciliation Commission in Canada is not an academic journal; however, it is a public policy report offering insight into the practice of carrying out reconciliation in Canada. Although considered "messy" or uncomfortable by some going through the process, this report offers a comprehensive perspective into the practice of carrying out truth and reconciliation. One of the key points in the report is the admittance of responsibility by the Canadian government of the wrongdoing done toward the First Nations people.

Indigenous Law versus Public Policy

Restorative justice has been used throughout legal traditions in Canada as well (Horn, 2016; Ross, 1996). The use of indigenous traditions in first nations communities has brought healing to a great many deal of people. Use of restorative justice is a common practice in tradition with the Canadian First Nations people and with other Canadian residents in the region (Ross, 1996).

Horn recognizes across almost all First Nations' use of restorative justice there is "promoting community healing, reconciliation, and the reintegration of the offender" (Horn, 2016). This report is more than fair in its recognition of different laws and declarations, such as the United Nations Declaration on the Rights of Indigenous Peoples (Horn, 2016). The researcher concludes with a point of indigenous groups now learning from the practice of restorative justice, which is fitting in a cyclical nature of life. This would stand to reason as Native Americans do believe a great deal in circles and the power of connection and interrelatedness (Horn, 2016; Ross, 1996). Horn's (2016) research appropriately identifies legislation on a world scale and nationally for Canada which connect the philosophies of indigenous legal traditions with the concepts of restorative justice.

Literature of Protocol for Talking Circles

Different authors describe defining guidelines and protocols of circle practices (Boyes-Watson et al., 2015). This includes introduction of the talking piece and other terms used in the circle . Kay Pranis does a particularly effective job across books and film in pointing out the logistics of holding a circle. What I admire about Pranis' practices are her continuous recognition of doing what works best for the researcher, or the "keeper of the circle." Pranis makes a methodical science out of what could potentially be perceived by others as an elusive art. Pranis tracks logistically and efficiently how to "as keeper of the circle" work on the self, through various reflective practice which include mediation, walks, and music. I have found as a practitioner of circle practices, this makes a great deal of difference for how an individual enters a space (Pranis et al., 2003). It is repeatedly pointed out by Pranis sometimes the keeper of the circle goes first or last, depending on the situation. Often times it is believed by researchers going first is important when the keeper of the circle wishes to set the tone for being vulnerable in the circle. I also believe this to be an effective practice through my own lived experiences, in being vulnerable so others may do the same. Pranis wisely argues the keeper of the circle is the last to speak when bringing together differing opinions (Pranis et al., 2003). This makes sense to myself, and I have heard this same notion across cultures, and even from a speech by Simon Sinek titled "Leaders Eat Last." I concur with Pranis in speaking last when bridging different opinions as others can be easily influenced by the leader or simply say what they think the leader wants to hear. I believe this is one of the strengths of circle practices, there is no one correct answer or response, it is simply the truth.

Granillo et al. (2010) listed the protocol of talking circles in an effective manner: efficient and encompassing of a grand idea in a short amount of text and are as follows:

Traditional native American Talking Circles are commonly composed of 5–10 participants who sit shoulder to shoulder in a circle facing one another. A facilitator opens a session with a traditional story and health topic, and then the floor is opened to the participants for discussion. Each member is typically afforded the opportunity to share information, ideas, and stories without fear or challenge of interruption by other members. The process is initiated by the facilitator and typically a stick, arrow, feather, rock, or other talisman is passed around the circle. The participant who wishes to talk holds the talisman and when finished, he or she passes it on. The sharing of information among participants is in a supportive, comforting environment.

The basic structure here really seems to be a foundation for many circle practices evolving from this design. While the above description of talking circles is intriguing, the authors go in further detail of description in a way I had never had the gift of reading or hearing before while describing a talking circle and is description of an Apache talking circle. The details of the talking circle are nearly similar to other descriptions of talking circles, with slight differences in the words to describe items or protocol. The author's describe the talking circle with Apache roots as (Granillo et al., 2010):

the following is a comprehensive list of talking circle elements: (1) exploring points of difference or difficulty balanced by protocols of listening and respect for varied viewpoints, (2) space is provided for productive possibilities rather than criticism and confrontation, (3) burden basket, (''an Apache ornately hand-woven basket typically hung outside door, where prior to entering one symbolically places their ''burdens'' into the basket so concerns do not disrupt the harmony of home or place.'') (4), [19] clearing ritual which starts the talking circle, (5) closing ritual, were the talisman or talking stick is passed around to ensure nothing remains unsaid prior to closing. The structure for the talisman includes speaking honestly and being brief. When the participant receives the talisman, he/she should state a feeling word describing the secret, burden or issue being addressed and states how he or she can relate, while other group participants should listen attentively with respect. Group members may speak only when holding the talisman, questions and verbal exchanges may take place, but only by permission from whoever is holding the stick or talisman [20]. When anyone is asked a question, they may choose to answer or pass the talisman while other group participants should listen attentively with respect. Group members may speak only when holding the talisman, questions and verbal exchanges may take place, but only by permission from whoever is holding the stick or talisman [20]. When anyone is asked a question, they may choose to answer or pass the talisman.

Another theme in the literature is circle process is about accessing collective wisdom (TheDRCA2, 2015). The protocol of the group is the agreed upon guidelines by the participants. These guidelines are about setting some agreements concerning how we are going to treat one another The use of the talking piece is also critical, as whoever is holding the talking piece is the only allowed to speak. The keeper of circle is also a participant and they have the responsibility of opening and closing protocol (TheDRCA2, 2015).

Burden Basket in Talking Circles

A description of the burden basket was given in further detail by a group of researchers comprised of members of the Anishnabe Nation, the Eastern Band of Cherokee, as well as a colleague and ally (Wilbur et al., 2001):

One such structure and ritual was the use of a burden basket in the talking circles, adopted from its Apache heritage and tradition. A burden basket is an ornately handwoven basket of various sizes typically hung at the outside door or entrance to one's home. Prior to entering their home or the homes of their friends and relatives, the Apache Indians symbolically placed their burdens into the basket so these concerns would not disrupt the harmony and balance of their homes and their interactions and relationships with family, friends, and loved ones (p. 372)

This teaching rings true with my personal experience, where I have heard the euphemism, "stuff your sorrys in a sack," along with another common euphemism, "leave your troubles at the door." These are reminiscent of the traditional practice of burden baskets.

The Theme of Vulnerability in Circles

Building off of the theme of vulnerability in the circle of the circle keeper, authors have pointed out how honesty and courage allows others to be vulnerable and open up and have real communication (Pranis et al., 2013). The authors further state being honest has the ability to be transforming. This theme will be revisited later in the oral history critique. I would further agree with this point of honesty and courage through my own experiences. However, I would assert all groups are different, and there certainly has to be a great deal of buy in from the participants, which authors recognize as well. It is noted participants must want to be in the circle and be willing and able to speak. For example, if there was not buy in and trust built in a group and you as the circle keeper try to open up by being vulnerable in the circle, you may get some raised eyebrows or side glances to the people around the circle. On the other hand, Pranis (2013) and other authors make it explicitly clear the importance of starting the circle with rapport and trust building questions people feel comfortable answering.

The other side of the coin of opening up and being vulnerable is the ability to have the option to remain silent. The recording musician Aubrey Drake Graham has a song where he notes a "You know, a wise man once said nothing at all" (Graham, 2018). Pranis and other authors also make it exceedingly clear when introducing every type of talking circle it must be an ability of the participants to choose to pass when called upon. In a western mindset, this notion of not speaking would seem as though the person is not participating. However, from an indigenous mindset, choosing not to speak at that time is a valid response, and the momentarily silence holds room for emotions to build. The ability for an individual to listen as fervently as they speak (TheDRCA2, 2015) is a concept in western culture which is rarely acknowledged. Also, in the silence is also where there is mystery, unknown, and our connection to something greater than ourselves (Batley, 2004; Blue & Blue,2001; Bender & Armour, 2007; Boyes-Watson, 2005; Mackey, 2000; Melton, 1995; Meyer, 2002; Hadley, 2001; Hazen, 2012; heartspeak, 2013; Huculak, 2001; King, 1997).

Oral Tradition of Circle Practice Protocol

In interesting conversations with family members who have used talking circles on my families reservation in Oneida, Wisconsin, my grandmother, Eleanor Bailey, told me stories of people having talking circles in Oneida where the leader of the ceremony would bring an eagle feather or other sacred object. My grandmother said it was told by the leader of the ceremony whoever was holding the feather was unable to tell a lie (E. Bailey, personal communication, February 3, 2020). This critical information is valid in Indigenous knowledge as it deals with the transmission of information from an elder and from a family resource. The comment of the eagle feather and speaking the truth was a protocol I had never heard articulated; however, the notion of telling the truth in circle practices is a common theme in the literature. My grandmother's teachings to me of the circle practices use of honesty aligns with other academics in the notion of being honest is transforming (Pranis et al., 2003). This triangulation of information creates a greater picture and depth of complexities within circle practices.

My cousin, Edi Cornelius-Grosskopf, also uses talking circles with approximately 12 to 14 other people (both native and non-native) at her book readings, and Edi said it was amazing the things you would hear when you really listen to others and allow them to speak (E. Cornelius-Grosskopf, personal communication, February 2, 2020). Edi described how Native and non-Native people would talk about abuse, trauma, addiction, among other troubling issues. Edi noted the greatest gift we can give to others is the gift of empathy and how talking circles teach these principles. Edi also noted the descent into the figurative hole with someone else and seeing it through their eyes can help build and shape an empathic skillset that may benefit the participants for life (E. Cornelius-Grosskopf, personal communication, February 2, 2020). Empathy in circles is an important theme in the literature. My cousin Edi's perspective was eye opening to me, and again was articulated in a way I had not comprehended from the literature. I find the nuance of word choice and delivery in oral tradition adds extra meaning in my own understanding of reality and leads to better understanding of these practices .

Seminal Talking Circle Workshop

A particularly thorough video is of a filmed workshop designed to give instruction on how to conduct a talking circle and explains why each step of the talking circle is taken. The keeper of the circle and facilitator of the workshop is Coyhis (2012) of the Mohican Nation and leader of the Wellbreity Movement. The film, titled "Recovery is a process not an event," begins with an explanation of the opening used as a reminder of interrelatedness. This specific workshop teaches of using an altar in the middle of the circle, and in the altar is a big red cloth, which represents our very big universe and all the circles and cycles moving in it such as solar systems, moons, and the four seasons. The circle keeper does a very clear job of explaining we are all a small part of something big and are all interrelated. The circle keeper of the workshop made an interesting point a person must not think the world revolves around them, for you must be able to see us all as interrelated things to enter the circle. When we sit in the circle, we recognize we are a small part of something big (Coyhis, 2012).

The workshop is notable for going into description on processes I had not seen explained in detail elsewhere. Another example of this is the description of the abalone shell which holds the sage in the middle of the altar, which is said to represent the womb of the earth. The keeper of the circle explains the shape of the shell attracts the heartbeat, the frequency of the Earth. The analogous example used by the keeper of the circle is how certain antennas are shaped like shells to attract certain frequencies. The heartbeat of Earth is where interconnectedness happens in the circle (Coyhis, 2012, 6:46). The keeper of the circle's description is profound in these spiritual teachings and are not noted elsewhere. The descriptions are in-line with other indigenous philosophies I have learned over the years.

Next the workshop film on conducting a talking circle does a thorough job in describing the use of the plant sage, and the plant's traditional calming properties. The keeper of the circle explains the medicine of the sage is released when it is burned, similar to how some plant's medicine is released in hot water such as a tea (Coyhis, 2012, 7:13). The circle keeper asks participants not to smudge wrong, first start with wafting the smudge smoke toward the heart area, and then up over our heads, "that connects the greatest distance that the human being must travel in his whole life, 18 inches, from the head to the heart" (Coyhis, 2012, 7:55).

Another important point is of the eagle feather fan. The fan is further described in importance by the circle keeper of the workshop as he states the eagle feather fan is a reminder to be willing to switch views, such as from the view of the eagle (Coyhis, 2012). The facilitator recognizes sometimes we can have the perspective of a mouse when we are stressed, however our ability to switch perspectives will allow us to grow. Again, my critique here is nothing but positive support as it speaks to me on an emotional, mental and spiritual level (Coyhis, 2012).

The literature points out the smudge is then lit, the fan is put through the smoke on both sides, and then there is a counter-clockwise rotation of the smudge being fanned four times around in a circle, as each circle shows respect for every color and direction. Then during the smudging, the circle keeper of this specific workshop let everyone know energy moves in a circle, not linearly, and participants must connect in a circle for the interrelatedness. The keeper of the circle makes a point all participants want to be at a place of interconnectedness with one another (Coyhis, 2012).

In addition, a principle of the circle is what you learn there, you leave it there. This is very interesting, particularly when trying to share information of participants, which would violate one of the proposed sacred protocol of the circle. Also, the keeper of the circle describes the circle gives first a gift of belonging, second a gift of trust, and then after this people have the ability to start sharing (Coyhis, 2012).

It is also pointed out anyone can lead a circle, and there is no degree required to run a circle (Coyhis, 2012). This a valid point and an essential reminder for myself and others in this work of circle practices. The circle keeper is told to welcome everyone, and then someone would light either sage, cedar, or sweet grass. That is when the smudge happens. The facilitator then starts a subject. In this description, the facilitator is to set to the left of the eastern door. The explanation is crucial as it defines clear roles, guidelines, and protocols for how to properly conduct a talking circle while honoring indigenous philosophies and all peoples.

It is noted how the talking circle must go around completely once it has started. The leader of the workshop noted talking circles should not be timed. This aligns with my understanding of the indigenous concept of time. A different type of talking circle is noted in the literature where it can be timed, and the person who chooses to speak grabs the talking piece out the middle and puts it back in the middle when done, in no particular order.

Native American Importance of Talking Circles

Talking circles are a traditional native American practice with cultural significance to different Native American people (Arthur & Porter, 2019; Conant, 2020; Doria et al., 2020; Luna et al., 2020; Wallace, 2019; Williams & Brant, 2019). In an extant study by Hodge (1996), 400 participants were involved in American Indian Women Talking Circles to address cervical cancer, it was determined Indigenous women were much more likely to respond positively to culturally sensitive information when delivered in a sensitive manner. This study was thorough in its methods of selecting eight different American Indian clinics randomly (Hodge, 1996). This step by the researcher ensures stronger validity of the study to gain a better representation of their population, which was reflective within the more recent literature for a greater theme of Native American importance on circles as a symbol and a framework for group communication (Colmant, 1999; Garrett et al., 2001; Tafoya & Kouris, 2003; Verbos et al., 2011).

An additional study by Winters (2014) found talking circles to be well received and can significantly improve in the training for Incident Command System. The study used talking circles as a delivery method, which was intended to be a culturally accepted way of communication. It focused on the oral tradition and storytelling aspect of talking circles, both common themes in the literature. A theme in the literature with talking circles is through storytelling, people build trust (Winters, 2014). Also, as reminded by Coyhis (2012), a guideline in the practice of talking circles is thinking circles are sacred.

Multicultural Use of Talking Circles

One example of a study examining the use of talking circles with nonindigenous participants was done in an alcohol and drug intervention program using six talking circles comprised of six to 10 people in each group and was found to be an effective tool across cultures (Wilbur et al., 2001). The circle of a traditional Donelawega, in Cherokee translates to mean people coming together for a special purpose, otherwise referred to as Pow-Wows (Wilbur et al., 2001). This was conducted by predominantly Indigenous researchers to a predominantly nonindigenous population while keeping the indigenous philosophy of a talking circle, and the example would be the use of indigenous language in the opening and closing. It was enlightening as a researcher to view the positive impact of talking circles on nonindigenous populations with a sample of approximately 36 to 60 different researchers. A critique of the study is it could have been clearer in sample size, and while I recognize the authors were also imploring technique to preserve the confidentiality of the student participants, the sample size may have been clearer in the data; however, the principle for using talking circles was sound in the research. The authors noted the idea of talking circles for their study emerged from the Cherokee tradition of Donelawega, which is building community through the life of the circle (Wilbur et al., 2001). This study conducted valid research by incorporating traditional knowledge successfully in an academic format.

A Word About Cultural Appropriation

The literature of talking circles also touches on the concept of cultural appropriation. This was illustrated by the perspective of one particular respondent to the workshop video put on by Coyhis (2012), which stated, "omg what a crappy white kinda' grasp for money." This response leads me to perceive diverse Native American peoples have different reactions to the same media, as I was profoundly moved by the same information which someone else refused. The issue of cultural appropriation in talking circles is a complex one, and an issue of importance for myself as an Indigenous person, and other Indigenous people may likely have their own perspective on the issue.

While some works recognize Circle taking place any time people are in a certain mindset of community (Baldwin, 1994), I would argue this is part of the Native American tradition of Talking Circles; however, I do feel the protocol involved is sound when Native practices are employed, such as smudging and use of an eagle feather as a talking piece. These procedures are both of figurative importance and physical importance. Smudging is used as a spiritual shield and an eagle feather is believed to have sacred importance to indigenous people across North America. Such spiritual symbols within the practice can provide figurative constructs for the guidelines within the circle and sense of protection within the circle.

When Talking Circles Are Missing the Indigenous Philosophical Foundation

When talking circles are used without alignment to the community, the talking circle seems to yield completely different results, which is rejection by the participants. An example in the literature of particular interest was one where native respondents from different tribes gave candid responses on their perspective of a "Second Wind" program aimed at the cessation of smoking for Native American people through the use of talking circles. The responses were probably some of the most honest I have ever read in a research journal concerning a western practice trying to take the place of an indigenous one. One Native participant from this program spoke to this subject (Daley et al., 2006):

To culturalize the program to fit our Native American needs including incorporating a talking circle, incorporating a self-help group, phone lines, and one of the biggest things I see is that this is so sterile. It's not culturally pleasing to me. Like with the 12 step program they incorporated the 12 steps in a medi-

cine wheel and gave every step a significance to our cultural identity. This (the Second Wind brochure, on the other hand) is just another government issued pamphlet and we've been inundated with them. I mean they're given to us all the time. ... They [Focus groups and programs] are always great starts and they mean well for us as Native people but the problem with that is when they're not culturalized and we can't relate to it then I lose interest as a Native person ... we have to tailor it to ... two things. That's oral history ... remember that our history is oral so we're just used to blowing off anything in writing, and secondly is visual, ... visual identity. Do you want to know what my opinion of it is? I think this gives lip service to Native Americans. I see nothing, other than the title, which is a catchy title. I see a design, other than that I don't see anything mentioned of the talking circle. I see nothing adapted (to Natives). (p. 430)

Where I would critique the study is in the reception of results. While the researchers (Daley et al, 2006) chose to list the participants' own words as a form of in vivo coding of data, the commentary on the results still did not seem to comprehend the point of cultural understanding and cultural differences the participant discussed. Stating the use of a talking circle without any of the cultural, philosophical, or spiritual connections to the practice is an example of cultural appropriation with talking circles. Cultural appropriation has the ability to occur with talking circles or traditional indigenous practices when not done with the help, consultation and insight of indigenous people themselves. However, the research by Daly and their colleagues in 2006 does close by inviting the input of all Native American researchers, which is a step in the right direction for validity and for future research to build upon.

CONCLUSION

Talking circles, circle practices and restorative justice have an importance to Native American people as well as lessons for all people. Circle practices are an indigenous process which encompass different decolonizing ideologies. This literature review initially examined the philosophical underpinnings behind similar practices of restorative justice, circles, circle practices, and talking circles. Thereafter, this literature review explored the explanation of protocol and guidelines for talking circles in the literature. Then, this literature review examined the actual implementation and use of talking circles present in literature. This literature review synthesized and critiqued a combination of different journal articles, books, films, and interviews. There are instances of this literature review also focused on the conversation of cultural appropriation.

A piece of literature I want to close with for this literature review was rearticulated by Kay Pranis and was originally written by Edwin Markham through a poem called "Outwitted." The poem encompasses the philosophy behind circle practices. The poem is of special importance to me because I was first introduced to this poem as a freshman in my undergraduate, and it played a pivotal role in my upbringing and view of the world. It is truly serendipitous this poem would come back into my life through my research on circle practices. While the piece of literature is not from an indigenous piece of wisdom, it is articulated eloquently through the gift of language from our white brothers and sisters in the English language. It goes as follows: "He drew a circle that shut me out-/ Heretic, rebel, a thing to flout./ But love and I had the wit to win:/ We drew a circle and took him In!" (Pranis et al., 2003). Talking circles and circle practices when done correctly create a sense of interconnectedness with others spiritually through a traditional indigenous process.

REFERENCES

Arthur, M., & Porter, C. (2019). Restorying Northern Arapaho food sovereignty. *Journal of Agriculture, Food Systems, and Community Development, 9*(B), 1-16.

Atkinson, J. (2002). *Trauma trails, recreating song lines: The transgenerational effects of trauma in Indigenous Australia*. Spinifex Press.

Baldwin, C. (1994). *Calling the circle: The first and future culture*. Bantam.

Batley, M. (2004). What is the appropriate role of spirituality in restorative justice? *Critical Issues in Restorative Justice*, 365-377.

Bender, K., & Armour, M. (2007). The spiritual components of restorative justice. *Victims & Offenders, 2*(3), 251–267. doi:10.1080/15564880701403967

Blue, A. W., & Blue, M. A. R. (2001). The case for Aboriginal justice and healing: The self perceived through a broken mirror. *The spiritual roots of restorative justice*, 57-79.

Bopp, J., & Bopp, M. (1989). *The sacred tree*. Lotus Press.

Boyes-Watson, C. (2005). Seeds of change: Using peacemaking circles to build a village for every child. *Child Welfare League of America, 84*, 191–208. PMID:15828408

Boyes-Watson, C., & Pranis, K. (2015). *Circle forward: Building a restorative school community*. Living Justice Press.

Colmant, S. A., & Merta, R. J. (1999). Using the sweat lodge ceremony as group therapy for Navajo youth. *Journal for Specialists in Group Work, 24*(1), 55–73. doi:10.1080/01933929908411419

Conant, C. M. (2020). *Recommendations for the effective treatment of methamphetamine addiction with Native American cultural specificity*. Academic Press.

Coyhis, D. (2012, March 21). *How to conduct Talking Circles.mp4* [Video]. YouTube.

Daley, C. M., James, A. S., Barnoskie, R. S., Segraves, M., Schupbach, R., & Choi, W. S. (2006). "Tobacco has a purpose, not just a past": Feasibility of developing a culturally appropriate smoking cessation program for a pan-tribal native population. *Medical Anthropology Quarterly, 20*(4), 421–440. doi:10.1525/maq.2006.20.4.421 PMID:17225653

Doria, C. M., Momper, S. L., & Burrage, R. L. (2020). "Togetherness:" The role of intergenerational and cultural engagement in urban American Indian and Alaskan Native youth suicide prevention. *Journal of Ethnic & Cultural Diversity in Social Work*, 1–18. doi:10.1080/15313204.2020.1770648

Garrett, M. T., Garrett, J. T., & Brotherton, D. (2001). Inner circle/outer circle: A group technique based on Native American healing circles. *Journal for Specialists in Group Work, 26*(1), 17–30. doi:10.1080/01933920108413775

Graham, A. D. (2018). *Emotionless. Scorpon* [CD]. OVO Music.

Granillo, B., Renger, R., Wakelee, J., & Burgess, J. L. (2010). Utilization of the Native American talking circle to teach incident command system to tribal community health representatives. *Journal of Community Health, 35*(6), 625–634. doi:10.100710900-010-9252-7 PMID:20300808

Hadley, M. L. (2001). Introduction: Multifaith reflection on criminal justice. In M. L. Hadley (Ed.), *The spiritual roots of restorative justice* (pp. 1–29). State University of New York Press.

Hazen, D. (2012, October 26). *Rupert Ross* [Video]. YouTube.

heartspeak. (2013, November 12). *Community healing programs with Rupert Ross Trailer* [Video]. YouTube.

Hodge, F. S., Fredericks, L., & Rodriguez, B. (1996). American Indian women's talking circle: A cervical cancer screening and prevention project. *Cancer: Interdisciplinary International Journal of the American Cancer Society, 78*(7), 1592–1597. doi:10.1002/(SICI)1097-0142(19961001)78:7<1592::AID-CNCR39>3.0.CO;2-T PMID:8839577

Horn, K. (2016). *A report on the relationship between restorative justice and Indigenous legal traditions in Canada.* Canada Department of Justice. https://www.justice.gc.ca/eng/rp-pr/jr/rjilt-jrtja/rjilt-jrtja.pdf

Huculak, B. (2001). Epilogue: Justice as hope. In M. L. Hadley (Ed.), *The spiritual roots of restorative justice* (pp. 217–223). State University of New York Press.

Jervis, L. L., Beals, J., Croy, C. D., Klein, S. A., Manson, S. M., & Team, A. S. (2006). Historical consciousness among two American Indian tribes. *The American Behavioral Scientist, 50*(4), 526–549. doi:10.1177/0002764206294053

Johnston-Goodstar, K., & VeLure Roholt, R. (2017). "Our kids aren't dropping out; They're being pushed out": Native American students and racial microaggressions in schools. *Journal of Ethnic & Cultural Diversity in Social Work, 26*(1-2), 30–47. doi:10.1080/15313204.2016.1263818

King, U. (1997). Spirituality. In J. Hinnells (Ed.), *A new handbook of living religions* (pp. 667–691). Blackwell Publishers.

Lavallée, L. (2007). Physical activity and healing through the medicine wheel. *Pimatisiwin, 5*(1), 127–153.

Luna, W. F., Malvezzi, C., Teixeira, K. C., Almeida, D. T., & Bezerra, V. P. (2020). Identity, care and rights: The experience of Talking Circles about the health of Indigenous People. *Revista Brasileira de Educação Médica, 44*(2), e067. doi:10.1590/1981-5271v44.2-20190309.ing

Lyons, O. (Ed.). (1992). *Exiled in the land of the free: Democracy, Indian nations, and the US Constitution.* Clear Light Pub.

Mackey, V. (2000). Holistic restorative justice: A response to McCold. *Contemporary Justice Review, 3*(4), 451–458.

McCabe, G. (2008). Mind, body, emotions and spirit: Reaching to the ancestors for healing. *Counselling Psychology Quarterly, 21*(2), 143–152. doi:10.1080/09515070802066847

Melton, A. P. (1995). Indigenous justice systems: Tribal society is a way of life. *Judicature, 79*, 126–133.

Meyer, J. (2002). It is a gift from the Creator to keep us in harmony: Original (verses alternative) dispute resolution on the Navajo Nation. *International Journal of Public Administration, 25*(11), 1379–1401. doi:10.1081/PAD-120013351

Native American Rights Fund. (2016, October 12). *About peacemaking - Robert Yazzie* [Video]. YouTube.

Nicolaidis, C., & Raymaker, D. M. (2015). Community based participatory research with communities defined by race, ethnicity, and disability: Translating theory to practice. In *The SAGE handbook of action research* (pp. 167–178). SAGE. doi:10.4135/9781473921290.n17

Pihama, L., Smith, L. T., Evans-Campbell, T., Kohu-Morgan, H., Cameron, N., Mataki, T., Te Nana, R., Skipper, H., & Southey, K. (2017). Investigating Māori approaches to trauma-informed care. *Journal of Indigenous Wellbeing: Te Mauri-Pimatisiwin, 2*(3), 18–31.

Pranis, K., Stuart, B., & Wedge, M. (2003). *Peacemaking circles: From crime to community*. Living Justice Press.

Quinn, A. (2007). Reflections on intergenerational trauma: Healing as a critical intervention. *First Peoples Child & Family Review, 3*(4), 72–82. doi:10.7202/1069377ar

Ross, R. (1996). *Returning to the teachings: Exploring Aboriginal justice*. Penguin Canada.

Sered, D. (2019). *Until we Reckon: Violence, mass incarceration, and a road to repair*. The New Press.

Smith, L. T. (2013). *Decolonizing methodologies: Research and indigenous peoples*. Zed Books.

Tafoya, T., & Kouris, N. (2003). Dancing the circle: Native American concepts of healing. *Modern psychology and ancient wisdom: Psychological healing practices from the world's religious traditions*, 125-146.

TheDRCA2. (2015, May 1). *Kay pranis: Using peacemaking circles in juvenile court, 4/22/2015* [Video]. YouTube.

Truth and Reconciliation Commission. (2015). *Honouring the truth, reconciling for the future*. Summary of the final report of the Truth and Reconciliation Commission of Canada.

University of California Television (UCTV). (2008, January 31). *Reconciling love: Archbishop Desmond Tutu* [Video]. YouTube.

Vansina, J. M. (1985). *Oral tradition as history*. University of Wisconsin Press.

Verbos, A. K., Gladstone, J. S., & Kennedy, D. M. (2011). Native American values and management education: Envisioning an inclusive virtuous circle. *Journal of Management Education, 35*(1), 10–26. doi:10.1177/1052562910384364

Wallace, M. (2019). *Timeless traditions: Council circles in a modern world*. Washington State University. http://hdl.handle.net/2376/14211

Wilbur, J. R., Wilbur, M., Garrett, M. T., & Yuhas, M. (2001). Talking circles: Listen, or your tongue will make you deaf. *Journal for Specialists in Group Work, 26*(4), 368–384. doi:10.1080/01933920108413785

Williams, K., & Brant, S. (2019). Good words, good food, good mind. *Journal of Agriculture, Food Systems, and Community Development, 9*(B), 1-14.

Wilson, S. (2008). *Research is ceremony. In Indigenous research methods*. Fernwood.

Winters, A., & America, N. (2014). Using Talking Circles in the classroom. *Heartland Community College*, 1-8.

ADDITIONAL READING

Baldwin, C., & Linnea, A. (2010). *The circle way: A leader in every chair*. Berrett-Koehler.

Hyslop, P. E., & Jarrett, B. N. (2019). Circle peace-making in Alaska: A return to Indigenous practice through intercultural dialogue. In S. Peleg (Ed.), *Intercultural and interfaith dialogues for global peace-building and stability* (pp. 146–164). IGI Global. doi:10.4018/978-1-5225-7585-6.ch007

Mosimege, M. D. (2017). Research protocols and ethical considerations in Indigenous Knowledge Systems. In P. Ngulube (Ed.), *Handbook of research on theoretical perspectives on Indigenous Knowledge Systems in developing countries* (pp. 156–172). IGI Global. doi:10.4018/978-1-5225-0833-5.ch007

Pranis, K. (2015). *Little book of circle processes: A new/old approach to peacemaking*. Simon and Schuster.

Walker, P. O. (2019). Indigenous ceremonial peacemaking: The restoration of balance and harmony. In M. W. Lutfy & C. Toffolo (Eds.), *Handbook of research on promoting peace through practice, academia, and the arts* (pp. 299–319). IGI Global. doi:10.4018/978-1-5225-3001-5.ch015

KEY TERMS AND DEFINITIONS

American Indian: A term commonly used to describe indigenous people who derive from the region which was inhabited before the United States of America (U.S.).

Burden Basket: Used in Apache style talking circles, this is a woven basket where individuals symbolically place their burdens or concerns into so as to release them from oneself.

Circles: Another common term to refer to circle practices, talking circles, or restorative justice.

Communication: The mechanism by which individuals share meaning between one another.

Decolonizing Ideologies: Smith (2013) outlined 25 decolonizing ideologies for indigenous people to reclaim indigenous ways of thinking in academia and life.

Eagle Feather: In certain Native American traditions, the eagle is the bird above all other birds and is a liaison between creation and the spirit world. Eagle feathers are sometimes used as sacred talismans, or talking pieces, during talking circles, and protected by U.S. federal legislation.

Native American: A term used to describe Indigenous peoples who derive from the countries that comprise the North, South, and Central Americas, and commonly used to refer to those indigenous to the continental U.S.

Restorative Justice: A practice which seeks to bring about reconciliation and healing for both the abused and the abuser through a circle practice of communication.

Spirituality: Difficult to describe in words, yet spirituality is often mystical, mysterious, and tied to a connection with the sacred space defined by the individual or culture.

Talisman: A sacred object which people use during a talking circle, and whomever holds the object has the right to talk while everyone else listens.

Talking Circles: A traditional Native American practice of communication which brings a group of people together in a circle and uses a talisman or other talking piece to distinguish who is speaking as everyone else listens.

Chapter 10
Accessibility of Land Claims Records at Kruger National Park of South Africa

Nkholedzeni Sidney Netshakhuma
University of Mpumalanga, South Africa

ABSTRACT

This chapter presents a study conceptualized to assess the accessibility of land claims records preserved at the Kruger National Park (KNP) of South Africa. The study used a qualitative method through document analysis and interviews. The sample of the study comprised land claimants and archivists based at the KNP archives. The key finding revealed land claimants use their democratic rights through the Promotion of Access to Information Act of 2000 to request land claim records from KNP archives. The findings aid tools were essential to assess records preserved in the archives even though some of the records were not found in the park.

INTRODUCTION

South African land claimants faced challenges to access records about forced removal in the park kept at the Kruger National Park (KNP) archives. Access in this chapter is described as the authority granted by an archivist, so that he or she may obtain records from or perform research using archival materials. The land claim was a form of restoring human rights for the people who were dispersed in the land to regain access to records. The land claims program aims to facilitate settlement of land claims in national parks in collaboration with the Land Claims Commission of South Africa (SANParks, 2019). Social justice and the power of records to recover hidden or forgotten memories have become an important memory (Bastian, 2017). Records about the removal of people from parks were kept in the KNP archives. Hence, it was the responsibilities of the KNP archives to provide access to all land records about the past removal of the people which were to be supported through the process of claiming the land to ensure their process into archives was a safe one that does not cause any personal damage to themselves or their families.

DOI: 10.4018/978-1-7998-3729-9.ch010

BACKGROUND

Land dispossession of Africans was central to colonialism and apartheid in South Africa (Kepe, 2013). The majority of South African people's loss of the heritage of land comes as a result of the apartheid laws of discriminating people based on race. The Native Land Act 27 of 1913 restricted the area of land for lawful black South African occupation of land (Jili & Masuku, 2017, p. 551). The Act ensured at least 10% of the South Africa land was being reserved for the Blacks. Other legislation such as the Group Areas Act No. 41 of 1950 denied people to live in areas reserved for white minority, which further extended the principle of removing people. Furthermore, in 1959, the Promotion of Bantu Self Government Act 46 of 1959 was enacted to establish the Bantustans homelands and to establish homeland states. Homeland states include countries such as Venda, Transkei, Bophuthatswana, Venda, and Ciskei (TBVC) (Netshakhuma 2017). These homelands were not recognized as sovereignty state because of the South Africa apartheid laws.

The above-mentioned legislation empowered the apartheid government to remove people from various areas to establish a national park. The removal of people was done through unfair dispossessions, limitation of land rights, human rights abuse, and restriction of the movements of people, all of which have characterized the oppressive period (Netshakhuma, 2017). Because of the apartheid legislation, most of the people were removed from their forefather land as a result of the apartheid law of forced removal. This statement was acknowledged by Tavuyanago (2017) who indicated the reasons for the government to remove black people from their land were to establish a national park system. In line with the racially discriminatory political system of apartheid and consistent with exclusionary approaches to conservation, many people were forcefully evicted from their land to make space for the establishment of protected areas known as the national parks (Krüger et al., 2016).

At the beginning of the 20th Century in South Africa, the colonial Transvaal government, under Paul Kruger, began the process of establishing the national park known as the Kruger National Park by removing the original inhabitants from their homestead to create and expand the park. The government removed inhabitants of the park through intimidation and selective use of violence and without consultations. The result has been the creation of a diaspora of various families and tribes in search of their historical roots (Skelcher 2003). It seems most of the people removed from the park lost their connection to the area and ancestral spirits for such a long time. By March 1991, disposed people demanded their land. Some went so far reoccupy their land. Under the new South African Constitution, the government enacted the Restitution of Land Rights Act. This act allowed people to file claims for the recovery of lost land resulting from the removal of black people going back to 1913.

The year 1994 was regarded in South Africa as a significant milestone of political transformation, although there are still disagreements about land distribution and unequal societies. South Africa gained democracy in 1994 and started the process to redistribute the land to the previously disadvantaged people. The distribution of land processes led to the people who were moved away from the parks to claim land in protected areas such as KNP. Kruger et al. (2016) echoed this statement and noted the majority of people laid legal claim to gain back the land lost on the establishment of KNP. This shows the issue of land reform was the spotlight and their appeared to be political pressure by people on various structures of government to deal with the concern of accessing land records (Iyer, 2017).

Several land claims lodged within the national park were at different stages of settlements, such as QwaQwa land claim at Golden Gate National Park and Colchester land claim (SANParks, 2019). It seems many peoples around the KNP possessed lands in the park of which they were unlawfully removed. The land claimants were removed from KNP and resettled in towns surrounding the national park. The fact that land reform is embedded in the Constitution Act 1996 of the Republic of South Africa dictates the government cannot disregard its responsibilities of distribution of land to dispossessed people in South Africa (Pienaar, 2015). This meant redistribution of land should be implemented within the context of the Constitution and specifically within the property clause, which is Section 25 of the Constitution of the Republic of South Africa (Iyer, 2017, p. 510). Further, this implied the redistribution of land should be done in compliance with national legislation (Iyer, 2017).

Land claims from dispossessed Black landowners were not considered until 1994 when the new democratic South Africa came to power. With the advent of the democratic system in South Africa in 1994, land inequalities were addressed through the land reforms program, which was also enshrined in the South Africa bill of Rights. The South Africa government launched a land project to repatriate the land to the people who were forcefully removed in the park. The land distribution to previously disadvantaged groups was a high priority set up by the first democratic government (Kruger et al., 2016).

Restitution is a restoration of the original land, provision of alternative land, or other state benefits or payments of financial compensation to the original inhabitants (Walker, 2005), as recognized in Section 25 of the Constitution of the Republic of South Africa, Act 108 of 1996. The claimants were required evidence of records to show they were forcefully removed from inside the park. Passage of the Restitution of Land Rights Act of 1994 provided both communities and individuals an opportunity to lodge land claims to regain access to the dispossessed land (Walker et al., 2011). The Act was the transformative legislation to be passed to handle the management of the land claims (Walker, 2005). The land restitution was done to redress the land dispossessions suffered by the people who were removed from the park during the apartheid system. The legislation had a significant impact on enforcing and encouraging public participation in communities to claim the land back especially at KNP (Thebe, 2016).

The KNP archives preserved most of the records about the removal of the people in and around the KNP. In 2001, the KNP archives opened the archives repositories to the public to provide opportunities for the land claimer to come and verify the land claim, as a representative from the South Africa National Parks stated in 2000 when speaking on archival and land claim records. The statement outlines the roles of archives and archivists in the KNP to play in retrieving information and documentation.

It appeared most of the people removed from the park visited the KNP to inquire about the original records about their removal from the park. The KNP established a special area room within the KNP archives repositories to handle the land claims of the people who were forcefully removed during the apartheid period. The claimants visited the special area room to enquire about the possession of records in the parks. The archivists ensured the following to assist the people who requested land claims records:

- Supervise the use of land claim records and ensure rules of archives, such as protecting the integrity of documents, proper handling of paper-based records, are followed
- Offer assistance to claimants as required. This implies a claimant was to produce written evidence of their connection to a particular land within the parks which they claimed. The evidence of the connection to the land which the land claimants claimed was necessary to retrieve needed information.

Problem Statement

The democratically constituted government had to deal with huge challenges of the backlog of centuries of the destructive system of land dispossession. Coupled with those challenges, there were expectations from the new government by the previous disadvantaged peoples who had been left landless. The accessibility of land claim records of people who were moved away from the park was a key challenge facing many countries including South Africa (Kruger et al., 2016). The KNP faced a challenge to provide access to land claims records of the people moved from the park as the result of the enactment of the Native Land Act 27 of 1913. It seems the unavailability to retrieve records was because of the lack of an archives management system to retrieve records. This study was conducted to assess the accessibility of land claims records to make a recommendation on the management of land claims records.

Despite the enactment of the National Archives and Records Service of South Africa Act No. 43 of 1996 guiding the management of records, many public institutions in South Africa were struggling to comply with the legislation with regards to the provision of access to information, especially land records (Ngoepe 2016: 270). These challenges happened despite several tools, such as finding aids and archival guidelines were designed to assist users to retrieve archives in the archival repository. Nevertheless, little research has been done in land records at Kruger National Parks. Hence, the preservation of archival material has a unique contribution to make towards the needs of society and holds the key of ensuring official records generated by both governments and private business are protected and preserved in a trustworthy and usable manner (Wamukoya, 2015).

ACCESS TO LAND CLAIM RECORDS

The purpose of the qualitative study was to investigate the accessibility of the land claims records at KNP with the view to answer the following research questions:

1. How was access control to assist to retrieve land records?
2. How was the process of systematic disposal of records?

Method

This research applied the qualitative method in the form of documentary analysis, observation, and interviews. The documentary analysis was archival material sourced from the KNP archives. This study draws heavily on the abundant secondary literature on people forcibly removed from the national park. The materials housed in KNP include land records, government/ statutory documents, and the National parks Department. The research was also enriched by information gathered from oral testimonies made by the claimants. Purposive sampling was used to collect data, archivists responsible for collecting data in the area were chosen to participate in the research. The 13 key informant interviews were conducted with individuals who engaged in the land claims, with two archivists responsible for land claims at KNP archives. This means there was a total number of 15 participants who were interviewed. All key informant interviews were semi-structured and centered around the respondents' experiences on the land claim.

Review of the Literature

The literature was reviewed base on the objectives of the study emanated from the research questions. According to Abioye (2009), the concept of access was considered as one of the most important aspects of archivists to retrieve records preserved in the archival repository. Segaetsho and Mnjama (2012) concurred archival services facilitate access of archival materials under their care, so these are accessible for research purposes, and available for land claims processes. In this book chapter, access implies accessibility through legal authorization and the existence of finding aids. Meeting information needs of claimants was an essential factor to reckon with by archivists, particularly in public archival agencies. The access and use of historical records collections in the custody of archival institutions is what gives these public information centers relevance to society (Chaterera, 2015). The rationale for the right to information is rooted in the concept of open and transparent government (Adams, 2006). This means the government needs to meet obligations to ensure a culture of openness and to facilitate access. However, the review of the literature shows there is no absolute freedom of access to government information in most of the African countries (Asogwa & Ezema, 2017).

According to Garaba (2016), access and utilization of archives were deemed fundamental for the reason archives' materials remain accessible to various stakeholders. Access of archives is fundamental of human rights, however, in many archival repositories, access and usage of archives is low because, as accessing records can be an unknown concept for people in an archival environment. This means the perspective of archives management is still unknown in most of the users. The trend worldwide was towards providing access to archives materials to foster good governance, accountability, transparency, and protection of human rights (Ngulube, 2009). Effective archives and records management systems promote public accountability and trust. This statement is alluded to by Thurston (2015) who indicated the significance of reliable and trustworthy records for public accountability and effectiveness when records are accessible. This provides an opportunity for citizens to enjoy the right to participate in their right to access the land records. This is because access to information is recognized as an aspect of one the goals for accountability, transparency, and openness.

In South Africa, the political transformation from the apartheid system to democratic governance promoted citizens to access historical records (Wood et al., 2014). The restitution of land in South Africa led to the demand by the public to retrieve records about the land claims. The focus of interested people in land claims in South Africa was placed on the retrieval of archives. The successful accessibility to land records is dependent on the preservation of archives materials in the archives' repositories. This implied an establishment of an archives management repatriation Centre. The archives division played a role to preserve any archival material for use in the future (Hallgrimsson, 2006). For records to be accessible by institutions, there was a need for an archives division to develop processes and procedures to retrieve records. This meant organizing and providing access to the collected content required an adaptation of methods and tools (Hallgrimsson, 2006).

Descriptive standards express relationships where contingency and uncertainty define the nature of archival materials preserved in the archives. Information contained in land claim records cannot be exploited and interpreted without being described and organized accordingly to provide access to archival materials (Maidabino, 2010). Metadata provides detailed information about records were useful to get the necessary information (Wood et al., 2014). Metadata offers an access point for users because they harmonize information describing the content of the document, such as author, title, and subject (Lecher, 2008). This implies transparent circumstances enabled metadata to be created and managed.

Metadata and conceptual reference models such as the Resource Description Framework (RDF) allowed a description of records not only to be upon multiple entities, but to include the nature of the relationships between those entities.

The archival inventory provides finding aids of an archival repository (Sundqvist, 2017). By using a finding aid, most land claimants at an archives institution identified records needed to process land claims. The finding aid was any description medium card or document, published or unpublished created to establish physical or administrative and intellectual control over records (Maidabino, 2010). The finding aids assisted archivists to retrieve files in the archives repository. The relevant records identified and located, the content must then be understood and interpreted. The finding aids played an essential role to search information in the archives repositories.

Archives institutions' mandate is to preserve historical, cultural, and scientific records (Marowa, 2015). A researcher or land claimants visit the archival institution to access land records (Menne-Haritz, 2001). This means archival institutions develop processes and procedures to enhance access to archival materials. Archivists developed a finding aid to assist users to assess archival materials (Cox, 2008). Procedures and processes in the form of a study aid and finding aid assist land claimers to access archival materials. The land claimers accessed land records preserved in the park. This implies the development of access and retrieval of archives systems such as the finding aid and repository guide. The findings aids provide contextual information about records and in representing the cohesive nature of records in a collection (Cox, 2008). The finding aids played a role in ensuring archival institutions were held accountable to society because the public used findings to aid in the access of the list of archives in the repositories (Cox, 2008).

It appeared archivists applied to finding aids to understand records preserved in archives repositories (Cox, 2009). Finding aids are designed according to the standard and conventions of the institutional networks in which they operate (Acker, 2017). Findings aids were adopted to influence accessible archival materials (Cox 2008, p. 10). The description of information is achieved through the Encoded Archival Description (EAD) and the EAD is an archival description which provided metadata about the collection. Access enabled the organization to choose the standards. Choosing the standards required an understanding of an effective ARM system (Menne-Haritz, 2001). The access paradigm reinforces theoretical challenges and the paradigmatic implementation of archival methods and ideas. Open and accessible archives define their places in the society of today and assure the capability to combine the past and future to present action (Menne-Haritz, 2001).

The land claimer was seeking access to and, in certain cases over land claim records. Archival institutions developed access to information policy to enhance access to archival materials. Russell (2005) indicated archival institutions developed access to information policy to their collections so people could better access the collection alludes to this statement. Government policy on archives is concerned with how archives can make contributions to the government's policy objective of public access (Horton, 2006). The absence of archives management policy affected the records management practices and access to information kept by the organization (Ndenje-Sichalwe & Ngulube, 2009). The study conducted by Sungvist (2017) indicated most archival institutions lack a strategy to promote access to archival materials. This weakness implied archival institutions need to develop an awareness strategy to promote access to archival materials (Menne-Haritz, 2001). Archival institutions developed a program to encourage various users to visit the archival institution. Archival awareness is a form of empowering citizens and to place citizens at the center of the development process by providing access to relevant, accurate, timely, and comprehensive information (Munge et al., 2014, p. 19).

Preservation of Archival Materials

It is through preservation that guarantees long-term preservation of archival materials for access, uses, and reuse (Mkuwira, 2015). Preservation policies provide a framework for the present, as well as the future, and ensure access to information is guaranteed (Nsibirwa, Hoskins, and Stilwell, 2014). The study conducted by Nsibirwa, Hoskins, and Stilwell shows most of the South African institutions lack a strategy to guide preservation, develop conservation facilities, or train and recruit staff. The survey conducted at the Nigerian institution found absences of preservation policy, lack of expertise and infrastructure for development, and inadequate funding on Nigerian institutions. In Malawi, the archives management system in the public service is poor due to a lack of adequate mechanisms of controlling the flow of records and this leads to loss of essential file (Limhoma, 2008).

The study conducted by Zaid, and Abioye (2010) as well as Segaetsho and Mnjama (2012) indicated the preservation of archival materials constitutes a challenge to heritage institutions in Africa. Segaetsho and Mnjama (2012) concurred archival materials preservation in Africa had not received adequate attention because of a lack of access to land records during colonialism and apartheid. This absence of an archives management standards practice had led to the institutions operating varying approaches to archives management practice, resulting in a lack of standard policies and procedures for the retention, disposal, and destruction of records in Nigeria. This practice is not in line with archives management standards in Southern Africa. The challenge includes the absence of preservation policy and lack of preservation awareness and training and appreciation of the importance, the sensitivity of heritage materials, and limited resources. In addition, Chaterera (2015) stated reaching out to the public archival institutions who operated within limited archival resources alludes to this statement. Furthermore, the study conducted to by (Mkuwira 2019) indicated limited funding was also reported to have negatively affected preservation at the National Archives of Malawi (Mkuwira, 2015). Hence, it is the strategic role of preservationists to ensure the long-term preservation of archival materials.

Disposal of Records

The disposal of records is an information governance process where the content of a regulated entity is systematically deleted with an audit based on the retention period. According to Marutha (2011), the records disposal is explained as the process of destruction of ephemeral records or the transfer of records of archival value to an archival institution for permanent preservation. The implementation of a disposal authority enables an organization to dispose of records regularly (Pereira 2018, p. 230). The file plan is a tool to conduct systematic disposal of records.

Archival institutions within the Eastern and Southern African Regional Branch of the International Council on Archives (ESARBICA) were facing a huge backlog of land records not disposed of (Garaba 2007). The reason stated for the backlog was the lack of expertise and cooperation by various departments to dispose of records. The challenge of a lack of skills and knowledge was experienced in countries such as Nigeria. Oweghoro (2015) indicated policies and procedures that guide the retention, disposal, and destruction of records were not available in Nigerian institutions, which alludes to this statement.

The review of the literature shows gaps in archives management in most of the African institutions because of the lack of an effective system to manage records within the park. The study conducted by Netshakhuma (2019) shows records about land claims were disposed of without issuing the disposal of authority by the National Archives of South Africa. Similarly, Williams, Thorpe, and Wilson (2014, p.

20) found that in Australia, records were disposed of without a disposal authority issued by the Australia National Archives. Adams (2006) alluded organizations need to establish and implement procedures for the timely disposal of public records (Adams, 2006). This means organizations are to develop and implement procedures for the transfer of public records of permanent value for preservation in the National Archives or other archival repository, as may be designated by the Act.

In South Africa, public entities are required to implement the provision on National Archives and Record Service Act such as obtain disposal authorities on all records from the national archives (Ngoepe & Makhubela, 2015). According to the National Archives and Records Service Act, no public records shall be deleted, destroyed, erased, or otherwise disposed of without the written authority of the national archivist. It is important to remember the institutions should keep records as long as required under the statute of limitations, retention for legal requirements or the country's records retention schedule (Oweghoro, 2015).

RESULTS

The 13 participants were asked to identify tools used to access the land claims records. The majority of participants (8) indicated the findings aids were a tool used by KNP to identify land records. The finding aids proved valuable to establish claims based on the land of disposing of people in the park. Some of the participants indicated the public experienced challenges to access land claim records because access, meaning related procedures and guidelines, were lacking in the park. However, the study conducted by Mnjama (2009) indicated access to archives material is an essential part of their function in society, and there is a need for the public to be made aware of the land records preserved by archival institutions.

The following highlights from interview session excerpts identify some of the challenges KNP experienced in regard to providing access to the land claims records

- There is a lack of an appropriate standard to manage information related records.
- It was a challenge to access and retrieve the records needed to do the specific tasks related to the management of land claims records
- KNP has not formulated any tool that can be used to benchmark land claims records with other stakeholders. This was confirmed by the various stakeholders who were interviewed during the session interviews.

Additionally, many participants raised concerns about the capabilities of archivists on making provision of access to institutional memory. The chapter author observed the step of the registration of the user to access the archives department, which requires preliminary registration of land claimants. The participants indicated when the land claimants visited the parks and were asked to sign the register to access land claims records preserved in the park. Most of the participants indicated land affairs records that were accessed include the geographical maps of the area where people were forcefully removed. To locate the geographical area where the land claimer was removed, identification was necessary to utilize the finding aids. The information sheets, brochures, and pamphlets about the history of relocation people from the park were provided to identify records related to the land claims.

Some of the participants indicated formal applications to access land claims records were made in writing. Some of the participants indicated that land claimants were entitled to seek access to the land claim records. Where a claimant requests access it must be made to the archivists in charge of keeping the records. Archivists played a role to disseminate information to society. Where access was given, there was no obligation to provide repeat access until a reasonable time interval had elapsed.

The chapter author observed finding aids used in the KNP archives were in the form of books or a register. There is a selective list of collections preserved in the archives to be accessible by various users. Finding aids were open to the chapter author, irrespective of restrictions on access to the archives they dealt with since it was a public right to know all accumulations of archives were held, at minimum in public financed repositories. The search room supervisor and his assistants were the focal points of the finding aid system.

In addition, it was observed KNP archivists designed their finding aids as far as possible to be self-explanatory. It appeared that the process of self–explanatory records was essential for the land claimer to understand the category of records preserved in the archives. The simplified language enabled the land claimer to access archival materials without seeking assistance from KNP archivists. Finally, it was observed a large part of the work of KNP archivists was to answer inquiries received by land claimers through post or telephone and physical visits. Although, the volume and nature of enquiring received would vary from one office to another. The duty of an archivist was to explain the nature of the KNP archives held, the nature of the finding aids available and to give what assistance was reasonably possible to enable an inquiring person to pursue his or her research.

KNP had an obligation to ensure the land claimer was aware of the land claims records preserved. Some of the participants indicated the KNP archivist identified and located records preserved in the KNP archives used an old filing system. The old filing system classified records according to the number and name of the collection. The land claimer who came to check the availability of the land claim records collection was allowed to check the great quantities of records in the hope of finding relevant records related to land claims.

Other participants reflected, "Archivists see that records provide the answer of the plot where our forefathers were based." This statement highlights the importance and significance of archivists to preserve land records for research purposes. In a case where the claimants could not allocate the records, oral information assisted to restore the records which were lost. The written and oral information was essential to provide a detailed narrative, not just of individual landholdings.

Other interviewees expressed the importance of preserving and facilitating access to land claims records need to be preserved in the archives. Other participants felt access to information was important to counteract a growing sense that not enough was done in terms of accessing land records preserved in the parks. Some of the participants said the following with regards to the management of parks records, "No effective efforts were done by the manager of the park to preserve land claim records." The government's policy statement suggested a series of negotiated settlements, wherein the black people would be extinguished in return for compensation whereby financial support was made available to the Black society.

Preservation of Archive Materials

The respondents were queried whether their park developed a strategy to preserve land records. Examples of the respondents reported as follows:

"There was no strategy or policy to preserve land records."

"Policy was not developed to ensure the preservation of historical land records."

"The inclusive National Archives and Records Management Act was enacted in 1996 which implied that there was no effective system in South Africa to preserve land records."

"There was a lack of clear- cut responsibilities for management of land records at the Kruger National Park."

"Component of land records management at Kruger National Parks was not fully explained and managed."

"There were limited resources allocated to the National park to manage land records."

The majority of participants (7) also indicated they were not aware of strategy and policies and preservation strategies to preserve archival materials. The fact there was a lack of strategy implied there was a limited process to manage land records within the park. Respondents were asked whether they were aware of the existence of land records preserved at the Kruger National Parks. The majority of participants (8) indicated they were not aware of archival materials preserved by archival institutions. From the outset, it was glaringly apparent the broader Kruger National Park staffs were unaware of the existence of land records, let alone the function, of the Kruger National Park. It was felt that for the Kruger National Park to position itself and make its purpose evident, it needed to create a visible and recognizable presence.

Another avenue, which has proved effective in creating an awareness of the function of the KNP and the nature of its holdings, was the regular mounting of exhibits across the university. The aim was not only to make staff and visitors aware of the rich history of the KNP but also to showcase the type of land records preserved by KNP. Exhibitions were mounted at various times for a range of occasions on both a temporary and permanent basis. Thus, by creating awareness through *visual identity* and *tangible* exhibits, the KNP believes it has become more evident in the broader South Africa community and in particular, among the land claimants. The increase in inquires and visits to the KNP by land claimants and staff makes this phenomenon apparent. This means there have been numerous capacity-building initiatives across the national park which raise awareness of the importance of land records at all levels from internal and external stakeholders from the park. To sustain an efficient and effective archives management system will depend to a larger extent on developing new skills and awareness within the public service as previously alluded to (Manyambula, 2009).

Disposal of Records

The purpose of this objective was to analyze the efficiency and effectiveness of records disposal of land records at the KNP. Participants were asked when the records destruction and transfer processes of records were taking place within the KNP archives. The land records were viewed as records necessary to be preserved. Some of the participants indicated that since the establishment of the parks, the KNP did not embark on the disposal of records. One participant said the following, "The problem with the land claims records was that there was no individual responsible for caring and management of records which posed a challenge for the effective management of land records within the park."

Some of the participants indicated most of the land claims records were not arranged, which posed a challenge for the management of records. It was found no microfilm project was embarked by the park to manage information. However, besides the lack of effective archives management system, it was surprising to found most of the land claims of dispersed people since 1913 were preserved by the park.

The Skukuza archives ensured the users participated in the design of the system. Given the generally haphazard methods of records management prevailing at the time, particularly at the field office level, it is of note so many records were not disposed of as the claimants demanded their evidence of forced removal records in the park. Many participants said the destruction of records was done without applying an approved retention schedule for land records. There was no systematic disposal of records of the land claims. It seems the Kruger National parks ensured the department continuously preserved land claims records. This finding illustrates the lack of systematic disposal in the parks for the management of records.

DISCUSSION AND RECOMMENDATIONS

The archivists, recognizing the significant importance of records without the recognition of the indigenous people and assisting in facilitating access to historical records, have conducted a significant amount of work over the past decade. Several factors such as finding aids and poor physical conditions reflected more negatively on inactive records than on current records restricting claimants to access land records in the parks. For example, some of the claimants were unable to access records of land. There was a challenge because accessing land claims records required an identified suitable time and compliance with archival legislation to facilitate easy retrieval of information is conducted through a registration book. It was essential for the archives storage to be made available to enable retrieval of information.

The development of a records management policy is necessary for the park to ensure land claims records are preserved. The policy establishes the framework within which archivists can allow access to records so future researchers can use them. A policy must be developed to suit the requirements of the KNP on the preservation of archival materials. The issues of legislation as well as protection of individual and community rights were to be considered by the community on the preservation of archives. Archivists at KNP were thus not able to deal with the request of the claimants because of a lack of finding aids or archival guideline system to manage archival materials.

It can be surmised land claims records were not listed or arranged in the KNP as anticipated which posed a challenge for the retrieval of information. Some of the records archivists could not trace in the archives. This implies such records were possibly disposed of by mistake. This posed challenges on the management of land claims records at KNP.

FUTURE RESEARCH DIRECTIONS

There is a need to develop an archives management policy to ensure land claims records are kept by the parks and are accessible. A clear policy is to assist KNP for improved access to records within the parks. SANParks work to engage in awareness so as to ensure people became aware of the importance of the preservation of land records. Outreach activities were essential to building a relationship between communities and the Kruger National parks. SANParks reviews a register of inquiries which form an index of subjects dealt with. The purpose of this index is to prevent duplication of research in response to inquiries, to coordinate research in some cases and to assist in determining the latent demand for extensions to the archival services.

It is recommended future research studies be conducted in other African countries to investigate the handling and management of land records as the result of colonialism. Such studies may supplement existing studies and contribute to a holistic and integrated approach in contextualizing archival management, concerning the management of land records.

CONCLUSION

In this study, the chapter author assessed the accessibility and disposal of records of the land records at KNP to make recommendations on the management of the land claim records. The development of finding aids is essential for the preservation of archival material. It was essential for archivists to develop findings aids to retrieve records in the archives. The study provides empirical evidence on different aspects, such as challenges experienced by users on accessing archival materials. There is also a challenge if organizations decided to dispose of records without authorization.

REFERENCES

Acker, A. (2017). When is a record? A research framework for locating electronic records in infrastructure. In A. J. Gilliland, S. McKemmish, & J. A. Lau (Eds.), *Research in the archival Multiverse*. Monash University.

Adams, M. (2006). Freedom of Information and Records Management in Ghana. *African Journal of Library Archives and Information Science*, (1), 29–38.

Asogwa, E. B., & Ezema, J. I. (2017). Freedom of access t government information in Africa: Trends, status and challenges. *Records Management Journal*, *27*(3), 318–338. doi:10.1108/RMJ-08-2015-0029

Bastian, A. J. (2017). Memory research/ Archival research. In A. J. Gilliland, S. McKemmish, & J. A. Lau (Eds.), *Research in the archival Multiverse*. Monash University.

Chaterera, F. (2015). Heading for a better understanding of outreach in the digital age: A look into the use of Web 2.0 as communication tool by state museums and archives in Zimbabwe. *Journal of the South African Society of Archivists*, *48*, 21–33.

Cox, R. J. (2008). Revisiting the archival finding aid. *Journal of Archival Organization*, *5*(4), 5–32. doi:10.1080/15332740802153245

Fachry, K. N., Kamps, J., & Zhang, J. (2008, October). Access to archival material in context. In *Proceedings of the second international symposium on Information interaction in context* (pp. 102-109). 10.1145/1414694.1414718

Garaba, F. (2007). The state of archival appraisal practices in the ESARBICA Region. *African Journal of Library Archives and Information Science*, *17*(1).

Hallgrimsson, T. (2006). Access and finding aids. In *Web Archiving* (pp. 131–151). Springer. doi:10.1007/978-3-540-46332-0_6

Horton, S. (2006). Social capital, government policy and public value: Implications for archive service delivery. *Aslib Proceedings*, *58*(6), 502–512. doi:10.1108/00012530610713588

(2011). Introduction. InWalker, C., Bohlin, A., Hall, R., & Kepe, T. (Eds.), *Land, memory, reconstruction and justice* (pp. 1–13). Ohio University Press.

Iyer, D. (2017). The role of government in expediting land expropriation: Reshaping the future of land reform. *Journal of Public Administration*, *52*(3), 508–519.

Jili, N., & Masuku, M. M. (2017). Access to land and women's participation in small-scale farming at uMlalazi local municipality. *Journal of Public Administration*, *52*(3), 548–561.

Kepe, T. (2004). Land restitution and biodiversity conservation in South Africa: the case of Mkambati, Eastern Cape Province. *Canadian Journal of African Studies/La Revue Canadienne des Études Africaines, 38*(3), 688-704.

Krüger, R., Cundill, G., & Thondhlana, G. (2016). A case study of the opportunities and trade-offs associated with deproclamation of a protected area following a land claim in South Africa. *Local Environment*, *21*(9), 1047–1062. doi:10.1080/13549839.2015.1065804

Lecher, H. E. (2006). Small scale academic web archiving: DACHS. In *Web Archiving* (pp. 213–225). Springer. doi:10.1007/978-3-540-46332-0_10

Lihoma, P. (2008). Situation of archives in Africa: The case of national archives of Malawi. *African Research & Documentation*, (106), 3.

Maidabino, A. A. (2010). The availability, organization, and use of archival records: A Study of Public Archives Agencies in the Northwestern States of Nigeria. *Library Philosophy and Practice*, 1.

Manyabula, M. (2009). Public service reform, accountability and records management: A case study of Tanzania. *ESARBICA Journal*, *28*(1), 28. doi:10.4314/esarjo.v28i1.44395

Marowa, I. (2015). Archives as Extended Memory of Communities: The Case of Dandawa Chiefdom in Hurungwe District, Zimbabwe. *ESARBICA Journal*, *34*, 104.

Menne-Haritz, A. (2001). Access—The reformulation of an archival paradigm. *Archival Science*, *1*(1), 57–82. doi:10.1007/BF02435639

Mkuwira, R. M. (2015). Preservation of documentary heritage in Malawi. *Journal of the South African Society of Archivists, 48*, 55–65.

Mnjama, N. (2009, July). Archival programming in the digital era: The challenge for ESARBICA archivists. In *XXth Bi-Annual East and Southern Africa Regional Branch of the International Council on Archives (ESARBICA) General Conference, Documentary Heritage Management in the Digital Age: Beauty and the Beast, Namibia, National Archives of Namibia, Windhoek July* (pp. 1-3). Academic Press.

Munge, E., Rotich, D. C., & Wamukoya, J. (2014). A situational analysis of information management in selected government ministries in the context of Kenya Vision 2030. *African Journal of Library Archives and Information Science, 24*(1), 15–26.

Ndenje-Sichalwe, E., & Ngulube, P. (2009). Records management and access to information: Key to fostering accountability, good governance and protection of human rights in Tanzania. *ESARBICA Journal, 28*(1), 28. doi:10.4314/esarjo.v28i1.44394

Netshakhuma, N. S. (2018). Assessing the appraisal, disposal and transfer of records from 1994 to 2014: The case of Mpumalanga provincial government in South Africa. *Mousaion, 36*(2), 1–20.

Netshakhuma, S. N. (2017). The role of archives on the incorporation of the former Kangwane homeland into Mpumalanga province. *Africanus, 47*(2), 1–16.

Ngoepe, M., & Makhubela, S. (2015). Justice delayed is justice denied. *Records Management Journal, 25*(3), 288–305. doi:10.1108/RMJ-06-2015-0023

Ngulube, P. (2009). Preserving South Africa's paper trail and making records available for present and future generations. *ESARBICA Journal, 26*, 45–69.

Nsibirwa, Z., Hoskins, R., & Stilwell, C. (2014). Building the South African nation through legal deposit: The impact of legislation on preservation of digital materials. *African Journal of Library Archives and Information Science, 24*(1), 53–65.

Oweghoro, B. M. (2015). Health Records Retention and Disposal in Nigerian Hospitals: Survey of Policies, Practices and Procedures. *African Journal of Library Archives and Information Science, 25*(1).

Pereira, R. (2018). Assessing the implementation of the National Archives and Records Services Act at Eduardo Mondlane University in Mozambique. *ESARBICA Journal, 37*, 221–244.

Pienaar, J. M. (2015). Land reform embedded in the constitution: Legal contextualisation. *Scriptura, 114*, 1–20. doi:10.7833/114-0-1116

Russell, L. (2005). Indigenous knowledge and archives: Accessing hidden history and understandings. *Australian Academic and Research Libraries, 36*(2), 161–171. doi:10.1080/00048623.2005.10721256

Segaetsho, T., & Mnjama, N. (2012). Preservation of library materials at the University of Botswana Library. *Journal of the South African Society of Archivists, 45*, 68–84.

Skelcher, B. (2003). Apartheid and the removal of black spots from Lake Bhangazi in KwaZulu-Natal, South Africa. *Journal of Black Studies, 33*(6), 761–783. doi:10.1177/0021934703033006003

South Africa National Parks. (2019). *Annual report 2018/19*. Author.

Sundqvist, A. (2017). Archival mediation: Studying users' interaction with access systems. In A. J. Gilliland, S. McKemmish, & J. A. Lau (Eds.), *Research in the archival Multiverse*. Monash University.

Tavuyanago, B. (2017). Our fathers and grandfathers were born here…" Shangaan eviction experiences from the Gonarezhou National Park, 1957-1968. *Historia (Wiesbaden, Germany)*, *62*(2), 46–67.

Thebe, T. P. (2016). Community participation: Reality and rhetoric in the development and implementation of the Integrated Development Plan (IDP) within municipalities of South Africa. *Journal of Public Administration*, *51*(4), 712–723.

Thurston, A. (2015). Access to reliable public records as evidence for freedom of information in Commonwealth Africa. *The Round Table*, *104*(6), 703–713. doi:10.1080/00358533.2015.1112095

Van Dalsen, A. (2017). *Land reform: Presidential policy statements on expropriation without compensation.* https://hsf.org.za/resource-centre/hsf-briefs/landreform-presidential-policy-statement

Wamukoya, M. J. (2015). Reflections on African archives: Their role in meeting societal needs in the 21st century. *Journal of the South African Society of Archivists*, *48*, 14–20.

Williams, L., Wilson, A., & Thorpe, K. (2006). Identity and access to government records: Empowering the community. *Archives and Manuscripts*, *34*(1), 8.

Wood, S., Carbone, K., Cifor, M., Gilliland, A., & Punzalan, R. (2014). Mobilizing records: Re-framing archival description to support human rights. *Archival Science*, *14*(3-4), 397–419. doi:10.100710502-014-9233-1

Zaid, Y., & Abioye, A. (2010). Museums, libraries and archives: Collaborating for the preservation of heritage materials in Nigeria. *African Research & Documentation*, 59–70.

ADDITIONAL READING

Mudzamatira, W. (2020). Heritage awareness and education in the Southern Gauteng Province, South Africa. In *Developing Effective Communication Skills in Archaeology* (pp. 200–222). IGI Global. doi:10.4018/978-1-7998-1059-9.ch010

Netshakhuma, N. S. (2019). The role of archives and records management legislation after colonialism in Africa. *Records Management Journal*, *29*(1/2), 210–223. doi:10.1108/RMJ-09-2018-0024

Shange, X. M. (2020). The ambit of ethics in the South African academic institutions: Experience of coloniality. In *Ethical research approaches to Indigenous knowledge education* (pp. 24–58). IGI Global.

Székely, I. (2010). The four paradigms of archival history. *Journal of Information Technology Research*, *3*(4), 51–82. doi:10.4018/jitr.2010100104

Walker, C. (2008). *Landmarked: Land claims and land restitution in South Africa*. Jacana Media.

Chapter 11
Settler Colonialism and the Capricious Seizure of Unwanted Land, or How the Huni Kuin were Expelled From Plácido de Castro, Acre, Brazil

Marcello Messina
https://orcid.org/0000-0002-8822-3342
Federal University of Paraíba, Brazil

Jairo de Araújo Souza
Federal University of Acre, Brazil

ABSTRACT

Situated in the Mesoregion of the Acre River, Plácido de Castro is a small municipality in the Brazilian state of Acre. In 2015, with the consent of the authorities, a group of people of Huni Kuin ethnicity occupied an abandoned, state-owned piece of land in the municipal territory, namely, the Parque Ecológico. For two years, the Huni Kuin group has lived in the Parque Ecológico, decontaminating and revalorising the land. Afterwards the Huni Kuin have been gradually dispossessed of the occupied land via various coercive actions, some of which were backed by the authorities. In this paper, the authors draw upon media releases as well as an interview with Hunk Kuin cacique Mapu, in order to signify the events in terms of a violent performance of settler colonialism in the face of the legitimate reclamation of Indigenous sovereignty over Brazilian land. In particular, they look at the ways in which political authorities, police forces, social services, and the broader non-Indigenous society unanimously cooperate towards the total effacement of Indigenous bodies, communities, and subjectivities from the land.

DOI: 10.4018/978-1-7998-3729-9.ch011

INTRODUCTION

With the capital Rio Branco, Acre is the westernmost state of the Federative Republic of Brazil. The state is proverbially characterized as the most remote territory within Brazilian national space, to the point of being the butt of a popular joke spread on social media, which purports "Acre doesn't exist" (Lucena & Barros, 2014). However distant from metropolitan Brazil, Acre is in fact extremely close to Bolivia and Peru, and is part of a tri-border region with the neighboring departments of Pando, in Bolivia, and Madre de Dios, in Peru[1]. Neglected and scorned in national popular culture, the state of Acre as part of Brazil is, as a matter of fact, the product of more or less conflictual negotiations with the two neighboring countries.

In particular, the chapter authors refer to the bellicose circumstances by which Brazil conquered a vast portion of land, previously belonging to Bolivia, in the Acre River Valley. Established by the 1903 Treaty of Petrópolis, this arrangement was actually the product of a violent war between the two countries, which eventually saw the victory of the Brazilian side, led by José Plácido de Castro. Glorified as "Acrean Revolution" within the Brazilian side, the conflict is remembered as "war" and "holocaust" by the Bolivians (Silva et al., 2017; Souza & Messina 2018). Plácido de Castro is also the name of the small Acrean town where the facts analyzed in this chapter took place. Many of the names of Acrean municipalities are direct references to the settler colonial heroes who facilitated the annexation of the region to Brazil. The state capital Rio Branco, for example, is named after José Paranhos, Baron of Rio Branco, the then Brazilian Minister of Foreign Affairs, who coordinated the last phases of the conflict with Bolivia between December 1902 and March 1903 (Tambs, 1996, pp. 271-272).

Bearing the name of one of the proud conquerors of Acre's own *Brazilianness*, the town of Plácido de Castro lies right at the border with Bolivia, being separated from Puerto Evo Morales by the river Abunã. In this geopolitical arrangement, Plácido de Castro emerges as a staunch bastion of Brazilianness that evokes settler colonial fantasies from its very name. Border narratives involve Bolivia and its Indigenous and settler colonial inhabitants as Acre's and Brazil's *Other*, to be scrutinized, marginalized, criminalized, and kept at a distance. These experiences need to be considered as a backdrop to the other fundamental conflict that inscribes the region, which involves the violent effacement of local Indigenous peoples, territories, and cultures from the sovereign horizon of the three colonial countries that occupy the region. In the state of Acre specifically, this is reflected in a tendency to ignore the trajectories of Indigenous population and their contribution to the present-day social, cultural and political configuration of the state (Albuquerque, 2015).

More in general, in western and northern Brazil, the chapter authors observe a tendency to conflate the "foreigner" and the "*indio*", both seen as comparable menaces against national sovereignty, and both a priori assigned to a space that exists beyond the boundaries of the national territory. As claimed by Cavalcante (2013) with regards to the situation in the state of Mato Grosso do Sul,

there is the attempt, by some sections of Brazilian society, to create an unsupported opposition between the ethnic identity of Indigenous people and their nationality. [...] For this reason, attempts are often made to characterize the Guarani as Paraguayans, which supposedly would represent them as opportunists who migrated to Brazil to illegitimately access the social and territorial rights guaranteed by Brazilian law, which would be allegedly more advantageous than those offered to the Guarani Indigenous people in Paraguay (p. 134)[2]

Incidentally, upon a visit to Plácido de Castro of Huni Kuin *cacique* Mapu, from the Acrean municipality of Marechal Thaumaturgo (another settler colonial toponym), he was immediately mistaken for Bolivian by the former mayor, Luiz Pereira. The *cacique* Mapu Huni Kuin relates that:

Former mayor Luiz Pereira happened to be there at the hotel where I was staying. He started talking to me, and asked if I was Bolivian. I told him I am Indigenous . He talked about the Parque Ecológico which had been inaugurated by him and was abandoned. (Mapu Huni Kuin as cited in Antunes, 2016)

This chapter focusses precisely on the events that involved Mapu and the group of Huni Kuin who occupied an abandoned piece of public land in Plácido de Castro, known as *Parque Ecológico* (Ecological Park). Among other things, at the time of the occupation, some of the Huni Kuin were also part of a musical group called *Forrozeiros da Floresta* (Machado, 2015) and there, in the Parque Ecológico, they created the cultural centre *Huwã Karu Yushibu.*

THE OCCUPATION AND REVITALISATION OF THE *PARQUE ECOLÓGICO*

In mid-2015, after the meeting with Luiz Pereira, there was another conversation between Mapu Huni Kuin, and the then mayor of Plácido de Castro, Roney Firmino. In this conversation, according to Mapu, "He accepted our proposal, which involved [the occupation of] an ecological park that was created thirty years ago, but had been abandoned 15 years ago" (Huni Kuin, 2017).

In a statement by Roney Firmino, reported in an online news story from 2015, one may find a confirmation as to the mayor's good disposition towards the Huni Kuin's occupation of the abandoned land:

The Director of [Cultural] Articulations spoke with Mayor Roney Firmino (PSB), who liked the idea and authorized the Indigenous group to build their homes within the park area. Firmino argues that it is better for the area to be occupied by the people of the band Forrozeiros da Floresta with their relatives and friends than to remain abandoned (Machado, 2015)

According to the official website of the Plácido de Castro City Council, the *Parque Ecológico*, created in 1991, counts with "34 hectares and 113 species of tropical flora", and is "considered one of the most important and complete [parks] in the Amazon Region" (PLÁCIDO DE CASTRO, AC, s / d). In 2011, several local blogs had been registering the fact that the park had been left in a serious state of neglect (Lima, 2011; Pereira, 2011). In his testimony, Mapu describes the state of the Ecological Park:

When we went in, when we got to know about this Parque Ecológico, my God, it was a lot of dirt, a lot of dirt, there it only served for prostitution, it only served people who used heavy drugs, drug dealers, there were deaths inside that space... so the town residents that lived nearby... they no longer had the courage to go there because it was very dangerous, right? And we went in, we worked three months to clean it, to take all the rubbish out, it was three whole months of that, in which we felt that the energy of that space only had bad things, it was a nightmare at night, it was so much that we felt (Huni Kuin, 2017)

Even with these difficulties, the Huni Kuin managed to clean the site and plant "more than 3000 seedlings" among bananas, maniocs, açaí palms, mulateiros, buritis, etc. (Huni Kuin, 2017). In March

2017, a note from the Missionary Council for Indigenous People (COMIN), recorded that, in the Ecological Park, the Huni Kuin

carried out a reforestation activity, with 800 seedlings of trees in the region. They organized their gardens with the planting of manioc, papaya, banana, açaí, cashew, watermelon, pumpkin, yams, potatoes [...] The presence of the Huni Kuin people within the Park created another reality for that place, which was revitalized and is living a new life, with names in the Huni Kuin language for the trees, the streams, the animals and the people. The Huni Kuin people found in this space a way of strengthening their culture, valuing their traditional knowledge and, most importantly, passing it on to future generations (COMIN, 2017)

It is important to emphasize that during this time of efforts to revitalize the public park, the relationship between the Huni Kuin and the local community was not always of mutual collaboration. Mapu reports that initially, the replanting work "was not easy", since

the residents did not want to give us banana seedlings or maniocs to plant... They wanted us to work, and then as a contribution they gave the banana seedlings, and we did it [...], we started to work for them in exchange for the seedlings, because they really didn't want to give them away (Huni Kuin, 2017)

After an initial period of work in exchange for the seedlings, a partnership was established with a widening participation project of the Forest Engineering Department of the Federal University of Acre. In the context of the project, around 800 seedlings were donated to the Huni Kuin (COMIN, 2017; Huni Kuin, 2017).

GEOCORPOGRAPHIES OF INDIGENEITY

Again, in the context of the difficult relations between the Huni Kuin and the Plácido de Castro community, it is important to point out an episode of serious relevance, contained in Mapu's narrative:

What happened was that one of the girls was pregnant, and she wanted to do prenatal care, and thus she went to the public health clinic over there. And they said that they did not serve Indigenous people: "No, here we do not serve Indigenous people" (Huni Kuin, 2017)

This last testimony might help unearth the vast arsenal of connotations normally associated with the signifier "Indigenous ". In this case, the attendants at the Plácido de Castro health centre felt in power to deny a basic and universally guaranteed service, based on a fundamental differential factor, condensed around the concept of "Indigeneity" or "Indigenous ness". Let us reflect a little more on this episode: (1) a woman arrives at a health clinic, which, as part of the Brazilian State-run Unified Health System (SUS), follows the principle of "universalisation", that is, the categorical imperative by which "health is a citizenship right guaranteed to all people" and "access to actions and services must be guaranteed to all people, regardless of sex, race, occupation or other social or personal characteristics" (Ministério da Saúde, n.d.); (2) when labelling this woman as "Indigenous ", the clinic employees refuse prenatal care, arguing that the structure does not serve Indigenous people, thus drawing an implicit border between the concept of "Indigeneity" and that of "citizenship".

In the light of the aforementioned conflation between "Indigenous " and "foreign", functional to an expungement of the former from the symbolic and moral space of the nation, as well as his/her exclusion from the set of rights that are guaranteed by the State to its citizens, here the authors of this chapter can undoubtedly argue that the health clinic staff categorized the Indigenous Huni Kuin woman, who solicited prenatal care, as "foreign", that is, as a person unprovided with Brazilian citizenship and, therefore, as a non-beneficiary of the national public service. This represents an arbitrary injustice, which also involves an unsolicited assessment of the person's ethnic/racial appearance, undoing the very principle of universalisation mentioned above.

Furthermore, even when unmasking the perverse logic that assimilates the concept of "Indigenous " to that of "foreigner", one cannot forget that the service to non-resident foreigners is a consolidated practice in the context of the Brazilian SUS, especially, but not exclusively, in border towns like Plácido de Castro: not only the authors are able to confirm this via the work of Branco and Torronteguy (2009) and Giovannella et al. (2007), but also based on their personal experiences, both in border and non-border regions of Brazil. Branco and Torronteguy also admit the existence of some isolated cases of border municipalities that refuse to offer health services to foreigners, depending on the demand and the financial resources available (Branco & Torronteguy, 2009, pp. 935-936), but this is hardly the case in Plácido de Castro.

Now, if a public service, based on a universal conception of citizenship that often transcends national boundaries (Giovannella et al., 2007), is denied when requested by a subject who is signified as "Indigenous ", this means that the Indigenous subject it is not only thought of as external to the Brazilian nation: s/he is also considered to be foreign to a more comprehensive and transnational concept of citizenship. In other words, the Huni Kuin woman who requests the prenatal care to which she is entitled is perhaps understood, in the particular view of the attendants of that particular health centre, as a non-citizen stateless person, an alien body who is not entitled to a universal service: the national Brazilian cliché affirming that *"índio não é gente"* ["*índios* are not people"] (Borges, 2014, pp. 82-83), seems to be the not-so-implicit subtext of this denied attendance.

Moreover, even recognising that, in this episode, the consequences of the "*índios* are not people" adage are exasperated *ad absurdum*, it is important to remember that the person requesting care was a pregnant woman, and that, according to the principle of *jus soli* adopted by the Brazilian legislation (Giovannella et al., 2007, p. S252), the yet-unborn child in her womb was, without any doubt, a future Brazilian citizen. In this context, not only the denial of citizenship and the dehumanisation triggered by the "*índios* are not people" logic — seemingly applied by the health centre staff — affect the mother, as they also affect her yet-unborn child.

The chapter authors argue both the mother and her foetus, in this context, are immediately and summarily visualized as extraneous and alien bodies, whose classification within the concept of "Indigenous " makes them embody the "geocorpographical" semblance of the non-citizen and non-human enemy. In his formulation of the concept of "geocorpographies", Joseph Pugliese intended to "to bring into focus the violent enmeshment of the flesh and blood of the body within the geopolitics of race, war and empire" (2007, p. 1).

In coining the term "geocorpographies" I want to encapsulate in one word the following thesis: that the body, in any of its manifestations, is always geopolitically situated and graphically inscribed by signs, discourses, regimes of visuality and so on. Its geopolitical markings can only be abstracted through a process of symbolic and political violence. The geopolitical significations that invest the body are constitutive of its cultural Intelligibility (Pugliese, 2007, p. 12)

In other words, the identification of the pregnant woman (and of her baby) as "Indigenous " and the consequent denial of her right to prenatal care are part of a process of decipheration of her ethnic, racial and cultural identity that involves the violent profiling of subjects in a context of tensions and geopolitical conflicts. In this particular episode, the violence occurred via the denial of a service that should be guaranteed for everyone. Furthermore, the authors' interview with Mapu revealed the planning of other violent interventions on the bodies of Huni Kuin women:

He wanted to build a motel in Bolivia, pick up the Indigenous women, and call foreigners who came from abroad, for [these women to then] offer themselves as prostitutes in Bolivia for them. [...] He came to me and said: "Mapu, here's the thing, I have a proposal for you: I give you a monthly wage of 3000 reais, I give you my car, but now your relatives are going to be in our hands, you and I will do that together". [...] He said: "I give that to you, and we build a motel in Bolivia because no one will find out, and then when the foreigners come, we take the Indigenous women who are living there in the park and they will have to be half-naked, they will be only in their panties with their breasts sticking out, they will not wear anything else, that's all, and they will have to stay like that all day, and it will be like this" (Huni Kuin, 2017)

The same testimony by Mapu can be found in press reports, with an attached response by the accused man, councilman Allison Lima, denying the allegations (Amazônia Real, 2016). Without needing to establish who is right, what is interesting in Mapu's complaint is the joint operativity and exploitation of two, or even three, geocorpographies of the other: on the one hand, the body of the Indigenous people to be stripped naked and offered to the "foreigners"; on the other hand, the border territory of Bolivia, the village Puerto Evo Morales, thought of as a lawless place where anything can be done and "no one will find out"; finally, the "foreigners", imagined as a uniform mass, all driven by the same desire of predatory consumption of the Indigenous women's bodies.

What emerges from these two different stories, that of the non-attendance at the health centre, and that of the councilman's indecent proposal, is the treatment of the bodies of these Indigenous women as *terrae nullius* to be discretionally conquered, exploited and violated, or left there, defenceless, and helpless, denying the assistance that is due to them. The bodies of the Indigenous women become, to paraphrase Pugliese's words again, "metonymic" images of "territories to be raped, mutilated into submission and conquered" (Pugliese, 2007, p. 12). In this way, the chapter authors argue that a sort of geocorpography of Indigeneity emerges, that allows the foreshadowing of a predatory intervention, or, alternatively, the denial of requested and due assistance, based on the same visualisation of the body of the Indigenous subject and its immediate interpretation as a body that is foreign, or even devoid of any citizenship whatsoever, or ultimately deprived of her/his very humanity.

THE GRADUAL EXPULSION FROM THE LAND

After settling down in the *Parque Ecológico* with all the aforementioned difficulties, the Huni Kuin were to encounter new and more daunting challenges due to the changing political situation in the town of Plácido de Castro:

Unfortunately, the mayor who was supporting us last year was already campaigning for re-election, and he lost. And then the other mayor who took office was against our project. [...] Right from the start, he said, "the first thing I want to do is to regulate the access to the land for you," – that was Gedeon Barros during the political campaign. "Oh, then okay, we Indigenous people are not divided into political parties, we are here for our right. We are not with that, with you, and such. We're going to support him, because we have to, but we have no political party [...] ". When he won and we sought him to talk, he was no longer available for us (Huni Kuin, 2017)

Since the change of the town mayor, the permanence of the Huni Kuin in the Ecological Park of Plácido de Castro began to be threatened. The previous year, two days after the first Plácido de Castro event, during the *Abril Indígena* festival, Mapu had already suffered a death threat on his way back from the school where he studied at night:

When I left school by nine o'clock, a dark car stopped by. I was on my bike with my nephew, then he asked me to stop on the way because he wanted to buy some ice cream. He crossed the street to get his ice cream...and I stood there on my bike waiting... suddenly, this car came up at high speed, a dark car... when they saw me... the car braked... that scared me... a guy pulled down the window glass, pointed at me and said "you're gonna die!!!" (Huni Kuin, 2017)

In addition to the flagrant death threat to Mapu, the conditions of the Huni Kuin's permanence on the site got even more complicated due to the loss of political support. On August 23rd, 2017, Mapu received a summons from the Civil police station: "When I got there, there was this chicken farmer over there saying he was going to enclose the area which was partially his." (Huni Kuin, 2017). This farmer, next to the *Parque Ecológico*, suddenly started claiming that he owned most of the land occupied by the Huni Kuin. Also, he started acting in a hostile manner against the permanence of the Indigenous group in the park.

Among other things, during a confrontation in the presence of Mapu, the farmer deliberately dropped a rifle cartridge, with the obvious intent to frighten him: "the day he was putting a fence in the area, we went to the police station to file a complaint. In front of a deputy and a prosecutor he dropped a cartridge case on the feet of a policeman." (HUNI KUIN apud CESAR, 2017). On the way back from the police station to the *Parque Ecológico*, as reported by Mapu, the farmer threatened the Huni Kuin again:

When we returned to the park, he said "from now on, in this area that is on my property, I don't want to see any Indigenous [...] even if there was a child dying there, I wouldn't let you collect a single medicinal leaf to give to this child. Let that child die, but I won't let anyone go beyond that limit to get medicinal plants or anything" (Huni Kuin, 2017)

The fence enclosure of most of the Ecological Park made by the farmer, turned the Huni Kuin's permanence extremely difficult, because "aside from making vulnerable the families who lived in the houses built by ourselves, he privatized the water [there is a brook in the area], he pulled out the plantings of cassava manioc, sugar cane, banana and trees, some of them hardwood" (Huni Kuin, as cited in Cesar, 2017).

According to Mapu's words, the death threats intensified at that point, and began to be extended to his relatives, who warned him that it would be better for him to leave Plácido de Castro and the *Parque Ecológico* before something more serious happened:

When I was out, as I was taking care of all these negotiations [with the farmer and the police], the guy [farmer] arrived and said to my sister: "do you want your brother to die? If you wish so, you may continue to transit here and seek support [with the authorities]. Now, if you don't want that to happen, you'd better get out of here, because my business is with him, not with you. My business is with your chief" (Huni Kuin, 2017)

Finally, the authorities also started backing the farmer, and Mapu reported a significant talk by some police officers about the Huni Kuin's stay in the *Parque Ecológico*: "No, not here, you *índios*, you are invaders, you are invading, let the guy build the fence, because it is his property, and you cannot, you are invaders, there is no Indigenous land here, it is not yours" (Huni Kuin, 2017).

The epithet of invaders resonates ironically when uttered by the authorities of a settler colonial state that actually sustains itself on the invasion of other people's lands and/or territories. Faced with a continuous usurpation of a sovereignty that was never ceded (cf. Pugliese, 2015), the settler colonial State also deliberately usurps the signifiers that are at disposal of Indigenous people in order to make sense of their own condition of oppression and dispossession.

CONCLUSION

When the chapter authors interviewed Mapu on December 13, 2017, he had already moved to Rio Branco. He and some of his relatives went to live in a rented house in a suburban area of the city. In terms of the other Huni Kuin of the *Parque Ecológico* of Plácido de Castro, some "returned to the Indigenous land of Jordão, others went to Tarauacá, and others went to Cruzeiro do Sul, some went back to Marechal Thaumaturgo, on the way to the Breu River region, which I originally came from" (Huni Kuin, 2017).

By the end of 2018, the Huni Kuin bought a land lot in the vicinity of the capital of Acre, 36 km from Rio Branco, and have resumed, since then, the activities of the *Huwã Karu Yushibu* centre interrupted with the expulsion of the *Parque Ecológico*. It seemed somehow that, due to the fact that they were finally able to purchase their own land lot, they could feel free, at least for a while, from all kinds of violence they had experienced up until then. However, the Huni Kuin were about to endure hard times once again.

As the authors have reported recently, on August 22nd, 2019, amid the record escalation of fires in a vast territory involving the Brazilian, Peruvian and Bolivian Amazon, which gained international repercussion, the land of the Huni Kuin was hit by a fire that completely destroyed its plantations (Souza, 2020). Interestingly, only the Huni Kuin lands were hit by fire in that perimeter, that is, the burning did not happen in farms and other surrounding lands (Souza, 2020). In an interview with the Instituto Humanitas Unisinos, Mirna Rosário, Mapu's wife, said that she was surprised by the fact that only their

Indigenous area had been affected by the fire in the forest, and highlighted: "We lost our swidden, which had banana, papaya, açaí, mundubi, which are things that are part of the Indigenous diet" (Amazônia em Chamas, 2019). Mapu and his family once again went to the local Police Station to report what happened and solicit further investigations due to the suspicious way in which the fire in their lands had occurred, but nothing followed up.

Finally, one of the critical points advanced in this chapter is that land issues for the Huni Kuin go beyond a mere discussion on possession–an apparent issue that imposes a limit on the political debate itself, and thus prevents observers from perceiving the quite distinctive life proposal inherent to Indigenous peoples, a proposal that distances itself from the parameters or paradigms established by non-Indigenous society. The common idea, even among those who are keen to support Indigenous struggles, that, quoting here again the officers from the *Parque Ecológico* in Placido de Castro, "there's no land for Indigenous peoples!" is symptomatic of a limited view of what Pugliese defines the "geopolitics of Indigenous sovereignty" (Pugliese, 2015), a vision that cannot overcome the categories imposed, even when granted as benefits by the same colonial state. Perhaps this is one of the main reasons why the Huni Kuin have found it so difficult to gain political support for their stay in Plácido de Castro.

This consideration should at least allow one the chance to further investigate the proposal of "occupation" brought by the Huni Kuin group, as well as to establish a dialogue from a paradigm of land use in the political vision Huni Kuin. Yet, such discussion remains challenging due to the legal status of the relationship with the land, implemented via the State, which likely remains outside of this vision. Consideration of the question and continued examination is necessary in order to overcome a vision of Indigenous juridical tutelage perpetrated, in many cases, by the current law in the country, despite some considerable progress over the past few years. Or at least, to enforce the Brazilian Constitution, which states that governments should

Consult with Indigenous peoples [...] as a general obligation under the Convention, in particular, through their representative institutions, whenever legislative or administrative measures affect them directly. (Article 6, paragraph 1, Convention 169, ILO)

The chapter authors understand situations like those experienced by Mapu and his relatives should be considered an opportunity, not only for Indigenous peoples from Acre, but for the society as a whole to strengthen a very important debate on the relationship with the land, beyond the issues of ownership and demarcation. The debate is increasingly urgent for the local, Brazilian, and global contemporary scene. Through this chapter, the authors expect to continue to engage in an open debate and strengthen the resistance against the structural racism historically perpetrated by the State and its colonialist actions.

Overall, this chapter continues ongoing research focused on land sovereignty and attempts to dispossession. Further research will also investigate other topics related to the Huni Kuin in Acre, such as the music of Mapu's group *Forrozeiros da Floresta* (Forró players from the forest) and its intercultural transitions, alongside the issue of school dropout due to settler-centered curricula.

REFERENCES

Albuquerque, G. R. d. (2014). História e historiografia do Acre: notas sobre os silêncios e a lógica do progresso. *Tropos: Comunicação. Society and Culture, 1*(4), 1–19.

Amazônia em Chamas. (2019). *Indígenas Huni Kuin perdem animais e árvores em incêndio, no Acre.* Author.

Antunes, F. (2016). *Cacique Mapu Huni Kuin acusa político de exigir que índios andem nus para atrair turistas em Plácido de Castro, no Acre.* Amazônia Real.

Branco, M. L., & Torronteguy, M. A. A. (2013). O SUS na fronteira e o Direito: Em que medida o estrangeiro tem direito ao SUS. *Cad. IberAmer. Direito. Sanit, 2*(2), 932–945.

Cavalcante, T. L. V. (2013). *Colonialismo, Território e Territorialidade: A luta pela terra dos Guarani e Kaiowa em Mato Grosso do Sul* (PhD Thesis). Universidade Estadual Paulista, Assis, SP.

Cesar, L. (2017). Índios acusam dono de granja de cercar terra onde funciona Parque Ecológico no interior do Acre. *G1 Acre.* https://glo.bo/2U2Gymn

COMIN. (2017). Grupo de Huni Kuin ocupa e revitaliza parque no Acre. *Conselho de Missão entre Povos Indígenas.* https://comin.org.br/?galleries=grupo-de-huni-kuin-ocupa-e-revitaliza-parque-no-acre

Constituição da República Federativa do Brasil de 1988. (2019). Convenção 169, da OIT. D5051.

Huni Kuin, M. (2017). *Interview with the authors. With the participation of Teresa Di Somma.* Universidade Federal do Acre.

Lima, E. (2011). *Parque ecológico de Plácido de Castro vira motel a céu aberto.* Blog do radialista Edizio Lima. https://bit.ly/2U2jggi

Lucena, G. X. D., & Barros, J. M. (2014). Memórias e Interações Midiatizadas: O Acre Existe? In *Anais do XII Congresso da Asociación Latinoamericana de Investigadores de las Ciencias de la Comunicación.* PUCP.

Machado, A. (2015). *Prefeito autoriza ocupação do Parque Ecológico de Plácido por indígenas.* Amazônia: Notícia e informação.

Ministério da Saúde. (n.d.). *Sistema Único de Saúde (SUS): Estrutura, princípios e como funciona.* Ministério da Saúde.

Pereira, L. (2011). *Eco Parque Municipal do Seringueiro: Ecologia do abandono.* Luiz Pereira Fala.

Plácido de Castro. (n.d.). Histórico. *Prefeitura de Plácido de Castro.*

Pugliese, J. (2007). Geocorpographies of torture. *Australian Critical Race and Whiteness Studies Association Journal, 3*(1), 1–18.

Pugliese, J. (2015). Geopolitics of Aboriginal sovereignty: Colonial law as 'a species of excess of its own authority', Aboriginal passport ceremonies and asylum seekers. *Law Text Culture, 19*, 84–115.

Senado Federal. (2009). *O tratado de limites Brasil-Peru.* Senado Federal, Conselho Editorial.

Silva, F. B., Souza, J. A., & Messina, M. (2017). Contentious narratives in Amazonian cities along the Brazil–Bolivia border: Memories and resentments turned heroic and glorious. *Bitácora Arquitectura*, (36), 130–137. doi:10.22201/fa.14058901p.2017.36.62277

Souza, J. A. (2020). Os Huni Kuin e a luta contra o colonialismo de Estado na fronteira acreana. *Muiraquitã, 9*(1).

Souza, J. A., & Messina, M. (2018). Narrativas contenciosas na fronteira das Amazônias Boliviana e Brasileira. *Revista Igarapé*, *5*(2), 332–349.

Tambs, L. A. (1966). Rubber, rebels, and Rio Branco: The contest for the acre. *The Hispanic American Historical Review*, *46*(3), 254–273. doi:10.1215/00182168-46.3.254

ADDITIONAL READING

Albuquerque, G. R. (2016). Acre. In G. R. Albuquerque & A. S. Pacheco (Eds.), *Uwa'kürü: Dicionário analítico* (pp. 13–29). Nepan Editora.

Ferreira da Silva, D. (2009). No-bodies: Law, raciality and violence. *Griffith Law Review*, *18*(2), 212–236. doi:10.1080/10383441.2009.10854638

Garvey, B., Alves, J., & Morais, M. J. (2019) Amazon in flames: Brazil's Huni Kuin Indigenous people count the social costs of fire and conflict. *The Conversation,* September 2.

Giovanella, L. Guimarães, L., Nogueira, V. M. R., Lobato, L. V. C. & Damacena, G. N. (2007). Saúde nas fronteiras: Acesso e demandas de estrangeiros e brasileiros não residentes ao SUS nas cidades de fronteira com países do MERCOSUL na perspectiva dos secretários municipais de saúde. *Cad. Saúde Pública*, Rio de Janeiro, 23 (Sup 2): S251-S266.

Messina, M. (2017). Performance-as-resistance and resistance-as-performance in the NO MUOS Movement in Sicily. *Muiraquitã - Revista de Letras e Humanidades, 5*(1), 50-94.

Messina, M., & Araújo Souza, J. (2018). Rios, pontes, balsas e fronteiras: uma provocação desde a brasilidade liminar e precária do Vale do Rio Acre. *Muiraquitã - Revista de letras e humanidades, 6*(1), 80-93.

Messina, M., & Di Somma, T. (2019). The "dispatch of education" to "rural communities" for "national unity"- The magical buzzwords of cultural genocide. *Muiraquitã - Revista de Letras e Humanidades, 7*(1), 74-83.

Perera, S., & Pugliese, J. (2020). In an impaired state: Settler racial logic and prosthetic citizenship in Australia. *International Journal of Politics Culture and Society*, *33*(4), 1–18. doi:10.100710767-020-09354-8

Pugliese, J. (2017). The Souths of" the West": Geocorpographical assemblages of plants, colonialism and race in Sergio Leone's metafigural Spaghetti Westerns. *Muiraquitã: Revista de Letras e Humanidades*, *5*(2), 11–59.

Rodrigues, M. G. M. (2002). Indigenous rights in democratic Brazil. *Human Rights Quarterly*, *24*(2), 487–512. doi:10.1353/hrq.2002.0028

Weber, I. (2006). *Um copo de cultura: os Huni Kuin (Kaxinawá) do rio Humaitá e a escola*. Edufac.

KEY TERMS AND DEFINITIONS

Acre: The Westernmost state in Brazil, situated in the Amazon region and bordering with Peru and Bolívia.

Geocorpographies: A term coined by Joseph Pugliese in 2009 that addresses the interplay between human bodies and the geopolitical representations associated to them.

Huni Kuin: Also known as Kaxinawá, they are an Indigenous people inhabiting the basin of the Purus river and its affluents, between Peru and Brazil.

Índio: The (sometimes derogatory) settler-colonial epithet commonly given to Indigenous people in Brazil. Cf. also the Spanish form *indio*.

Jus Soli: A system of assignation of birthright citizenship, based on the principle anyone born within the territorial premises of a specific sovereign country automatically gain the right to be a citizen of said country. This system is dominant in the Americas, but not in Europe, for instance.

Plácido de Castro: Refers to (1) the Brazilian military leader José Plácido de Castro, who led the Acre war against Bolivia; and (2) the town in the Brazilian State of Acre, bordering with Bolivia.

Settler Colonialism: A specific type of colonial occupation that achieves or at least envisages the replacement of the local populations with settlers.

ENDNOTES

1 This chapters expands on, translates to English, and furthers the research published in a previous conference paper in Portuguese by the chapter authors. See Messina, M., & Souza, J. A. (2019). Colonialismo e confisco de terras, ou como os Huni Kuin foram expulsos de Plácido de Castro, no Acre. Linguística e Literaturana Amazônia: Políticas de pesquisa para as margens: anais. Manaus: UEA.

2 All translations from Portuguese are by the chapter authors.

Chapter 12
Intergenerational Trauma and Other Unique Challenges as Barriers to Native American Educational Success

Thomas Reed
University of San Diego, USA

ABSTRACT

This chapter examines unique challenges in the way of Native American educational success as well as solutions to overcoming. The chapter addresses why intergenerational trauma matters, the impacts of public policy on Native American people such as the Native American Languages Act of 1990, and the importance of Native American people being connected to the land, protecting traditions, language, and their ancestors. The purpose of this literature review is to shed light on Native American educational barriers and to critique existing literature. Areas analyzed include the trend of low rates of educational attainment among Native Americans, the history of abuse towards Indigenous people and other minorities, the impact on individuals, and solutions for the future. There is a need for Native American students to stay connected to cultural tradition, cultural relevancy in education, role models for Native American people, and an importance of Native American students staying connected to family.

INTRODUCTION

This chapter presents the results of a literature review of more than 60 journal articles and books with a focus on unique challenges stunting Native American educational success. In synthesizing different themes found in the literature on the current state of Native American education, the author explores the history, context, historical trauma and abuse experienced by Indigenous peoples and minority groups while pursuing an education (Adams, 1995; Anderson, n.d.; Blackhawk, 1995; Boyer, 1997; Harmon, 2010; Lawrence, 2000; Lewis & McLester, 2005; Mello & Wolf, 2010; Pacheco et al., 2013; Powers, 1932; Torpy, 2000). Subsequently, the chapter also offers solutions for overcoming educational obstacles

DOI: 10.4018/978-1-7998-3729-9.ch012

for Native Americans based on best practices from ethnic groups around the world and will discuss the necessity for Native Americans to remain immersed in cultural values to ensure educational success (Coladarci, 1983; Covarrubias & Fryberg, 2015; Guillory & Wolverton, 2008; Kanu, 2006; Tierney, 1992).

The purpose of this literature review is to shed light on Native American educational barriers and to critique existing literature. As a clarification of terms, the label of Native American will be used interchangeably with American Indian, Indian, Indigenous, Aboriginal, First Nations, and Native depending on how it was used by researchers in the literature. This chapter highlights the trend of low rates of educational attainment among Native Americans, the history of abuse towards Indigenous people and other minorities, the impact on individuals, and solutions for the future.

Within the overarching theme of a history of abuse in the Native American community, this literature review will discuss the prominent subthemes of perceptions of bias in history towards Native Americans (Blackhawk, 1995; Powers, 1932; Tierney, 1992), researchers misleading Native Americans through harmful studies that take place against Indigenous people (Harmon, 2010; Lawrence, 2000; Mello & Wolf, 2010; Pacheco et al., 2013; Torpy, 2000), and the traumatic impact of the forced boarding school system in the early 20th century (Adams, 1995; Anderson, n.d.; Boyer, 1997; Lewis & McLester, 2005). Finally, this literature review will synthesize best practices from around the world in battling historical trauma and the importance of Native Americans preserving their cultural traditions while striving for educational success. Three subthemes emerge in Native Americans staying connected to cultural tradition for educational success: the value of cultural relevance in the curriculum (Coladarci, 1983; Covarrubias, Fryberg, 2015; Guillory & Wolverton, 2008; Kanu, 2006; Tierney, 1992), the importance of Native American role models (Covarrubias & Fryberg, 2015; Guillory & Wolverton, 2008), and the significance of family (Guillory & Wolverton, 2008; Tierney, 1992).

A brief introduction and context for framing unique challenges in the way of Native American educational success is followed by an examination of current western educational attainment rates of Native American students, then the unique challenges to Native American students pursuing a western education is considered. The history of abuse, deception and discrimination to Native American people in research and the impact to individuals and communities with potential solutions to unique challenges in the way of Native American educational success followed by a conclusion and summary. The objective of this chapter is to identify unique challenges in the way of Native American educational success and to provide solutions for overcoming those challenges.

BACKGROUND

Native American people's connection to land, spirit, their ancestors, and our Creator is at the very core of understanding this chapter and in understanding the unique obstacles in the way of Native American people receiving a western education. A person should not separate the past from having relevance to Native American people, as for many Native American people the concept of seven generations is a notion in which all of our actions are to be done with recognition to seven generations to our past and simultaneously have actions be done for seven generations into our future. Chief Oren Lyons who is Faith keeper of the Onondaga Nation stated when making decisions it is best not to make decisions for yourself, or even for your family, but to make decisions while keeping in mind how this will impact generations to come (Johns Hopkins Center for American Indian Health, 2020). A linear, Gregorian calendar of time is not always aligned with a Native American construct of time, where time and events are connected in the past, present and future simultaneously. To discount events which occurred to Native Americans in the past is to invalidate their experiences as human beings.

A dictionary definition of genocide may infer an intentional and systematic destruction of a specifically-defined group, and the past genocide is what Native American students continue to overcome in the current decade. To the point of relevancy of inherited post-traumatic-stress-disorder (PTSD) being passed down through generations, known as intergenerational trauma, has been an obstacle in achieving an education for Native American students. The term "blood memories" is used when discussing inherited traumatic memories by Native American people (Duran et al., 1998). For example, Duran et al. (1998) discussed a Native American individual in a community who would feel strange, negative feelings, and overall incredible sadness when the individual would walk by a certain place in their community, and elders notified this individual the place where they experienced feelings of trauma is where a massacre happened to their people over a 100 years ago (Duran et al., 1998). Without foreknowledge of the event, this Native American person, as have other Native American people, experienced blood memories through intergenerational trauma.

In support of blood memories, the chapter author pursued a Certificate in American Indian Studies as part of a master's degree program and recalled taking an American Indian studies course where the Native American professor discussed blood memories and how they are experienced by Native American people. When this occurred, a Native American classmate began to cry from their desk in the back of the classroom. Through tears, the classmate stated how they had experienced those blood memories, and other family members and friends they had known did as well. The person continued to uncontrollably cry for what felt like a few minutes as a somber class soberly attempted to regain composure. This anecdote illustrates the existence of blood memories, intergenerational trauma, and why these concepts are of crucial importance when considering unique obstacles in the way of Native American education. In a more recent example, the chapter author played a video game where the protagonist is a Mohawk, or Kanien'keha:ka (pronounced gwen-yay-gahn-ha-ga) person, and the character's village is burned down, which is based on actual events of George Washington burning down the villages of certain Haudenosaunee, also known as Iroquois villages, including the Oneida (the chapter authors' relatives and ancestors). When the protagonist called out for their mother through the flames in their traditional Kanien'keha:ka language, the game was paused and the chapter author sobbed uncontrollably, feeling the blood memory and pain experienced by the ancestors, as if it was happening in real time. These intergenerational trauma and blood memories are of great relevancy for understanding unique obstacles in the way of Native American educational success.

To summarize what may at first appear as unrelated points about Native Americans are actually quite connected and essential to understand the unique obstacles that impede Native American pursuit of an education. Native American artist and activist, Gregg Deal (2018a), whose work, "deals with Indigenous identity and pop culture, touching on issues of race relations, historical consideration and stereotype" stated, "Today I was asked: 'What is most important to Indigenous people? The Land? Protecting traditions? Your language? Or your people' I told him: 'Those are all the same things" (Deal, 2018b). What Deal said rings true; Native American people are connected to their community and ancestors, the soil of Turtle Island, preserving generational knowledge, and reclaiming Native American languages which were only made legal to speak by the federal government in 1990 (Native American Languages Act, 1990). The Native Americans Languages Act of 1990, "declares to preserve, protect and promote the rights and freedom of Native Americans to use practice and develop Native American Languages" (Native American Languages Act, 1990). A Native American student's grandparents first language was illegal to speak until 1990, which impacts how parents are able to help and support through their children with their studies, and this cycle is perpetuated intergenerationally. The past matters, especially for Native American people pursuing an education and concurrently experiencing the aftermath of colonization remains challenging.

Current Western Educational Attainment Rates for Native American Students

Past researchers have indicated a considerable disparity in the current state of educational attainment for Native Americans. Numerous researchers observed Native American people tend to have low rates of education (Covarrubias & Fryberg, 2015; Field, 2016; Guillory, 2009; Ladson-Billings, 2006; Office of Minority Health [OMH], 2018; Ogunwole et al., 2012; Perna, 2000). Literature reports findings of Native American students: low high school graduation rates (Coladarci, 1983; Covarrubias & Fryberg, 2015; Field, 2016; Ladson-Billings, 2006), low higher education graduation rates (Covarrubias & Fryberg, 2015; Guillory, 2009; Ogunwole et al., 2012; Perna, 2000), and challenges in the way of Native American educational success (Covarrubias & Fryberg, 2015; Field, 2016; Ladson-Billings, 2006). All of the aforementioned variables contribute to a significantly lower academic achievement rate for Native Americans.

Low Graduation Rates for Native American High School Students

Research emphasizes Native Americans have low high school graduation rates when compared to other ethnicities and races (Coladarci, 1983; Covarrubias & Fryberg, 2015; Field, 2016; Ladson-Billings, 2006). Literature indicates the graduation rate is approximately 57% for Native American high school students (Ladson-Billings, 2006). It is important to bear in mind research by Ladson-Billings fails to describe the distinction of educational attainment among the culturally specific 574 unique federally recognized tribes and refers to all the distinct tribes as simply "Native Americans." Future research would benefit from examining one specific Native American tribe culturally in relation to educational attainment. Coladarci's (1983) study provides an insightful examination of 46 Native American high school dropouts in Montana. Coladarci outlined the unique cultural factors influencing dropout rates, such as Native American students' perception of their teachers' apathy and the irrelevance of the curriculum to Native American culture. The methodology for this case study used interviews from 46 participants and identified cultural factors unique to the Native American community. Coladarci concluded Native American high school dropouts report withdrawing from school because of perceived cultural insensitivity or irrelevance of their culture in the curriculum. Furthermore, students who dropped out articulated a perception of teachers' apathy toward their education (Coladarci, 1983). Although the case study in Montana offers a unique depiction of Native American dropout rates, further research is needed to identify Native American tribes in different regions and their educational challenges to help researchers gain a more comprehensive view of the issue at large.

Low Rates of Native Americans in Higher Education

Low high school graduation rates logically lead to low higher education rates for Native Americans because a diploma is a prerequisite for a college or university degree. American Indians have the lowest college enrollment rates (less than 1% nationally), as well as the lowest graduation rates compared to any other student cohort in the United States university system (Guillory, 2009). Researchers found Native Americans have the lowest rate for attaining a bachelor's degree (Covarrubias & Fryberg, 2015; Guillory, 2009; Ogunwole et al., 2012) and doctoral degree compared to other ethnic groups (OMH, 2018). Statistics from the U.S. Census recognized 13% of Native Americans receive bachelor's degrees, as opposed to the total population rate of 27% (Ogunwole et al., 2012). Research also shows 6% of American Indians have an advanced degree (i.e., medical., law, master's, or Ph.D.) compared to 12% of the non-Hispanic white student population (OMH, 2018). American Indians comprise 0.6% of all associate's, bachelor's, and advanced degrees completed in the United States (Guillory, 2009). While Guillory's (2009) implementation of a multiple case study approach to recognize specific variables impacting Native Americans in higher education has benefits, perhaps employing a quantitative study of a document analysis by assessing the number of Native American students at each institution of higher education nationally could be helpful in gaining a more accurate understanding of the percentage of Native Americans in higher education.

Furthermore, with very few Native American role models in academia, Native American students can feel a lack of belonging in the educational system (Covarrubias & Fryberg, 2015). Covarrubias and Fryberg (2015) stated the underrepresentation negatively impacts a sense of belonging as well as adversely impacting academic performance

A lack of role models in education plays a pivotal role in the success of Native American students. In a 2007 study by Walton and Cohen, the methodology of two experiments with White and Black students measuring their sense of belonging in academia is insightful; in this study, Black students felt stigmatized in academia because of a lack of role models. However, the study fails to include a Native American sample of students yet makes assertions about Native Americans' sense of belonging in academia. For some studies about ethnicities in education, there were limited Native American students enrolled and thus, the data were deemed insufficient information for detailed analysis (Perna, 2000). While research recognizes Native Americans are not adequately represented in higher education, research on students deciding to go to college (Perna, 2000) would have been more compelling if the methodology for the study were to conduct data gathering of their own for compiling Native American data in higher education. Instead the researchers in the 1994 National Education Longitudinal study stated they did not have enough data to analyze Native Americans in higher education.

Research studies consistently show a low rate of educational attainment for Native American people. It is interesting to note educational journals like *The Journal of Higher Education*, *Journal of Developmental Education,* and *Educational Researcher*, focus on this issue as opposed to Native American journals. Different educational publications conducting independent studies and reporting the same conclusions regarding the disparity in education for Native Americans strengthen the validity of the findings (Covarrubias & Fryberg, 2015; Guillory, 2009; Ogunwole et al., 2012).

UNIQUE CHALLENGES TO NATIVE AMERICAN EDUCATIONAL SUCCESS

There is little disagreement among current and past researchers as to the vast educational gap for Native Americans. Researchers have acknowledged the unique challenges Native Americans encounter in the journey toward educational attainment (Anyon et al., 2014; Covarrubias & Fryberg, 2015; Field, 2016; Ladson-Billings, 2006; Krezmien et al., 2006). In addition, researchers reported Native Americans face different barriers in attaining education, of which include hurdles from the United States Congress through federal government policy (Native American Languages Act, 1990). In 1864, the U.S. Congress passed legislation making it illegal for Native Americans to learn their own Indigenous language (Ladson-Billings, 2006). Until 1990, it was illegal for Native Americans to speak their own language (Native American Languages Act, 1990). It would only be through the Native American Languages Act of 1990 which would allow Native Americans to speak their native languages (Native American Languages Act, 1990). Prior to 1990, all education was to be delivered in the English language; this legal requirement inhibited individual learning at one's fullest capacity as this was a second language to many Native Americans. Additionally, the ability to have parental support with homework or guide the student along their educational journey was more difficult due to a language barrier. Covarrubias and Fryberg (2015) also observed a lack of belonging for Native American people in education.

Minorities are often taught a different culture and sometimes language at school than in their own homes (Ogbu, 1990). A predominantly White Anglo Saxon culture taught in school reinforces systematic oppression, which leads to disparities in education for minorities. In a study of 45 textbooks, Kane (1970) showed the perspective of history is portrayed from a white, Protestant, Anglo Saxon view, and that the perspective of minorities was largely ignored. Future research methodologies would benefit from improving upon previous literature's textual analysis by conducting surveys and interviews on the perspective of history from White communities and marginalized communities (specifically Native American people) to gain a better understanding of how history is predominantly told from an Anglo Saxon view.

The National Center for Education Statistics (NCES) stated the dropout rate among the Native American population was roughly 15%, which is higher than Asian/Pacific Islanders, Blacks, or Whites (Ladson-Billings, 2006). The literature took into consideration different races by comparison and made a clear conclusion from the data. Researchers found expulsions were disproportionately high for Native American students (Anyon et al., 2014; Krezmien, Leone, & Achilles, 2006). Researchers argued disproportionate suspensions towards Native American students cause them to fall behind and can be a contributing factor in a Native American student's decision to drop out of school (Anyon et al., 2014; Krezmien, Leone, & Achilles, 2006). A possible critique of this literature is the conclusions made (Anyon et al., 2014; Krezmien, Leone, & Achilles, 2006) could suffer from endogeneity, in which there could be other variables not controlled for other than the students being Native American. It could be logical there are specific factors Native American students share, but accurate assertions would require further research or else claims would be speculative at best.

Historical Abuse, Deception, and Discrimination

Literature about Native American people and culture stresses the negative experiences endured by Native American people through abuse, deception, and discrimination, particularly since the formation of the United States (Adams, 1995; Anderson, n.d.; Blackhawk, 1995; Boyer, 1997; Harmon, 2010; Lawrence, 2000; Lewis & McLester, 2005; Mello & Wolf, 2010; Miller, 2011; Pacheco et al., 2013; Powers, 1932; Schuman et al., 2005; Torpy, 2000). Since the dawn of the United States until now, the federal government has broken every single treaty made with tribal nations (Lyons, 1992). It is described by tribal elders, who are well-respected, senior citizen community members, that when Native Americans were forced onto reservations, they would be removed from the land if it was found to have any desirable traits. For example, if a reservation had land that was desirable for farming, the tribe would be relocated to a different area (Lyons, 1992). If the land the Native American tribes lived on had abundant natural resources, the Native American tribe would be transferred elsewhere.

It is a revelatory statement to unveil that Native Americans are exiled in the land of the free. These accounts are available from Native American scholars and the oral tradition, which are the firsthand experiences of Native American people, rather than from a public administration scholarly journal. A lack of references to other scholarly sources or government research discussing Native Americans being exiled in the land of the free has to do with an overall lack of research from a western perspective on Native American people. Within the theme of a history of abuse to Native American communities are perceptions of bias in history against Native Americans (Blackhawk, 1995; Powers, 1932; Tierney, 1992), misleading research by researchers done against the Native American community (Harmon, 2010; Lawrence, 2000; Mello & Wolf, 2010; Pacheco et al., 2013; Torpy, 2000), and the negative impact of the boarding school system towards Native Americans.

Researcher Bias Towards Native Americans in Writing History

Researchers observed perceptions of bias in history exist against Native Americans. For instance, history books usually gloss over the original presence of Native Americans in the United States with perhaps a paragraph of text when discussing the approximate 250 year history of the country (Lyons, 1992). Furthermore, there is limited reference in literature (Lyons, 1992; Miller, 2011) to the presence of over 2,000 Native American tribal nations who lived for thousands of years in North America before the existence of European colonists and the formation of the United States. There are also perceptions of bias in history in terms of how historical events are framed. For example, people often state that Christopher Columbus discovered North America, when in fact this statement is biased against Native Americans and is untrue. How can Columbus have discovered a place where people had already been existing for thousands of years (Miller, 2011; Schuman et al., 2005)?

Even some contemporary research that examines people's perception of Christopher Columbus (Schuman et al., 2005) has bias in the reporting of their findings as it notes that Native American activists are the primary disputers of Christopher Columbus' legacy, as opposed to the general population. Why would primarily Native Americans care to correct the history of the past when it applies to all inhabitants of North America and worldwide? A further example of bias in history against Native American people is the idea of "manifest destiny," where westward expansion was deemed as a right from God for colonists, also referred to as settler society (Miller, 2011). Paintings depicting this era of westward expansion display Indigenous inhabitants being pushed out with industry and developments (Miller, 2011). Reflecting further on the perception of bias in history against Native Americans summons the hundreds of western films made, the majority of which depict wars against Native Americans, with cowboys as the hero (Diamond et al., 2009).

Native Americans' perspective on history is not generally taken into account (Blackhawk, 1995; Powers, 1932; Tierney, 1992). Native American lives in history have not always been valued the same as those of their colonial counterparts. A seminal articulation of this perspective is from Mary Powers (1932), who stated:

It was only as the white man encroached more and more, as he drove the Indian farther and farther toward the setting sun, that the red man did retaliate and take a stand for national existence. Every white man who fought for home, country, or religion is considered a patriot; but every Indian who did likewise is termed a murderous savage. (p. 11)

This statement was written by Powers, an Iroquois woman, and is still not readily found in academic journals to this day. Native Americans were deemed murderous savages for trying to protect the land they lived on for thousands of years. History is written by the victors and the history of the United States is generally from the colonial settler perspective and for the most part, ignores the Native American narrative and presence in the formation and history of the United States (Lyons, 1992; Miller, 2011).

The Native American voice and perspective is left out of public policy decision making through a lack of representation in political leadership (Ladson-Billings, 2006), with the exception of two recent congresswomen elected into office which was further celebrated as a historic moment due to their Native identity. Ladson-Billings (2006) argued research could go further in offering solutions to having Native Americans be a part of the civic process by recognizing an Indigenous people's history in the United States. Tierney (1992) pointed out how differences in perception of history stem from differing perspectives on life. Tierney noted Vine Deloria, Jr. in *The Metaphysics of Modern Existence* asserts Indians and non-Indians have two entirely different perceptions of the world. Literature which considers the Native American perspective in history produces a type of a counter-narrative to the mainly accepted notion of history from a colonial perspective (Blackhawk, 1995; Powers, 1932; Schuman et al., 2005; Tierney, 1992). Research that accounts for Native American perspectives recognizes Indigenous voices are often excluded from the mainstream narrative.

Abuse Through Misleading and Harmful Actions in Research

Researchers further noted deceitful and harmful scientific and medical research towards Native Americans (Harmon, 2010; Lawrence, 2000; Mello & Wolf, 2010; Pacheco et al., 2013; Torpy, 2000). One particular misleading form of medical malpractice researchers noted was the sterilization of Native American women without their knowledge or consent prior to and through the 1970s (Lawrence, 2000; Torpy, 2000). During the 1970s, thousands of women of color and poor women, including Chicanos, Puerto Ricans, and Blacks were sterilized without their full knowledge (Torpy, 2000). Native American women were particularly susceptible targets to forced sterilization due to tribal dependence on the Bureau of Indian Affairs, Department of Health, Education and Welfare, and the Indian Health Service (Torpy, 2000). Forced sterilization is a fundamental violation of human rights, as no group of people should try to exterminate another group of people through genocide without their permission or knowledge. Based on orders derived from federal policy, hysterectomies were performed on Native Americans without their consent while undergoing surgery for an entirely different procedure. It is fascinating the journal articles that note this travesty (Lawrence, 2000; Torpy, 2000) are from the publishers *The American Indian Quarterly* and *American Indian Culture and Research Journal* and not from more non-native research journals. While this issue of sterilization of Native American women concerns Native American people and it would be reasonable that the journal articles would be available in publications specifically about Native American people, the forced sterilization of Native American women against their will should be recorded in medical journals, as well as, journals on ethics.

The unethical research done towards the Havasupai tribe under the pretenses of diabetes research is an additional example in the literature of deceitful and harmful medical research done to Native Americans by researchers (Harmon, 2010; Mello & Wolf, 2010; Pacheco et al., 2013). Researchers indicated the Havasupai tribe gave blood samples in the 1990s in hopes of improving diabetes research. Arizona State University used those blood samples to determine mental illness and to deny the right to geographic ownership of land for the Havasupai people (Harmon, 2010; Mello & Wolf, 2010; Pacheco et al., 2013).

The New England Journal of Medicine does advantageous work for future research when they frame the misleading research done against the Havasupai people as a conversation on the ethical nature of using biospecimen samples for further research in the future (Mello & Wolf, 2010). The researchers do an adequate job of considering the Native American participants as people and not solely as test subjects (Harmon, 2010; Mello & Wolf, 2010; Pacheco et al., 2013).

Abuse to Native Americans Through the Boarding School System

For many Native American people, the boarding school system of the early 20th century is synonymous with trauma and abuse (Adams, 1995; Anderson, n.d.; Boyer, 1997; Lewis & McLester, 2005). The First Nations people in Canada experienced similar abuse through the residential school systems (Elias, 2012). Researchers identify the last of the "Indian Wars" were in classrooms in the boarding school system (Adams, 1995). Researchers have documented the negative warlike experience of the boarding school systems by thoroughly examining government documents, boarding school newspapers, and student and teacher autobiographies (Adams, 1995). Research in the future would be more comprehensive by employing a methodology of interviews from former boarding school students and their descendants to gain an extensive picture of everything that transpired during the boarding school era. For some Native American people, the abuse was so severe some students chose to run away even if it meant becoming an enemy of the country (Anderson, n.d.). The records of Carlisle Indian Boarding School are now accessible to the public. From the released Carlisle Boarding School Records, the subhuman treatment of Native American people is made clear from the perspective of students and administration (Anderson, n. d.). Carlisle is where my great grandfather Anderson Cornelius was forcibly taken from his home to go to school in Pennsylvania, and Carlisle was used as an archetype other Indian boarding schools across the United States. Canada also had what are known as residential schools.

Information concerning specific abuse towards Native Americans at boarding schools is sparser in academic literature. To provide a sense of these educational institutions, Indian Boarding Schools had cemeteries on site for children who passed away during their schooling and jails for students who did not abide by institutional rules (Adams, 1995). Similar to the aftereffects of war, research specify how post-traumatic stress disorder (PTSD) through intergenerational trauma is a common association for descendants of those who experienced the Indian boarding school systems (Adams, 1995).

Researchers also stressed the negative impact of the boarding school systems (Adams, 1995; Anderson, n.d.; Boyer, 1997; Lewis & McLester, 2005). Unless literature strictly ignores the Native American perspective during the forced boarding school era, it would be difficult to draw a conclusion which was not one of damage done by the Indian boarding schools to the Native American community culturally, emotionally, and mentally. A 1940 interview with Anderson Cornelius, an attendant of the boarding school system between 1908 and 1914, reveals Anderson initially only knew the words "yes" and "no" in the English language as he only spoke his native tongue of Oneida (Anderson, n.d.). During classes at Carlisle Boarding School, Anderson would guess between "yes" or "no" to say in school in response to questions (Anderson, n.d.). Cornelius revealed if he said the wrong phrase, he would be beaten (Anderson, n.d.). If he was caught speaking his traditional language, he would be beaten (Anderson, n.d.). Adams (1995) noted the lessons taught in boarding schools of "kill the Indian to save the man" was not taught passively, and the lasting impact, as researchers assert, is an obstacle to overcome of mistrust of the educational system in the Native American community in the century since Indian boarding school era. There is a justifiable need in research for the methodology of future studies to include interviews on the impact of the Indian boarding schools on former students and their descendants. This resonates with the theme of accounts being present in first-hand Native American documents, yet largely absent in scholarly literature.

Impact on Individuals and Community

Historical trauma is a research term, with use across the world, to refer to the intergenerational trauma that is passed down from ancestors, often impacting groups of people who have experienced a collective traumatic event (Atkinson, 2002; Bombay et al., 2009; Denham, 2008; Fast & Collin-Vézina, 2010; Giladi & Bell, 2013; Gray & Beresford, 2008; Elias, 2012; Jervis et al., 2006; Johnston-Goodstar & VeLure Roholt, 2017; Lambert et al., 2014; Lyons, 1992; Menzies, 2007; O'Loughlin, 2009; Pihama et al., 2017; Quinn, 2007; Raphael et al., 1998; Rowland-Klein & Dunlop, 1998; Steel et al., 2002). There is evidence to support that the annihilation of culture and resulting loss of identity can lead to the intergenerational transmission of trauma and can negatively impact the individual by giving rise to addictive and self-destructive behaviors, and can negatively impact the community with loss of collective hope (O'Loughlin, 2009). These research findings gain strength in their validity from similar findings for First Nations people in Canada and their experiences of historical trauma due to a history of colonization and oppression (Bombay et al., 2009; Elias, 2012; Fast & Collin-Vézina, 2010; Menzies, 2007; Quinn, 2007). Also, the aboriginal people of Australia experience historical trauma (Atkinson, 2002; Gray & Beresford, 2008; O'Loughlin, 2009; Raphael et al., 1998), as well as, the Maori in New Zealand (Pihama et al., 2017). There has also been evidence to support Holocaust survivors and their descendants experiencing historical trauma (Giladi, & Bell, 2013; Rowland-Klein & Dunlop, 1998).

Furthermore, the devastating impact trauma can have on the health and wellbeing of a whole population is further supported by research regarding refugees (Momartin et al., 2003; Momartin et al., 2004; Silove et al., 2007). For different refugees, such as for trauma-affected refugees seeking refuge in Australia, PTSD occurs from the trauma of displacement (Momartin et al., 2003; Momartin et al., 2004; Silove et al., 2007; Steel et al., 2002). The case of Native Americans is particularly egregious since they are displaced and exiled from their original land. Where do Native Americans seek refuge while being occupied by a nation known for being "the land of the free and the home of the brave" (Lyons, 1992)?

A history of abuse towards minorities also adversely affects mental health (Chou et al., 2012; Karlsen & Nazroo, 2002; Nazroo, 2003; Schraufnagel et al., 2006). The negative mental health impact associated with the perception of racial discrimination towards minorities in the United States is connected to major depressive disorder, PTSD, panic disorder with agoraphobia, agoraphobia with no history of panic disorders, as well as substance abuse, regardless of gender, age, level of education, and socioeconomic status (Chou et al., 2012). Chou et al. examined 2,795 African Americas, 951 Hispanic Americans, and 793 Asian Americans through a Composite International Diagnostic Review; however, researchers failed to take into account any Native American participants in their study. Also, previous research methodologies may be subject to further investigation in terms of validity and reliability, as participants of the survey may have more strongly polarized opinions than those who choose not to participate in the study. This response bias may cause results to not reflect accurate findings of the population.

There is evidence racial discrimination leads to health inequalities in the U.S. and the U.K. (Nazroo, 2003), as studies have been done measuring the similar adverse health impacts through racial discrimination in England and Wales (Karlsen & Nazroo, 2002). Evidence further supports a history of abuse towards minorities negatively impacts educational success (Wallace Jr. et al., 2008). Researchers in the

U.K. have done an effective job of conducting a series of regression analysis on data from the Fourth National Survey of Ethnic Minorities on 5,196 marginalized people from different ethnic groups with a comparison sample of 2,867 white people in examining perceptions of racism. Future research could shed light on Native American people's perceptions to racism if the same study done in the U.K. (Wallace Jr. et al., 2008) were to be replicated in the United States. Overall, considerable research shows trauma, continuous and systemic abuse, and continued discrimination can impact the physical and mental well-being of individuals and whole communities. Such trauma is the undeniable and ever present background to the academic challenges Native Americans consistently face.

Solutions to Impediments of Native American Educational Success

Various best practices have been utilized to combat historical trauma and abuse in different countries and with different groups of people. In Canada, where Indigenous people have endured a similar history of colonization and oppression, some First Nations best practices include self-government and a connection to spirit and culture (Fast et al., 2010). Further, best practices from the First Nations in Canada include social political advocacy, developing critical consciousness, role modeling, self-healing, decolonization (Sinclair, 2004), and preserving aboriginal healing practices (Quinn, 2007). Best practices from aboriginal people in Australia are to truly listen to one another (through what is known as the "aboriginal gift," known as Dadirri) and to truly contemplate every person's place in society (Atkinson, 2002). Research on aboriginal people overcoming historical trauma in Australia recommends restorative educational practices, where aboriginal youth are educated in cultural narratives, a sense of purpose, and in ancestral memories (O'Loughlin, 2009). Best practices for Holocaust survivors and their children for reducing secondary traumatic stress associated with historical trauma include a better sense of self differentiation, as well as, better communication in families (Giladi & Bell, 2013). Best practices in the research of minorities overcoming a history of abuse is encouraging education and informing students that it is plausible to be agents of change who work in conjunction alongside civil rights movements (Kane, 1970).

Many approaches have been used to intervene on these problems and some of have worked while others have not had a positive impact for Native Americans to overcome the obstacles in the journey of educational attainment. There is evidence, however, that use of best practices for Native American people to overcome historical trauma include (a) framing intergenerational trauma into a narrative of resiliency (Denham, 2008), (b) staying connected to traditional practices, (c) fostering a sense of belonging for connectedness (Hill, 2006), (d) using repatriation to return ancestors to Indigenous communities so communities can heal (Thornton, 2003), and (e) answers to healing lie with the Native American people themselves (Grayshield, 2015).

Importance of Native Americans Staying Connected to Cultural Tradition

There is a body of past literature which notes the importance of Native American people staying connected to their cultural tradition (Coladarci, 1983; Covarrubias & Fryberg, 2015; Guillory & Wolverton, 2008; Kanu, 2006; Tierney, 1992). Native Americans are considered a collectivist culture, as opposed to the individualist culture in the United States. There is evidence to support that individualist cultures put themselves first, whereas collectivist cultures put the good of the collective or group first (Dickson et al., 2012). Often, Native American students are placed with the same lens for success as Non-Native students in the United States, when in fact more collectivist cultural values exist for Native American students as opposed to more individualistic cultural views by their Non-Native counterparts. This impacts Native American students' learning because a collectivistic mindset takes into consideration the success of the group and the wisdom from people's family members as a means of education, and Non-Native students tend to view education as a competition and focuses on the individual's success.

Literature points out the value and importance of Native Americans staying connected to their cultural tradition (Coladarci, 1983; Covarrubias & Fryberg, 2015; Guillory & Wolverton, 2008; Kanu, 2006; Tierney, 1992). Evidence is strong that in order to achieve success, Native American children should stay connected to their cultural traditions (Coladarci, 1983; Covarrubias & Fryberg, 2015; Guillory & Wolverton, 2008; Kanu, 2006; Tierney, 1992). For example, in 1975 the American Academy of Child Psychiatry urged that Native American children not be placed in white homes, as the children were twice as likely as Native American youth living on reservations to commit suicide due to a lack of identity caused by the loss of their ties to tribal customs (Americans, 1998). Within the importance of Native Americans staying connected to their cultural traditions is the value of cultural relevance in education (Coladarci, 1983; Guillory & Wolverton, 2008; Kanu, 2006; Tierney, 1992), importance of Native American role models (Covarrubias & Fryberg, 2015; Guillory & Wolverton, 2008), and importance of family for Native American students and people (Guillory & Wolverton, 2008; Tierney, 1992). Evidence supports that perceived irrelevance and insensitivity in curricula is a large reason for Native American students dropping out (Coladarci, 1983).

Importance of Native American Cultural Relevance in Education

Having culturally-relevant curriculum has been pinpointed by researchers as a key factor for Native American success (Coladarci, 1983; Covarrubias & Fryberg, 2015; Guillory & Wolverton, 2008; Kanu, 2006; Tierney, 1992). Whereas Kanu (2006) stated:

the transformative power of integration of Native culture to enhance the understanding of all students about Native issues, to increase the self-esteem and pride of Native students, and to alleviate ignorance and racism among dominant cultural groups. For this reason, he [Teacher A in the study] integrated Native perspectives into not only in his social studies course, but also his other courses, and even his extracurricular activities with students (p. 176)

The methodology of the Kanu (2006) study uses case studies and interviews in a qualitative study to make a strong argument for the importance of Native Americans being taught with culturally relevant curricula. A further example of a teacher incorporating culturally relevant curriculum is by playing the traditional Native American game of lacrosse to combat diabetes. Kanu used interviews with concrete details to show the impact of culturally relevant curriculum. A study done in the state of Montana with 46 high school dropout students found that perceived cultural insensitivity in curricula, as well as, perceived cultural irrelevance were key reasons for dropping out (Coladarci, 1983).

Future research is needed to examine other geographic areas and tribes' relation to education, which could offer different results of data than those respondents in 1983 due to technological or other societal changes over the last 37 years. Literature recognizes Native Americans have a unique cultural factor of history that transpired before colonists arrived in North America. Further research noted a solution would be for universities to shift from an atmosphere of competition and achievement to one that encourages collaboration and cooperation, (Tierney, 1992) which connects with the theme of the collectivistic mindset of Native Americans. It is evident Native Americans have a different idea of success in education than mainstream colonial culture does.

Importance of Native American Role Models

Researchers described the detrimental impact of a lack of Native American role models (Covarrubias & Fryberg, 2015; Guillory & Wolverton, 2008). The authors stated:

Native American students encounter limited exposure to positive representations (i.e., role models) in the academic domain. This underrepresentation threatens students' identities in the classroom, subsequently decreasing feelings of school belonging and negatively impacting academic performance. (Covarrubias & Fryberg, 2015, p. 1099)

The two experiments on belonging by Covarrubias and Fryberg (2015) with White and Black students support the notion of the importance of role models for marginalized groups of people. The findings of the research were that Black students were negatively impacted by being told in experiment one that they would have few friends in the intellectual domain and were positively impacted in their academic achievement in experiment two through an intervention that reduced doubt about social belonging in college.

Importance of Family for Native American People

Researchers have identified family being a prioritized value for Native Americans (Guillory & Wolverton, 2008; Tierney, 1992). As noted before, family connects back to this notion of a collectivistic mindset. Literature records a major contributor to high attrition rates for disadvantaged youth is a failure of institutions to recognize the difference between Native American values centered around family and institutional values (Guillory & Wolverton, 2008). The importance of the value of family was evident in literature for Native American people. An alternative framework with the intent to improve Native American academic achievement would be to incorporate the Native American cultural value of family into education, including framing higher education, not as a sudden shift from one world to a different one. Rather, a solution could be to frame college as incorporating, as well as reinforcing what an individual has learned from their extended family (Tierney, 1992). Proponents for incorporating family and cultural relevance into curriculum for Native American students have argued for those students to hold onto their family connections through their education while also forming community with the local Native American tribes and families (Tierney, 1992). The research articulated that by having students connected to family and tribe, the tribal communities can help shape the educational experience through the use of Indigenous values, beliefs, and knowledge to create a more appropriate and relevant education for the Native American students (Guillory & Wolverton, 2008). Guillory and Wolverton used previously accrued data from 2002 to explore similarities and differences of Native American student perceptions versus those of university presidents, faculty, and state representatives on barriers to Native American education at Washington State University, University of Idaho, and Montana State University. While it is understood there are logistical constrictions in retrieving data from more universities across the United States, this research could be improved in examining more universities. Increasing retrieval from different universities across the United States and seeing if the data supports or refutes their initial findings from the three universities around the northwest region of the United States would support the reliability and validity of findings. Future research would benefit from exploring different universities across the United States and specific cultural factors and barriers to Native American success for unique tribes, as opposed to blanket statement findings on Native Americans as a whole. Since the cultural factor of family for Native Americans is held with great importance, the connection to a Native American student's family, as well as with a local tribe, can make a positive impact. Native American people's world view is often more consistent with that of a collectivist culture (Dickson et al., 2012), with important values being family and staying connected to an individual's tribe and other Indigenous peoples.

CONCLUSION

In conclusion, this chapter focused on unique challenges for Native American educational success and solutions for the future and discussed the history and context of the abuse towards Native Americans, as well as other groups around the world and the negative impact on the individuals and communities as a key background factor for understanding and addressing educational disparities, followed by best solutions and key Native American cultural values for educational success. This chapter also focused on the current state of Native American education, history of abuse, impact on individuals, and solutions for the future. A review of over 60 different journal articles and books discussed the current state of Native American education, as well as, examined the impact of historical trauma on Indigenous peoples across the world and minority groups. Specifically, the subthemes of perceptions of bias in history towards Native Americans (Blackhawk, 1995; Powers, 1932; Tierney, 1992), misleading and harmful research done against Native American people by researchers (Harmon, 2010; Lawrence, 2000; Mello & Wolf, 2010; Pacheco et al., 2013; Torpy, 2000), and the negative impact on Native Americans from the forced boarding school system in the early 20th century (Adams, 1995; Anderson, n.d.; Boyer, 1997; Lewis & McLester, 2005) were presented. For solutions, this literature review synthesized best practices from around the world in battling historical trauma and the importance of Native Americans preserving their cultural tradition for educational success. The three subthemes of Native Americans staying connected to cultural tradition for educational success are the value of cultural relevance in curriculum for Native Americans (Coladarci, 1983; Covarrubias & Fryberg, 2015; Guillory & Wolverton, 2008; Kanu, 2006; Tierney, 1992), the importance of Native American role models (Covarrubias & Fryberg, 2015; Guillory & Wolverton, 2008), and the importance of family for Native Americans (Guillory & Wolverton, 2008; Tierney, 1992). Future research could improve upon previous literature by incorporating Native American perspectives in future experiments of academic achievement in relation to the theoretical constructs of community, a sense of belonging, and role models. It has previously been shown a role model from underrepresented populations can boost self-esteem for the underrepresented members (Covarrubias & Fryberg, 2015; Guillory & Wolverton, 2008). Additional research is also needed to address the effects of a lack of belonging in academia in relation to purpose, meaning, and a sense of value.

REFERENCES

Adams, D. W. (1995). *Education for extinction: American Indians and the Boarding School Experience, 1875-1928*. University Press of Kansas.

Anderson, W. (n.d.). Anderson Cornelius student file. In *Carlisle Indian School Digital Resource Center*. http://carlisleindian.dickinson.edu/student_files/anderson-cornelius-student-file

Anyon, Y., Jenson, J. M., Altschul, I., Farrar, J., McQueen, J., Greer, E., Downing, B., & Simmons, J. (2014). The persistent effect of race and the promise of alternatives to suspension in school discipline outcomes. *Children and Youth Services Review*, *44*, 379–386. doi:10.1016/j.childyouth.2014.06.025

Atkinson, J. (2002). *Trauma trails, recreating song lines: The transgenerational effects of trauma in Indigenous Australia*. Spinifex Press.

Blackhawk, N. (1995). I can carry on from here: The relocation of American Indians to Los Angeles. *Wicazo Sa Review*, *11*(2), 16–30. doi:10.2307/1409093

Bombay, A., Matheson, K., & Anisman, H. (2009). Intergenerational trauma. *Journal de la santé autochtone.*

Boyer, P. (1997). *Native American colleges: Progress and prospects. A special report*. Jossey-Bass, Inc.

Chou, T., Asnaani, A., & Hofmann, S. G. (2012). Perception of racial discrimination and psychopathology across three US ethnic minority groups. *Cultural Diversity & Ethnic Minority Psychology*, *18*(1), 74–81. doi:10.1037/a0025432 PMID:21967527

Coladarci, T. (1983). High-School Dropouts among Native Americans. *Journal of American Indian Education*, *23*(1), 15–22.

Covarrubias, R., & Fryberg, S. A. (2015). The impact of self-relevant representations on school belonging for Native American students. *Cultural Diversity & Ethnic Minority Psychology*, *21*(1), 10–18. doi:10.1037/a0037819 PMID:25181325

Deal, G. (2018a, March 26). *Indigenous identity and existence: Fighting erasure and racism*. Colorado College.

Deal, G. [@greggdeal]. [2018b, October 21). *Today I was asked: 'What is most important to Indigenous people? The Land? Protecting traditions? Your language? Or your people' I told him: 'Those are all the same things'* [Tweet]. Twitter.

Denham, A. R. (2008). Rethinking historical trauma: Narratives of resilience. *Transcultural Psychiatry*, *45*(3), 391–414. doi:10.1177/1363461508094673 PMID:18799640

Diamond, N., Bainbridge, J., & Hayes, C. (2009). *Reel injun (motion picture)*. National Film Board of Canada.

Dickson, M. W., Castaño, N., Magomaeva, A., & Den Hartog, D. N. (2012). Conceptualizing leadership across cultures. *Journal of World Business*, *47*(4), 483–492. doi:10.1016/j.jwb.2012.01.002

Duran, B., Duran, E., & Yellow Horse Brave Heart, M. (1998). Studying Native Americans and the trauma of history. In R. Thornton (Ed.), Studying Native America: Problems and prospects. University of Wisconsin Press.

Duran, E., Duran, B., Brave Heart, M. Y. H., & Yellow Horse-Davis, S. (1998). Healing the American Indian soul wound. In Y. Danieli (Ed.), *The Plenum series on stress and coping. International handbook of multigenerational legacies of trauma* (pp. 341–354). Plenum Press. doi:10.1007/978-1-4757-5567-1_22

Elias, B., Mignone, J., Hall, M., Hong, S. P., Hart, L., & Sareen, J. (2012). Trauma and suicide behaviour histories among a Canadian Indigenous population: An empirical exploration of the potential role of Canada's residential school system. *Social Science & Medicine*, *74*(10), 1560–1569. doi:10.1016/j.socscimed.2012.01.026 PMID:22464223

Fast, E., & Collin-Vézina, D. (2010). Historical trauma, race-based trauma and resilience of Indigenous peoples: A literature review. *First Peoples Child & Family Review*, *5*(1), 126–136. doi:10.7202/1069069ar

Giladi, L., & Bell, T. S. (2013). Protective factors for intergenerational transmission of trauma among second and third generation Holocaust survivors. *Psychological Trauma: Theory, Research, Practice, and Policy*, *5*(4), 384–391. doi:10.1037/a0028455

Gray, J., & Beresford, Q. (2008). A 'formidable challenge': Australia's quest for equity in Indigenous education. *Australian Journal of Education*, *52*(2), 197–223. doi:10.1177/000494410805200207

Grayshield, L., Rutherford, J. J., Salazar, S. B., Mihecoby, A. L., & Luna, L. L. (2015). Understanding and healing historical trauma: The perspectives of Native American elders. *Journal of Mental Health Counseling*, *37*(4), 295–307. doi:10.17744/mehc.37.4.02

Guillory, R. M. (2009). American Indian/Alaska Native college student retention strategies. *Journal of Developmental Education*, *33*(2), 12.

Guillory, R. M., & Wolverton, M. (2008). It's about family: Native American student persistence in higher education. *The Journal of Higher Education*, *79*(1), 58–87. doi:10.1353/jhe.2008.0001

Harmon, A. (2010, April 10). Indian tribe wins fight to limit research of its DNA. *The New York Times*. https://www.nytimes.com/2010/04/22/us/22dna.html

Hero, R. E., & Tolbert, C. J. (1996). A racial/ethnic diversity interpretation of politics and policy in the states of the US. *American Journal of Political Science*, *40*(3), 851–871. doi:10.2307/2111798

Hill, D. L. (2006). Sense of belonging as connectedness, American Indian worldview, and mental health. *Psychiatric Nursing*, *20*(5), 210–216. doi:10.1016/j.apnu.2006.04.003 PMID:17010824

Jervis, L. L., Beals, J., Croy, C. D., Klein, S. A., Manson, S. M., & Team, A. S. (2006). Historical consciousness among two American Indian tribes. *The American Behavioral Scientist*, *50*(4), 526–549. doi:10.1177/0002764206294053

Johns Hopkins Center for American Indian Health. (2020, November 21). *Oren Lyons: Indigenous lessons for the world: Native American Heritage Month lecture* [Video]. YouTube.

Johnston-Goodstar, K., & VeLure Roholt, R. (2017). "Our Kids Aren't Dropping Out; They're Being Pushed Out": Native American students and racial microaggressions in schools. *Journal of Ethnic & Cultural Diversity in Social Work, 26*(1-2), 30–47. doi:10.1080/15313204.2016.1263818

Kane, M. B. (1970). *Minorities in textbooks: A study of their treatment in social studies texts.* Quadrangle Books.

Kanu, Y. (2006). Getting them through the college pipeline: Critical elements of instruction influencing school success among Native Canadian high school students. *Journal of Advanced Academics, 18*(1), 116–145. doi:10.4219/jaa-2006-348

Karlsen, S., & Nazroo, J. Y. (2002). Relation between racial discrimination, social class, and health among ethnic minority groups. *American Journal of Public Health, 92*(4), 624–631. doi:10.2105/AJPH.92.4.624 PMID:11919063

Katz, R. V., Kegeles, S. S., Kressin, N. R., Green, B. L., James, S. A., Wang, M. Q., Russell, S. L., & Claudio, C. (2008). Awareness of the Tuskegee Syphilis Study and the US presidential apology and their influence on minority participation in biomedical research. *American Journal of Public Health, 98*(6), 1137–1142. doi:10.2105/AJPH.2006.100131 PMID:17901437

Krezmien, M. P., Leone, P. E., & Achilles, G. M. (2006). Suspension, race, and disability: Analysis of statewide practices and reporting. *Journal of Emotional and Behavioral Disorders, 14*(4), 217–226. doi:10.1177/10634266060140040501

Ladson-Billings, G. (2006). From the achievement gap to the education debt: Understanding achievement in US schools. *Educational Researcher, 35*(7), 3–12. doi:10.3102/0013189X035007003

Lambert, J. E., Holzer, J., & Hasbun, A. (2014). Association between parents' PTSD severity and children's psychological distress: A meta-analysis. *Journal of Traumatic Stress, 27*(1), 9–17. doi:10.1002/jts.21891 PMID:24464491

Lawrence, J. (2000). The Indian health service and the sterilization of Native American women. *American Indian Quarterly, 24*(3), 400–419. doi:10.1353/aiq.2000.0008 PMID:17089462

Lewis, H. S., & McLester, L. G. (Eds.). (2005). *Oneida Lives: Long-Lost Voices of the Wisconsin Oneidas.* University of Nebraska Press.

Lyons, O. (Ed.). (1992). *Exiled in the land of the free: democracy, Indian nations, and the US Constitution.* Clear Light Publishers.

Mello, M. M., & Wolf, L. E. (2010). The Havasupai Indian tribe case—Lessons for research involving stored biologic samples. *The New England Journal of Medicine, 363*(3), 204–207. doi:10.1056/NEJMp1005203 PMID:20538622

Menzies, P. (2007). Understanding Aboriginal intergeneration trauma from a social work perspective. *The Canadian Journal of Native Studies, 27*(2), 367.

Miller, R. J. (2011). American Indians, the doctrine of discovery, and manifest destiny. *Wyoming Law Review, 11*, 329.

Momartin, S., Silove, D., Manicavasagar, V., & Steel, Z. (2003). Dimensions of trauma associated with posttraumatic stress disorder (PTSD) caseness, severity and functional impairment: A study of Bosnian refugees resettled in Australia. *Social Science & Medicine, 57*(5), 775–781. doi:10.1016/S0277-9536(02)00452-5 PMID:12850105

Momartin, S., Silove, D., Manicavasagar, V., & Steel, Z. (2004). Comorbidity of PTSD and depression: Associations with trauma exposure, symptom severity and functional impairment in Bosnian refugees resettled in Australia. *Journal of Affective Disorders, 80*(2), 231–238. doi:10.1016/S0165-0327(03)00131-9 PMID:15207936

Native American Languages Act, S.2167, 101st Cong. (1990). https://www.congress.gov/bill/101st-congress/senate-bill/2167

Nazroo, J. Y. (2003). The structuring of ethnic inequalities in health: Economic position, racial discrimination, and racism. *American Journal of Public Health, 93*(2), 277–284. doi:10.2105/AJPH.93.2.277 PMID:12554585

O'Loughlin, M. (2009). A psychoanalytic exploration of collective trauma among Indigenous Australians and a suggestion for intervention. *Australasian Psychiatry, 17*(1, suppl), S33–S36. doi:10.1080/10398560902948746 PMID:19579103

Office of Minority Health. (2018, March 28). *Profile: American Indian/Alaska Native*. https://minorityhealth.hhs.gov/omh/browse.aspx?lvl=3&lvlid=62

Ogbu, J. U. (1990). Minority education in comparative perspective. *The Journal of Negro Education, 59*(1), 45–57. doi:10.2307/2295291

Ogunwole, S., Drewery, M., & Rios-Vargas, M. (2012). *The population With a bachelor's degree or higher by race and Hispanic origin: 2006- 2010.* American Community Survey Briefs. https://www.census.gov/prod/2012pubs/acsbr10-19.pdf

Pacheco, C. M., Daley, S. M., Brown, T., Filippi, M., Greiner, K. A., & Daley, C. M. (2013). Moving forward: Breaking the cycle of Mistrust between American Indians and researchers. *American Journal of Public Health, 103*(12), 2152–2159. doi:10.2105/AJPH.2013.301480 PMID:24134368

Perna, L. W. (2000). Differences in the decision to attend college among African Americans, Hispanics, and Whites. *The Journal of Higher Education, 71*(2), 117–141. doi:10.2307/2649245

Pihama, L., Smith, L. T., Te Nana, R., Cameron, N., Mataki, T., Skipper, H., Te Nana, R., Skipper, H., & Southey, K. (2017). Investigating Māori approaches to trauma-informed care. *Journal of Indigenous Wellbeing: Te Mauri-Pimatisiwin, 2*(3), 18–31.

Powers, M. (1932). The Indian as peacemaker. Fleming H. Revell Company.

Quinn, A. (2007). Reflections on intergenerational trauma: Healing as a critical intervention. *First Peoples Child & Family Review, 3*(4), 72–82. doi:10.7202/1069377ar

Raphael, B., Swan, P., & Martinek, N. (1998). Intergenerational aspects of trauma for Australian Aboriginal people. International handbook of multigenerational legacies of trauma, 327-339.

Rowland-Klein, D., & Dunlop, R. (1998). The transmission of trauma across generations: Identification with parental trauma in children of Holocaust survivors. *The Australian and New Zealand Journal of Psychiatry*, *32*(3), 358–369. doi:10.3109/00048679809065528 PMID:9672725

Schraufnagel, T. J., Wagner, A. W., Miranda, J., & Roy-Byrne, P. P. (2006). Treating minority patients with depression and anxiety: What does the evidence tell us? *General Hospital Psychiatry*, *28*(1), 27–36. doi:10.1016/j.genhosppsych.2005.07.002 PMID:16377362

Schuman, H., Schwartz, B., & d'Arcy, H. (2005). Elite revisionists and popular beliefs: Christopher Columbus, hero or villain? *Public Opinion Quarterly*, *69*(1), 2–29. doi:10.1093/poq/nfi001

Silove, D., Austin, P., & Steel, Z. (2007). No refuge from terror: The impact of detention on the mental health of trauma-affected refugees seeking asylum in Australia. *Transcultural Psychiatry*, *44*(3), 359–393. doi:10.1177/1363461507081637 PMID:17938152

Sinclair, R. (2004). Aboriginal social work education in Canada: Decolonizing pedagogy for the seventh generation. *First Peoples Child & Family Review*, *1*(1), 49–62. doi:10.7202/1069584ar

Steel, Z., Silove, D., Phan, T., & Bauman, A. (2002). Long-term effect of psychological trauma on the mental health of Vietnamese refugees resettled in Australia: A population-based study. *Lancet*, *360*(9339), 1056–1062. doi:10.1016/S0140-6736(02)11142-1 PMID:12383986

Thornton, R. (2003). Repatriation as healing the wounds of the trauma of history: Cases of Native Americans in the United States of America. In *The dead and their possessions* (pp. 35–42). Routledge.

Tierney, W. G. (1992). An anthropological analysis of student participation in college. *The Journal of Higher Education*, *63*(6), 603–618. doi:10.2307/1982046

Torpy, S. J. (2000). Native American women and coerced sterilization: On the Trail of Tears in the 1970s. *American Indian Culture and Research Journal*, *24*(2), 1–22. doi:10.17953/aicr.24.2.7646013460646042

Van Dijk, T. A. (2000). New(s) racism: A discourse analytical approach. *Ethnic Minorities and the Media*, *37*, 33–49.

Wallace, J. M., Goodkind, S., Wallace, C. M., & Bachman, J. G. (2008). Racial, ethnic, and gender differences in school discipline among US high school students: 1991-2005. *Negro Educational Review*, *59*(1-2), 47. PMID:19430541

ADDITIONAL READING

Battiste, M. (2017). *Decolonizing education: Nourishing the learning spirit*. UBC press.

Cromer, L. D., Gray, M. E., Vasquez, L., & Freyd, J. J. (2018). The relationship of acculturation to historical loss awareness, institutional betrayal, and the intergenerational transmission of trauma in the American Indian experience. *Journal of Cross-Cultural Psychology*, *49*(1), 99–114. doi:10.1177/0022022117738749

Ferebee, S. S., & Lawlor, A. C. (2020). Native American cultural identity exploration in their postsecondary education: A narrative inquiry. In K. Setzekorn, N. Patnayakuni, & T. Burton (Eds.), *Socioeconomics, Diversity, and the Politics of Online Education* (pp. 142–164). IGI Global. doi:10.4018/978-1-7998-3583-7.ch009

Harjo, J. (2020). *An American sunrise, poems.* W. W. Norton.

Houck, J. A. (2018). *When ancestors weep: Healing the soul from intergenerational trauma.* Abbott Press.

Orange, T. (2018). *There there: A novel.* Vintage.

Weaver, H. N. (2019). *Trauma and resilience in the lives of contemporary Native Americans: Reclaiming our balance, restoring our wellbeing.* Routledge.

KEY TERMS AND DEFINITIONS

Blood Memories: A term coined by Kiowa author N. Scott Momaday, where memories are passed down genetically to the next generations.

Carlisle Indian Boarding School: Located in Pennsylvania, Carlisle's motto was to "kill the Indian, save the man" and was used as an archetype for hundreds of other Indian boarding schools.

Cultural Relevancy: A concept in which beliefs and practices by a group of people are recognized as having importance in education.

Cultural Tradition: Practices, beliefs and customs practiced by a group of people which have been passed down from previous generations.

Genocide: The purposeful destruction of a group of people and their culture by another group of people.

Indigenous: As a clarification of terms, the word Native American will be used interchangeably with American Indian, Indian, Indigenous, Aboriginal, First Nations, and Native, depending on how it was used by researchers in the literature.

Intergenerational Trauma: Inherited post-traumatic-stress-disorder caused by abuse and trauma and passed down through generations.

Seven Generations: A Native American notion of belief in which all our decisions and actions are done with recognition to seven generations in the past and for seven generations in the future.

Chapter 13
Dancing With the Dreamweavers:
A Narrative Discourse of the T'bolis of the Southern Philippines

Emmanuel Villoria Hernani
Cebu Normal University, Philippines

Ma Rosita Ampoyas Hernani
Cebu Normal University, Philippines

Delmo Amfan Dulay
Ateneo de Davao University, Philippines

ABSTRACT

This chapter revolves around the impact of socio-political diaspora to the concept of tribal-ancestral land, which is sacred to the community and the cultural identity of the T'boli, an ethno-linguistic group. A narrative discourse approach is used to illustrate the tribe's struggles to the existing hegemony, particularly with the dynamics between the tribe and other inhabitants, the intrusions of other values and exploitations of their ancestral domains as explored across a changing sociocultural milieu. In an attempt to provide understanding of cultural identity amidst the changing social landscapes, the authors describe, identify, explore, and interpret the subject. Hence, the chapter provides the worldview of T'boli people and offers a narrative juxtaposition of the three opuses from three different fields. Further research is needed to ensure protection and preservation of the T'boli culture and its identity and indigenous significance within Southeast Asia and, specifically, the Philippines to better understand this land-based culture.

DOI: 10.4018/978-1-7998-3729-9.ch013

INTRODUCTION

The Philippines, an archipelago of around 7,000 islands is culturally diverse. Most Filipinos identify themselves by their ethnic identity or by their language (Reid, 2005). Inhabitants of the uncolonized regions are generally categorized as indigenous and tribal—two terms that have negative stereotypes. Low than being called provincial, which debases the person' social and economic status, the term "indigenous" connotes that a person is unschooled, illiterate, unbaptized, wild and uncivilized. Regarded with contempt and indifference, persons from the indigenous societies are considered as *the other*.

Approximately 17 million indigenous peoples reside in the Philippines belonging to 110 ethnolinguistic groups according to the survey report of United Nations Development Program (UNDP, 2003). There around 150 languages that represents the different ethnic groups that spread across the Philippine archipelago. One of these groups, the T'bolis has preserved their culture amidst the series of intrusion from their local neighbors and from colonial societies. Amidst the different maelstroms from the outside and from within their own group, they have been trying to preserve their ancestral territories and their ethnic identities from erosion. In this chapter, the authors are using the terms "indigenous," "tribal," "native," and "ethno-linguistic groups" interchangeably. These terms agree to the adopted definition of the United Nations (UN) and International Labor Organization (ILO) on indigenous peoples. The authors also used *lumad*, a Visayan term, which encapsulates the same adopted definition. The term is often used locally by the indigenous inhabitants in reference to their ethnic identity and their ethno-cultural lineage.

Culture is the constitution of geographical and socio-environment dimensions, which is human-made. To understand behavior or its determinants, cultural influences must be understood (Triandis, et al.,1973). In this chapter, culture is glimpsed using the person who is in the foreground; thus, aside from participating in the discourse, a T'boli scholar participates in the narrative as a T'boli member. His experiences are interdependent to the situation of the tribe (Wollants, 2012). As the grandson of a Tboli female leader named as one of the country's national artists before she died, their constant communion and affection to one another contributed to his psychological environment, which is interdependent to the physical or geographical environment. His late grandmother passed on to him a legacy embedded in his memory in the form of lores, songs, and dances. He would provide glimpses and voices to the presented issues.

The chapter explores the meanings of T'boli dances, which have been used to preserve their traditions. T'nalak weaving is also explored, the pride and glory of the tribe whereby women weavers are referred to as dream weavers as T'nalak weaving signifies the tribe's connection to the transcendental realms. The objective of the chapter is to discuss the impact of the diaspora to the concept of tribal-ancestral land, which is sacred to the community and the cultural identity of the new generation T'bolis. The chapter also explores the meanings of T'boli dances and the sacred dreaming weaving, which have been used to preserve their culture and traditions.

BACKGROUND

Indigenous communities thrive in the entire island archipelago of the Philippines. These ethno-linguistic groups have been trying to preserve their cultural and traditional practices against the changing social and political landscape. Mindanao, of the southern Philippine region, was undaunted by the centuries of foreign intrusion. Prejudice and disdain between major ethnic groups are matters of concerns because even the Visayans and Mindanaons, the inhabitants of the two major island-regions outside of Manila, the capital, are also often subjected to ridicules and discriminations. At times subtle and at times direct, puns and gibes insinuate the other as low class, inferior, ignorant. Labels such tribal, indigenous, people from the mountain and from the cave are embodied in ethnic slurs and slanders. Undeniably, layers of ethnic discrimination are embedded in the social fabric of Philippine society and indigenous peoples or the ethno-linguistic groups are the most vulnerable (Arquiza, 2007). A socio-political divide embeds animosity and apathy breeds ostracism, prejudice and discrimination; it heaves the marginalized and minorities farther away, widening the gap of inequality.

Discussions and debates over the definition of "indigenous peoples" have been resounding for decades but no definition has ever been adopted by any UN-system body (Banda, 2004). Anthropologists believe that the T'boli are part of the Austronesian-speaking population (Casal & Bueza 2017; Reid, 2009; Zorc, 1986). Casal and Bueza (2017) impressed they are strongly associated with the Proto-Malay race who arrived in Mindanao through the Balangay expedition. The T'boli or Tagabili is an ethnolinguistic group that inhabits parts of Saranggani Province, South Cotabato and Sultan Kudarat, Philippines. As a land-based culture, T'boli means people of the slopes or hills although some inhabit the lakeshores. The T'bolis of Lake Sebu, declared as the ancestral domain of the T'bolis, are known as the summer and economic, tourism, cultural center of South Cotabato. T'bolis were previously classified as a hunter-gatherer group before they resolved into farming. Aside from farming and fishing, T'bolis also cultivate wood products such as bamboo and rattan. At present, farmlands and lakesides fish cages have superimposed the T'bolis homesteads. The T'bolis are also skilled in weaving and metalcrafts. Tinalak, a distinctive cloth, and metal crafts and other personal effects have been sold around the country as souvenir items. T'bolis are also unique due to their cultural identity and ethnicity as they are "known to be conservative, shy, humble, hospitable, sensitive to the needs of others, and have close family ties" (Cudera et al., 2020, p. 2538).

The land life because everything sprouts from it. *Fu*, the spirit of the land, has a dual character. At times benevolent, that *Fu* would help people especially farmers by blessing them with bountiful harvests or healing the sick member of a family, malevolent, in other times, that Fu causes illness and destroys crops. Understanding on the duality of the spirit's characteristics gives each T'boli reverence to the environment that extends to the different elements that communes with it. In fact, trees, animals, and water are not considered as mere elements but other spiritual entities. This belief system guides them to commune with nature and all entities that co-exist from it. From this belief, they anchor their respect and regard to all things that exist. They conserve, protect, and manage their natural resources like how they treat their relationship to each other. They build and strengthens their relationship with the spirits by taking care of its manifestations, the things that exists, the physical world.

Conceptual Approach and Lens to Describe the T'bolis

The chapter is structured as a discourse narrative so as to incorporate the perspective of T'boli members as situated within the scholarship discussion. The narrative excerpts from T'boli members provide glimpses and voices to further illustrate each issue. The chapter authors use the concept of emic and etic in ethnographic research. Thus, there is the juxtaposition of the opus of three writers. Theoretical and conceptual emphases and the phenomenological-personal elements will be presented side by side. However, the main anchor of the discourse is on the experiences of the T'boli scholar who offers the discourse narrative as a T'boli member. The authors also opine on the incognizance and indifference of the new generations T'boli to the socio-political issues that have been hounding the tribe. They have become enthralled by the outsiders' lifestyles that they already take their tribal identity for granted.

There have been several pressing issues of the tribe even before the turn of the century. Thus, the chapter's central theme revolves around the impact of the diaspora on the concept of tribal-ancestral land, which is sacred to the community and the cultural identity of the new generation T'bolis. Socio-cultural concerns are framed by the narrative discourses on ancestral domain, land and water resources, and tribal identity. The authors also opine on the incognizance and indifference of the new generations T'boli to the socio-political issues that have been hounding the tribe. They have become enthralled by the outsiders' lifestyles that they already take their tribal identity for granted. The recent and historical scholarship surrounding T'boli arts and crafts (Endaya, 2015: Mora, 2012; Quizon, 2019) and environmental conservation and utilization (Lasalita-Zapico et al., 2008: Magbanua, et al., 2017: Zapico, et al., 2014) are considered.

Tudbulul and the T'boli People

The legend of *Tudbulul*, a Filipino oral epic, played significant role in the life of every T'boli. *Tudbulul* is a cultural icon, a legendary hero whose character influences the perceptions and ideology of the T'bolis. Just like any mythic heroes' journey, he overcame each struggle and defeated even the fiercest enemies who have magical powers. An inspiration, a creative imagination, among us T'bolis, his legend inspires everyone to see the better end of their struggles. *Tudbulul* and his innate power is an inspiration especially in protecting Lemlunay, the paradise where there is peace and prosperity. The dedication of *Tudbulul* in guarding his territory encouraged us to take responsibility for the environment and community.

The legend of *The Tudbulul* also played a significant role in the life of every T'boli. *Tudbulul* is a cultural icon a legendary hero whose character influences the perceptions and ideology of the T'bolis. Just like any mythic heroes' journey, he overcame each struggle and defeated even the fiercest enemies who have magical powers. An inspiration, a creative imagination, among us T'bolis, his legend inspires the community to see the better end of these struggles. *Tudbulul* and his innate power is an inspiration especially in protecting *Lemlunay*, our paradise where there is peace and prosperity. The dedication of *Tudbulul* in guarding his territory encouraged the T'bolis to take responsibility of their environment and our community.

T'bolis value everything that exists in a surrounding. The valuation of entities makes everything sacred. *T'nalak* weaving is a sacred ceremonial from the pre-harvest of abaca until its use. Sacred to the tribe, harvesters and weavers adheres to rituals and beliefs that aims to revere and to avoid offending *Fu,* the spirit of trees. The abaca plant can only be harvested after a male T'boli recites an incantation to the spirit. Special attention and care are also needed in handling the fiber, which must never touch the ground and when these are already on the loom. Children and non-weavers must never play with the abaca fiber. The complex and intricate processes emphasize the sacredness of T'nalak (Castro, 2013) as described by the grandson:

Our reverence to our land extends to the different elements that communes with it. In fact, trees, animals, and water are not considered as mere elements but other spiritual entities. This belief system guides us on how to commune with nature and all entities that co-exist from it. From this belief, we anchor our respect and regard to all things that exist. We conserve, protect, and manage our natural resources like how we treat our relationship to each other. We build and strengthens our relationship with the spirits by taking care of its manifestations, the things that exists, the physical world.

MYRIADS OF PERENNIAL ISSUES PROBLEMS

The T'boli tribe has been suffering from endless debacles especially from inappropriate government intervention even during the time of the American regime (Arquiza, 2007). Aside from the required cadastral survey and payment, there was a declaration that all unregistered lands were considered public territories. The privileged few, the educated elite and those who held economic and political leverage, exploited the laws that deprived the tribal members who were unaware of the registration procedures (Cunanan, 1980). This is the first of the many onslaughts against the ethnic minorities who were driven farther from the mainstream.

Exploitation of mineral resources did not start with the local migrants. It started in 1905, during the American occupation when a law declared that all public lands in the Philippines are free for exploration, occupation, and purchase by the citizens of the United States and the Philippines (McKenna, 2017). First to befall were the mountains and forests of Luzon. Displaced and neglected, the tribal members suffered worse than exploitation because they were not seen and heard—they were nonexistent in their own land. Come 70 years later, at that time of the Martial Law regime, when exploitation of resources became a nationwide campaign and in the guise of utilization of resources, logging, mining, land conversions and infrastructures overwhelmed the ethnic minorities. Tribal territories and resources became the melting pot of oppression since vast majorities of the national ethnic minorities were still deprived and impoverished (Cunanan, 1980; McKenna, 2017).

The pervasive incognizance of the government on ancestral domain led to myriads of problem to the T'bolis. The wrongful identification of ancestral lands as uninhabited is an incursion to the identity of indigenous communities whose understanding of land ownership is communal—that land is not something to be expropriated; That it belongs to the present and succeeding generations (Duhaylungsod, 1993). It is "user right" through membership in clan groups identified with the names of their landscape (Agbayani, 1993; Duhaylungsod, 1993; Duhaylungsod & Hyndman, 1993). To articulate this, the grandson stated,

Nor is the land vested in anyone's proper name or quantified over a given period of area. Land tenure for appropriation of territory follows ancestral rights. Each settlement has defined property rights over territorial lands around which members of the community usually take up land for cultivation. When cultivation is abandoned, its ownership reverts to the community. Ownership is circumscribed by extensive and intimate knowledge of the place.

Local Migrants and Conflict

In the 1950s, Mindanao was dubbed as the land of promise. Of the three major islands in the Philippines, it was a land unexplored, untouched, and uncivilized. Unthought-of and unheard of by others, and unaware that there were already functioning communities, people from other regions touted it as wilderness frontier that only the bold and adventurous would be willing to come. Because of government campaign and assurance of support, migrants from Ilocos and the Visayas regions participated in the state sponsored colonization; another assault to the tribes, the tribal domains, and their socio-cultural landscape (Duhaylungsod, 1993).

Without regards to the original habitats who were considered uncultured and hinged to their laidback indigenous practices, the state declared the ancestral lands as public domain. The chaotic situation inflamed the frenzy of the local colonialists who dispersed the tribes from their original habitats. The state sponsored socio-cultural invasion altered the way of life of the T'bolis. They were displaced and became mere tenants of their own lands. The dramatic rise of outsiders sunk the minority status of the T'bolis and other groups further. However, the majority were displaced and required to flee to the mountains for refuge and survival. The significant changes of the landscape altered the traditional lifestyle of the people.

Even at the turn of the new century, the T'bolis remain besieged with socio-political problems. Conflicts have escalated into a larger scale with religious entanglements adding to the socio-political conflicts in some parts of the regions. Other ethnolinguistic groups, also struggling to retain their identity amidst the changing landscape, persist. The T'bolis have weathered many storms and persist amid the protracted conflicts; yet, the conflicts have led to an erosion of identity of the T'boli people.

The neighboring communities also posed a problem as other groups proselytized behaviors atypical to the tribe. During casual and business transactions, outsiders bring with them blueprints of their own identity that would leave a mark on the group. Because of their business knowledge, they are sometimes more familiar with business and economy and thus easily influence the tribe as they gradually assert their socio-political leverages against the tribe. The T'boli lake, and its rims, the primary source of food of the tribe, has now fettered with rest houses and resorts owned not by the tribe or any of its members but outsiders who welded influences to the tribe and to other outside entities that manage the habitat.

Exploitation of Cultural Identity and Natural Resources

For the tribe, *Fu*, the spirit of the land, has a dual character. At times benevolent, that Fu would help people especially farmers by blessing them with bountiful harvests or healing the sick member of a family, malevolent, in other times, that Fu causes illness and destroys crops. Their deep respect to the duality of *Fu*, and its spirits characteristics, magnified their reverence to the environment. Their reverence to their land extends to the different elements that communes with it. In fact, trees, animals, and water are not considered as mere elements but other spiritual entities. This belief system guides them on how to commune with nature and all entities that co-exist from it. From this belief, they anchor their respect and regard to all things that exist. They conserve, protect, and manage their natural resources like how they treat their relationship to each other. They build and strengthens their relationship with the spirits by taking care of its manifestations, the things that exists, the physical world.

The land of the T'bolis is endowed with good climate, fertile lands with pastoral ambience, rolling hills and mountains, clear rivers, clear lakes, and emerald waterfalls. All these nature endowments are the key factors why their place is famous spots in Mindanao. However, Lake Sebu, the largest of the three lakes, is in dire state due to man-made problems. It is in a sorry state due to over population of fish cages, pollution due to the unconsumed feeds, and siltation caused by surrounding agricultural lands. This has occurred even when Lake Sebu and its surrounding areas is a protected area. Environmental problems are prevalent. T'boli communities are besieged with ecological challenges. It is in the light of this type of problem that marginalization has a face. Mining operations, deforestations, and conversions of ancestral lands into other purposes are decades old form of marginalization because these are always conducted without regards to tribal significance. Sadly, perpetrators of these transgressions operate with the guidance and protection of their T'boli accomplices.

In Lake Sebu, operators, who are mostly outsiders, have been able to continue with their trade through the support of the tribe. Settlements in the areas around the lake and the conversion of forest areas to agricultural lands contributed to the problem. Papa and Briones (2014) highlighted the extensive lake-shore town development. Intensive aquaculture and unsustainable farming also affected the lake's ecosystem. Absence of collaboration between government agencies also contributes to the problem. Some water systems have been depleted due to government-sponsored irrigation projects for the agricultural lands that affected the ecological integrity of Lake Sebu (Porras & Buot, 2016). The local government unit failed to regulate the construction of fish cages because of political consideration. There are families who are dependent on the industry who are mere tenants and operators working for others. Calls for moratorium to revive the lake to its past glory remain unanswered (Sarmiento, 2013).

The pollution of the water system and denudation of the forests with the tribe's ancestral domain are caused by artificial factors. Firstly, the influx of tourists contributed to the pollution of the lake. Local agriculture officers also admitted some difficulties in implementing laws because of political interventions. Noted the fact that the fish cages belong to higher government officials. The issue is not only between economic and environmental sustainability; Aside from usurpation of sacred waterscape, but exploitation of the tribe is also gleaning over the capitalistic collaboration. The profitable eco-tourism overshadows the sorry plight of community (Cudera et al., 2020). It does not only kill the life out of the lake, it also extinguished hope, a critical state necessary for indigenous life of T'boli residents. The state of Lake Sebu, the *Lemlunay,* a paradise of the past generations, contrasts with the inspirations of *Tudbulul*. Responsibility and stewardship of nature are inundated by other inspirations. This is perhaps a sign that the power of mythic characters and its ingrained values have already eroded and replaced by modern and foreign values. Or could it be, as some T'boli would surmise, the ecological crisis is the manifestation of *Fu*'s ambivalence. The degradation of the lake is a reminder of the cycle of opposites and *Fu* is now trying to turn the wheel to the other pole.

Dreaming, Weaving and Living Traditional Values

T'boli people are known to be one of the most creative and artistic ethnolinguistic group in the Philippines (Cudera et al., 2020). Among the different T'boli art forms, *T'nalak* is one of the most popular and admired around the globe. A *t'nalak,* a woven textile made of abaca or Manila hemp, has many traditional uses for the T'boli. The textile can be used as a dowry, as an instrument of sacrifice to cure an illness, as currency for bartering livestock and most of all the emblem of the tribe's inspiration. The level of skill involved in creating *t'nalak* determines a weaver's status and position in the village (Paterno & Oshima, 2001). Be Lang Dulay, a national artist, popularized *T'nalak* weaving with her over 100 different *T'nalak* designs. The national and international recognition and the appreciation of her art has left a legacy. Her valuable craft carries with it the T'boli identity. *T'nalak,* a tedious craft, manifests the passion for every T'boli to preserve their culture. Her intricate and picturesque *T'nalak* designs embody the resiliency of the tribe's cultural identity. Despite the challenges that are brought about by the mainstream culture, the new generations are cognizant of the art. However, the younger generations, especially those who have embraced the fads in social media and those who have adopted western orientations have looked at it as a mere art and overlook the living treasures that the art embodies—the traditional living values. In reflection, a chapter author narrates:

As a young T'boli professional, I still embodied the identity and practices as according to what and who we are. My parents are still engaging T'nalak weaving that became means of economic sustainability and a way of instilling cultural practice. However, because of various factors ironically, young people are more interested in adapting new trend of practices as millennials. Gadgets and social media alter their interest in learning traditional knowledge and practices that are essential in the preservation of both material and non-material culture.

Be Lang Dulay inculcated the T'boli living values and principles through T'nalak weaving. For almost two decades, Be Lang Dulay taught over a hundred of weaver-apprentices. She transmitted her knowledge and skills, the techniques, and procedures in weaving like a mother teaching a young child to walk, which she drew from the inspirations of *Tudbulul.* T'boli families thrive and sustain their needs through weaving. Her masterpiece has left a sustainable legacy. Aside from cultural promotion, it has enhanced the socio-economic life dimensions of the community. As described by a T'boli member,

Weaving has been the means of livelihood among the people that helped in the provision of their needs and for education for their children. This is what I personally experienced, that weaving played an important role in my life to what I am today. Intrinsically, the principles and beliefs that embedded in this art and in the life of Be Lang Dulay, were the same thing that enlightened my perception and motivated me in the practice of other art forms. However, not only weaving, but also music and dances, which are essential part of our culture should also be enlivened and transmitted to the next generation. The legacy of my grandmother that she left to us is in the image of the T'nalak, within it, are patience, kindness, beliefs, passion, and love for culture and people.

T'boli traditional practices and belief systems embed the transmitted beliefs, costumes, and traditions of their community. Hence, T'boli activities remain governed by their indigenous beliefs. T'nalak is a product of the weaver's dream. A weaver draws her signature patterns from her dream. It is easy for a member of a tribe to be inspired, even from a dream, because of their affinity with the spirit and nature. The tribe, despite of the intrusion of other belief systems, is still able to connect with their primordial beliefs. Dream is the royal road to the unconscious (Freud,1901); It is also the storehouse of creativity. Perhaps, the centuries of recognition and practices of taking inspiration from a dream fortified the collective unconscious (Jung, 1936). For others, it is merely a dream; yet, for a T'boli the dream conceptualizes a weave design, and in the T'nalak, embodied the identity of the tribe. Nature and its spirits communicate with the T'bolis through dream, a direct pipeline between people and nature as evident in their indigenous knowledge systems and practices.

The growing market demands for indigenous products of both tourists and the textile industry lead to the commercialization of *T'nalak*. The commodification and commercialization of indigenous treasures erodes the symbolic significance of weaving. The textile preserves the experiences of the weaver and the memories of the generations, losing the cultural and tribal significance means losing the collective story of the tribe (Clariza, 2019). Because of the clamor of the indigenous sectors and advocates of cultural preservations, the country's culture, and arts commission, to preserve the group's cultural heritage, through its legal mandate, show mitigating policies, cultural promotions and among others. Artefacts, stories, music, dances, and songs are treasuries of cultural identities. Without these vessels, individual and collective identities are easily eroded into oblivion. Thanks to the gatekeepers, like Be Lang Dulay, the culture is preserved through artistic expressions that embed the stories of the community's struggles, aspirations, and dreams.

T'boli Dances and Music

At the core of a ritual is an underlying belief that has been embedded in the community for generations. The T'boli people spirit for survival has been inspired and strengthened by their close encounter with nature. Thus, their rituals and incantations, which is usually in dance forms, symbolize nature and its different elements. As part of their cultural preservation, T'boli songs, dances and its accompaniments have become integral to their community way of life. Also, their music, songs and dances are important because these conveys the stories of the pre-colonial Filipinos; These give glimpses of the country's past (Yamut, 2008).

The T'bolis have a repertoire of songs and dances intended for every occasion. These expressive art forms are the highlights of Helobong, a festival that is held from September to November every year in Lake Sebu, South Cotabato. The festival reflects the T'boli belief in *Lemlunay,* which can roughly translate as a paradise, which they aspire to build in the land. Paradise, it is, *Lemlunay* suggests peace and prosperity that it is a form of thanksgiving and convocation of unity and solidarity of the tribe and with other communities as well. Other tribe in South Cotabato like Ubo, Manobo, Kalagan, Maguindanao and Tasaday) and tribes from neighboring regions like Tirurays, Mandaya, Surigao tribes, Langilan, Bilaan, Bagobo, Mansaka converge in Lake Sebu for this grand occasion. The festival is said to originate from their town fiesta celebration for feast day of Sta. Cruz. In the 1970s, *MoNinum,* the thanksgiving ritual of the T'bolis was incorporated with elements of the Catholic tradition for the commemorative mass that concludes the celebration is a blend of Roman Catholic and traditional T'boli rituals. Every July, T'nalaks are showcased in a form of festival, hence known as T'nalak Festival. The exhibition of the different fabrics and parade of cultural attires are not complete without music, dances, and its accompaniments.

Because dance is believed to be a gift from the divine, dance rituals are performed as a commune with the spirit. In the world of the T'boli where nature, spirit, humankind, and other elements are one, music, dancing and the sound of its accompaniments are communions with god. T'boli dances has multitudes of forms dependent to the situation and intentions. However, at the core of its ritualistic movements and expressions is the underlying beliefs in the existence of the connection between humanity, nature, and the spirits. Thus, there are ritual dances and music that intend to mimic nature and its elements as a way of appeasing the spirits, appreciate a good harvest, heal the sick, and for social engagements.

T'boli dances have their corresponding nature and background and it is related to the social events in the T'boli tribe. Their dance also shows the interaction between human being and other living and non-living elements. T'boli dances are said to be authentic and genuine since it is originally from Lake Sebu. This is clearly emphasized in *Madal Tahu* which means True Dance. Other dances such as *Madal Temelek, Madal Soyow, Madal Be-Hegelung, Madal Sewol* and *Madal Mit Mata* are more on social interactions between men and women. They would only differ in their intention and their purpose in interacting with each other. Madal Temelek and Madal Mit Mata is a seduction dance using body movement and facial expressions. Dances like Madal Sewol, Madal Soyow and Madal Be-Hegelung is more on expressing someone's emotion and showing their love and affection to each other. T'boli dances are also mimetic in nature. They imitate the movements of animals. *Madal Tahaw* and *Madal Iwas* respectively emulates the movements of bird and monkey. Choreography and artistry were added to make the dance more creative and so that people will be more motivated to watch and learn the dance. The essence of

T'boli dances, as noted, if one delves further into its intentions, is the reverence of nature and spirit. If one would wonder if flirting and seductive dances are also served as forms of devotion, the instant answer lies in the social context of the dance.

Christian Dogmas in the Backdrop of Indigenous Practices

T'bolis understand the relationship of nature or spirits and human life. T'bolis believe in *D'wata*, which is quintessential in every element found in nature. Thus, the tribe responsibly interacts with nature; Spirits inhabit trees that T'bolis forbid any form activities that would disturb the spirits. As a sign of veneration and acknowledgement to the spirit, a T'boli would a dip finger into a river that he encounters for the first time as an act of initiation or salutation. It is also a form of familiarization and seeking blessings from the spirit of river. Stopping from one's task when someone sneezes or when one would hear a sound from a certain bird are acts of reverence. Though these mentioned exhibits are not Christian in aspirations, the chapter authors assert that these are examples of Christian and T'boli belief systems complimenting each other because regardless of perspectives, the intention is still the same—its purposes are for human good. For a T'boli, the *Dwata* wants them to be compassionate, accommodating, understanding and altruistic for the good of others and for the benefits of the community. As recalled by a T'boli member,

I have been raised with Christian orientation; My mother was one of the early converts of the first waves of protestant missionaries that arrived in our community. My Christian upbringing brought me out from ignorance of life's reality. I saw the gap of our traditional spirituality through the teachings of the Bible. The Christian principles have become my tools to deepen my understanding on the interconnectivity of human life to supreme powers, nature and human beings. Christianity has illuminated and guide me, my compass that gives me clear directions to my life decisions and actions. Indeed, it gives awareness that promotes responsible choices in life. In my observation, Christianity brought positive influences in our traditional practices. For instance, the practice of polygamy, early marriage and arranged marriages are decreasing not because of practical reasons but because of our deeper understanding on what is beneficial to humanity. I would say that the traditional belief system compliments with Christianity. Being a T'boli, I cannot deny the fact that I am still adhering to our traditional belief system which I see as complimenting rather than contradicting my own Christian principles.

Early and arranged marriages, and polygamy are acceptable and practiced in the T'boli culture. Early and arranged marriages are usually done not because of practical or financial reasons. In usual cases, T'boli parents usually arrange their children's marriages when a child becomes ill. To alleviate the illness, the village shaman facilitates the arrangement by looking for suitable partner for their child. This is based on the Tribe's presumption that the child needs a lifetime partner who is obliged to give an accessory, an instrument of healing, like a ring or bracelet. Polygamy in T'boli culture is an emulation of *D'wata,* a spirit who has multiple wives. There are customs to follow especially the rule that men must be adequate and capable of satisfying the needs of his wives and who can only become part of the family, in marriage with the permission of the first wife. These two practices run adverse with Christianity and western traditions. Like most Filipinos, T'bolis are split-level Christians. They still believe in nature spirits which is contrary to Christian faith. Bulatao (1992) codified split-level Christianity as a "phenomenon that consists in a man holding in his mind a set of rote learned religious and moral formulae, which is nevertheless fail to become principles of actual behavior."

Challenges for the Contemporary Generations

The different generations of T'bolis have already changed a great deal. Generation Y and Z, who are considered as the younger generations, and even Generation X, born in the later 60s through the 70s, were raised with influences from contemporary culture. At present, the disparity of preferences between the older and the generations are no longer ubiquitous. The community already embraced modernization that their behaviors, attitudes and their way of life no longer reflects their cultural identity. This is largely because these three generations have better education which is partly responsible for acculturation of lifestyles novel to the tribe. In fact, the third author, a new generation T'boli, has been thanking of the religious missionaries who indirectly proselytized the T'boli community giving them educational materials side by side with the Christian Bible. This was illustrated by a T'boli member:

I grew up with my parents who belong to the early generation T'bolis of the modern era. Their orientation, principles and system are purely T'boli. We had a simple family life. My parents have been farmers and weavers. Our livelihood has always revolved around horticulture and weaving that have sustained us. Education then was not part of our parents' priorities since they did not experience it themselves. Just like the other T'bolis of their generation, they got married earlier than usual compared to other westernized cultures. Education is a foreign concept to T'boli culture. My dream of attaining formal education is inspired by these realities that I witnessed when I was a kid. Of all the changes that the religious missionaries introduced to the community, I considered education as one of the most significant and most impactful in the life of the T'bolis.

Having attained formal education is a form of leverage among Filipinos. Having a college diploma is every parent's dream. It is typical for a household to hang the family members certificates aside from family pictures and other memorabilia. Education attainment is an heirloom that can be passed to the next generation. It is part of the intangible resources that every person can also tap during trying times. Ingrained social reputation comes with one good educational background. Honor, integrity, discipline and resolve fare equally with material and monetary resources- it is a ticket to one's dream, a way out of poverty and a social prestige not only to the individual but also to the family as noted by a T'boli member:

Though it cannot be denied that the introduction of education has caused socio-cultural changes, but looking at it in another angle, it has been beneficial to the T'bolis as well. After I finished my baccalaureate degree and when I become a schoolteacher, things started to transform. My daily tasks before of working in the field and herding farm animals are now substituted by teaching numbers of students. Admittedly, teaching, which is another form of livelihood, is somehow convenient and simple way of supporting my family.

CONCLUSION

The problems of the T'boli tribe are diverse and interrelated. The continued intrusion of outsiders and extrusion of the generation to the outside world created a wide array of problems. Traditional indigenous practices that have sustained the group to keep their heritage have been threatened anew by multi-faceted debacles. Deforestation cut the cord between the tribe and nature. Denudation of the forest would not only devalue thriving flora and fauna; it would also disconnect the present generation from their primordial engagement with nature. Other debacles such as exploitation of water resources, can incapacitate the community from doing their usual rituals and routine; Human settlement augment the threats of values because of cross communication and engagement like business activities, inter-marriages, informal exchange of ideas and vicarious learning. Encroachment of their ancestral domain is worse than water pollution and siltation.

Other than its natural resources, Lake Sebu is also known as the ancestral domain of the T'bolis. However, the group was displaced from their own lands because of the massive influx of settlers from Luzon and Visayas after the Philippine government implemented its resettlement programs. Aside from the usurpation of ancestral land, mining activities pose a threat to tribal culture (Lozano, 1991). The effect of the changes of the general socio-political structures and functions of the country to the T'boli culture may not be readily visible; however, it remains apparent in the changing landscapes and identity of the new generations. The new generations now prefer modern clothing and technology and would rather own a motorbike than tend a carabao or a horse. The internet and other media also contributed to the erosion of community identity and live more typically to other Filipino households. This is a burden on the elders and leaders of the tribe as the new generations tangle with other cultures. The more contemporary generations of T'bolis, such as Generation X, Y, and Z, are inevitably inculcated with influences from contemporary culture. The younger generations of T'boli often lack the assertiveness of their elders, who continue the fight for their rights since the exodus of outsiders.

At present, the disparity of preferences between the older and the younger generations are no longer ubiquitous. The community has embraced modernization that their behaviors, attitudes and their way of life no longer reflects their cultural identity. Despite this assimilation, the T'bolis remain marginalized. They are vulnerable to the threats within themselves and from the dominant sectors of society. Their attempts to preserve and transmit their ethno-cultural distinctions, the basis of their existential identity as people, are very much impacted by the changes of the socio-political landscape. Further research is needed to ensure protection and preservation of the T'boli culture and its identity and indigenous significance within Southeast Asia and specifically, the Philippines, to better understand this land-based culture.

REFERENCES

Agbayani, R. (1993). Some cultural traditions of the indigenous cultural communities in the Philippines: Their implications to the environmental conservation. *PSSC Social Science Information*, *20*, 9–17.

Arquiza, Y. (2007). *The road to empowerment: Strengthening the Indigenous Peoples Rights Act* (Vol. 1). International Labour Organization.

Banda, J. P. (2004, January). Data collection pertaining to indigenous peoples: issues and challenges. In *Workshop on Data Collection and Disaggregation for Indigenous Peoples*. Department of Economic and Social Affairs, United Nations.

Bulatao, J. C. (1992). *Phenomena and their interpretation: Landmark essays, 1957-1989*. Ateneo University Press.

Casal, G., & Bueza, R. V. (2017). T'boli. In N. G. Tiongson (Ed.), *Peoples of the Philippines* (Vol. 3). Cultural Center of the Philippines.

Castro, S. (2001). Kedungon: The abaca fiber. In Dreamweavers (pp. 34-45). Bookmark.

Clariza, M. E. (2019). Sacred texts and symbols: an indigenous Filipino perspective on reading. *The International Journal of Information, Diversity, & Inclusion, 3*(2).

Cudera, R., Razon, B., & Millondaga, K. J. (2020). Cultural and ecological significance of Odonata (Insecta) to the T'boli of Lake Sebu, Mindanao, Philippines. *Biodiversitas Journal of Biological Diversity, 21*(6).

Cunanan, J. P. (1980). Differential access to resources: its impact on environmental activity. *Agham-Tao, 3*(1).

Duhaylungsod, L. (1993). Ancestral domain and cultural identity: missing notes in development. *PSSC Social Science Information, 20*, 19-23, 41.

Duhaylungsod, L. (1996). Higaonons and Bukidnons forests incorporated:" Will the twain ever meet?" *Agham-Tao, 8*(5).

Duhaylungsod, L., & Hyndman, D. (1993). Where T'boli bells toll: A political ecology voices behind the Tasaday hoax. Copenhagen, Denmark: International Working Group on Indigenous Affairs (IWGIA).

Endaya, I. (2015). *Towards a herstory of Filipino women's visual arts*. National Historical Commission of the Philippines (NHCP), Roundtable Conference on Women in History and History of Women.

Freud, S. (1901). *The psychopathology of everyday life* (SE, 6). Hogarth.

Jung, C. G. (1936). *The concept of the collective unconscious. Collected Works, 9*(1), 42.

Lasalita-Zapico, F., Martin, T. T., Pena, R. J., & Gonzales, J. (2008). Farming and seed conservation practices of rice farmers in the marginal uplands of Lake Sebu, South Cotabato, Philippines. *Philippine Journal of Crop Science, 16*(1), 7–11.

Magbanua, F. S., Fontanilla, A. M., Ong, P. S., & Hernandez, M. B. M. (2017). 25 years (1988-2012) of freshwater research in the Philippines: What has been done and what to do next? *Philippine Journal of Systematic Biology, 11*(1).

McKenna, R. T. (2017). *American imperial pastoral: The architecture of US colonialism in the Philippines*. University of Chicago Press. doi:10.7208/chicago/9780226417936.001.0001

Mora, M. (2012). Tune and textile: interrelatedness in the music and weaving arts of the T'boli, Philippines. *Humanities Diliman: A Philippine Journal of Humanities, 9*(2).

Nolasco, R. M. (n.d.). *Proto-Austronesian transitivity revisited: Reviewing the Philippine evidence*. http://citeseerx.ist.psu.edu/viewdoc/download?doi=10.1.1.557.5948&rep=rep1&type=pdf

Papa, R. D., & Briones, J. C. (2014). Climate and human-induced changes to lake ecosystems: What we can learn from monitoring zooplankton ecology. *Journal of Environmental Science and Management, 17*(1).

Paterno, M. P., & Oshima, N. M. (2001). *Dreamweavers*. Bookmark.

Porras, R. E., & Buot, I. E. (2016). Profiling Lake Sebu and the indigenous community in the vicinity. *Journal of Wetlands Biodiversity*, *6*, 85–96.

Quizon, C. (2019). The weaver's house: Ethnography, translation, and video in the highlands of Mindanao. *Visual Anthropology Review*, *35*(2), 148–161. doi:10.1111/var.12189

Reid, L. (2019). The reconstruction of a dual pronoun to Proto Malayo-Polynesian. In B. Evans (Ed.), *Discovering history through language: Papers in honour of Malcolm Ross* (pp. 461–477). Pacific Linguistics.

Sarmiento, B. S. (2013, Mar. 10). A paradise lost. Lake Sebu, South Cotabato. *Mindanews*.

Triandis, H. C., Malpass, R. S., & Davidson, A. R. (1973). Psychology and culture. *Annual Review of Psychology*, *24*(1), 355–378. doi:10.1146/annurev.ps.24.020173.002035

United Nations Development Programme. (2003). *Country level impact assessment: The Philippines.* http://web.undp.org/evaluation/documents/CLIA-Philippines.pdf

Wollants, G. (2012). *Gestalt therapy*: *Therapy of the situation. Sage (Atlanta, Ga.).*

Yamut, V. T. (2008). Ritual dances of the T'Boli. *Journal of Higher Education Research*, *5*(2).

Zapico, F., Aguilar, C. H., Eroy, M., Marie, J. R., Barbosa, D. S., & Banisil, S. R. (2014). Morpho-agronomic variability and gxe interactions of manila hemp (musa textilis l. Née) genotypes grown in varying agro-ecozones in Southern Mindanao, Philippines. *International Journal of Agronomy and Agricultural Research*, *4*(2), 12–20.

Zorc, R. D. (1986). The genetic relationships of Philippine languages. In *FOCAL II: Papers from the Fourth International Conference on Austronesian Linguistics* (pp. 147-173). Canberra: Department of Linguistics, Research School of Pacific Studies, Australian National University.

ADDITIONAL READING

Boquet, Y. (2017). The diversity of the Philippine population. In *The Philippine Archipelago* (pp. 159–179). Springer. doi:10.1007/978-3-319-51926-5_7

Clariza, M. E. (2019). Sacred texts and symbols: An Indigenous Filipino perspective on reading. *The International Journal of Information, Diversity, & Inclusion (IJIDI)*, *3*(2).

Cudera, R., Razon, B., & Millondaga, K. J. (2020). Cultural and ecological significance of Odonata (Insecta) to the T'boli of Lake Sebu, Mindanao, Philippines. *Biodiversitas Journal of Biological Diversity*, *21*(6).

Dove, M. R., Sajise, P. E., & Doolittle, A. A. (Eds.). (2011). *Beyond the sacred forest: Complicating conservation in Southeast Asia*. Duke University Press.

Handayani, B., Seraphin, H., & Korstanje, M. (2019). Dark tourism in the Philippines Islands. In *Special Interest Tourism in Southeast Asia: Emerging research and opportunities* (pp. 23–42). IGI Global. doi:10.4018/978-1-5225-7393-7.ch002

Mora, M. (2005). *Myth, mimesis and magic in the music of the T'boli*. Ateneo de Manila University Press.

Quizon, C. (2019). The Weaver's house: Ethnography, translation, and video in the Highlands of Mindanao. *Visual Anthropology Review*, *35*(2), 148–161. doi:10.1111/var.12189

KEY TERMS AND DEFINITIONS

Dream Weavers: The craft of weaving among the T'boli is a sacred spiritual tradition. Designs are believed to arrive from *Fu Dalu*, the spirit of the Abaca.

T'boli: An ethnolinguistic group that inhabits parts of Saranggani Province, South Cotabato and Sultan Kudarat, Philip

*Tudbulul***:** A Filipino oral epic. Oral epics of Southeast Asia are often genealogically related for claims to the right of succession and moral order.

Chapter 14
The Hauntings and Heart of a Place:
Reconnecting to Grandmother Lands

John-Paul Peter Joseph Chalykoff
Michigan State University, USA & Michipicoten First Nation, Canada

ABSTRACT

This autoethnographic research presents personal stories from the author, connecting family, land, and music. He recounts stories his Ojibwe grandmother shared about her time in Franz, a small railroad village in northeastern Ontario that is now a ghost town. The connection to Franz is established through memories from his grandmother. Inspired to write a song, the author aimed to reconnect to Franz itself. The study follows the author's personal journey to visit his grandmother's land for the first time, making new connections and stories along the way. The research utilizes Indigenous autoethnography, Indigenous storytelling, and arts-based methods, such as a/r/tography, to link his stories to those of his grandmother, resulting in a reflection of storytelling, community history, and (re)connection to land, woven together by stories from the family matriarch.

INTRODUCTION

The year was 1944, maybe 1945. We're at a small railroad town in northern Ontario, north of Lake Superior. There's a young Ojibwe girl, about 4 or 5 years old, walking home on a dirt road along the rail-track. Her name is Frances; she's the baby of the family. World War II was still raging in other parts of the world. Her oldest brother, Allan, left some time ago to go fight in the war.

Her grandma, Mary, was working around the yard when Frances arrived, singing "Praise the Lord and pass the ammunition!" Astonished, Mary burst into laughter,

"Aaniindi gaa-noondaman iw nagamon?" (Where did you hear that song?)

DOI: 10.4018/978-1-7998-3729-9.ch014

"Ningii-noondaan radio-ing." (I heard it on the radio.)

"Gi-debwe na? Gi-nisidotaan na?" (Are you for real? Do you understand it?)

"Gaawiin." (No.)

The girl and her grandmother laughed heartily.

Somewhat puzzled, yet amused at having gotten a fit of laughter out of her grandmother, Frances began singing again, "Praise the Lord, and pass the ammunition!"

This is a story I remember my grandmother, Frances, sharing. It was one of many that she told of her early childhood in Franz, a tale from northern Ontario, in the heart of the Michipicoten First Nation's traditional territory. Franz was a small railroad town (Figure 1) along the Algoma Central Railway, near the midpoint between Sault Ste. Marie and Hearst. It is now only a shadow of what it once was—a ghost town. However, for it to now be deserted, it must have once had much life. This chapter explores a period when the region was alive, a time when my grandmother and her family lived there. I share stories I remember her telling, the kind that brought life to a place that I never knew, and about which I have been trying to learn.

Figure 1. Algoma Central Railway (ACR) car running through Franz
Source: Author's grandparents' collection, circa early 1960s

Much of the inspiration for this research comes from the final course I took to complete my Master of Education degree from Lakehead University in Thunder Bay, Ontario. I enrolled in the course "Place-Based Education" with Dr. David Greenwood in the early summer of 2019. In this course, we were encouraged to think about place and, more importantly, connections to place. One of our textbooks was *Hearth: A Global Conversation on Community, Identity, and Place* (Smith & O'Connor, 2018). The book offered many perspectives on what relationships to place can mean. However, two essays that I did not expect to stand out in this collection are what most inspired my reflection. Andrew Lam's essay, "Enchantment," described his experience growing up in Vietnam, then having to flee in times of war. Boey Kim Cheng's essay, "Home is Elsewhere," spoke of the complex boundaries between Singapore and Australia as home. These were stories of movement, displacement, and making new homes in new places, with memories and connections to the motherlands remaining intact. Their stories and experiences could not have been more different than my own, and yet they resonated with me. I could understand what they were writing about, or at least I wanted to understand more. The way they spoke of the homes of their youth was not so different from how I remember my grandmother speaking of her own childhood. I have spent my life living in Anishinaabewakiing, our Anishinaabe homelands, and the vast majority of my time has been spent in northern Ontario. Yet there were places of familial significance that I had never visited. Franz is one of these places.

In a sense, I was familiar with where my grandmother had grown up, as I had heard stories about Franz for much of my life. I knew it was only about an hour away from Wawa, where I was raised, yet I had never been there. During my college course, I was reading these complex stories of motherlands that were so far away, yet still very personal. It led me to reflect on what my own motherlands are. I realized that, in some ways, my story of reconnecting to Indigenous lands may not be so different. Most of my connection to Franz has come from stories from my grandmother and grandfather. These are, quite literally, stories of my *mother's motherlands*.

BACKGROUND

Boozhoo, John-Paul Chalykoff nindizhinikaaz. Wawa, Ontario, nindoonjibaa, mii gaye gii-ondaadiziyaan iwidi. Michipigodong Ojibwe Anishinaabe miinawaa Wemitigoozhi nindaaw.

(Hello, my name is John-Paul Chalykoff. I'm from Wawa, Ontario, where I was born. I'm Ojibwe, from the Michipicoten First Nation, and French-Canadian.)

Although the chapter focuses on my grandmother, I offer some details here about my background. I was born in Wawa, a small town in northern Ontario known for the large goose statue that is perched where Highway 17 branches off into town (Figure 2). I spent the first 11 years of my life there, then moved to Sault Ste. Marie, where I spent the remainder of my youth. For a few years, I attended school in Thunder Bay, and I returned to Wawa after the passing of my grandmother in 2015. Currently, I teach introductory Anishinaabemowin and Introduction to American Indian and Indigenous Studies in Lansing, Michigan, and I am a second-term elected councillor on the Michipicoten First Nation's Council.

"The truth about stories is that's all we are" (King, 2003, p. 2). With this recognizable phrase from his seminal work, Thomas King (Cherokee) laid a foundation for Indigenous storytelling that continues to inspire many of us to this day. I used to think about his statement on stories a lot. I wondered if there was a deeper, perhaps more esoteric, meaning behind it that I was not fully grasping. There is probably a lot more to glean from the statement, but as I reflect on my grandmother, it becomes very simple.

Gii-maajaa nookomisiban gaa-niibing 2015. My grandmother passed away in the summer of 2015. It was one of those moments that everyone in a family has to reckon with—we lost the family matriarch.

Figure 2. Map of significant family locations
Source: Google

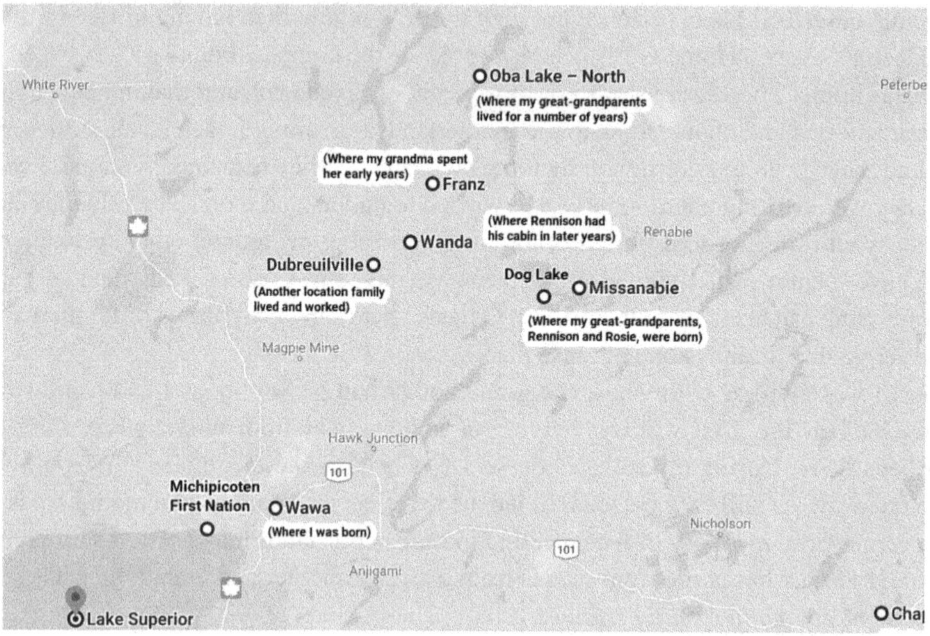

Since her passing, what we are left with is her stories: the kinds of stories that bring her to life for me; the kinds that brought life to my great-grandparents, her siblings, as well as the town of Franz, itself. These stories have been one of the only ways that I have been able to get to know many of these people, the only way I got to know this place. I had never been to Franz, but I felt connected to it. The stories were and are the connection.

For this research, I utilize Indigenous autoethnography. Much of the material in this chapter comes from my own experiences and memories. Many of the stories shared here are those I remember my grandmother sharing throughout my life. While discussing stories as Indigenous methodology, Margaret Kovach (2009; Nêhiyaw and Saulteaux) states that "stories remind us of who we are and of our belonging" (p. 94). Paul Whitinui (2013; Maori) explains that "Indigenous autoethnography by its very definition asks us to consider epistemological perspectives equally and to draw together self (auto), ethno (nation), and writing (graphy)" (p. 12). Bishop (2020; Gamilaroi) challenges the concept of auto/self being confined to only an individual, arguing that "the concept of 'self' needs broadening to recognise that this is a bigger entity than an individual" (p. 6). The stories presented here are a mix of family tales, some of which are pieced together with family and census records, stories from elders, and engaging with academic research. However, this chapter also utilizes storytelling. Simard (2020; Anishinaabe), while referencing Koch (1998) explains that "storytelling is a lived process designed to facilitate change, whether internal or external, within an individual, family, community, nation or environment." He goes on to state that, "through reflection and praxis, storytelling methods allow for the discovery of social meanings related to the natural process of cultural development" (p. 141). Likewise, Bishop (2020) reminds us that, as "Indigenous researchers, we are responsible and accountable first and foremost to our families, community members, Elders, Ancestors, and Country" (p. 4).

Through my research, I have verified that the local pronunciation of Michipicoten is *Michipigodong*. I asked a speaker in the Batchewana First Nation (in southeast Ontario), a speaker in Chapleau (east Ontario), a speaker in the Pic Mobert First Nation (northwest Ontario), and an elder in the Michipicoten First Nation itself. They all pronounced it as *Michipigodong*. Expanding on this, Michipicoten elder Bill Swanson (Ojibwe, Michipicoten First Nation, Ontario) says it is *Michipigodong Ziibiing Anishinaabewakiing*, referring to the traditional village that was situated along the mouth of the Michipicoten River near where it flows into *Gichi-Gami* (Lake Superior).

It is more challenging to identify what Michipicoten means. Most of the people I interviewed struggled to define it. A Google search indicates the translation as "big bluffs." I have not broken down the term, apart from labeling *michi-/mishi-* as meaning something big or very large. In *The Decolonial Atlas* (Lippert & Engel, 2014), it is written as *Mishibikwadinaang*. Neither Swanson nor another elder from the region had ever heard it described in this way. When I was attending an Ojibwe immersion academy with Ojibwemotaadidaa Omaa Gidakiiminaang in Fond Du Lac, Minnesota, I raised the topic with some colleagues. Although they did not recognize the term *Michipigodong*, they were able to make sense of *Mishibikwadinaang*. Using *The Ojibwe People's Dictionary*, the latter term can be identified as follows:

- *Mishi*: Giant, of legendary size.
- *bikwadinaa*: A knoll or hill.
- *-ng*: A locative, making it a location.

Thus, the term describes giant banks or cliffs, which matches the "big bluff" definition. My theory is that *Michipigodong* is possibly a shortened form of *Mishibikwadinaang* that took shape over the years. While I do not have a linguistics background and I cannot say this is the correct interpretation, it is my hypothesis for the time being.

Michipicoten has a rich yet complex history. Michipicoten was historically made up of two groups, a coastal group and an inland group. These populations were fairly independent from one another, yet inter-connected through trade and marriage (Gray & Morrison, 2019, pp. 5–6). My family belongs to the interior group, formerly known as *les gens de terres*, or *les têtes de boules*, the "round-heads," by the French. The name "round-heads" apparently comes from a former chief known as *Gichi-oshtigwaan*, which means "large head" (p. 6). It is said that *les gens de terres*, people of the land/inland, came from *noopiming dazhi-ininiwag*, or "backwoodsmen," referring to the Indians who "reside in the interior of the shores of Lake Superior, in the North" (Ojibwe writer George *Gaagigegaabaw* Copway, 1851, as quoted in Ningewance Nadeau & Valentine, 2013). Gray and Morrison (2019) point out that the term was used in a joking, and sometimes pejorative, tone, the way that the word "hicks" is used by some of the Ojibwe in the south (p. 11). This was most likely not a term we used to describe ourselves.

GRANDMA'S STORIES

These stories take place in the interior of northeastern Ontario, north of Lake Superior. These are stories from Michipigodong Anishinaabewakiing (the traditional lands of the Michipicoten First Nation). The landscape is rugged, in the midst of the Boreal Forest. Complex river systems connect communities in all directions. The Michipicoten River system played an important part in the north–south connection from Lake Superior to James Bay. Generations of residents enjoyed hunting, trapping, fishing, and trading. Several the lakes in the surrounding area feature old red ochre pictographs along the cliffs. One of these lakes is Dog Lake, where our story begins.

My great-grandfather, Rennison Tangie, was born in 1905 in Missanabie, Ontario, near Dog Lake. His wife—my great-grandmother—Rosie Quackagezick, was born in 1907, also in Missanabie. I have very few details about their early lives besides their birthplaces, which I obtained from their marriage certificate. I know that Rennison eventually spent a significant portion of his childhood at St. John's Indian Residential School in Chapleau. These schools were, as the Truth and Reconciliation Commission of Canada (2015) puts it, "an education system in name only" (p. v). They were designed to remove Indigenous children from their families and communities, forcing them to assimilate into Euro-Canadian culture over a period of more than a hundred years (Truth and Reconciliation Commission of Canada, 2005, p. v). They were known for atrocious abuse of the students, creating long-lasting social impacts that our communities deal with to this day. St. John's Indian Residential School had a terrible reputation for such abuse. It was haunting to read how closely the research by northern Ontario historian Bill McLeod matched the few stories that Rennison had shared, such as children being "ill fed, ill clothed, and beaten for the most trivial offences" (Leeson, 2018). Many of my great-grandfather's experiences at St. John's followed him throughout his life, with the memories haunting him until his passing.

Rennison and Rosie lived close to one another throughout their lives. The records in the 1911 Canadian Census of the East Algoma region indicate that their families lived next-door to one another, with Rennison and Rosie aged 6 and 4, respectively, at the time. Eventually, they both wound up in Oba Lake, Ontario. Before they were married, Rosie had two sons, Allan (b. 1924) and John (b. 1927), by another man. By 1928, they were living together in Franz, where they wed. Rennison raised Allan and John as his own, giving them the Tangie name. By 1930, Rennison and Rosie had their first child together, Dorothy, followed by Charlotte (b. 1932), Alice (b. 1934), and Samuel (b. 1935). My grandmother, Frances, was the baby of the family, born in 1940 (Figure 3).

While working on a family-tree assignment in the 1970s, Rennison explained to his granddaughter, my mother, that Tangie had started out as a nickname for his father, William. It then was recorded on an

Figure 3. My grandmother, Frances, with her father, Rennison (right), and her brother, Sam (left)
Source: Author's grandparents' collection, circa early 1960s

official document as Tangie, and the name stuck. Prior to this, the family name was Step. I have thus far been unable to trace a family name of Step, or to find out what the Ojibwe name would have been before that. My grandmother translated Quackagezick as "Turnover Day." While I still do not fully understand the meaning of the name, I was recently able to make more sense of it while reading a historical report for Michipicoten; here, it was written by a French Jesuit missionary as Gwekigijig (Gray & Morrison, 2019, p. 42). I suddenly recognized parts of the word: *gwek-* is the root for turning, and *giizhig* means day or sky. I am still unsure what "turning of the day" means—whether it refers to the transition from day to night, or from clear skies to overcast, or to some other changes—but I am glad to have a clearer understanding of my grandmother's description.

I know very little of Rosie's life; she passed away from tuberculosis (TB) less than two years after Frances was born. Because of this, my grandmother never had the chance to get to know her mother. I have seen only one photo of Rosie. There is a whole story—a whole life—that I know so little about, yet it is such an important part of our family history. Since Rennison was still trapping and hunting or working for the ACR at this point—both of which required a lot of time away from home—he was unable to take care of Frances while he was working. Thus, Frances was raised by her paternal grandmother, Mary Matchininie. My grandmother recalled this time fondly for the rest of her life, and she described how Mary would speak to her primarily in Ojibwe. After Mary passed away in 1945, it was rare for adults to continue speaking Ojibwe to Frances. Because of this, she lost her familiarity with the language, which was something she would mourn for the rest of her life. She would, however, often find comfort in hearing certain speakers talk, as they would remind her of Grandma Mary. She held on to bits of the language, and she remembered an Ojibwe lullaby that Mary sang to her through her early childhood. Frances would go on to sing it to her own children and grandchildren. It is a short and simple vocable, repeating *memejewee* to a gentle melody.

Memejewee, memejewee, meme,

Memejewee.

After Mary's passing, Frances went to live with her uncle and aunt, as Rennison began working for the ACR, and was unable to watch her during the day. These were tough years for Frances. Her aunt was unkind and put her through many hardships. I remember these stories coming up several times around the dinner table. They were tales of hardship and tears, but there was always a happy ending. Many people told Frances that she needed to write a book, that her stories were so good. She would, however, usually dismiss the idea. She was worried, and never wanted to offend her family by sharing these details. The difficult times involved much hardship. Residential schools had taken their toll on so many in our communities. Patterns and behaviours that children had learned in these schools, ripe with abuse, meant that they did not know how to show love to their own families, from whom they had been separated. This was in the 1940s, and many of the victims did not come to terms with what happened at the schools until much later.

While these were difficult years for Frances, there were beautiful moments as well—bright spots that she would share, small stories that have stayed with me. I remember one anecdote in which Frances said she was walking along the tracks outside of Franz with a friend. Suddenly, a large bull moose appeared out of the forest line in front of them. Her friend thought it would be fun to tease him, so she stuck her tongue out and began blowing raspberries at him. The moose did not approve and took an aggressive pose, preparing to charge. Quickly realizing their mistake, the girls turned and ran as fast as their little legs would take them, as the large bull began to sprint after them. Luckily, there was a large boulder nearby, and they scrambled up to safety. The moose, unable to reach them as they clung for their lives to the large stone, eventually calmed down and returned to the forest. They went back to revisit the boulder the following day, and no matter how hard they tried, they could not get back on top of the stone that provided them sanctuary. Needless to say, they knew not to tease a moose again.

Frances also remembered secret ceremonies that took place during her youth. The secrecy was required because, at the time, the Canadian government had banned Indigenous ceremonies from taking place. By 1885, Canada had enacted the Potlatch Ban in the Indian Act, prohibiting the Potlatch ceremony from being practiced on the west coast of Canada. This barring of traditional ceremonies eventually made its way throughout the rest of the country and lasted until 1951 (Monkman, 2017). Because of the ban, the adults had to practice the ceremonies carefully and clandestinely; there was a very real threat of punishment if they were caught. Because of this, the parents kept the children from actively participating or witnessing what took place. This protected both the parents and the children, and made it less likely that the children would accidentally reveal any details of the practices. The families walked deep into the woods, up the railway tracks, where they could not be seen or heard. My grandmother remembered hearing singing and drumming, as well as smelling burning medicines coming from the ceremonial structure. She remembers peeking her head under the canvas, only to be quickly shooed away, sent out to play with the other children. I often wonder what ceremonies they were practicing and which songs they might have been singing. I wonder where they were and if I can someday find that place.

Small stories would often come back to my grandmother while we sat at the dinner table. She would laugh to herself, reminded that the older family members called beans *boogijimin*—the farting fruit. Other times, she would recall a simple word, like *kayaashk*, or seagull. These were the kinds of words she remembered from her childhood. She also reminisced about old-timers telling stories about travelling by canoe to *Baawiting*, Sault Ste. Marie, where many of our family members ended up living.

As we delve deeper into these stories, it is important to revisit the topic of TB. The disease had devastating effects in many communities, and its reach affected the town of Franz and the entire region of northern Ontario. For our family, it was a very real threat. Rennison lost a little sister, Ester, to it decades before. Rosie lost her father, Louis, in 1922, and her mother, Charlotte, in 1925, both taken by the sickness. As noted above, Rosie passed from TB in 1941. This was unfortunately still not the end of the sickness's impact on the family. In what was the beginning of a devastating three years, Frances lost her oldest sister, Dorothy, to TB complications in 1947. Her sister, Alice, would soon follow, passing from TB in 1948. Finally, another sister, Charlotte, passed from a kidney infection in 1949. By 1951, Frances herself contracted TB and was sent to a sanitorium to recover. She would go on to spend a few years of her life in the institution, leaving around 1954. In some ways, her time at the sanitorium was an escape from her aunt and gave her time to recover from more than just the TB. Her brother, Sam, also contracted the disease and spent several years in a sanitorium, as well; thankfully, he also recovered. When her health improved, Frances spent a year in the Shingwauk Indian Residential School in Sault Ste. Marie before returning to Franz in 1956.

My grandmother was a very musical person. Sometime after her return to Franz, she learned how to play the guitar. Sam had a guitar, and it was one of his prized possessions. As he was heading out for work, he would tell Frances to not touch his guitar—he did not want anything to happen to it. Of course, not long after he would leave, Frances would pick up the guitar and teach herself how to play (Figure 4). She began figuring out chords and how to strum the instrument. One day, her brother returned and saw

Figure 4. My grandmother playing guitar
Source: Author's grandparents' collection, circa early 1960s

her playing. Astonished, he asked her if she had learned how to play on his guitar. She looked at him, smiling, and said, "Yep!" She would keep a guitar with her for the rest of her life, entertaining many with her songs, while also inspiring many of us in the family, both children and grandchildren, to take up music as well.

At some point in the late 1950s, my grandfather, Jean-Louis, left Québec and made his way to Ontario for work. He joined the ACR and was eventually stationed in Franz. Soon, my grandmother spotted him, and he did the same. They would often catch one another sneaking glances at each other. I remember Frances telling stories of being love-struck, writing her beau's name in the snowbanks in the middle of winter. Before long, the two met and became a couple. Young and in love, they married in 1960, the beginning of a new chapter for Frances (Figure 5). Though it was a joyous moment, it was also bittersweet.

Rennison did not approve of Frances marrying Jean-Louis because he had some negative experiences with some of the French workers in Franz. Some of them had pelted him with rocks, bloodying his face. He, understandably, never forgot that moment and assumed that all French workers were racist and ignorant. Rennison told Frances that he did not like Jean-Louis—that he was too strict (Jean Louis did not drink), and that he thought of the suitor almost like a priest. On the wedding day, Rennison decided that he would not attend. He was having some drinks at the little bar in Franz when his friend arrived after the wedding ceremony. "How could you do that? That's your only daughter, and you didn't even show up to her wedding!" With the weight of the realization of his mistake, Rennison wept. He knew that his friend was right—he had missed his baby girl's wedding. It was something he knew he could never take back, and he would have to live with it.

Rennison's relationship with Jean-Louis improved over time, as he came to know that his daughter and son-in-law were truly in love. Moreover, Rennison would have a great relationship with his grandchildren, and all of them remember him fondly. He had nicknames for all of them and would teach them little bits of the native language. They all remember him teaching them to count from one to ten, and they came to

Figure 5. My grandparents as a young couple in Franz
Source: Author's grandparents' collection, circa early 1960s

realize that his way of counting was slightly different from other dialects of Anishinaabemowin. While the majority count in a similar way—*bezhig, niizh, niswi, niiwin, naanan, ningodwaaswi, niizhwaaswi, nishwaaswi, zhaangswi, midaaswi*—Rennison's method was slightly different: *pezhig, niizhin, nisin, niiwin, naanan, ningodaachin, niizhwaachin, nishwaachin, zhaangchin, mitaachin.* I remember hearing that some would say that it was Oji-Cree, however, my grandmother's brother, John, would insist, "I know Oji-Cree, and we don't speak Oji-Cree! We speak Ojibwe!" I eventually came across some fellow language learners who count that way; they were from the Temagami First Nation, also in northeastern Ontario, a few hundred kilometers east. Numbers may be a small thing, but they are little treasures that Rennison passed on, clues of the under-documented inland dialect. Near the end of his life, when he had cancer and knew he was going to pass, Rennison wept once again. He cried knowing he had so little time and still so much more he wanted to share with his grandchildren. Language, trapping, hunting, and stories were among some of what he wished he could have shared further.

Within a few years of marrying, Frances and Jean-Louis left Franz, following the work and raising their seven young children. Throughout her life, Frances shared all kinds of stories—of love, of sadness, of joy, of coming of age, of loss of innocence, of redemption, of strength, of loss, of discovery, of music. These are just some of the tales that I remember her telling; for each one I know, there are dozens that I do not. Though I never heard Frances refer to herself as such, she was a gifted storyteller, transporting many listeners to places we had never been, but which we had all experienced by the end of her stories. Whether it was with her guitar on stage, or around the various family dinner tables, she would share all kinds of details from her life. I realize now that these stories are treasures that no amount of gold or riches can buy. I cannot help but feel regret for not having understood their true value sooner. I wish I had listened more, that I would have asked for one more story during each of those visits. I wish I would have visited just a little bit longer instead of taking off to do other things that seemed important at the time. No doubt many people understand this sentiment. Perhaps this will serve as a reminder for some; I know I can use them from time to time.

My grandmother had a tough go at times, but even with all the stories of sadness and pain, she never let this define her. She would go on to live a full life, sharing 55 years of marriage with Jean-Louis.

They raised their seven children and one of her nephews, and they would have 15 grandchildren and a dozen great-grandchildren as of this writing. The family matriarch, Frances has been and remains an inspiration to many of us.

MUSIC-INFORMED ARTS-BASED RESEARCH

I have long admired the methodology of a/r/tography, where the roles of artist, researcher, and teacher work in tandem. There are many layers to the approach, and many complexities, but I prefer its basic version, where the roles we hold are inseparable. The duties of artist, researcher, and teacher cannot be separated or compartmentalized. They are part of who we are, and the art is not an afterthought—it is part of what we do. Springgay et al. (2005) cycle through six renderings of a/r/tography. Of these, Reverberations matches me best, as it speaks of movement, quaking, measures, and rhythm, all factors that sync well with music. They exclaim that "these vibrations allow art making/researching/teaching to sink deeply, to penetrate, and to resonate with echoes of each other" (pp. 906–907).

Music is my art form of choice. The connecting of stories and land acts as reverberations that come through musically with my art. After seeing some variations on it, such as dis/a/r/tography (Roman et al., 2020), where disability is part of the identity of the artist/researcher/teacher, I revisited an idea of adapting it to aa/r/tography. There are a few elements at play here that result from adding a second "a" at the beginning of the term. This changes the phrase to "Anishinaabe/artist/researcher/teacher." Part of the play on words comes from Anishinaabemowin (the Anishinaabe/Ojibwe language), which uses double vowels to convey long vowels in written form, such as aa, ii, oo. The double-a in aa/r/tography is a play on this idea. The goal is to merge Indigenous identity with a/r/tography. Irwin and Springgay (2008) speak of the flexibility of a/r/tography, but also the tension that is inherent to it. They explain that there is no rigid structure or way to define it, which leaves room for creativity that is sometimes complementary and other times discordant, all while working with a/r/tography (p. xix). My understanding is that these pieces cannot be separated, and they inform the work as a whole, rather than as separate pieces. With that in mind, I weave the extra layer of Indigenous methodology within this argument, as my identity cannot be removed from this discussion.

Music is not the easiest art form to examine in arts-based research. There is no visual element, and it is not easy to put sound to print. However, I learned through experience that there are ways to work with music in research. In the winter of 2014, I collaborated with Dr. Pauline Sameshima, as a graduate assistant. Sameshima specializes in arts-based research/arts-integrated research, and this was my first exposure to the field. She had been working on a project titled *Women & Meth* (2014), which is an arts-integrated research project about female meth addicts in recovery, utilizing different arts-based projects. I had never utilized music as an academic medium, and Sameshima explained that it was still an under-utilized art form for arts-based research; this gave me some freedom to explore. I was given transcripts from an interview with "Jill," a pseudonym for one of the study participants. I looked at some of the other art projects and began reading the transcripts. Stories took shape in my mind, and I began working on creating the music. I wrote short pieces to create moods and atmospheres that reflected what I had read. I then wrote artist statements at the end of the recording process to give insight to the music and help the audience reflect on what they had heard. This is the process I have continued to use in my arts-based research. Dr. Daniel Bakan's dissertation (2014) has also been very helpful in integrating elements of a/r/tography, autoethnography, and music into my work. His manuscript finds a beautiful balance between a/r/tography, autoethnography, and music, all of which I highly admire.

As a part of my final assignment for my course with Dr. Greenwood in the summer of 2019, I composed and recorded a song that shares the title of this chapter, "The Hauntings and Heart of a Place." It is an instrumental piece that began to take shape as I worked on the musical arrangement. The tools I had were limited, as I had only brought my acoustic guitar to Thunder Bay for the semester. Using my guitar and my voice, I created a layered sound. The more I worked and the more the piece began to take shape, I realized it was telling a story of its own. Since it was an instrumental, I knew it was not a story that most others would be able to see immediately, so I began something new. I began to write about my grandmother and Franz. Three minutes is not much time to work with, so I sculpted my words carefully, retaining only what was needed to clarify the story. This was a new style of writing. It took the shape of prose, and I did not worry about rhyme or meter, but kept the time in mind. I began by reading the lyrics aloud to the music, and I edited the words to fit within the three-minute timespan. The song began to take its own shape, with unplanned moments synchronizing beyond any expectation I had. The music begins slowly and pensively, building the foundation of my grandmother's story. Then, a shift to a more aggressive strum syncs with the tale of the charging moose. A gentle romantic air sets in as we reach the beginning of my grandparents' love story. I had a vague idea in my mind, with images and emotions flowing through the music, but the ultimate product was unplanned. These were the kind of serendipitous moments that we only sometimes find as we let the art guide the way (Chalykoff, 2020).

Following the creation and performance of this song, I had one remaining desire. I knew that I had started something that I needed to complete, and I could not leave it the song as empty words. I was sincere in expressing the need to find my way to Franz. Once the words were committed to the page and to the recording, I knew I had to find my way there, and I began planning the trip.

MY JOURNEY TO FRANZ

The summer of 2019 was coming to a close. I was preparing for a major move, leaving Wawa and northern Ontario to begin work at Michigan State University in East Lansing. I knew my time to visit Franz was running short, and I was beginning to figure out how to get there. In my mind, it was a long, epic drive through dirt roads and woods, and I needed to be ready for anything. I told my cousin, Brandon, that I was planning to go. We had discussed a similar trip for a number of years, yet we were never able to sync our schedules to make it work. He said he needed to finish some shingling on his garage, and he'd be able to make the trip to Franz once the project was completed. I joined him and helped as best I could. Afraid of heights, I worked doing clean-up on the ground level—sweeping, gathering nails, and throwing the old shingles onto a trailer to be taken to the dump, as Brandon worked above with my uncles and other family. Within two days, the job was done, and we were ready to make our first trip to Franz.

Getting there from Wawa is straightforward. You travel west on Highway 17, then turn onto the Dubreilville Highway and take a dirt road the rest of the way to Franz. I had been close to the town a number of times throughout my life without realizing it. I could not help but laugh to myself when I realized this. The road was not nearly as rough as I had imagined, and it is fairly well maintained to provide access for the railroad by CN rail, as they have a bunkhouse in Franz.

After a little more than an hour of driving, we arrived at the "grandmother-lands." We were among the beautiful northern trees of the Boreal Forest. To be honest, I do not know what kinds of trees they were. I should know more, but my tree knowledge is unfortunately lacking. I know how to identify some more common ones, like birch, cedar, and maple trees (unless the maple leaves have fallen off—then it is a 50/50 chance). I can even name a decent number of trees in Ojibwe off the top of my head: *zhing-waak, giizhik, ininaatig, zhingob, wiigwaas*. I would, however, be in trouble if I had to put the names to the trees themselves. It is something that I want to work on, something important. Doing a Google search feels like cheating.

Even though Franz was a ghost town, it was not deserted. A portion of the town serves as a bunkhouse for CN Rail workers to keep the rails maintained. We spent a few hours walking around and exploring. We had nowhere in particular to go and nothing to look for, so we took our time and explored the houses that still stood. There are some abandoned homes that are slowly falling apart, with no doors or windows remaining. We were walking through ruins of a different time. It was a peaceful feeling, being able to walk and freely explore. We went a little way down the tracks, seeing several train maintenance buckets along the side of the trail. We saw remnants from a time before, slowly deteriorating. We got a few views of Lake Hobon from different vantage points, and I saw some large boulders that made me think of my grandmother's story about escaping the moose. I do not think any of them were big enough to fit that story, but it was nice to think about.

After a few hours of this, it was time to go home. We slowly walked back to the truck, looked around, and drove back to Dubreilville for some lunch. It was, and is, important for me to remember that this was only the first visit. I will return, perhaps with one of our older cousins—one my grandmother's brother's sons—who spent more time there, to guide us through the area and put more pieces together.

Months later, as the COVID-19 pandemic changed the pace of our lives, I began to scan old photographs. After my grandparents passed away, I was given their old 35 mm collection of slides. I kept them safe and invested in a scanner. However, the project fell to the wayside and, before I knew it, close to three years had passed. With life slowing down, I decided it was time to finally start scanning. Between March 26 and April 23, I scanned 451 slides. I began to see a small snapshot into my grandparents' early life together. I saw photos of them as a young couple, as newlyweds, and as young parents. As I continued scanning the photos, I realized that I recognized some of the locations—I recognized Franz. After some detective work using the photos I had taken in August 2019, I was able to match some locations to the 35 mm slides that were produced in the early to mid-1960s (Figures 6 and 7). Some of the buildings and structures are still standing; many of them are no longer there. The photos bring to light the shadows of what once was. Without realizing it, I had stood in spots where my family had stood years before, some of them eerily close to where the old pictures had been taken. When I return to Franz, I want to recreate more of the images to document the changes that have taken place in the past 50–60 years. Other family members have even older photos going back to the 1930s and 1950s, which will also help piece together this history.

Though we had planned to return to Franz during the summer of 2020, as almost everyone in the world has experienced, times have changed drastically. Our new goal is to return in 2021. It is also important to remember that Franz is only the first chapter. I need to visit Oba Lake, where my great-grandparents lived before moving to Franz, as well as Wanda, which is also along the ACR line and where my great-grandfather lived after Franz. All these places of importance are components of the family story.

Figure 6. Past and present

Note: The top photo is from my visit to Franz in the summer of 2019. The building on the left is the porch where my great-grandfather is sitting with my aunt and uncle in the second photo, below, from 1962 or 1963. The structures in the background of the old photo are no longer there, and the foliage has grown in.

Source: Top photo from author's collection; bottom photo from author's grandparents' collection

CONCLUSION

The cold north wind is blowing,

And the snow is wet and cold.

As I make my way through this woodland,

I'm thinking of my love.

He's gone from me, I know,

To where I'll never know.

Oh, how could he ever leave me,

When he knows I still love him so?

Figure 7. Past and present: 1966 and 2019
Note: My mother is sitting on the family car in 1966. You can see the large building behind her in both photos. The building on the right was eventually torn down, and the more modern house was erected sometime later.
Source: Top photo from author's collection; bottom photo from author's grandparents' collection

As I make my way through this woodland,

I'm thinking of my love.

The cold north wind is blowing.

--The Cold North Wind, by Frances Beaupré (née Tangie)

It is difficult to describe the feeling of exploring Franz. Though it is easy to romanticize the town and fall into certain tropes of events that magically fall into place, I never expected a magical revelation to occur, where some monumental understanding would appear before me. Rather, the process was much more subtle, like getting to know someone for the first time—someone I had heard a lot about, but whom I had never met. During such explorations, you never really know how it will go. Once I was there, I realized I knew very little about what I was seeing. I was unsure of where my grandmother had lived, or whether the house even stood. I knew that my great-grandfather Rennison's cabin was no longer in Wanda from reading an interview a cousin had done for Michipicoten (Morton, 2019). With that said, the trip was a pilgrimage of sorts. Franz was less than 100 km from me for much of my life, and still it took me over 30 years to get there. It was a special place to visit. Making it to Franz brought the stories to life in a way that I could not have anticipated, while the stories in turn had brought life to this place that I had heard so much about.

As I near the end of this narrative, I cannot help but reflect on a few final stories. I never got to know my great-grandfather, Rennison; he had passed away seven years before I was born, so I only know him through stories and pictures. As I began teaching Anishinaabemowin, one of my uncles told me that Rennison would be proud. Before he passed, he had been asked by the Sault College satellite campus in Wawa to teach Anishinaabemowin. He did not know how to write it with the Latin alphabet, but he knew how to use the syllabic writing system. Because he was ill, he was unable to take the job. I never knew this, but it is a nice connection to my own work.

The last time I spoke with my grandmother, Frances, also comes to mind. She had been struggling with dementia and was in the hospital. The challenges grew, and she would have good moments, then harder moments. I had written a little song in Anishinaabemowin several years before. It is a simple tune about the colors of some animals that can be found in Ojibwe country. Even though I had written it years earlier, I had never shown it to her. I was afraid; I was worried that it might not be good enough. Frances really loved music. She had written a song, *The Cold North Wind*, about her and Jean-Louis. It is a northern love song about love and the cold. It is a towering song in the family, one she would perform whenever on stage.

My aunt and cousin were both there, visiting with her in the hospital. Frances was starting to shift from a good moment to feeling distressed when I asked her if she wanted to hear a song. She started to calm at the idea of hearing music. I pulled my phone out of my pocket and played *Enaanzowaad Awesiinyag*, the colors of the animals, for her.

Omakakii ozhaawashkwaazo, omakakii ozhaawashkwaazo (The frog is green, the frog is green.)

Aaniin enaanzod omakikii? (What color is the frog?)

Her eyes lit up. "You're singing in the language!"

Makwa makadewizi, makwa makadewizi (The bear is black, the bear is black.)

Aaniin enaanzod makwa? (What color is the bear?)

She choked back tears, understanding the words being sung in Ojibwe. Then she smiled. I remember her frail little hands tapping in rhythm to the song on the hospital bed. Suddenly, the fear had disappeared.

Waagosh ozaawaazo (The fox is orange.)

The moment was soon replaced with a feeling of regret. I wished that I had put that fear aside much sooner, that I had shown her that song years earlier. Perhaps we could have even written a few together. It is easy to get lost in these kinds of thoughts, but I came back to the moment of watching her enjoy the song.

Mii sa enaanzowaad awesiinyag (So those are the colors of the animals.)

The song fended. Frances looked at me and said, "You speak the language better than me now." I was humbled and proud. It meant so much to me that she had enjoyed the song. I treasure that I was able to share this with her before she passed. The last words I remember her saying were, "Grandpa and I are so proud of you. We're so proud of all you grandkids. You all make us so proud." That was the last time I spoke with her, as she was no longer conscious the next time I saw her a few months later in the final days before her passing.

Even though Frances left Franz, Franz never really left her. She spent much of her early life there. When she had dementia in her final years, many of her memories returned to Franz. She would ask about a lot of old names, many of which I had never heard. It was hard for her to understand that they had all passed on long ago. While many in our family have never been to Franz, we all carry a part of it with us. We carry this connection through stories—stories that maintain the memory of my grandmother, of our family; stories that bring life to a little ghost town in northeastern Ontario. These are only a small fraction of the stories that I remember. They are not meant as possessive or exclusionary. There are many stories that are lost that we will never know.

Now that I have visited Franz, there is a new aspect to consider. I shift from being a passive listener to becoming actively engaged in making my own memories. This moves beyond preserving and remembering to the realm of creating. Creating new memories, new stories, new art, informed not only by the past but also by the present. The connection to Franz evolves beyond a static understanding of place on a map to a dynamic relationship with a living, breathing locale of the grandmotherlands. Even with this new understanding, this new relationship, I must pay respect to the history that lives within the land. These are not the only stories. Many came before me, and their influence remains. More will come, as reconnecting is not a one-time act. It is something that takes place over time. I will be returning, revisiting, reconnecting to Franz again. Future work will include continuing to gather stories from family, going to the land itself, making new music based on my time there, and sharing with family and community this place my grandmother called home, where hauntings and heart remain.

REFERENCES

Bakan, D. (2014). *A song of songs: A/r/tography, autoethnography, and songwriting as music education research* [Dissertation, University of British Columbia]. UBC Theses and Dissertations. https://open.library.ubc.ca/cIRcle/collections/ubctheses/24/items/1.0167101

Bishop, M. (2020). 'Don't tell me what to do' encountering colonialism in the academy and pushing back with Indigenous autoethnography. *International Journal of Qualitative Studies in Education: QSE*, 1–12. doi:10.1080/09518398.2020.1761475

Chalykoff, J. P. (2019). *The hauntings & heart of a place* [Recorded by artist].

Cheng, B. K. (2018). Home is Elsewhere. In A. Smith & S. O'Connor (Eds.), *Hearth: A global conversation on community, identity, and place* (pp. 117–128). Milkweed Editions.

Dernoi, C. (2007). *Traditional territories of the Michipicoten First Nation*. Christine Dernoi & Associates.

Gray, S. E., & Morrison, J. (2019). *History of Michipicoten First Nation*. Academic Press.

Irwin, R. L., & Springgay, S. (2008). *A/r/tography as practice-based research. Being with A/r/tography*. Sense Publishers.

King, T. (2003). *The truth about stories: A native narrative*. The House of Anansi Press.

Kovach, M. (2009). *Indigenous methodologies: Characteristics, conversations, and contexts*. University of Toronto Press.

Lam, A. (2018). Enchantment. In A. Smith & S. O'Connor (Eds.), *Hearth: A global conversation on community, identity, and place* (pp. 31–47). Milkweed Editions.

Leeson, B. (2018, November 5). Author details dark history of Chapleau's residential schools. *The Timmins Daily Press*. https://www.timminspress.com/news/local-news/author-details-dark-history-of-chapleaus-residential-schools

Lippert, C., & Engel, J. (2014, April 14). The Great Lakes: An Ojibwe perspective. *The Decolonial Atlas*. https://decolonialatlas.wordpress.com/2015/04/14/the-great-lakes-in-ojibwe-v2/

Monkman, L. (2017, March 25). Historical ban on potlatch ceremony has lingering effects for Indigenous women, author says. *CBC*. https://www.cbc.ca/news/indigenous/historical-ban-spirituality-felt-indigenous-women-today-1.4036528

Morton, A. (2019). *Michipicoten First Nation elder interviews*. Bluestone Research.

Ningewance Nadeau, P., & Valentine, J. R. (2013). *Western Ojibwe dictionary*. [Software].

Roman, L. G., Gobbi, R. D. P., Beaudry, J. S., & Blackbridge, P. (2020). Rippling excesses: A/r/tography becoming dis/a/r/tography. *International Journal of Art, 16*(1), 63–82. doi:10.1386/eta_00017_1

Simard, E. (2020). Critical Indigenous ways of knowing: Research, narratives, and self-actualisation. *International Journal of Critical Indigenous Studies, 13*(2), 135–153. https://ijcis.qut.edu.au/article/view/1636/1002

Smith, A., & O'Connor, S. (Eds.). (2018). *Hearth: A global conversation on community, identity, and place*. Milkweed Editions.

Specht, J. (n.d.). *Indian genealogical records volume 1: Lake Nipigon, Michipicoten, Grand Portage, Wikwemikong*. Academic Press.

Springgay, S., Irwin, R. L., & Wilson, S. (2005). A/r/tography as living inquiry through art and text. *Qualitative Inquiry, 11*(6), 897–912. doi:10.1177/1077800405280696

Truth and Reconciliation Commission of Canada. (2015, December). *Honouring the truth, reconciling for the future: Summary of the final report of the Truth and Reconciliation Commission of Canada*. http://www.trc.ca/assets/pdf/Executive_Summary_English_Web.pdf

Whitinui, P. (2013). Indigenous autoethnography: Exploring, engaging, and experiencing "Self" as a Native method of inquiry. *Journal of Contemporary Ethnography*, 1–32.

ADDITIONAL READING

Chalykoff, J. P. (2014). *Chalykoff response*. Women & Meth. https://www.womenandmeth.com/chalykoff-response.html

KEY TERMS AND DEFINITIONS

A/r/tography: Art-based methodology based around the idea of maintaining the inseparable roles of being artist, researcher, and teacher.

Anishinaabe: Ethnonym of Anishinaabe peoples, which includes Ojibwe, Odawa, and Pottawatomi. Used interchangeably with Ojibwe in this context, but not always a synonym in all contexts.

Anishinaabemowin: The language of the Anishinaabeg. Sometimes used as a synonym for Ojibwe.

Anishinaabewakiing: The land of the Anishinaabeg, or Anishinaabe territory.

Michipicoten First Nation: Michipicoten First Nation is an Ojibwe community with reserve lands along the northeast coast of Lake Superior, as well as in the interior, with reserve lands at Dog Lake at Missinabie, and at Chapleau.

Chapter 15
Struggles With Historical Trauma:
Cognitive Awareness and Native American Culture

Kirsten A. Koenig
Northcentral University, USA

ABSTRACT

The chapter presents results from a qualitative phenomenological heuristic study of the perceptions of historical trauma across Native American nations. Historical trauma has been established as a by-product of cultural and physical suppression. Cultural psychology details the impact of an individual's culture on the psychological development of the individual. Therefore, by examining the change to the culture that resulted in historical trauma, determination could be made regarding how the individual was impacted. This research addressed these contentions by interviewing Native American persons from the Eastern and Northern nations of North America and Canada and determined how historical trauma had influenced their psychological development via symptoms they experienced. The research identified several areas that differed from the extant literature regarding the Eastern and Northern nations.

INTRODUCTION

Culture is an intrinsic part of an individual's psychological development; as such, wounding of the culture results in wounding of the individual's psyche (Denham, 2008; Duran et al., 2008). Various cultures (e.g., American Indian, Jews) have suffered loss of their culture through physical and cultural genocide (Crawford, 2013; Ehlers et al., 2013; Goodkind et al., 2012; Gone, 2013; Waldram, 2013). For the American Indian, this loss of culture encompasses relocation to reservations, enforced attendance at boarding schools, removal of traditions, and outlawed ceremonies (Arndt & Davis, 2011; Brave Heart et al., 2011; Gone 2013, 2013a; Walls & Whitbeck, 2013; Weaver, 1998, 2000, 2001). Additionally, many of the individuals in these cultures suffer survivor syndrome and/or survivor's child complex, both of

DOI: 10.4018/978-1-7998-3729-9.ch015

which create anxiety and impulsivity (Brave Heart & DeBruyn, 1998; Brave Heart et al., 2011; Granbois & Sanders, 2012). There is indication of elevated alcohol/chemical dependency, child abuse, homicide, unintentional injury, poverty, and unemployment (Braveheart et al., 2012 Gone, 2013, 2013a). Additionally, there is evidence of increased physical challenges (e.g., heart disease, cancer, diabetes, chronic stress, cirrhosis of the liver and shorter life spans), nightmares, sadness, and increased suicidal ideations when compared to those that have not experienced survivor syndrome and/or survivor's child complex (Brave Heart & DeBruyn, 1998; Brave Heart et al., 2011; Granbois & Sanders, 2012; Stumblingbear-Riddle & Romans, 2012). Others show signs of disenfranchised grief, which Brave Heart and DeBruyn (1998) and Evans-Campbell (2008) described as grief that cannot be openly acknowledged or mourned in public. When combined, survivor syndrome and disenfranchised grief create historical trauma (Brave Heart & DeBruyn, 1998). Historical trauma (also called intergenerational historical trauma), is defined as the cumulative emotional and psychological wounding across a person's life and across generations (Brave Heart, 2003; Crawford, 2013; Gone, 2013, 2013a, 2014; Granbois & Sanders, 2012; Kristianto, 2013; Lajimodiere, 2012; Nebelkopf et al., 2011; Trembinski, 2011; Waldram, 2013; Walls & Whitbeck, 2013; Wright et al., 2011). Unfortunately, historical trauma has become part of the historical consciousness, which is defined as an awareness of the past, of the Jews in Europe and the American Indian population (Arndt & Davis, 2011; Brave Heart, 1998; Jervis et al., 2006). However, Jervis et al. (2006) have also stated memories transcend the individual and intergenerational boundaries, meaning; the memories continue generationally, and individuals remember them through stories and life experiences. Thus, this suffering has become a fundamental and ongoing part of many individual lives. James and Renville (2013) supported the contention that the memories are intergenerational stating that the children's brains have been rewired for survival, which is based on historical trauma. There are more recent findings that indicate that trauma affects the DNA of the individual, and that the altering of the DNA is generationally passed forward (Yehuda, et al. 2015).

Historical trauma often results in historical traumatic response, which is defined as a collection of features precipitated by historical trauma, including sadness, self-destructive behaviors, low self-esteem, suicidal ideations, rumination, anger issues, and a general inability to express emotion (Goodkind et al., 2012; Jacob, 2012; Sarche & Whitesell, 2012; Stumblingbear-Riddle & Romans, 2012; Ward, 2013). Historical traumatic response aligns with many of the diagnostic criteria for psychological disorders such as dysthymic disorder, major depressive disorder, bipolar disorder, post-traumatic stress disorder (PTSD), and anxiety disorders (American Psychiatric Association, 2000). Yehuda et al. (2001) found an increase in depressive disorders in the children of parents who had been exposed to trauma as holocaust survivors. Additionally, Evans-Campbell (2008) indicates that there is a risk of physical health problems, impaired family communication and interaction, and a total breakdown of traditions and ceremonies.

Researchers have established historical trauma as a by-product of cultural and physical suppression/genocide (Brave Heart et al., 2012). Thus far, research has examined the Apache, and Lakota; however, exploration of the lived experience of the above stated symptoms outside these specific populations is lacking (Evans-Campbell, 2008). There is little or no exploration of historical trauma among the Eastern and Northern nations and it was not known what it was like to live and experience the above-mentioned symptoms as a Native American person. It was possible the experiences would be the same regardless of the traditions or ceremonies practiced by the individual. Therefore, by exploring historical trauma individually, across the different nations within the blanket term Native American, a clearer understanding of historical trauma and its effect on the American Indian population was obtained. Brave Heart (2003) stated that the exploration of historical trauma is critical for a clearer understanding of how historical trauma affects all cultures and other persons experiencing trauma (e.g. oppressed persons, rape victims, injured workers) and will offer a basis for developing an intervention model in the future. Thus, the exploration of how other nations experience historical trauma begins to build the foundation for understanding. The objective of this chapter is to understand the essence of the lived experience of historical trauma across a small cross section of cultures within the blanket term Native American, specifically members of the Eastern and Northern nations.

BACKGROUND

Past researchers have reported such diverse groups such as the Lakota nation, the Apache nations, Japanese Americans, and Korean Americans have experienced historical trauma, with responses similar to those of the Jewish population in Europe (Brave Heart, 1998; Liem, 2007). In fact, although the Jewish population in America has experienced historical trauma, their response appears to be different from their counterparts in Europe. The research revealed that the Jewish population that remained in Europe has continued to struggle with stunted emotions, feelings of unresolved loss, and anger due to not leaving the geographical area where the historical trauma occurred (Brave Heart, 1998). Similarly, the American Indians have not left the area where the historical trauma occurred, and their historical traumatic response is most consistent with the European Jews (Brave Heart, 1998).

Researchers also implied there is a parallel between the Apache nation and the Lakota nation with historical traumatic response, specifically drug and alcohol use/abuse, uncontrolled anger, and stunted emotions (Jervis et al., 2006). Geographically and culturally, the Apache and Lakota nations differ significantly; however, their response to historical trauma is comparable (Jervis et al., 2006). The impact of historical trauma on both nations provided striking results, showing that both the Apache and Lakota nations remember and experience historical trauma at a similar level (Braveheart et al., 2012, Jervis et al., 2006).

Since the Apache and Lakota nations exist in the western United States, and the Europeans landed, in part, on the eastern coastlines, the Eastern and Northern nations (e.g., Mohawk, Mohican, Narragansett) experienced contact with the Europeans more than 100 years prior to the Lakota and Apache. Therefore, it would be logical to assume that their experience could differ from the Lakota and Apache. This is supported by Whitbeck (2006) who stated that each nation's traditions are different; as such, their individual responses to historical trauma may be different as well. However, the generalized information on historical trauma discusses how the reservation life affected the nations in the western U.S, including stories of Custer and the massacre at Stone Creek. Based on the previously stated differences, Whitbeck and other researchers (Evans-Campbell, 2008; Gone, 2013, 2013a; Trimble & Clearing-Sky, 2009) further substantiated that regardless of tribal differences, historical traumatic response would be the same. Therefore, this research extended what is known to include the experiences of the Eastern and Northern nations.

The Eastern nations, including the Iroquois confederacy have records of their association with the Europeans, which cover more than 100 years of interactions prior to the massacre at Wounded Knee in 1890. Due to the 100+ year time span, and the differences of cultural norms and traditions within each individual nation, it cannot be generalized that their lived experiences of historical trauma would be the same as those 100+ years later and with a different nation. This is because each tribe is a sovereign nation by themselves, and it would be like comparing the United States and Canada, or England and

Scotland. History has shown that these particular sovereign nations have fought one another to maintain their individual identities.

In addition, Jordan (2013) indicated sovereignty as a concept relies on a Western model of politics that is fought against by Native Americans in general. The Iroquois confederacy was bound together in an alliance, which created a community that acted in concert to pursue common goals (Starna, 2008). However, they found themselves powerless after the European encroachment even while attempting to maintain self- governance (Jordan, 2013). Additionally, there are such differences between the European way of understanding and the Native American ways of being, the only effective way to determine the similarities or differences was to enmesh oneself in the research, hence the use of a phenomenological study for this research.

Culture, Ways of Being

Beginning in the 1800s, the United States government implemented policy that would systematically destroy the Native American population (Duran & Duran, 1995). Essentially, this marked the beginning of an attempt to assimilate the American Indian into the European culture (Duran & Duran, 1995). The process was designed to absorb the Native American/American Indian in to the mainstream culture by removing their identity through the prohibition of cultural and spiritual practices, forced removal of children to boarding schools, introduction of new diseases, genocidal policies, and community massacres (Evans-Campbell 2008.) This process continues to this day within the reservations in the western and southern portions of the United States (Arndt & Davis, 2011; Brave Heart, 1998; Jervis et al., 2006). Hence, when the research began on historical trauma, the researchers went to the reservations to collect their data (Braveheart et al., 2012, Jervis et al., 2006).

Each of the more than 500 + recognized nations experienced their own particular version of historical trauma. The Cherokee, Choctaw, and others suffered along the "Trail of Tears" and were forced to march for days on end (Drew, 2014). The Cheyenne suffered loss and trauma at the "Sand Creek massacre" (Horwitz, 2014). The Wampanoag and Abenaki suffered traumatic events when they were taken as captives, survived epidemics, and had the graves of their ancestors ransacked (Dow & Slapin, 2004). Additionally, the Pequot suffered the traumatic massacre of over 700 men, women and children, which the colonized society earmarked as a day of thanksgiving; hence, this U.S. national holiday may be better honored as a day of mourning (Dow & Slapin, 2004). Each of the more than 500 federally recognized nations, and more than 200 non-federally recognized nations suffered a different traumatic event, and responded differently to the event, however, each of the researched nations in the west and south has exhibited similar historical traumatic responses (Evans-Campbell, 2008; Gone, 2013, 2013a; Trimble & Clearing-Sky, 2009). Therefore, this study has added to the body of knowledge to compare the lived experience from eastern and northern nations to what is already established from the study of western and southern nations.

Much research has focused on validating the symptoms of historical trauma (Brave Heart & DeBruyn, 1998; Brave Heart et al., 2011; Granbois & Sanders, 2012; Stumblingbear-Riddle & Romans, 2012). Those studies cite symptoms such as sadness, anger, addiction, impulse control problems etc. (Brave Heart & DeBruyn, 1998; Brave Heart et al., 2011; Granbois & Sanders, 2012; Stumblingbear-Riddle & Romans, 2012). However, a gap exists in the research for the repercussions of historical trauma, and what daily living activities are impacted by the said trauma. For instance, the research has shown that the Jewish community had directly suffered as a result of the holocaust, and still today, there is a stigma associated with the Germans, and the Jewish population (Brave Heart, 1998; Liem, 2007). Additionally, Dias and Ressler (2014) contend that there is evidence to suggest that traumatic events are passed forward genetically from parent to child. Since the exploration requires naturalistic observation, qualitative study was the method of choice.

Culture determines how thoughts are organized, what is felt, if things are felt, and how the world is perceived (Ratner, 2011). Culture changes, evolves, and grows across the generations (Gray, Coates, & Hetherington, 2007). Culture plays an important role in the understanding of the psyche (Duran & Duran, 1995). Psychology is the process of understanding the human mind, how it thinks, feels, and emotes (Duran & Duran, 1995). Therefore, Cultural Psychology is the process of understanding how a person thinks, feels, emotes, and functions within the culture that organizes those thoughts and feelings (Duran & Duran, 1995; Gray et al., 2007; Ratner, 2011). The understanding of the Native American/American Indian begins with an understanding of how the culture is enmeshed within their psychological identity (Gray et al., 2007). It is distinctly possible that the assimilation and incorporation of the American Indian in to the westernized (dominant) culture has potentially harmed their psychological growth causing irreparable harm (Gone, 2008, 2011, 2013, 2013a; Gray et al., 2007).

Multiculturalism is generally another term that describes the westernized (dominant) cultural view (Brave Heart, 2011; Gone, 2008; Gray et al., 2007). Since culture is transmitted generationally, it is learned, and is innate, harm is also transmitted generationally leading to historical trauma (Brave Heart et al., 2012; Gone 2008, 2013, 2013a; Sarche & Whitesell, 2012; Walls & Whitbeck, 2013; Weaver,1998, 2000, 2001; Weaver & Brave Heart 1999). Duran and Duran (1995) had stated that there is a code of honor that the Native American/American Indian lives by which was oppressed by the historical trauma and was also transmitted generationally.

The culture of the American Indian remains intertwined and affected by historical trauma, and historical traumatic response and cannot be separated and one of the many lost cultural components contributing to the transmission of historical trauma includes the loss of language (Arndt & Davis, 2011; Brave Heart, 2003; Brave Heart & DeBruyn, 1998; Duran & Duran, 1995; Duran et al., 2008; Grey et al., 2007; Gone 2008, 2013, 2013a; Gray & Rose, 2011; Jacob, 2012; Walls & Whitbeck, 2013; Weaver, 1998, 2000, 2001, 2004). Language is enmeshed within the culture and is ongoing and never ending (Gergen & Gergen, 1997; Grey et al., 2007; Ratner, 2003). Language being central to the cultural development, its loss breaks the foundation of the culture (Evans-Campbell, 2008; Grey et al., 2007). The knowledge from the elders in the community is steeped in culture, stating there are no teachers, and all individuals learn from one another (Coe & Palmer, 2009; Coyhis & Simonelli, 2008; Gray & Rose, 2011; Waldram, 2013; Whitbeck, 2006). Whitbeck (2006) repeatedly discovered that his research provided no new information to the elders of the community, implying they already knew what his results would be. Heuristic inquiry allows for the voices of the lived experience to be heard, validating the voices telling the story from their personal experiences (Moustakas, 1990). Therefore, sensitivity to the diversity of the culture is imperative (Gergen & Gergen, 1997).

As noted, the American Indian has experienced cultural genocide, loss of traditions and ceremonies, loss of spirituality, loss of language, loss of children, and loss of their homes. Their loss did not stop with the colonization and relocation to reservations; the loss continued and includes environmental assaults, flooding of the homelands, and toxic dumping (Evans-Campbell 2008). The future generations have been impacted causing pervasive mental health problems, alcohol and drug abuse, and increased incidents of suicide among adolescents (Ehlers et al., 2013; Ehlers et al., 2013a; Gone, 2011, 2013, 2013a, 2014; Kenyon & Hanson, 2012; Sarche & Whitesell, 2012; Stumblingbear-Riddle & Romans,

2012; Trembinski, 2011; Weaver,1998, 2000, 2001, 2004; Young et al., 2001). This ongoing dysfunction is attributed to the inability of the Native American/American Indian to express his anger toward the oppressor, and to have his voice heard (Duran & Duran, 1995). The implication is a cyclic history of traumatic experiences that has now become a part of the evolving culture (Duran & Duran, 1995). The cultural loss has led to changes in the ways of being that is their spiritual and traditional components of living (White Shield, 2009). This change has disrupted the continuity and sense of community that is intrinsic to the American Indian (White Shield, 2009). Sufficient literature supports the contention that culture is enmeshed with the psychological well-being of the individual (Crawford, 2013; Gone, 2008, 2010; 2013a ; Kristianto, 2013; Lajimodiere, 2012; Waldram, 2013; Wright et al., 2013).

The Native American/American Indian 'way of being' is alien to the dominant colonized worldview (White Shield, 2009). They are unable to separate culture from identity (Brave Heart 1998, 1999). Thus, it is important that the culture of the individual be addressed incorporating whatever traditions and ceremonies their belief system holds as a holistic means of treatment and healing. Whitbeck (2006) indicated that the understanding of the situation is within the culture itself. Therefore, the understanding of the lived experience of historical trauma and loss is within the culture of the Native American/American Indian. Whitbeck (2002) urged the acknowledgement of the diversity of Native American/American Indian nations, stating there is a significant difference between nations regarding traditions and ceremony and thus each nation must be explored individually. Cultural identity is connected inseparably to tradition, ceremony, and spiritual ways (Blankenau et al., 2010; Crawford, 2013; Goodkind et al., 2010; Gone, 2008, 2013a ; Granbois & Sanders, 2012; Kristianto, 2013; Waldram, 2013; Wright et al., 2013). It is evident, whether examined through culturally traditional means, or scientific methodology, that cultural psychology, specifically dialectic contextualism, offers a key to unlock the mystery of understanding the lived experience of historical trauma among the American Indian nations.

Dialectic Contextualism

Culture evolves and changes as the participants within the culture evolve and change, for example urban American Indians are different from reservation American Indians. Dialectic contextualism's definition of psychological phenomena is cultural in essence (i.e., the element of artifacts) social in nature (i.e., cultural concepts) organized socially, mentally, and environmentally (i.e., social institutions) and is devised individually by humans, and incorporated socially through participation (Ratner, 1999).

Dialectic contextualism espouses the ideation that culture is composed primarily of several factors (i.e. social institutions, artifacts, and cultural concepts), which are the lens through which the individual feels, thinks, and perceives the world (Grey et al., 2007; Ratner, 2008, 2011). The social institutions (e.g., church and community gatherings) determine tradition, and ceremonies that the individual incorporates into their identity. The artifacts (e.g., clothing, shopping habits) are the outward expression of the cultural psychological thinking. The cultural concepts (e.g., personal values and views) are the inward manifestation and thought process that determine the psychological phenomena of the individual (Ratner, 2003, 2008, 2011). In essence, everything affects everything and is intertwined with everything else. Therefore, when psychological phenomena are described outside of the presiding culture, researchers have noted the observer is unable to capture the person's vibrant nuances and indigenous features (Geortzen, 2010; Ratner, 2009; Sameroff, 2010). For instance, anecdotal evidence suggests, when the Native American/American Indian wear Native American clothes outside of a Native American gathering they would be considered odd and be judged accordingly. Without those nuances, the true essence of the cultural phenomena is not experienced (Ratner, 2009). Gray et al. (2007) stated that the indigenous people are engaged in a quest to maintain their cultural traditions. Culture varies with its tradition, and it varies within the cultural factors that interpenetrate it (Geortzen, 2010; Ratner, 2009).

The idea of dialectic contextualism and the different elements that influence the psychological growth of the individual is not new. Wundt (as cited in Gergen & Gergen, 1997) discussed that there were individuals who were different and not in accordance with the social or psychological norm. Duran and Duran (1995) further stated the incorporation of Jung's belief of a bridge between cultures is essential to restore balance and harmony to the psyche; which is what the process of psychotherapy has intended to do; therefore, the exploration of the cultural element within dialectic contextualism is vital. Jung (as cited in Duran & Duran, 1995) stated culture is an intrinsic part of balance, and development and cannot be accomplished by intent alone, he continues; if man lived together instinctively then the change could come about purely by biological laws. Dialectic contextualism, which began with the work of Vygotsky (1978), implies that every process in the mental development occurs two times, first socially within the family, then individually within the individual (Gergen & Gergen, 1997; Ratner, 2003, 2006, 2008, 2011; Sameroff, 2010). Evans-Campbell (2008) concurred and related the impact of historical trauma to individual, family, and community.

Given the importance of addressing culture while assessing the individual, it can be posited with the Native American/American Indian population that the more enmeshed they become with the European society (which may lead to a predisposition to addiction and other physical and emotional disturbances) the less they are impacted by racial slurs and historical trauma (Coyhis & Simonelli, 2008). However, as they return to their traditional cultural ceremonies and traditions, they begin to see how the historical trauma has affected their lives (Brave Heart & DeBruyn, 1998; Coyhis & Simonelli, 2008). In essence, they are working toward becoming acculturated to the western traditions and completing advanced degrees while maintaining their traditions and ceremonies (Coyhis & Simonelli, 2008). Some individuals choose to remain more traditional: living with the old 'ways of being' adding some modifications accommodating modern life (Coyhis & Simonelli, 2008).

Denham (2008) related resilience and strength are the cornerstones of what the Native American/American Indian has exhibited through the long years of oppression and genocide. The resilience is attributed to the ability to adapt and spring back (Denham, 2008; Granbois & Sanders, 2012). It is a factor in maintaining positive health outcomes, and assists in decreasing depressive symptomology (Goodkind et al., 2010; Schure et al., 2013). The elders, in particular, have lived the experience of historical trauma and shown resilience (Granbois & Sanders, 2012; Stumblingbear-Riddle & Romans, 2012). The level of adaptability is directly related to the immersion in the culture and traditions (Denham, 2008; Granbois & Sanders, 2012; James & Renville, 2012).

Ratner (2008) had also stated the experiential patterns that were formed by an individual's experience were holistic in nature. The author further noted the highest form of methodological holism recognizes the internal relationship between a psychological phenomenon and the cultural phenomena (Ratner, 2008). Holism, a concept within dialectic contextualism, is the idea that individuals reciprocally influence each other, and by doing this, the culture as a whole is affected by the individuals, while simultaneously affecting them (Geortzen, 2010; Ratner, 2008; Sameroff, 2010). These elements are intertwined within the psychological wellbeing of the individual creating a culture that becomes embedded in the psychological identity of the individual (Geortzen, 2010; Ratner, 2008; Sameroff, 2010). For instance, in the Native American/American Indian community, the phrase "we are all related" is often used to communicate community and connectedness one with another (Evans-Campbell, 2008).

Culture is described as a flexible process, and the culturally appropriate approach is to be aware, and uncritical of the other culture, allowing the indigenous individual to feel accepted (Gray et al., 2007). Peoples' identities are linked to their culture and individuals are embedded in cultural practices from the inside out (Coyhis & Simonelli, 2008; Gone, 2008, 2011, 2013, 2013a, 2014; Morgan & Freeman, 2009; Waldram, 2013). As Grey et al. (2007) posits, a client is an expert, and the psychotherapist is the learner where there is only learning and understanding the Native American. The Native American/American Indian traditions also state there are no teachers, but that all individuals learn from one another (Bombay, Matheson, & Anisman, 2013; Denham, 2008; Nebelkopf et al., 2011). Whitbeck (2006) empirically validated what the elders had already told him, verifying the concept that all individuals learn from one another. Finally, Grey et al. (2007) quotes Canadian Indians to illustrate this end:

...the good life is a life in which people and communities take responsibility for healing and growth. The 'good life' includes wellness in all aspects of life, physical, spiritual, emotional, and cognitive (p. 62)

In agreement with contextualism, Grey et al. (2007) contends that if you can reach the client where they live, eat, and play, and embrace the things that are meaningful to them within their culture, then psychotherapy will be relevant to their needs. Therefore, within cultural psychology, dialectical contextualism specifically identifies the individual is comprised of all the elements they encounter, creating the unique and wonderful psychological phenomenon that is the human being (Geortzen, 2010; Sameroff, 2010).

Historical Trauma

The American Indian population's cultural loss included relocation to reservations, enforced attendance at boarding schools, and the outlawing of traditions and ceremonies (Bombay, Matheson, & Anisman, 2013; Gone, 2013a; Trembinski, 2011; Weaver, 1998, 2000, 2001). It is estimated that as many as 13 million original inhabitants were killed (Weaver & Brave Heart, 1999). The study further examines the legacy left by the holocaust of the Jewish community and compares it to the American Indian (Brave Heart & DeBruyn, 1998). The removal of culturally related spirituality, traditions, and ceremonies (called ways of being) has negatively affected the personality of the American Indian (Duran & Duran,1995; Gryczynski & Johnson, 2011; White Shield, 2009). The personal exploration of these ways of being led to the understanding that something different must be addressed by the American Indian if they are to heal from these traumatic experiences. Anecdotal observation of friends and acquaintances speaking of their personal trauma and grief due to these experiences revealed that nothing seemed to help their healing, which has been supported by other research (Bombay et al., 2013; Crawford, 2013; Ehlers et al., 2013, 2013a; Gone, 2011, 2013, 2013a, 2014; Gryczynski & Johnson, 2011; Jacob, 2012; Lajimodiere, 2012; Ward, 2013).

Evans-Campbell (2008) stated that the assaults on tribal sovereignty, corruption within the government, and "thieving" of traditions and ceremony perpetuated the ongoing historical trauma. Unfortunately, historical trauma has become part of the historical consciousness of the American Indian population (Crawford, 2013; Evans-Campbell, 20028; Gone, 2011, 2013, 2013a, 2014; Jacob, 2012; Lajimodiere, 2012). Gone (2008) suggests that the key to understanding American Indians (within their culture) is to understand nation-specific ways of being, including living energy and personal relationships, both of which merge with everything else contained within the culture to create the psychological personality of the individual. Living energy is defined as the life essence that flows through all things (e.g., plants, animals, and insects) which exist in connection with human beings (Gone, 2008). The separation from that connection, caused by the encroachment of the western culture, resulted in a distinctive change in the American Indian culture (Gone, 2011, 2013, 1013a, 2014; Kristianto, 2013; Stumblingbear-Riddle & Romans, 2012; Waldram, 2013; Wright et al., 2013). Where once the American Indian population was connected to all living energy (through ceremonies and traditions), after contact with the western culture, they were forced to abandon their connection with the land, ceremonies, and traditions, changing their ways of being (Brave Heart & DeBruyn, 1998; Brave Heart et al., 2012; Coyhis & Simonelli, 2008; Evans-Campbell, 2011; Hodge & Limb, 2011; Morgan & Freeman, 2009). Evans-Campbell (2008) stated that this loss of connection with the living energy had caused intergenerational transmission of trauma, which affects interpersonal interactions and community interactions. Duran and Duran (1995) imply that the reactive behaviors of historical trauma are learned, passed on generationally, and become the norm for the new generation, which perpetuates the historical trauma.

The concept of historical trauma is based on the theory of survivor syndrome (Brave Heart & DeBruyn, 1998; Gray & Rose, 2011). Weaver and Brave Heart (1999) stated past events shape current reality. The genocide altered the sense of self of the Native American/American Indian (Weaver & Brave Heart, 1999). Historical trauma begins with genocide, which is defined as the intent to destroy, in whole or in part, a national, ethical, racial, or religious group (Brave Heart et al., 2012; Evans-Campbell, 2011; Gone, 2011, 2013, 1013a, 2014; Goodkind et al., 2012; Granbois & Sanders, 2012; Hodge & Limb, 2011; Jacob, 2012; James & Renville, 2012; Kristianto, 2013; Lajimodiere, 2012; Morgan & Freeman, 2009; Nebelkopf et al., 2011; Novins et al., 2012; Stumblingbear-Riddle & Romans, 2012; Waldram, 2013; Wright et al., 2013). Denham (2008) had suggested ceremony, traditions, and community support can increase the likelihood of healing. Historical trauma may be best understood when looking at the individual within a family within a community (Evans-Campbell, 2008). For example, Whitbeck et al. (2004) and Brave Heart (2003) delved into the measurement of historical trauma and historical traumatic response among the American Indian. Cultural loss is the foremost aspect of the historical trauma and historical traumatic response, beginning with language, and moving through to traditions, and ceremonies (Ehlers et al., 2013; Gone, 2011, 2013a; Jacobs, 2013; Kristianto, 2013; Waldram, 2013; Walls & Whitbeck, 2013; Ward, 2013; Wright et al., 2013).

Mental Health Concerns, Historical Traumatic Response

Historical traumatic response has been described as a constellation of features in direct reaction to the specific trauma (Bombay, Matheson, & Anisman, 2013; Brave Heart et al., 2012; Ehlers et al., 2013; Ehlers et al., 2013a ; Gone, 2011, 2013, 2013a, 2014; Klest et al., 2013; Kristianto, 2013). These features often include symptoms congruent with Major Depressive Disorder, PTSD, and Impulse Control Disorders with a high incidence of abuse and significant traumatic experiences. (Brave Heart, 1999, 2003; Goodkind et al., 2010; Granbois & Sanders, 2012; Gryczynski & Johnson, 2011; Mays et al., 2009; Morgan & Freeman, 2009; Turner & Pope, 2009). The symptoms can include low self-esteem, suicidal ideation and intent, self-destructive behavior, anger, difficulty recognizing and expressing emotion, and anxiety (Bombay et al., 2013; Brave Heart et al., 2012; Ehlers et al., 2013; Ehlers et al., 2013a ; Gone, 2011, 2013, 2013a, 2014; Kenyon & Hanson, 2012; Klest et al., 2013; Kristianto, 2013). Additionally, there has been evidence of memory problems, sleep disturbances, irritability, and emotional dreams (Brave Heart, 1999, 2003; Brave Heart et al., 2012; Ehlers et al., 2013; Ehlers et al., 2013a; Goodkind et al., 2010; Mays et al., 2009; Morgan & Freeman, 2009; Sarche & Whitesell, 2012; Stumblingbear-Turner &

Pope, 2009). There is indication of self-medication with drugs and alcohol due to an avoidance of painful memories (Brave Heart, 1999, 2003). In addition, Morgan and Freeman (2009) and other researchers have linked alcohol as a pervasive destructive health problem among Native American/American Indians.

Due to the persistence of the ethnic cleansing, which did not end with military defeat and occupation, the Native American/American Indians have experienced ongoing remembrance of what they have lost (Brave Heart, 1999, 2003; Brave Heart & DeBruyn, 1998; Crawford, 2013; Whitbeck et al., 2004). The loss continues currently with racism, toxic dumping, and assaults on tribal sovereignty (Brave Heart 1999, 2003; Brave Heart & DeBruyn, 1998; Evans-Campbell, 2008; Whitbeck et al., 2004). There is evidence of socioeconomic inequality, which leads to social disadvantage and poverty (Gryczynski & Johnson, 2011; Klest et al., 2013). Poverty levels among the Native American/American Indians are twice as high as the general populations, even though they are the smallest in population size (Brave Heart et al., 2012; Gryczynski & Johnson, 2011). Their death rate is five times higher than the general population, and there are indications of a higher comorbidity with anxiety and affective disorders (Ehlers et al., 2013a). There is evidence to suggest that Native American/American Indians have the highest suicide rate with individuals aged between 15 and 24: at a rate that is three times higher than the national average (Goodkind et al., 2012). Researchers have determined that the population tests in the normal range on the current depression scales; however, appears to have significantly higher than average suicide rates. This is attributed to historical trauma response, which often manifest with symptoms similar in nature to PTSD, depression, and suicidal ideations (Goodkind et al., 2012; Gone, 2013a). There is evidence of a broader range of dysfunction, which includes a demoralization, which extends beyond PTSD (Gone, 2013a).

The above-mentioned factors often contribute to increased depressive symptomology (Brave Heart et al., 2012; Gryczynski & Johnson, 2011; Mays et al., 2009; Whitbeck et al., 2002). It appears that the weaker the cultural ties, the more susceptible the negative effects of discrimination leading to increased depression (Brave Heart et al., 2011; Evans-Campbell, 2008 Whitbeck et al., 2002). Additionally, depressive symptoms increased with alcohol use and drug use. Specifically, suicide is often a manifestation of Major Depressive Disorder, which is the most common co-morbid condition with PTSD (Brave Heart, 1999; Ursano et al., 1996). The suicide rate within an unnamed Lakota reservation is nearly 7 times higher than the national average (Brave Heart, 1999). It is estimated that 61% percent of the successful suicides among the Apache, were in youths younger than 25, and the White Mountain Apache suicide rate is 13 times higher than the national average (Mullany et al., 2009). It is evident that symptoms of Major Depressive Disorder are prevalent.

Thrane et al. (2004) measured depression among the American Indian adolescents and discovered a need for a culturally specific form of measurement. Words such as "depressed" and "anxious" are not present in many of the American Indian dialects (Thrane et al., 2004). For the Navajo, feelings of sadness and sorrow are discouraged (Thrane, et al., 2004). Many traditional American Indians do not always understand the word depression. Therefore, it is often difficult for American Indians to answer questions about depression. In contrast, for the Hopi, the words sickness of mind or sad in heart are often better understood than depression (Allen, 1998; Beals et al., 2005). Thus, asking them questions about sickness of mind is likely to reveal descriptions of depression. In addition, the American Indian, especially the elders, prefer speaking in their first language (their native tongue), and have difficulty understanding Western dialect, and the meanings of the words being used (Gray et al., 2007).

Whitbeck et al. (2009) endeavored to clarify how depression is an extension of historical loss, they posit that the individual that grows up within the cultural context of historical trauma with all the reminders of genocide and ethnic cleansing contribute to the depressed affect and self-medication with alcohol and substances (Whitbeck et al., 2009). Additionally, they contend that the historical trauma and loss originated a long time ago however has persisted throughout the generations contributing to ongoing symptoms (Whitbeck et al., 2009). Their findings indicate that the sense of traumatic loss is on the minds of a significant percentage of American Indian adolescents and adults, impacting daily functioning (Whitbeck et al., 2009).

Along with symptoms congruent with Major Depressive Disorder, there is evidence of Impulse Control Disorders manifesting in Alcohol/Substance use and abuse (Brave Heart, 1998, 1999, 2003; Crofoot et al., 2008; Goodkind et al., 2010; Plumb, & Smith, 2008; Tann et al. 2007). Brave Heart (1999) suggested the death rate among American Indians due to alcoholism was 89.3 per 100,000 individuals whereas the national average is 6.8. Further, Wright et al., (2013) stated increased alcohol and drug use have increased mortality rates with indications that those rates are higher than any other race. Life expectancy remains lower and infant mortality is twice as high as the general population (Blankenau et al., 2010). Additionally, life expectancy is reduced by as much as 20 years (Blankenau et al., 2010). The Native American/American Indian's have up to 579% higher alcoholism, and 70% higher suicide compared to the national average (Stumblingbear-Riddle & Romans, 2012). Tann et al. (2007) contends there are multi-morbidities, which affect the depressive state of the Native American/American Indian. Crofoot et al., (2008) relate the importance of crisis care, and lack thereof, to deal with the specific needs of the families suffering from substance abuse. Myhra (2011) reported that nearly all participants connected their drinking, or substance use to a need to numb themselves from cumulative stress from historical trauma, and ongoing racism and discrimination, which includes current traumatic events. Sawchuck et al., (2005) concur with the above stated articles and add additional risk factors of PTSD.

There is a high prevalence of lifetime PTSD among the American Indian population (Sawchuck et al., 2005). Posttraumatic Stress Disorder is generally cumulative, generationally moving forward as the unresolved trauma perpetuates the dysfunctional behavior and the children then grow up with fear and rage, which continues the cycle (Duran & Duran, 1995). Ultimately, oppression becomes internalized and assimilated into the psyche of the Native American/American Indian culture making it nearly impossible to differentiate healthy from unhealthy function (Duran & Duran, 1995).

Occurring along with the PTSD are symptoms associated with Depressive Disorder, and cardiovascular disease, (Sawchuck et al., 2005). Brave heart (1999) indicates that physical health has been an ongoing historical problem with the Lakota Nation since the inception of reservations in 1871. There is evidence of increased diabetes, homicide, mortality rates, psychopathology, shorter life span, cancer, and heart disease (Blankenau et al., 2010; Granbois & Sanders, 2012; Stumblingbear- Riddle & Romans, 2012). Additionally, untreated Major Depressive Disorder, and Anxiety Disorders have been shown to have a negative effect of physical health, with PTSD contributing significantly (Brave Heart, 1999). Whitbeck et al. (2009) conclude that defeat and ethnic cleansing of the Native American/American Indian resulted in ongoing internalization of symptoms. It was further stated this internalization is directly related to perceptions of historical loss, which is similar to perceived discrimination (Whitbeck et al., 2009). Duran and Duran (1995) stated the individual's self-worth has sunk to a level of self-hatred, which is due to the effect of historical trauma.

Whitbeck et al. (2004) suggest that historical loss interrupts functioning, and is at the root of maladaptive behaviors, however further research is necessary for complete understanding. Since historical trauma and historical traumatic response are enmeshed in culture, understanding cultural competence while providing treatment of historical trauma and historical traumatic response appears inevitable. Brave Heart (2003) opined individuals may feel as though they carry around a weight related to historical trauma.

Denham (2008) related a different side of historical trauma and its ensuing response, choosing to focus on strength and resiliency. Trauma has occurred historically and ranged from the past through current times with racism, health care difficulties and discrimination (Denham, 2008). Embedded within the history of trauma among the American Indian is resilience and strength (Denham, 2008). This is corroborated with anecdotal evidence, which indicated the nations would survive as long as the rivers run, and the green grass grows. The nations will survive as long as the last Native woman remains standing.

METHOD

The qualitative phenomenological heuristic research design allowed for insights into hidden stories within participants lived experiences in their natural settings and ensures insights into life with historical trauma (Patton 2002). This research requires tolerance, openness, and trust between the participant and the researcher, which works toward overcoming the mistrust fostered by the events, which have contributed to the historical trauma (Patton, 2002). Since a heuristic phenomenological design searches for meaning through the essence of an experience, this design allowed the researcher to immerse themselves in the data thereby answering a question that provided patterns of the experience of historical trauma (Douglass & Moustakas, 1985; Moustakas, 1990). It allowed for procedures that encourage open expression and dialogue (Moustakas, 1994). Heuristic phenomenological research takes on a life of its own; therefore, the results allow for deep revelation of the phenomenon in question (Moustakas, 1994). Research in clinical depression, suicide attempts, PTSD, and addictions indicated American Indians suffer from these mental health challenges in large numbers (Bombay et al., 2013; Ehlers et al., 2013; Gone, 2011, 2013, 2013a, 2014; Turner & Pope, 2009). Thus far, research has examined the Jews in America and Europe, Korean Americans, and several nations, including the Apache, Navajo, Hopi, and Lakota; however, exploration of the lived experience of the above stated symptoms outside these specific populations is lacking (Evans-Campbell, 2008). The exploration of how other nations experienced historical trauma begins to build the foundation for understanding. Researchers have established historical trauma as a by-product of cultural and physical suppression/genocide (Brave Heart et al., 2012). This study sought to clarify how these symptoms are experienced.

There is little or no exploration of historical trauma among the Eastern and Northern nations. Researchers have reported that historical trauma contains symptoms related to many disorders and includes high levels of addiction and suicide attempts/successes (Brave Heart et al., 2013). However, we do not know what it is like to live and experience those symptoms as a Native American/American Indian person. By exploring historical trauma individually, across the different nations within the blanket term Native American, a clearer understanding of historical trauma and its effect on the American Indian population was attained. Thus, the exploration of how other nations experience historical trauma builds the foundation for understanding for Native American/American Indians. The purpose of this heuristic phenomenological qualitative study was to understand the essence of the lived experience of historical trauma across a small cross section of cultures within the blanket term Native American, specifically members of the Eastern and Northern nations. The use of a heuristic phenomenological design resulted in a cultural and phenomenological picture of themes or patterns of the lived experience of historical trauma. The information gathered of the lived experience of historical trauma identified similarities and differences among the cultures interviewed.

The research question and sub questions for this study included:

Q1a. How is historical trauma experienced within the Eastern and Northern nations?
Q1b. How is historical traumatic response manifested similarly and/or differently when comparing the experience of the Eastern and Northern nations to extant research?

As the American Indian culture provided a unique picture of historical trauma, a final sample 12 individuals were interviewed from a group that answered nine pre-screen questions with "yes." The persons interviewed represented the following nations Blackfoot, Lenape, Cherokee, Passamaquoddy, Catawba, Haudenosaunee, Choctaw, Ponca, Mi'kmac, Mingo, and Lakota.

COGNITIVE AWARENESS OF GENERATIONAL TRAUMA AMONG NATIVE AMERICAN CULTURE

The Native American/American Indian population has undergone extensive scrutiny, and survived the longest, most intense cultural extermination ever perpetuated upon a race (Brave Heart & DeBruyn, 1998; Duran & Duran, 1995; Whitbeck, 2006). As such, it is understandable they are resistant to research, and changes from those within the European culture (Whitbeck, 2006). Therefore, it is necessary to be sensitive and aware of the cultural differences while researching this population. Many well- intentioned prevention programs have imposed values that do not incorporate the Native American/American Indian way of being (Whitbeck, 2006). Often elders in the Native American/American Indian community "know" when something is right, therefore, it is essential they are respected and honored when doing research (Whitbeck, 2006). Several findings resulted from this research, the first being prevention efforts must proceed nation by nation (Whitbeck, 2006). Additionally, the author states cultural ways and knowledge must be viewed as equal to empirically scientifically tested results (Whitbeck, 2006). The American Indian population offers a unique view of the effects of historical trauma/historical traumatic response on different cultures because each individual nation is distinctive from the others. Given the contention that historical trauma and historical traumatic response are intertwined within the American Indian culture, and cannot be separated (Grey et al., 2007; McCabe, 2007; White Shield 2009), it is evident an in-depth phenomenological qualitative inquiry will ensure understanding of the stories within the culture (McCabe, 2007). The interview experience will offer the American Indian population the opportunity to tell their stories of historical trauma and historical traumatic response. Additionally, the research community will gain a clearer understanding of the symptoms associated with historical trauma, and the influence on different sub-cultures, leading to further research and clarity of historical traumatic response.

This study was limited to the following nations, Passamaquoddy, Catawba, Ponca, Cherokee, Blackfeet, Lakota, Mi'kmac, Haudenosaunee (Seneca), Choctaw, and Lenape nations. The findings were internally validated, depicting the lived experience of the individuals interviewed. However, similar interviews and research would need to occur to expand the findings to determine the lived experience of the Southern and Western nations. Comparing the results to the existing research from the Lakota and Apache nations offered external validation. Additionally, this study was limited with its necessary use of some verbiage (i.e. genocide, extermination, made white, forced to be absorbed). These are terms used within the study to indicate preconceptions on the part of the researcher; however, many of the terms were suggested in personal conversations with both expert evaluators. As the study was heuristic in nature, which required immersion into the research topic, the determination was made that the language is appropriate to explain the events that occurred. Finally, study results may be limited due to the small sample; however, results offer illustrate understanding of the experiential portion of historical trauma.

The problem addressed in this study was a cognitive awareness of historical trauma and a realization of the experiences associated with it (Brave Heart et al., 2011). However, in literature, the understanding of the lived experience of historical trauma across nations within the Native American culture is incomplete, as the bulk of the literature has examined the Western and Southern nations (Bombay, Matheson, & Anisman, 2013; Brave Heart et al., 2011). Historical trauma is an ongoing problem within the Native American community, despite research and ongoing efforts to ameliorate the challenges.

RESULTS AND DISCUSSION

The findings in this study were consistent with the theory presented by Brave Heart and DeBruyn (1998). All of the participants cited experiences consistent with the existing body of literature, which speaks of symptoms congruent with depressive disorder, posttraumatic stress disorder, anxiety disorders, mood disorders, and impulse control disorders (Arndt & Davis, 2011; Brave Heart, 2003; Brave Heart et al., 2012; Lane & Simmons, 2011; Morgan & Freeman, 2009). All participants spoke of a *loss of culture* (identified as Theme #1), which is considered the primary catalyst of historical trauma (Ehlers et al., 2013; Gone, 2011, 2013a; Jacobs, 2013; Kristianto, 2013; Waldram, 2013; Walls & Whitbeck, 2013; Ward, 2013; Wright et al., 2013). They spoke of a loss of heritage, and they were not included in the existing federally recognized nation, nor were they allowed to participate or learn about the nation's traditions or ceremonies.

The second theme (*effects of colonization*) runs throughout the existing literature, and covered the effects of colonization, both positive and negative. Genocide resulted in an altered state of the Native American/American Indian sense of self (Weaver & Brave Heart, 1999). There seems to be two parts to the genocide which were discussed by the informants. One was the eradication of their ancestors, perpetuated by the U.S. military. The second was cultural genocide, whereby the individual was spared, however there was a loss of traditions, ceremonies, language, and ways of being. All the participants felt they were negatively impacted by colonization. However, there was some divergence from the existing body of literature here. Many participants spoke of their ancestor's attempts at assimilation and total immersion into the existing colonized culture. Since many of the Eastern nations were eradicated, there is an ongoing sense of loss, connection, and sadness. Many of the participants felt this was due to the lack of acceptance by the colonials for Native American/American Indian persons. A startling difference was noted by five participants, which was the recognition of positive effects of colonization. They felt that the effects of colonization bred tenacity, and an ability to survive and recognized colonization brought technology that assists with personal comfort and a better lifestyle.

The most remarkable difference discovered and discussed by all of the participants was the third theme, *hiding*. There was nothing in the existing body of literature that discussed hiding, as it was presented by these participants. Entire families reported that they were not Native American, to protect themselves from the government. Generations of families did not know they were descended from nations that had been eradicated by the Europeans. Families hid in the mountains and "hollers." Children were punished for asking about Native American heritage or talking about ceremony and traditions. However, through all of it, they survived, and found their way back to their true heritage. The participants spoke of total immersion into the colonized culture, which resulted in a loss of a part of themselves. They identified with their heritage; however, found it was inaccessible to them, as they were not "enrolled" in a "federally recognized" nation. Thus, they were subject to dual racism. The members of the dominant culture did not accept them, and those "enrolled members" of the "federally recognized" nations did not accept them either.

The existing body of literature also supports the fourth theme of *identifying with nation or culture*. Identity, as a component of culture, is shaped by recognition within the culture (Weaver, 2001). Identity is also shaped by appearance (Weaver, 2001). The most crucial component of identity is self-perception. All the participants identified with their culture, even if they were denied access to ceremonies and traditions because of the rejection by the enrolled members of the nation as discussed above. They did everything they could to do to find more information, and connect with their spirituality, and way of being. Literature describes the identification of culture as a process that grows from inside the person, and changes and evolves over time (Gone, 2013, 2013a, 2014; Waldram, 2013). All of the participants supported this; however, as they were not recognized because their ancestors decided to hide, they were subject to additional losses. They lost all access to remaining cultural traditions, as they were considered "wannabes" to the enrolled Native American/American Indian population. This rejection is likely a result of fear of cultural appropriation, which is considered the final loss of a way of being. Many Native American's believe a way of being cannot be understood, explained, or documented unless one experiences it, lives it, and breathes it (Weaver, 2001). Even though the rejection likely comes from a fear of appropriation on the part of the 'federally enrolled' Native Americans/American Indian, it still negatively affected those interviewed. Many Native American/American Indians feel they are not given rights as citizens. They are required to prove their blood quantum to be federally recognized (Turner & Pope, 2009). If they are unable to prove their heritage, and blood quantum, they are not considered American Indian/Native American. Although the existing body of literature supports racism as a byproduct of historical trauma, there is no discussion about racism within the Native American community toward those who carry mixed blood, or against those whose ancestors hid. All of the participants experienced *racism*, the next theme, from the colonized culture. They spoke of difficulties they experienced, and ignorance of the truth behind many Hollywood views of Native American/American Indians. Racism runs rampant toward those that the colonized culture deems different; however, there was no discussion in the existing body of literature, which examined dual racism. The first component is described above and came from Caucasians. The second component came from those who were federally enrolled and was directed at those who self-identify as Native Americans.

The theme *mental illness* evolved from nearly all of the participants citing their personal experiences with symptoms of depression, anxiety, worry, problems with focus, problems with impulse control, and hypersensitivity. They talked about feelings of insecurity, decreased self-esteem, suicidal ideations, and ongoing pervasive sadness. Participants talked about a feeling of detachment within themselves, as though they belong nowhere. They reported their ancestors had engaged in destructive behavior and spoke of a lot of anger in their family history, which often resulted in different types of abuse. They also talked about family members did not express emotions or were cold and distant. There was evidence of irritability, and angry outbursts. They experienced difficulty associating with those in the dominant culture and expressed the feeling they were more comfortable among people in the "powwow community," or among their own family. All of these feelings and experiences are congruent with the existing body of literature, and it can be determined the participants of this study all experienced historical traumatic response as a direct result of historical trauma.

There is indication of self-medication with drugs and alcohol due to an avoidance of painful memories (Brave Heart, 1999, 2003). This leads to the final theme that emerged from the research: *abuse, drugs/alcohol* evolved from all of the participants discussing their personal experience with physical and sexual abuse, drug/alcohol use and abuse, as well as experiences in their extended families. Duran and Duran (1995) contend the spirit of the warrior inside the Native American individual was not able to compete with the oppression resulting from colonization and genocide. Subsequently, the emotions were repressed and turned inward resulting in the use of coping tools such as drugs, alcohol, and familial abuse to deal with the internalized anger, shame, and fear. The loss of identity, combined with the poverty, has often resulted in physical and sexual abuse, drug/alcohol use/abuse. All of the participants experienced abuse, including sexual, mental, and physical abuses. The informants recalled stories of personal violation related to alcohol/drug use. They recalled stories of physical and sexual abuse. They were emotionally abused, and told they were worthless, and they were not wanted. Again, the existing body of literature supports this experience as being pervasive through Indian country, on the reservations, and also in Canada. This results in a high suicide rate, and higher levels of morbidity. Gone (2013a) stated the members of the group experienced the collective and deliberate conquest and genocide frequently share the above-mentioned collective features.

SOLUTIONS AND RECOMMENDATIONS

The findings from this research indicate the possibility that there are more insidious components of historical trauma which were not examined. It is likely future research that explores the experiences of the Eastern and Northern nations may reveal similar results. Perhaps it would be beneficial for the existing federally recognized nations to look closer at the mixed bloodlines, and the self-identified individuals, and to assist them with finding the correct traditions and ceremonies. Additionally, culturally responsive education and appropriate therapeutic settings may help those individuals still hiding to gain acceptance and enhance wellbeing. Arnt and Davis (2011) indicated mentoring the upcoming generations, and assisting the current generations to heal, will go a long way toward reconciliation of historical trauma. It is recommended individuals be treated as whom they identify as, rather than then what the federal government, and enrolled nations judge them to be. As always, educating the population regarding these findings, and incorporating the new knowledge into the existing body of literature would be beneficial. Finally, working to accept those who self-identify as Native American, and assisting them with dealing with their historical traumatic response symptoms as such, rather than some combination of Depressive Disorder, Anxiety Disorder, or Posttraumatic Stress Disorder, would be beneficial. This is a result of an alteration in the DNA, and a pervasive, ongoing wound, and it needs to be addressed as such.

FUTURE RESEARCH DIRECTIONS

It is clear from the Medicine Wheel that the loss of culture and ensuing effects of colonization have influenced the functioning of the individual (see Figure 1). The communities had been impacted by loss of culture, racism, and loss of members. Others self-identified Native Americans have been ostracized and experienced racism at the hand of existing members of federally recognized nations. The life experience has been disrupted causing some members of the nations to hide, thereby losing their culture, spirituality, traditions, and ceremonies. This has ultimately resulted in abuse, mental illness, and the excessive use of drugs, and alcohol as a coping tool for the pervasive feelings of loss. The symptoms experienced have affected generations of the people, and will likely continue to impact them, unless something is done to stop the chain. Ongoing research may clarify opportunities to do so.

Figure 1. The Medicine Wheel Model

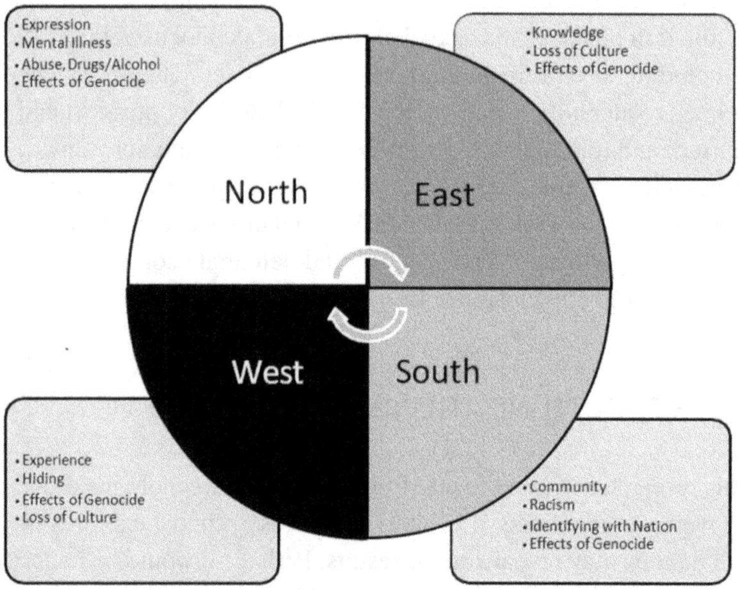

CONCLUSION

This qualitative phenomenological heuristic study researched the perception of historical trauma among the Native American Nations. The existing body of literature has primarily studied the effects of historical trauma among the Apache and Lakota nations. Other studies have explored the experiences with the Gros Ventre [a nation primarily located in north central Montana], the Korean Americans, the Jewish community, the Dine, and the Japanese Americans. Studies have also explored the Canadian Native American population, as well as other nations. However, until now, there has been little discussion regarding the perception of historical trauma among the Eastern and Northern nations. This study continued the work began by Brave Heart (1998), and Brave Heart and DeBruyn (1998). The findings identified six themes consistent with the existing body of literature; however, there was an additional theme that emerged not previously identified in the existing body of literature. Additionally, there were components of three other themes had not been previously discussed in the existing body of literature.

Theme one, *the loss of culture*, was consistent with the existing body of literature. All of the participants experienced the feeling they had lost something precious. Several participants discussed the experiences with the Western nations talking about Wounded Knee and indicated 100 years earlier their ancestors had experienced similar losses. This is in keeping with traditions and ceremonial statements many Native American/American Indians use today. They say, "We are a pitiful people…" Both the existing body of literature and the participants talked about living in two different worlds to the best of their ability. Anecdotal evidence indicated it is like walking on the edge of a knife. There is a sense of loss, which permeates everything. The participants felt a sense of not belonging anywhere, which translated to anger, irritability, and frustration. Many Native people now are challenged, and find it impossible, to live a life full of traditions and ceremony, because many things were lost, and nations eradicated. However, among all the loss, there is an ongoing sense of survival and resilience, which is also congruent with the existing body of literature. They shared their way of being, and way of understanding things. All of the loss was discussed was attributed to the mass genocide and colonization by the European culture.

Theme 2, *effects of colonization both positive and negative*, is where the findings of this study differ from the existing body of literature. All participants concur with the existing body of literature speaks of the negative effects of colonization. Geographically, the participants of this study are from different area of the country. They were self-identified members of different nations, however overwhelmingly they endorse all of the symptoms of the existing research. Their experience differed from the existing body of knowledge by speaking of total assimilation into the white culture. Many of the participants had relatives who wholly denied their heritage. They had ancestors who reported on the federal Census their heritage was white, Irish, German, Scottish, Amish, or something other than native. If the children looked white, that meant they could "fit in" and not be ostracized or sent away. Many of the participants remembered their grandparents were fearful the children would be removed. The children were sent to catholic schools, to learn new customs. A fear was instilled in the children carried forward to this day. The children were warned of the government and the "boogeyman" who would come and take them away. Entire generations were raised with this distrust of the colonized culture and the governmental authorities. Contrary to the existing body of literature, there were participants who saw positive effects with the effects of colonization. There was a sense of community that became stronger as a result of having to "pull together." One of the participants felt that the effects of colonization forced the people to survive, building their resilience, and thereby making them stronger. Another thought it was a positive thing to work with the people today and assist them in dealing with the rampant drug/alcohol abuse, and mental illness challenges. Living conditions improved as a result of colonization. There are positive results such as air conditioning, electricity, and medical services, which have resulted due to the industrial revolution.

The most startling difference revealed in this research was the third theme, *hiding*. The participants talked about leaving the Trail of Tears and hiding out in the mountains, or the "hollers" and reported a pervasive fear, generationally passed forward by the governmental authorities as being taken away by the "boogeyman." Families reported they were a different race on the federal Census to escape being forced to live on the reservations. Thus, their families were never part of the federally recognized census and the Dawes Rolls had been created by the federal government to document the Native Americans. Additionally, the ensuing generations who did not report their true heritage on the Census, were no longer identified as Native American/American Indian. The result is a total loss of culture, and estrangement from the existing federally enrolled nations. The government refuses to acknowledge these members of eradicated tribes' existence with their bloodlines. Hence, the 200+ non-federally recognized Native American nations (Trimble & Clearing-Sky, 2009). As a result of hiding, and the lack of enrollment in a federally recognized nation, a dual discrimination permeates the nations. Western nations are often critical of Eastern nations, and those who are self-identified as Native American/American Indian are often seen as stealing the culture. This is likely due to a fear of appropriation on the part of the existing federally recognized enrolled members. Thus, the participants talked of trying to find about their heritage to the best of their ability, and they are often subject to racism from the enrolled members of the federally recognized nations. This represents the fourth divergence from the existing body of literature. The theme of *racism* offers consistence with the existing body of literature in that the experience of racism from the dominant culture is the same as that experienced by other nations. Of note, however, is the response from the tribally enrolled Native Americans toward the participants in this study and their ancestors. This dual racism is significantly different enough to be mentioned, as five of the participants experienced it.

The last two themes can be combined, as they are entirely consistent with the existing body of literature. The last two themes are *mental illness, physical and sexual abuse, and drug/alcohol use/abuse*. The symptoms that have been recognized and associated with historical trauma can include low self-esteem, suicidal ideation and intent, self-destructive behavior, anger, difficulty recognizing and expressing emotion, and anxiety (Bombay et al., 2013; Brave Heart et al., 2012; Ehlers et al., 2013; Ehlers et al., 2013a ; Gone, 2011, 2013, 2013a, 2014; Kenyon & Hanson, 2012; Klest et al., 2013; Kristianto, 2013). Additionally, symptoms include memory problems, sleep disturbances, irritability, and emotional dreams (Brave Heart, 1999, 2003; Brave Heart et al., 2012; Ehlers et al., 2013; Ehlers et al., 2013a; Goodkind et al., 2010; Mays et al., 2009; Morgan & Freeman, 2009; Sarche & Whitesell, 2012; Stumblingbear-Riddle & Romans, 2012; Turner & Pope, 2009). The body of literature speaks of poverty as a contributing factor in abuse, and drugs and alcohol use. Eight participants talked about directly experiencing mental illness, while all of the participants have experienced some form of mental illness within their families. Many of the participants struggle to remain free from drug and alcohol use, and others struggle with the physical and/or sexual abuse suffered as a direct result of alcohol/drug abuse from a relative. Again, this is consistent with the existing body of literature. Therefore, it can be safely stated the experiences of the participants in this study are consistent with the responses to historical trauma previously researched.

A notable consistent response among all of the participants, and in some of the existing body of literature, is resilience, and pride in being Native American. Despite the abuse, racism, and genocide that had been suffered by the participants, and their direct ancestors, there is an ongoing sense of continuing their traditions. The participants continue to gather during the warmer months to celebrate their heritage and who they are. There is a joy and openness to their celebrations that is not visible to the observing public yet is evident when you are a member of their community. Even when the government was persecuting their ancestors, there were gatherings, in which their heritage was celebrated. Several of the participants spoke of teaching their children the traditions that they had discovered, in the manner that they were taught. As they found information and connections within their communities, they would pass the information to the children, so the next generation will remember. There is a sense of community where elders are cared for, and the extended family is connected. Several participants spoke of the "aunties and uncles" feeding them when their family had not food. There is a sense of honor and pride in being connected to the community. Even those who lost their connection, and their families denied their heritage, found their way back to the community, and now actively seek knowledge to pass on to the next generation. Therefore, the circle will not be broken.

The participants spoke of quietly maintaining their beliefs, away from others to avoid judgment. Yet they still practice the traditions. There was pride and as a participant stated, "Sometimes doing right makes you proud." He spoke emphatically stressed the need to continue on, despite the racism, and oppression as another participant fittingly concluded:

I follow the red road; I follow and pray in the old ways. It's a way of being, it's a heart, it's a way of understanding… it's a circle with colors, it's a circle with people, it's a circle with the belief system, it's a circle of acceptance.

REFERENCES

Allen, J. (1998). Personality assessment with American Indians and Alaska Natives: Instrument considerations and service delivery style. *Journal of Personality Assessment, 70*(1), 17–42. doi:10.120715327752jpa7001_2

American Psychiatric Association. (2000). *Diagnostic and statistical manual of mental disorders* (4th ed., text rev.). Author.

Arndt, L., & Davis, A. (2011). Warrior spirit: Soul wound and coping among American Indians in law enforcement. *The Counseling Psychologist, 39*(4), 527–569. doi:10.1177/0011000010389827

Beals, J., Manson, S. M., Whitesell, N. R., Mitchell, C. M., Novins, D. K., Simpson, S., & Spicer, P. (2005). Prevalence of major depressive episode in two American Indian reservation populations: Unexpected findings with a structured interview. *The American Journal of Psychiatry, 162*(9), 1713–1722. doi:10.1176/appi.ajp.162.9.1713 PMID:16135632

Birks, M., & Mills, J. (2011). Grounded theory: A practical guide. *Sage (Atlanta, Ga.).*

Blankenau, J., Comer, J., Nitze, J., & Stabler, W. (2010). The role of tribal experiences in shaping Native American Health. *Social Work in Public Health, 25*(5), 423–437. doi:10.1080/19371918.2010.498699 PMID:20818590

Bombay, A., Matheson, K., & Anisman, H. (2013). The intergenerational effects of Indian residential schools: Implications for the concept of historical trauma. *Transcultural Psychiatry, 0*, 1–19. PMID:24065606

Bowen, G. (2008). Naturalistic inquiry and the saturation concept: A research note. *Qualitative Research, 8*(1), 137–152. doi:10.1177/1468794107085301

Brave Heart, M. (1999). Oyate ptayela: Rebuilding the Lakota nation through addressing Historical trauma among Lakota parents. *Journal of Human Behavior in the Social Environment, 2*(1-2), 109–126. doi:10.1300/J137v02n01_08

Brave Heart, M. (2003). The historical trauma response among natives and its relationship with substance abuse: A Lakota illustration. *Journal of Psychoactive Drugs, 35*(1), 7–13. doi:10.1080/02791072.2003.10399988 PMID:12733753

Brave Heart, M., Chase, J., Elkins, J., & Altschul, D. (2011). Historical trauma among indigenous peoples of the Americas: Concepts, research, and clinical considerations. *Journal of Psychoactive Drugs, 43*(4), 282–290. doi:10.1080/02791072.2011.628913 PMID:22400458

Brave Heart, M., & DeBruyn, L. M. (1998). The American holocaust: Healing historical unresolved grief. *American Indian and Alaska Native Mental Health Research, 8*, 56–78. PMID:9842066

Brave Heart, M., Elkins, J., Tafoya, G., Bird, D., & Salvador, M. (2012). Wicasa was'aka: Restoring the traditional strength of American Indian boys and men. *American Journal of Public Health, 102*(S2), 177–183. doi:10.2105/AJPH.2011.300511 PMID:22401529

Coe, B., & Palmer, C. T. (2009). How elders guided the evolution of the modern human brain, social behavior, and culture. *American Indian Culture and Research Journal*, *33*(3), 15–21. doi:10.17953/aicr.33.3.b53t752702p4h767

Coyhis, D., & Simonelli, R. (2008). The Native American healing experience. *Substance Use & Misuse*, *43*(12-13), 1927–1949. doi:10.1080/10826080802292584 PMID:19016172

Crawford, A. (2013). The trauma experienced by generations past having an effect in their descendants: Narrative and historical trauma among Inuit in Nunavut Canada. *Transcultural Psychiatry*, *0*, 1–31. PMID:23475452

Crofoot, T., Harris, N., Plumb, M., & Smith, K. (2008). Mental health, and substance abuse service needs for the Native American rehabilitation association northwest (Nara NW) in the Portland, Oregon metropolitan area. *American Indian and Alaska Native Mental Health Research*, *14*(3), 1–24. doi:10.5820/aian.1403.2007.1 PMID:18286444

Denham, A. R. (2008). Rethinking historical trauma: Narratives of resilience. *Transcultural Psychology*, *45*(3), 391–414. doi:10.1177/1363461508094673 PMID:18799640

Dias, B., & Ressler, K. (2014). Parental olfactory experience influences behavior and neural structure in subsequent generations. *Nature Neuroscience*, *17*(1), 89–98. doi:10.1038/nn.3594 PMID:24292232

Douglass, B., & Moustakas, C. (1985). Heuristic inquiry: The internal search to know. *Journal of Humanistic Psychology*, *25*(3), 39–55. doi:10.1177/0022167885253004

Dow, J., & Slapin, B. (2004). Deconstructing the myths of the first Thanksgiving. *Multicultural Review*, *13*, 44–53.

Drew, B. (2014). The great amnesia. *Southwest Review*, *99*, 556–569.

Duran, E., & Duran, B. (1995). *Native American post colonial psychology*. State University of New York Press.

Duran, E., Firehammer, J., & Gonzalas, J. (2008). Liberation psychology as the path toward healing cultural soul wounds. *Journal of Counseling and Development*, *86*(3), 288–296. doi:10.1002/j.1556-6678.2008.tb00511.x

Ehlers, C., Gizer, I., Gilder, D., Ellingson, J., & Yehuda, R. (2013). Measuring historical trauma in an American Indian community sample: Contributions of substance dependence, affective disorder, conduct disorder, and PTSD. *Drug and Alcohol Dependence*, *133*(1), 180–187. doi:10.1016/j.drugalcdep.2013.05.011 PMID:23791028

Ehlers, C., Gizer, I., Gilder, D., & Yehuda, R. (2013a). Lifetime history of traumatic events in an American Indian community sample: Heritability and relation to substance dependence, affective disorder, conduct disorder, and PTSD. *Journal of Psychiatric Research*, *47*(2), 155–161. doi:10.1016/j.jpsychires.2012.10.002 PMID:23102628

Evans-Campbell, T. (2008). Historical trauma in American Indian/native Alaskan communities: A multilevel framework for exploring impacts on individuals, families, and communities. *Journal of Interpersonal Violence*, *23*, 316–338. doi:10.1177/0886260507312290 PMID:18245571

Geortzen, J. R. (2010). Dialectical pluralism: A theoretical conceptualization of pluralism in psychology. *New Ideas in Psychology*, *28*(2), 201–209. doi:10.1016/j.newideapsych.2009.09.013

Gergen, K. J., & Gergen, M. M. (1997). Toward a cultural constructionist psychology. *Theory & Psychology*, *7*, 31–36. doi:10.1177/0959354397071003

Gone, J. (2008). So I can be like a whiteman: The cultural psychology of space and place in American Indian mental health. *Culture and Psychology*, *14*(3), 369–399. doi:10.1177/1354067X08092639

Gone, J. (2009). A community-based treatment for Native American historical trauma: Prospects for evidenced based practice. *Journal of Consulting and Clinical Psychology*, *77*(4), 751–762. doi:10.1037/a0015390 PMID:19634967

Gone, J. (2011). The red road to wellness: Cultural reclamation in a native First Nations community treatment center. *The American Journal of Psychology*, *47*, 187–202. PMID:21052824

Gone, J. (2013). A community-based treatment for Native American historical trauma: Prospects for evidenced-based practice. *Spirituality in Clinical Practice*, *1*(S), 78–94. doi:10.1037/2326-4500.1.S.78

Gone, J. (2013a). Redressing first nations historical trauma: Theorizing mechanisms for Indigenous culture as mental health treatment. *Transcultural Psychiatry*, *50*(5), 683–706. doi:10.1177/1363461513487669 PMID:23715822

Gone, J. (2014). Reconsidering American Indian historical trauma: Lessons from an early Gross Ventre war narrative. *Transcultural Psychiatry*, *51*(3), 1–26. doi:10.1177/1363461513489722 PMID:23765681

Gone, J. P., & Kirmayer, L. J. (2010). On the wisdom of considering culture and context in psychopathology. In T. Millon, R. F. Krueger, & E. Simonsen (Eds.), *Contemporary directions in psychopathology: Scientific foundations of the DSM- V and ICD-11* (pp. 72–96). Guilford Press.

Goodkind, J., Hess, J., Gorman, B., & Parker, D. (2012). We're still in a struggle: Dine' resilience, survival, historical trauma, and healing. *Qualitative Health Research*, *22*(8), 1019–1036. doi:10.1177/1049732312450324 PMID:22707344

Goodkind, J., Ross-Toledo, K., John, S., Hall, J., Ross, L., Freeland, L., Coletta, E., Becenti-Fundark, T., Poola, C., Begay-Roanhorse, R., & Lee, C. (2010). Promoting healing and restoring trust: Policy recommendations for improving behavioral health care for American Indian/Alaska Native adolescents. *American Journal of Community Psychology*, *46*(3-4), 386–394. doi:10.100710464-010-9347-4 PMID:20857331

Granbois, D., & Sander, G. (2012). Resilience and stereotyping: The experiences of Native American elders. *Journal of Transcultural Nursing*, *23*(4), 389–396. doi:10.1177/1043659612451614 PMID:22786944

Gray, J., & Rose, W. (2011). Cultural adaptation for therapy with American Indians and Alaska Natives. *Journal of Multicultural Counseling and Development*, *40*(2), 82–92. doi:10.1002/j.2161-1912.2012.00008.x

Gray, M., Coates, J., & Hetherington, T. (2007). Hearing indigenous voices in mainstream social work. *The Journal of Contemporary Social Services*, *88*(1), 55–67. doi:10.1606/1044-3894.3592

Gryczynski, J., & Johnson, J. (2011). Challenges in public health research with American Indians and other small ethnocultural minority populations. *Substance Use & Misuse*, *46*(11), 1363–1371. doi:10.3109/10826084.2011.592427 PMID:21810071

Guest, G., Bunce, A., & Johnson, L. (2006). How many interviews are enough?: An Experiment with data saturation and variability. *Field Methods*, *18*(1), 59–82. doi:10.1177/1525822X05279903

Hodge, D., & Limb, G. (2011). Spiritual assessment and Native Americans: Establishing the social validity of a complementary set of assessment tools. *Social Work*, *56*(3), 213–223. doi:10.1093w/56.3.213 PMID:21848086

Horwitz, T. (2014). Hundreds of women and children were coming towards us, and getting on their knees for mercy. *Smithsonian*, *14*, 50–57.

Jacob, M. (2012). We wanted those people to see that Indians aren't stupid: Identity, Representation, and resistance in the cultural tourism of the Wapato Indian Club. *American Indian Quarterly*, *36*(4), 465–478. doi:10.5250/amerindiquar.36.4.0465

Jacobs, M. (2013). Remembering the forgotten child: The American Indian child welfare crisis of the 1960s and 1970s. *American Indian Quarterly*, *37*(1-2), 136–159. doi:10.1353/aiq.2013.0014

James, A., & Renville, T. (2012). Ohiyesa's path: Reclaiming native education. *Reclaiming Children and Youth*, *21*, 27–30.

Jervis, L., Beals, J., Croy, C., Klein, S., Manson, S., & Team, A. I.-S. U. P. E. R. P. F. P. (2006). Historical consciousness among two American Indian tribes. *The American Behavioral Scientist*, *50*(4), 526–550. doi:10.1177/0002764206294053

Jordan, K. (2013). Incorporation and colonization: PostColumbian Iroquois satellite communities and processes of indigenous autonomy. *American Anthropologist*, *115*(1), 29–43. doi:10.1111/j.1548-1433.2012.01533.x

Kenyon, D., & Hanson, J. (2012). Incorporating traditional culture into positive youth development programs with American Indian/Alaska Native youth. *Child Development Perspectives*, *6*(3), 272–279. doi:10.1111/j.1750-8606.2011.00227.x

Klest, B., Freyd, J., & Foynes, M. (2013). Trauma exposure and posttraumatic symptoms in Hawaii: Gender, ethnicity, and social context. *Psychological Trauma: Theory, Research, Practice, and Policy*, *5*(5), 409–416. doi:10.1037/a0029336 PMID:24660048

Kristianto, B. (2013). The notion of the body and the path to healing. *The International Journal of Religion and Spirituality in Society*, *2*(3), 41–53. doi:10.18848/2154-8633/CGP/v02i03/51006

Lajimodiere, D. (2011). Ogimah Ikwe: Native women and their path to leadership. *Wicazo Sa Review*, *26*(2), 57–82. doi:10.1353/wic.2011.0011

Lajimodiere, D. (2012). A healing journey. *Wicazo Sa Review*, *27*(2), 5–19. doi:10.5749/wicazosareview.27.2.0005

Lane, D., & Simmons, J. (2011). American Indian youth substance abuse: Community- driven interventions. *The Mount Sinai Journal of Medicine, New York, 78*(3), 362–372. doi:10.1002/msj.20262 PMID:21598263

Liem, R. (2007). Silencing historical trauma: The politics and psychology of memory and Voice. *Peace and Conflict, 13*(2), 153–174. doi:10.1080/10781910701271200

Mays, V., Gallardo, M., Shorter-Gooden, K., Robinson-Zanartu, C., Smith, M., McClure, F., Puri, S., Methot, L., & Ahhaitty, G. (2009). Expanding the circle: Decreasing American Indian mental health disparities through culturally competent teaching about American Indian mental health. *American Indian Culture and Research Journal, 33*(3), 61–83. doi:10.17953/aicr.33.3.b27481242q461u25 PMID:25284917

McCabe, G. (2007). The healing path: A culture and community-derived indigenous therapy model. *Psychotherapy (Chicago, Ill.), 44*(2), 148–160. doi:10.1037/0033-3204.44.2.148 PMID:22122207

Morgan, R., & Freeman, L. (2013). The healing of our people: Substance abuse and historical trauma. *Substance Use & Misuse, 44*(1), 84–98. doi:10.1080/10826080802525678 PMID:19137484

MoustakasC. (1990). *Heuristic research: Design, methodology, and applications*. SAGE.

MoustakasC. (1994). *Phenomenological research methods*. SAGE.

Mullany, B., Barlow, A., Goklish, N., Larzelere-Hinton, F., Cwik, M., Craig, M., & Walkup, J. T. (2009). Toward understanding suicide among youths: Results from the White Mountain Apache tribally mandated suicide surveillance system, 2001-2006. *American Journal of Public Health, 99*(10), 1840–1848. doi:10.2105/AJPH.2008.154880 PMID:19696377

Myhra, L. (2011). It runs in the family: Intergenerational transmission of historical trauma among urban American Indians and Alaska natives in culturally specific sobriety maintenance programs. *American Indian and Alaska Native Mental Health Research Journal, 18*(2), 17–40. doi:10.5820/aian.1802.2011.17 PMID:22302280

Nebelkopf, E., King, J., Wright, S., Schweigman, K., Lucero, E., Habte-Michael, T., ... Cervantes, T. (2011). Growing roots: Native American evidenced-based practices. *Journal of Psychoactive Drugs, 43*, 263–268. doi:10.1080/02791072.2011.628909 PMID:22400455

Novins, D., Boyd, M., Brotherton, D., Fickenscher, A., Moore, L., & Spicer, P. (2012). Walking on: Celebrating the journeys of Native American adolescents with substance use problems on the winding road to healing. *Journal of Psychoactive Drugs, 44*(2), 153–159. doi:10.1080/02791072.2012.684628 PMID:22880543

PattonM. J. (2002). *Qualitative research & evaluation methods*. SAGE.

Ratner, C. (1999). Three approaches to cultural psychology; A critique. *Cultural Dynamics, 11*(1), 7–31. doi:10.1177/092137409901100102

Ratner, C. (2006). Contextualism and Positivism in Cross-Cultural psychology. In G. Zheng, K. Leung, & J. Adair (Eds.), *Perspective and progress in contemporary cross-cultural Psychology* (pp. 35–48). Light Industry Press.

Ratner, C. (2007). A macro cultural-psychological theory of emotions. In P. Schultz & R. Pekrun (Eds.), *Emotions in Education* (pp. 85–100). Academic Press. doi:10.1016/B978-012372545-5/50007-1

Ratner, C. (2008). Methodological individuism and holism. In L. Given (Ed.), *SAGE encyclopedia of qualitative research methods*. SAGE.

Ratner, C. (2009). The cultural psychology of oppression and liberation. *Journal of Social Distress and the Homeless*, *18*(3-4), 213–268. doi:10.1179/105307809805365190

Ratner, C. (2011). Macro Cultural Psychology, The psychology of oppression, and cultural-psychological enrichment. In P. Portes & S. Salas (Eds.), *Vygotsky in 21st century: Advances in cultural historical theory and praxis with non-dominant communities*. Peter Lang.

Ratner, C., & Hui, L. (2003). Theoretical and methodological problems in cross-cultural psychology. *Journal for the Theory of Social Behaviour*, *33*(1), 67–94. doi:10.1111/1468-5914.00206

Sameroff, A. (2010). A unified theory of development: A dialectic integration of nature and nurture. *Child Development*, *81*(1), 6–22. doi:10.1111/j.1467-8624.2009.01378.x PMID:20331651

Sarche, M., & Whitesell, N. (2012). Child development research in North American native communities: Looking back and moving forward: Introduction. *Child Development Perspectives*, *6*(1), 42–48. doi:10.1111/j.1750-8606.2011.00218.x

Sawchuck, C. N., Roy-Byrne, P., Goldberg, J., Manson, S., Noonan, C., Beals, J., & Buchwald, D. (2005). The relationship between post- traumatic stress disorder, depression, and cardiovascular disease in an American Indian tribe. *Psychological Medicine*, *35*(12), 1785–1794. doi:10.1017/S0033291705005751 PMID:16300692

Schure, M., Odden, M., & Goins, T. (2013). The association of resilience with mental and physical health among older American Indians: The native elder care study. *American Indian and Alaska Native Mental Health Research*, *20*(2), 27–41. doi:10.5820/aian.2002.2013.27 PMID:23824641

Starna, W. (2008). Retrospecting the origins of the league of the Iroquois. *Proceedings of the American Philosophical Society*, *152*, 279–321. PMID:19831230

Stumbling-Riddle, G., & Romans, J. (2012). Resilience among urban American Indian adolescents: Exploration into the role of culture, self-esteem, subjective well- being, and social support. *American Indian and Alaska Native Mental Health Research*, *19*(2), 1–19. doi:10.5820/aian.1902.2012.1 PMID:22875470

Tann, S., Yabiku, S., Okamoto, S., & Yanow, J. (2007). Triadd: The risk for alcohol abuse, depression, and diabetes multimorbidity in the American Indian and Alaska Native population. *American Indian and Alaska Native Mental Health Research*, *14*(1), 1–23. doi:10.5820/aian.1401.2007.5 PMID:17602410

Thrane, L., Whitbeck, L., Hoyt, D., & Shelley, M. (2004). Comparing three measures of depressive symptoms among American Indian adolescents. *American Indian and Alaska Native Mental Health Research*, *11*(3), 20–43. doi:10.5820/aian.1103.2004.20 PMID:15536587

Trembinski, D. (2011). Comparing premodern melancholy/mania and modern trauma: An argument in favor of historical experiences of trauma. *History of Psychology*, *14*(1), 80–99. doi:10.1037/a0020430 PMID:21688753

Trimble, J., & Clearing-Sky, M. (2009). An historical profile of American Indians and Alaska Natives in psychology. *Cultural Diversity & Ethnic Minority Psychology, 15*(4), 338–351. doi:10.1037/a0015112 PMID:19916669

Turner, S., & Pope, M. (2009). North America's native peoples: A social justice and trauma counseling approach. *Journal of Multicultural Counseling and Development, 37*(4), 194–205. doi:10.1002/j.2161-1912.2009.tb00102.x

Ursano, R. J., Grieger, T. A., & McCarroll, J. E. (1996). *Prevention of posttraumatic stress: Consultation, training, and early treatment.* Guilford Press.

Vygotsky, L. (1978). *Mind in society*. Harvard University Press.

Waldram, J. (2013). Healing history? Aboriginal healing, historical trauma, and personal Responsibility. *Transcultural Psychiatry, 0*, 1–17. PMID:23788570

Walls, M., & Whitbeck, L. (2013). The intergenerational effects of relocation policies on ingenious families. *Journal of Family Issues, 33*(9), 1272–1293. doi:10.1177/0192513X12447178 PMID:23024447

Ward, A. (2013). Understanding postcolonial traumas. *Journal of Theoretical and Philosophical Psychology, 33*(3), 170–184. doi:10.1037/a0033576

Weaver, H. N. (1998). Indigenous people in a multicultural society: Unique issues for human services. *Social Work, 43*(3), 203–211. doi:10.1093w/43.3.203 PMID:9597944

Weaver, H. N. (2001). Indigenous identity. *American Indian Quarterly, 25*(2), 240–256. doi:10.1353/aiq.2001.0030

Weaver, H. N., & Brave Heart, M. (1999). Examining two facets of American Indian identity: Exposure to other cultures and the influence of historical trauma. *Journal of Human Behavior in the Social Environment, 2*(1-2), 19–33. doi:10.1300/J137v02n01_03

Whitbeck, L. (2006). Some guiding assumptions and a theoretical model for developing culturally specific preventions with Native American people. *Journal of Community Psychology, 34*(2), 183–192. doi:10.1002/jcop.20094

Whitbeck, L., Adams, G., Hoyt, D., & Chen, X. (2004). Conceptualizing and measuring historical trauma among American Indian people. *American Journal of Community Psychology, 33*(3-4), 119–130. doi:10.1023/B:AJCP.0000027000.77357.31 PMID:15212173

Whitbeck, L., McMorris, B., Hoyt, D., Stubben, J., & LaFromboise, T. (2002). Perceived discrimination. Traditional practices, and depressive symptoms among American Indians in the upper Midwest. *Journal of Health and Social Behavior, 43*(4), 400–418. doi:10.2307/3090234 PMID:12664673

Whitbeck, L., Walls, M., Johnson, K., Morriseau, A., & McDougall, C. (2009). Depressed affect and historical loss among north American indigenous adolescents. *American Indian and Alaska Native Mental Health Research, 16*(3), 16–41. doi:10.5820/aian.1603.2009.16 PMID:20052631

White Shield, R. (2009). Identifying and understanding indigenous cultural and spiritual strengths in the higher education experiences of indigenous women. *Wicazo Sa Review*, *24*(1), 147–163. doi:10.1353/wic.0.0022

Wright, S., Nebelkopf, E., King, J., Maas, M., Patel, C., & Samuel, S. (2011). Holistic system of care: Evidence of effectiveness. *Substance Use & Misuse*, *46*(11), 1420–1430. doi:10.3109/10826084.2011.592438 PMID:21810076

Yehuda, R., Daskalakis, N., Bierer, L., Bader, H., Klengel, T., Holsboer, F., & Binder, F. (2015). Holocaust exposure induced intergenerational effects on FKBP5 methylation. *Biological Psychiatry*. Advance online publication. doi:10.1016/j.biopsych.2015.08.005 PMID:26410355

Yehuda, R., Halligan, S. L., & Bierer, L. M. (2001). Relationship of parental trauma exposure and PTSD to PTSD, depressive and anxiety disorders in offspring. *Journal of Psychiatric Research*, *35*(5), 261–270. doi:10.1016/S0022-3956(01)00032-2 PMID:11591428

Young, R. S., Joe, J. R., Hassin, J., & St. Clair, D. (2001). Addressing psychosocial issues and problems of co-morbidity for Native American clients with substance abuse problems: A conference proceedings. *American Indian and Alaska Native Mental Health Research*, *10*(2), 1–7. doi:10.5820/aian.1002.2001.ed PMID:11698986

ADDITIONAL READING

Anderson, K. (2016). *A recognition of being: Reconstructing Native womanhood* (2nd ed.). Canadian Scholars' Press.

Branson, D. C. (2020). Student trauma, the hidden curriculum, and cultural humility: This trio needs a team approach. In S. G. Taukeni (Ed.), *Addressing multicultural needs in school guidance and counseling* (pp. 82–105). IGI Global. doi:10.4018/978-1-7998-0319-5.ch005

Duran, E. (2019). *Healing the soul wound: Trauma-informed counseling for Indigenous communities*. Teachers College Press.

Kopacz, D. R., & Rael, J. (2016). *Walking the Medicine Wheel: Healing trauma & PTSD*. Pointer Oak.

Nicholson, R. (2021). *Natural healing as conflict resolution*. IGI Global. doi:10.4018/978-1-7998-3665-0

Weaver, H. N. (2019). *Trauma and resilience in the lives of contemporary Native Americans: Reclaiming our balance, restoring our wellbeing*. Routledge.

KEY TERMS AND DEFINITIONS

Genocide: Intentional obliteration, in whole or in part, of a national, ethical, racial, or religious group.

Historical Consciousness: An awareness of the past that includes transcendent memories beyond individual and intergenerational boundaries and related through stories and life experiences.

Historical Trauma: Often begins with genocide, acculturation, or forced assimilation and is defined as the intent to destroy, in whole or in part, a national, ethical, racial, or religious group and results in cumulative emotional and psychological wounding across generations of individuals.

Living Energy: Defined as the life essence that flows through all things (e.g., plants, animals, and insects) and exists in connection with human beings.

Compilation of References

(2011). Introduction. InWalker, C., Bohlin, A., Hall, R., & Kepe, T. (Eds.), *Land, memory, reconstruction and justice* (pp. 1–13). Ohio University Press.

Absolon, K. E. (2016). Wholistic and ethical: Social inclusion with indigenous peoples. *Social Inclusion (Lisboa)*, *4*(1), 44–56. doi:10.17645i.v4i1.444

Achieve3000, Inc. (2016a). *The 5-step literacy routine.* http://doc.achieve3000.com/marketing/5stepCard_student/5stepCard_student.pdf

Achieve3000, Inc. (2016b). *Curriculum resources.* https://hub.achieve3000.com/pro-teacher-customize-curriculum/curriculum-resources/

Acker, A. (2017). When is a record? A research framework for locating electronic records in infrastructure. In A. J. Gilliland, S. McKemmish, & J. A. Lau (Eds.), *Research in the archival Multiverse*. Monash University.

Adams, D. W. (1995). *Education for extinction*. University Press of Kansas.

Adams, D. W. (1995). *Education for extinction: American Indians and the Boarding School Experience, 1875-1928.* University Press of Kansas.

Adams, M. (2006). Freedom of Information and Records Management in Ghana. *African Journal of Library Archives and Information Science*, (1), 29–38.

Adkins, T. A. (2012). "Can't nobody sleep" and other characteristics of culturally responsive English instruction. *Multicultural Perspectives*, *14*(2), 73–81. doi:10.1080/15210960.2012.673308

Agbayani, R. (1993). Some cultural traditions of the indigenous cultural communities in the Philippines: Their implications to the environmental conservation. *PSSC Social Science Information*, *20*, 9–17.

Agyeman-Yeboah, S. (2018). Land rights documentation in Ghana: Experiences from low-income key workers. *European Journal of Research in Social Sciences*, *6*(1), 13–26.

Albuquerque, G. R. d. (2014). História e historiografia do Acre: notas sobre os silêncios e a lógica do progresso. *Tropos: Comunicação. Society and Culture*, *1*(4), 1–19.

Allen, J. (1998). Personality assessment with American Indians and Alaska Natives: Instrument considerations and service delivery style. *Journal of Personality Assessment*, *70*(1), 17–42. doi:10.120715327752jpa7001_2

Allen, W. F., Ware, C. P., & Garrison, L. M. (1867). *Slave songs of the United States.* A. Simpson & Co. doi:10.5479il.78680.39088002074508

Altaha, N., & Kraus, S. (2017). "Kill the Indian, save the man": Native American historical trauma in college students. *Metamorphosis*. Retrieved from http://metamorphosis.coplac.org/index.php/metamorphosis/article/view/67

Amazônia em Chamas. (2019). *Indígenas Huni Kuin perdem animais e árvores em incêndio, no Acre*. Author.

American Indian College Fund. (2008). Retrieved from https://www.collegefund.org/downloads/FactSheet_2007.pdf

American Indian Higher Education Consortium. (2008). *Sustaining tribal colleges and universities and the tribal college movement: Highlights and profiles*. Systemic Research Inc.

American Psychiatric Association. (2000). *Diagnostic and statistical manual of mental disorders* (4th ed., text rev.). Author.

Ametepee, L. K., Tchnisala, Y., & Agbeh, A. O. (2014). The No Child Left Behind Act, the Common Core State Standards, and the school curriculum. *Review of Higher Education and Self-Learning*, *7*(24), 111–119.

Anderson, W. (n.d.). Anderson Cornelius student file. In *Carlisle Indian School Digital Resource Center*. http://carlisleindian.dickinson.edu/student_files/anderson-cornelius-student-file

Anderson, G. C. (2016). The Native peoples of the American West: Genocide or ethnic cleansing? *The Western Historical Quarterly*, *47*(4), 407–433. doi:10.1093/whq/whw126

Antunes, F. (2016). *Cacique Mapu Huni Kuin acusa político de exigir que índios andem nus para atrair turistas em Plácido de Castro, no Acre*. Amazônia Real.

Anyon, Y., Jenson, J. M., Altschul, I., Farrar, J., McQueen, J., Greer, E., Downing, B., & Simmons, J. (2014). The persistent effect of race and the promise of alternatives to suspension in school discipline outcomes. *Children and Youth Services Review*, *44*, 379–386. doi:10.1016/j.childyouth.2014.06.025

Aragon, S. R. (2002). An investigation of factors influencing classroom motivation for Postsecondary American Indian/Alaska students. *Journal of American Indian Education*, *41*(1).

Arizona Department of Education. (2014). *The basics*. https://www.azed.gov/assessment/files/2014/11/azmerit-overview_the-basics_final_english.pdf

Arizona Department of Education. (2015a). *2013 Arizona NAEP results by achievement-level Percentage*. https://azreportcards.com/Assessments/NAEP

Arizona Department of Education. (2015b). *Arizona report cards – Accelerating student achievement*. https://azreportcards.com/Assessments/Ela

Arizona Department of Education. (2015c). *AzMERIT*. https://www.azed.gov/assessment/azmerit

Arizona Department of Education. (2015d). *AzMERIT and NCSC 2015*. https://www.azed.gov/research-evaluation/files/2015/11/azmerit_ncsc_2015.xlsx

Arizona Department of Education. (2016). *AzMERIT 2016*. https://www.azed.gov/research-evaluation/files/2016/09/2016-azmerit.xlsx

Arizona Department of Education. (2016). *School year 2015-2016 state report card*. https://www.azed.gov/research-evaluation/files/2017/03/state-of-arizona_022417_final.pdf

Arndt, L., & Davis, A. (2011). Warrior spirit: Soul wound and coping among American Indians in law enforcement. *The Counseling Psychologist*, *39*(4), 527–569. doi:10.1177/0011000010389827

Arquiza, Y. (2007). *The road to empowerment: Strengthening the Indigenous Peoples Rights Act* (Vol. 1). International Labour Organization.

Arthur, M., & Porter, C. (2019). Restorying Northern Arapaho food sovereignty. *Journal of Agriculture, Food Systems, and Community Development, 9*(B), 1-16.

Asogwa, E. B., & Ezema, J. I. (2017). Freedom of access t government information in Africa: Trends, status and challenges. *Records Management Journal, 27*(3), 318–338. doi:10.1108/RMJ-08-2015-0029

Atkinson, J. (2002). *Trauma trails, recreating song lines: The transgenerational effects of trauma in Indigenous Australia*. Spinifex Press.

Atsbha, G. A., & Satinder, K. (2019). The structural relationship between tourist satisfaction and sustainable heritage tourism development in Tigrai, Ethiopia. *Heliyon, 5*(3), e01335. Advance online publication. doi:10.1016/j.heliyon.2019.e01335 PMID:30957037

Attali, J. (2017). *Noise: The political economy of music*. University of Minnesota Press.

Augustinus, C., & Lemmen, C. (2011, April). What is required to bring the social element into land administration: moving from the land administration domain model to the social tenure domain model+ powerpoint. In *Annual World Bank Conference on Land and Poverty*. World Bank.

Bakan, D. (2014). *A song of songs: A/r/tography, autoethnography, and songwriting as music education research* [Dissertation, University of British Columbia]. UBC Theses and Dissertations. https://open.library.ubc.ca/cIRcle/collections/ubctheses/24/items/1.0167101

Baldwin, C. (1994). *Calling the circle: The first and future culture*. Bantam.

Banda, J. P. (2004, January). Data collection pertaining to indigenous peoples: issues and challenges. In *Workshop on Data Collection and Disaggregation for Indigenous Peoples*. Department of Economic and Social Affairs, United Nations.

Bastian, A. J. (2017). Memory research/ Archival research. In A. J. Gilliland, S. McKemmish, & J. A. Lau (Eds.), *Research in the archival Multiverse*. Monash University.

Batley, M. (2004). What is the appropriate role of spirituality in restorative justice? *Critical Issues in Restorative Justice*, 365-377.

Batterbury, S., & Ndi, F. (2018). Land-grabbing in Africa. In *The Routledge Handbook of African Development. Routledge International Handbooks*. Routledge.

Beals, J., Manson, S. M., Whitesell, N. R., Mitchell, C. M., Novins, D. K., Simpson, S., & Spicer, P. (2005). Prevalence of major depressive episode in two American Indian reservation populations: Unexpected findings with a structured interview. *The American Journal of Psychiatry, 162*(9), 1713–1722. doi:10.1176/appi.ajp.162.9.1713 PMID:16135632

Behura, N. K. (1982). Forest and tribal world view. *Journal of Social Research, 25*(1).

Bender, K., & Armour, M. (2007). The spiritual components of restorative justice. *Victims & Offenders, 2*(3), 251–267. doi:10.1080/15564880701403967

Bevacqua, M. L. (2015). The song maps of Craig Santos Perez. *Transmotion, 1*(1), 84–88.

Bevacqua, M. L., & Bowman, I. K. (2016). Histories of wonder, futures of wonder: Chamorro activist identity, community, and leadership in "The Legend of Gadao" and "The Women Who Saved Guåhan from a Giant Fish.". *Marvels & Tales, 30*(1), 70–89. doi:10.13110/marvelstales.30.1.0070

Bippert, K., & Harmon, J. (2017). Middle school teacher's perceptions of computer-assisted reading intervention programs. *Reading Psychology, 38*(2), 203–230. doi:10.1080/02702711.2016.1245691

Birks, M., & Mills, J. (2011). Grounded theory: A practical guide. *Sage (Atlanta, Ga.).*

Bishop, M. (2020). 'Don't tell me what to do' encountering colonialism in the academy and pushing back with Indigenous autoethnography. *International Journal of Qualitative Studies in Education: QSE*, 1–12. doi:10.1080/09518398.2020.1761475

Blackhawk, N. (1995). I can carry on from here: The relocation of American Indians to Los Angeles. *Wicazo Sa Review*, *11*(2), 16–30. doi:10.2307/1409093

Blankenau, J., Comer, J., Nitze, J., & Stabler, W. (2010). The role of tribal experiences in shaping Native American Health. *Social Work in Public Health*, *25*(5), 423–437. doi:10.1080/19371918.2010.498699 PMID:20818590

Blauner, R. (1969). Internal colonialism and ghetto revolt. *Social Problems*, *16*(4), 393–408. doi:10.2307/799949

Blue, A. W., & Blue, M. A. R. (2001). The case for Aboriginal justice and healing: The self perceived through a broken mirror. *The spiritual roots of restorative justice*, 57-79.

Boche, M., & Anseeuw, W. (2013). *Unraveling" land grabbing"-Different models of large-scale land acquisition in Southern Africa.* LDPI Working Paper 46.

Bombay, A., Matheson, K., & Anisman, H. (2009). Intergenerational trauma. *Journal de la santé autochtone.*

Bombay, A., Matheson, K., & Anisman, H. (2013). The intergenerational effects of Indian residential schools: Implications for the concept of historical trauma. *Transcultural Psychiatry*, *0*, 1–19. PMID:24065606

Bopp, J., & Bopp, M. (1989). *The sacred tree*. Lotus Press.

Bottazzi, P., Goguen, A., & Rist, S. (2016). Conflicts of customary land tenure in rural Africa: Is large-scale land acquisition a driver of 'institutional innovation'? *The Journal of Peasant Studies*, *43*(5), 971–988. doi:10.1080/03066150.2015.1119119

Bourke, B. (2014). Positionality: Reflecting on the research process. *Qualitative Report*, *19*, 1–9. http://nsuworks.nova.edu/cgi/viewcontent.cgi?article=1026&context=tqr

Bowen, G. (2008). Naturalistic inquiry and the saturation concept: A research note. *Qualitative Research*, *8*(1), 137–152. doi:10.1177/1468794107085301

Boyer, P. (1997). *Native American colleges: Progress and prospects. A special report.* Jossey-Bass, Inc.

Boyer, P. (2004, November/December). Tribal colleges: Building native communities. *Native Peoples*, *17*(7), 24–28.

Boyes-Watson, C. (2005). Seeds of change: Using peacemaking circles to build a village for every child. *Child Welfare League of America*, *84*, 191–208. PMID:15828408

Boyes-Watson, C., & Pranis, K. (2015). *Circle forward: Building a restorative school community*. Living Justice Press.

Branco, M. L., & Torronteguy, M. A. A. (2013). O SUS na fronteira e o Direito: Em que medida o estrangeiro tem direito ao SUS. *Cad. IberAmer. Direito. Sanit*, *2*(2), 932–945.

Brave Heart, M. (1999). Oyate ptayela: Rebuilding the Lakota nation through addressing Historical trauma among Lakota parents. *Journal of Human Behavior in the Social Environment*, *2*(1-2), 109–126. doi:10.1300/J137v02n01_08

Brave Heart, M. (2003). The historical trauma response among natives and its relationship with substance abuse: A Lakota illustration. *Journal of Psychoactive Drugs*, *35*(1), 7–13. doi:10.1080/02791072.2003.10399988 PMID:12733753

Brave Heart, M., Chase, J., Elkins, J., & Altschul, D. (2011). Historical trauma among indigenous peoples of the Americas: Concepts, research, and clinical considerations. *Journal of Psychoactive Drugs, 43*(4), 282–290. doi:10.1080/02791072.2011.628913 PMID:22400458

Brave Heart, M., & DeBruyn, L. M. (1998). The American holocaust: Healing historical unresolved grief. *American Indian and Alaska Native Mental Health Research, 8*, 56–78. PMID:9842066

Brave Heart, M., Elkins, J., Tafoya, G., Bird, D., & Salvador, M. (2012). Wicasa was'aka: Restoring the traditional strength of American Indian boys and men. *American Journal of Public Health, 102*(S2), 177–183. doi:10.2105/AJPH.2011.300511 PMID:22401529

Brayboy, B. M. J. (2005). Toward a tribal critical race theory in education. *The Urban Review, 37*(5), 425–446. doi:10.100711256-005-0018-y

Bremer, J. (2017). Land was the main basis for business: Markets, merchants, and communities in Frontier Iowa. *Annals of Iowa, 76*(3), 261–289. doi:10.17077/0003-4827.12401

Brooks, A. (2007). Feminist standpoint epistemology: Building knowledge and empowerment through women's lived experience. In S. N. Hesse-Biber & P. L. Leavy (Eds.), *Feminist research practice* (pp. 53–82). SAGE. doi:10.4135/9781412984270.n3

Bulatao, J. C. (1992). *Phenomena and their interpretation: Landmark essays, 1957-1989.* Ateneo University Press.

Byrne, G. (2017). Narrative inquiry and the problem of representation: "Giving voice", making meaning. *International Journal of Research & Method in Education, 40*(1), 36–52. doi:10.1080/1743727X.2015.1034097

Cabral, A. (1993). National liberation and culture. In P. Williams & L. Chrisman (Eds.), Colonial discourse and postcolonial theory: A reader (pp. 53-65). Hertfordshire, UK: Harvester Wheatsheaf.

Carlsen, J., & Butler, R. (Eds.). (2011). Island tourism: Towards a sustainable perspective. Oxforshire: UK: CABI. doi:10.1079/9781845936792.0000

Carter, A., & Kruzic, A. (2017). Centering the Commons, Creating space for the collective: Ecofeminist# NoDAPL praxis in Iowa. *Journal of Social Justice*, 7.

Casal, G., & Bueza, R. V. (2017). T'boli. In N. G. Tiongson (Ed.), *Peoples of the Philippines* (Vol. 3). Cultural Center of the Philippines.

Castro, S. (2001). Kedungon: The abaca fiber. In Dreamweavers (pp. 34-45). Bookmark.

Cavalcante, T. L. V. (2013). *Colonialismo, Território e Territorialidade: A luta pela terra dos Guarani e Kaiowa em Mato Grosso do Sul* (PhD Thesis). Universidade Estadual Paulista, Assis, SP.

Cesar, L. (2017). Índios acusam dono de granja de cercar terra onde funciona Parque Ecológico no interior do Acre. *G1 Acre*. https://glo.bo/2U2Gymn

Chaloult, N., & Chaloult, Y. (1979). The internal colonialism concept: Methodological considerations. *Social and Economic Studies, 28*(4), 85–99.

Chalykoff, J. P. (2019). *The hauntings & heart of a place* [Recorded by artist].

Chaterera, F. (2015). Heading for a better understanding of outreach in the digital age: A look into the use of Web 2.0 as communication tool by state museums and archives in Zimbabwe. *Journal of the South African Society of Archivists, 48*, 21–33.

Chen, C.-M., & Huang, S.-H. (2014). Web-based reading annotation system with an attention-based self-regulated learning mechanism for promoting reading performance. *British Journal of Educational Technology, 45*(5), 959–980. doi:10.1111/bjet.12119

Cheng, B. K. (2018). Home is Elsewhere. In A. Smith & S. O'Connor (Eds.), *Hearth: A global conversation on community, identity, and place* (pp. 117–128). Milkweed Editions.

Chopra, S. S. (2016). Tribal identity concerns in literature: A critical study of Gopinath Mohanty's The Ancestor. *International Journal of Research, 3*(5).

Chou, T., Asnaani, A., & Hofmann, S. G. (2012). Perception of racial discrimination and psychopathology across three US ethnic minority groups. *Cultural Diversity & Ethnic Minority Psychology, 18*(1), 74–81. doi:10.1037/a0025432 PMID:21967527

Chu, J. M. (2013). *Creating a Zambian breadbasket: 'Land Grabs' and foreign investments in agriculture in Mkushi District, Zambia.* https://www.gov.uk/research-for-development-outputs/ldpi-working-paper-33-creating-a-zambian-breadbasket-land-grabs-and-foreign-investments-in-agriculture-in-mkushi-district-zambia

Chu, J., Young, K., & Phiri, D. (2015). *Large-scale land acquisitions, displacement and resettlement in Zambia.* Institute for Poverty, Land and Agrarian Studies, University of Western Cape.

City of Savannah. (2018). *Framework for Savannah's tourism management plan.* Retrieved from https://www.savannahga.gov/DocumentCenter/View/14245/Tourism-Management-Plan?bidId=

Clariza, M. E. (2019). Sacred texts and symbols: an indigenous Filipino perspective on reading. *The International Journal of Information, Diversity, & Inclusion, 3*(2).

Cleary, L. M., & Peacock, T. D. (1998). *Collected wisdom: American Indian education.* Allyn and Bacon.

Coe, B., & Palmer, C. T. (2009). How elders guided the evolution of the modern human brain, social behavior, and culture. *American Indian Culture and Research Journal, 33*(3), 15–21. doi:10.17953/aicr.33.3.b53t752702p4h767

Coladarci, T. (1983). High-School Dropouts among Native Americans. *Journal of American Indian Education, 23*(1), 15–22.

Coleman, T. (2009). *Putting tribal culture in school lessons.* Retrieved from http://www.reznetnews.org/article/putting-tribal-culture-school-lessons-27310

Colmant, S. A., & Merta, R. J. (1999). Using the sweat lodge ceremony as group therapy for Navajo youth. *Journal for Specialists in Group Work, 24*(1), 55–73. doi:10.1080/01933929908411419

COMIN. (2017). Grupo de Huni Kuin ocupa e revitaliza parque no Acre. *Conselho de Missão entre Povos Indígenas.* https://comin.org.br/?galleries=grupo-de-huni-kuin-ocupa-e-revitaliza-parque-no-acre

Conant, C. M. (2020). *Recommendations for the effective treatment of methamphetamine addiction with Native American cultural specificity.* Academic Press.

Constituição da República Federativa do Brasil de 1988. (2019). Convenção 169, da OIT. D5051.

Council, M. R. III, Cartledge, G., Green, D., Barber, M., & Gardner, R. III. (2016). Reducing risk through a supplementary reading intervention: A case study of first- and second-grade urban students. *Behavioral Disorders, 41*(4), 241–257. doi:10.17988/bedi-41-04-241-257.1

Covarrubias, R., & Fryberg, S. A. (2015). The impact of self-relevant representations on school belonging in Native American students. *Cultural Diversity & Ethnic Minority Psychology, 21*(1), 10–18. doi:10.1037/a0037819 PMID:25181325

Cox, R. J. (2008). Revisiting the archival finding aid. *Journal of Archival Organization*, *5*(4), 5–32. doi:10.1080/15332740802153245

Coyhis, D. (2012, March 21). *How to conduct Talking Circles.mp4* [Video]. YouTube.

Coyhis, D., & Simonelli, R. (2008). The Native American healing experience. *Substance Use & Misuse*, *43*(12-13), 1927–1949. doi:10.1080/10826080802292584 PMID:19016172

Cramer, E. D., Pellegrini-Lafont, C., & Gonzalez, L. (2014). Towards culturally responsive and integrated instruction for all learners: The integrated learning model. *Interdisciplinary Journal of Teaching and Learning*, *4*(2), 110–124.

Crawford, A. (2013). The trauma experienced by generations past having an effect in their descendants: Narrative and historical trauma among Inuit in Nunavut Canada. *Transcultural Psychiatry*, *0*, 1–31. PMID:23475452

Crofoot, T., Harris, N., Plumb, M., & Smith, K. (2008). Mental health, and substance abuse service needs for the Native American rehabilitation association northwest (Nara NW) in the Portland, Oregon metropolitan area. *American Indian and Alaska Native Mental Health Research*, *14*(3), 1–24. doi:10.5820/aian.1403.2007.1 PMID:18286444

Cudera, R., Razon, B., & Millondaga, K. J. (2020). Cultural and ecological significance of Odonata (Insecta) to the T'boli of Lake Sebu, Mindanao, Philippines. *Biodiversitas Journal of Biological Diversity, 21*(6).

Cuevas, J. A., Russell, L. R., & Irving, M. (2012). An examination of the effect of customized reading modules on the diverse secondary students' reading comprehension and motivation. *Educational Technology Research and Development*, *60*(3), 445–467. doi:10.100711423-012-9244-7

Cunanan, J. P. (1980). Differential access to resources: its impact on environmental activity. *Agham-Tao, 3*(1).

Daley, C. M., James, A. S., Barnoskie, R. S., Segraves, M., Schupbach, R., & Choi, W. S. (2006). "Tobacco has a purpose, not just a past": Feasibility of developing a culturally appropriate smoking cessation program for a pan-tribal native population. *Medical Anthropology Quarterly*, *20*(4), 421–440. doi:10.1525/maq.2006.20.4.421 PMID:17225653

Damron, A. D. (2006). *Tribal colleges look for ways to retain students.* Retrieved from http://www.iaiachronicle.org/archives/ RetainStudents.htm

Darling-Churchill, K. E., DeVoe, J. F., & Snyder, T. D. (2008). *Status and trends in the education of American Indians and Alaska Native: 2008.* Retrieved from https://nces.ed.gov/pubs2008/2008084.pdf

Datta, R. (2019). Clarifying the process of land-based research, and the role of researcher(s) and participants. *Ethics in Science and Environmental Politics*, *19*, 1–11. doi:10.3354/esep00187

Davis, J. (Winter 2001). American Native American boarding school experiences: Recent studies from native perspectives. *Organization of American Historians, 15*. Retrieved from https://www.oah.org/pubs/magazine/deseg/davis.html

De Silva, M., & Gandhi, K. (2019). "Daughter" as a positionality and the gendered politics of taking parents into the field. *Area*, *51*(4), 662–669. doi:10.1111/area.12525

Deal, G. (2018a, March 26). *Indigenous identity and existence: Fighting erasure and racism.* Colorado College.

Deal, G. [@greggdeal]. [2018b, October 21). *Today I was asked: 'What is most important to Indigenous people? The Land? Protecting traditions? Your language? Or your people' I told him: 'Those are all the same things'* [Tweet]. Twitter.

Dean, J., Furness, P., Verrier, D., Lennon, H., Bennett, C., & Spencer, S. (2017). Desert island data: An investigation into researcher positionality. *Qualitative Research*. Advance online publication. doi:10.1177/1468794117714612

DeGeer, M. E. (2003). Biopiracy: The appropriation of indigenous peoples' cultural knowledge. *New England Journal of International and Comparative Law*, *9*, 179–208.

Deininger, K., Ali, D. A., & Alemu, T. (2011). Impacts of land certification on tenure security, investment, and land market participation: Evidence from Ethiopia. *Land Economics*, *87*(2), 312–334. doi:10.3368/le.87.2.312

DeLisle, C. T. (2016). Destination Chamorro culture: Notes on realignment, rebranding, and post-9/11 militourism in Guam. *American Quarterly*, *68*(3), 563–572. doi:10.1353/aq.2016.0052

Deloria, V. Jr. (1994). *Indian education in American.* American Native American Science & Engineering Society.

Delos, R. C. (2009). *Tribal colleges' top priority for Obama: 'Full and forward funding'.* Retrieved from http://www.diverseeducation.com/artman/publish/article_12160.shtml

DeLoughrey, E. M. (2019). Toward a critical ocean studies for the anthropocene. *English Language Notes*, *57*(1), 21–36. doi:10.1215/00138282-7309655

DeMarni Cromer, L., Gray, M. E., Vasquez, L., & Freyd, J. J. (2018). The relationship of acculturation to historical loss awareness, institutional betrayal, and the intergenerational transmission of trauma in the American Indian experience. *Journal of Cross-Cultural Psychology*, *49*(1), 99–114. doi:10.1177/0022022117738749

Demmert, W. G., & Towner, J. C. (2003). *A review of the research literature on the influences of culturally based education on the academic performance of Native America students.* Retrieved from https://educationnorthwest.org/sites/default/files/resources/cbe.pdf

Denham, A. R. (2008). Rethinking historical trauma: Narratives of resilience. *Transcultural Psychiatry*, *45*(3), 391–414. doi:10.1177/1363461508094673 PMID:18799640

Dernoi, C. (2007). *Traditional territories of the Michipicoten First Nation.* Christine Dernoi & Associates.

Deschenie, T. (2004, November/December). Following the Dakota Way: Sisseton Wahpeton College. *Native Peoples*, *17*(7), 30.

Devalle, S. (1990). Tribe in India: The fallacy of a colonial category. In D. Lorenzen (Ed.), *Studies on Asia and Africa from Latin America* (pp. 71–116). El Colegio de Mexico. doi:10.2307/j.ctv3f8qc7.8

DeVoe, J. F., & Darling-Churchill, K. E. (2008). *Status and trends in the education of American Indians and Alaska natives* (NCES 2008-084). Retrieved from https://nces.ed.gov/pubs2008/2008084.pdf

Dey, D. (2019). India: The context of its current internal colonialism. In D. Schorkowitz, J. Chávez, & I. Schröder (Eds.), *Shifting forms of continental colonialism.* doi:10.1007/978-981-13-9817-9_10

Diamond, N., Bainbridge, J., & Hayes, C. (2009). *Reel injun (motion picture).* National Film Board of Canada.

Dias, B., & Ressler, K. (2014). Parental olfactory experience influences behavior and neural structure in subsequent generations. *Nature Neuroscience*, *17*(1), 89–98. doi:10.1038/nn.3594 PMID:24292232

Diaz, V. M., & Kauanui, J. K. (2001). Native Pacific Cultural Studies on the Edge. *The Contemporary Pacific*, *13*(2), 315–342.

Diaz, V. M., & Kauanui, J. K. (2001). Native Pacific cultural studies on the edge. *The Contemporary Pacific*, *13*(2), 315–342. doi:10.1353/cp.2001.0049

Dickson, M. W., Castaño, N., Magomaeva, A., & Den Hartog, D. N. (2012). Conceptualizing leadership across cultures. *Journal of World Business*, *47*(4), 483–492. doi:10.1016/j.jwb.2012.01.002

Doria, C. M., Momper, S. L., & Burrage, R. L. (2020). "Togetherness:" The role of intergenerational and cultural engagement in urban American Indian and Alaskan Native youth suicide prevention. *Journal of Ethnic & Cultural Diversity in Social Work*, 1–18. doi:10.1080/15313204.2020.1770648

Doss, C., Meinzen-Dick, R., & Bomuhangi, A. (2014). Who owns the land? Perspectives from rural Ugandans and implications for large-scale land acquisitions. *Feminist Economics*, *20*(1), 76–100. doi:10.1080/13545701.2013.855320

Douglass, B., & Moustakas, C. (1985). Heuristic inquiry: The internal search to know. *Journal of Humanistic Psychology*, *25*(3), 39–55. doi:10.1177/0022167885253004

Dow, J., & Slapin, B. (2004). Deconstructing the myths of the first Thanksgiving. *Multicultural Review*, *13*, 44–53.

Dragouni, M. (2017). *Sustainable heritage tourism: Towards a community-led approach.* Retrieved from https://discovery.ucl.ac.uk/10025949/1/E-thesis.pdf

Drew, B. (2014). The great amnesia. *Southwest Review*, *99*, 556–569.

Du Cros, H. (2001). A new model to assist in planning for sustainable cultural heritage tourism. *International Journal of Tourism Research*, *3*(2), 165–170. doi:10.1002/jtr.297

Duhaylungsod, L. (1993). Ancestral domain and cultural identity: missing notes in development. *PSSC Social Science Information, 20*, 19-23, 41.

Duhaylungsod, L. (1996). Higaonons and Bukidnons forests incorporated:" Will the twain ever meet?" *Agham-Tao, 8*(5).

Duhaylungsod, L., & Hyndman, D. (1993). Where T'boli bells toll: A political ecology voices behind the Tasaday hoax. Copenhagen, Denmark: International Working Group on Indigenous Affairs (IWGIA).

Duran, B., Duran, E., & Yellow Horse Brave Heart, M. (1998). Studying Native Americans and the trauma of history. In R. Thornton (Ed.), Studying Native America: Problems and prospects. University of Wisconsin Press.

Duran, E., & Duran, B. (1995). *Native American post colonial psychology*. State University of New York Press.

Duran, E., Duran, B., Brave Heart, M. Y. H., & Yellow Horse-Davis, S. (1998). Healing the American Indian soul wound. In Y. Danieli (Ed.), *The Plenum series on stress and coping. International handbook of multigenerational legacies of trauma* (pp. 341–354). Plenum Press. doi:10.1007/978-1-4757-5567-1_22

Duran, E., Firehammer, J., & Gonzalas, J. (2008). Liberation psychology as the path toward healing cultural soul wounds. *Journal of Counseling and Development*, *86*(3), 288–296. doi:10.1002/j.1556-6678.2008.tb00511.x

Ehlers, C., Gizer, I., Gilder, D., Ellingson, J., & Yehuda, R. (2013). Measuring historical trauma in an American Indian community sample: Contributions of substance dependence, affective disorder, conduct disorder, and PTSD. *Drug and Alcohol Dependence*, *133*(1), 180–187. doi:10.1016/j.drugalcdep.2013.05.011 PMID:23791028

Ehlers, C., Gizer, I., Gilder, D., & Yehuda, R. (2013a). Lifetime history of traumatic events in an American Indian community sample: Heritability and relation to substance dependence, affective disorder, conduct disorder, and PTSD. *Journal of Psychiatric Research*, *47*(2), 155–161. doi:10.1016/j.jpsychires.2012.10.002 PMID:23102628

Elias, B., Mignone, J., Hall, M., Hong, S. P., Hart, L., & Sareen, J. (2012). Trauma and suicide behaviour histories among a Canadian Indigenous population: An empirical exploration of the potential role of Canada's residential school system. *Social Science & Medicine*, *74*(10), 1560–1569. doi:10.1016/j.socscimed.2012.01.026 PMID:22464223

Endaya, I. (2015). *Towards a herstory of Filipino women's visual arts*. National Historical Commission of the Philippines (NHCP), Roundtable Conference on Women in History and History of Women.

Erguvan, I. D. (2014). Instructor's perceptions towards the use of an online instructional tool in an academic English setting in Kuwait. *The Turkish Online Journal of Educational Technology, 13*(1), 115–130.

Erguvan, I. D. (2015). Kuwaiti undergraduate students' perceptions of ICT in writing classes. *Arab World English Journal, 6*(1), 280–297. doi:10.24093/awej/vol6no1.22

Eubanks, J. P. (2014). Potential ramifications of Common Core State Standards adoption on information literacy. *Communications in Information Literacy, 8*(1), 23–31. doi:10.15760/comminfolit.2014.8.1.162

European Union. (n.d.). *Sustainable heritage tourism.* Retrieved from https://europa.eu/cultural-heritage/sites/eych/files/sustainable-cultural-tourism-recommendations_en.pdf?token=PsePI9T4

Evans-Campbell, T. (2008). Historical trauma in American Indian/native Alaskan communities: A multilevel framework for exploring impacts on individuals, families, and communities. *Journal of Interpersonal Violence, 23*, 316–338. doi:10.1177/0886260507312290 PMID:18245571

Fachry, K. N., Kamps, J., & Zhang, J. (2008, October). Access to archival material in context. In *Proceedings of the second international symposium on Information interaction in context* (pp. 102-109). 10.1145/1414694.1414718

Faircloth, S. C., & Tippeconnic, J. W. III. (2010). *The dropout/graduation rate crisis among American Indian and Alaska native students: Failure to respond places the future of native peoples at risk.* The Civil Rights Project/Proyecto Derechos Civiles at UCLA. Retrieved from https://www.civilrightsproject.ucla.edu/research/dropouts/faircloth-tippeconnic-native-american-dropouts-2010.pdf

Fann, A. (2004). *Tribal colleges: An overview.* Retrieved from https://www.ericdigests.org/2003-2/tribal.html

Fast, E., & Collin-Vézina, D. (2010). Historical trauma, race-based trauma and resilience of Indigenous peoples: A literature review. *First Peoples Child & Family Review, 5*(1), 126–136. doi:10.7202/1069069ar

Federal education policy & off-reservation schools 1870-1933. (1999). Retrieved from http://clarke.cmich.edu/NativeAmerican/treatyeducation.htm#nas

Fenty, N., Mulcahy, C., & Washburn, E. (2015). Teacher-led fluency instruction on students at risk of reading failure. *Learning Disabilities (Weston, Mass.), 13*(2), 141–156.

Fitzgerald, S. J. (2015). *Native women and land: Narratives of dispossession and resurgence.* University of New Mexico Press.

Fletcher, M. L. M. (2008). *American Native American education: Counternarratives in racism,struggle, and the law.* Routledge.

Fowler, L. (2002). *Tribal sovereignty and the historical imagination: Cheyenne-Arapaho politics.* University of Nebraska Press.

Freedman, S. G. (2011, June 16). *A black cultural tradition and its unlikely keepers.* Retrieved from https://www.nytimes.com/2011/06/18/us/18religion.html

Freeman, B. M. (2019). Promoting global health and well-being of Indigenous youth through the connection of land and culture-based activism. *Global Health Promotion, 26*(3, suppl), 17–25. doi:10.1177/1757975919831253 PMID:30964409

Freire, P. (2000). *Pedagogy of the oppressed* (30th ed.). Bloomsbury Academic.

French Development Cooperation. (2009). *Land governance and security of tenure in developing countries.* White Paper, Technical Committee on "Land Tenure and Development". French Development Cooperation.

Freud, S. (1901). *The psychopathology of everyday life* (SE, 6). Hogarth.

Gall, M. D., Gall, J. P., & Borg, W. R. (2007). *Educational research* (8th ed.). Pearson.

Garaba, F. (2007). The state of archival appraisal practices in the ESARBICA Region. *African Journal of Library Archives and Information Science*, *17*(1).

Garrett, M. T., Garrett, J. T., & Brotherton, D. (2001). Inner circle/outer circle: A group technique based on Native American healing circles. *Journal for Specialists in Group Work*, *26*(1), 17–30. doi:10.1080/01933920108413775

Garrod, B., & Fyall, A. (2000). Managing heritage tourism. *Annals of Tourism Research*, *27*(3), 682–708. doi:10.1016/S0160-7383(99)00094-8

Geortzen, J. R. (2010). Dialectical pluralism: A theoretical conceptualization of pluralism in psychology. *New Ideas in Psychology*, *28*(2), 201–209. doi:10.1016/j.newideapsych.2009.09.013

Gergen, K. J., & Gergen, M. M. (1997). Toward a cultural constructionist psychology. *Theory & Psychology*, *7*, 31–36. doi:10.1177/0959354397071003

German, L., Schoneveld, G., & Mwangi, E. (2011, April). Processes of large-scale land acquisition by investors: case studies from sub-Saharan Africa. In *International Conference on Global Land Grabbing* (pp. 6-8). University of Sussex.

Ghai, R. (2018). Tribal rights in India are a grey picture: experts. *Down To Earth.* Retrieved from https://www.downtoearth.org.in/news/environment/tribal-rights-in-india-are-a-grey-picture-experts-62230

Ghebru, H., & Lambrecht, I. (2017). Drivers of perceived land tenure (in) security: Empirical evidence from Ghana. *Land Use Policy*, *66*, 293–303. doi:10.1016/j.landusepol.2017.04.042

Giladi, L., & Bell, T. S. (2013). Protective factors for intergenerational transmission of trauma among second and third generation Holocaust survivors. *Psychological Trauma: Theory, Research, Practice, and Policy*, *5*(4), 384–391. doi:10.1037/a0028455

Gilberthorpe, E., Agol, D., & Gegg, T. (2016). 'Sustainable mining'? Corporate social responsibility, migration and livelihood choices in Zambia. *The Journal of Development Studies*, *52*(11), 1517–1532. doi:10.1080/00220388.2016.1189534

Gist, C. D. (2014). The culturally responsive teacher educator. *Teacher Educator*, *49*(4), 265–283. doi:10.1080/08878730.2014.934129

Gone, J. (2008). So I can be like a whiteman: The cultural psychology of space and place in American Indian mental health. *Culture and Psychology*, *14*(3), 369–399. doi:10.1177/1354067X08092639

Gone, J. (2009). A community-based treatment for Native American historical trauma: Prospects for evidenced based practice. *Journal of Consulting and Clinical Psychology*, *77*(4), 751–762. doi:10.1037/a0015390 PMID:19634967

Gone, J. (2011). The red road to wellness: Cultural reclamation in a native First Nations community treatment center. *The American Journal of Psychology*, *47*, 187–202. PMID:21052824

Gone, J. (2013). A community-based treatment for Native American historical trauma: Prospects for evidenced-based practice. *Spirituality in Clinical Practice*, *1*(S), 78–94. doi:10.1037/2326-4500.1.S.78

Gone, J. (2013a). Redressing first nations historical trauma: Theorizing mechanisms for Indigenous culture as mental health treatment. *Transcultural Psychiatry*, *50*(5), 683–706. doi:10.1177/1363461513487669 PMID:23715822

Gone, J. (2014). Reconsidering American Indian historical trauma: Lessons from an early Gross Ventre war narrative. *Transcultural Psychiatry*, *51*(3), 1–26. doi:10.1177/1363461513489722 PMID:23765681

Gone, J. P., & Kirmayer, L. J. (2010). On the wisdom of considering culture and context in psychopathology. In T. Millon, R. F. Krueger, & E. Simonsen (Eds.), *Contemporary directions in psychopathology: Scientific foundations of the DSM- V and ICD-11* (pp. 72–96). Guilford Press.

Goodkind, J., Hess, J., Gorman, B., & Parker, D. (2012). We're still in a struggle: Dine' resilience, survival, historical trauma, and healing. *Qualitative Health Research, 22*(8), 1019–1036. doi:10.1177/1049732312450324 PMID:22707344

Goodkind, J., Ross-Toledo, K., John, S., Hall, J., Ross, L., Freeland, L., Coletta, E., Becenti-Fundark, T., Poola, C., Begay-Roanhorse, R., & Lee, C. (2010). Promoting healing and restoring trust: Policy recommendations for improving behavioral health care for American Indian/Alaska Native adolescents. *American Journal of Community Psychology, 46*(3-4), 386–394. doi:10.100710464-010-9347-4 PMID:20857331

Government of the Republic of Zambia. (2006). *Report on the Environmental Impact Assessment Carried Out for Development of Nansanga Farm Block in Serenje District*. Ministry of Agriculture and Cooperatives.

Government of the Republic Zambia. (2005). *Farm Block Development Plan*. Ministry of Finance and National Planning.

Graham, A. D. (2018). *Emotionless. Scorpon* [CD]. OVO Music.

Granbois, D., & Sander, G. (2012). Resilience and stereotyping: The experiences of Native American elders. *Journal of Transcultural Nursing, 23*(4), 389–396. doi:10.1177/1043659612451614 PMID:22786944

Granillo, B., Renger, R., Wakelee, J., & Burgess, J. L. (2010). Utilization of the Native American talking circle to teach incident command system to tribal community health representatives. *Journal of Community Health, 35*(6), 625–634. doi:10.100710900-010-9252-7 PMID:20300808

Gratani, M., Sutton, S. G., Butler, J. R., Bohensky, E. L., Foale, S., & Stevenson, M. (2016). Indigenous environmental values as human values. *Cogent Social Sciences, 2*(1), 1185811. Advance online publication. doi:10.1080/23311886.2016.1185811

Gray, S. E., & Morrison, J. (2019). *History of Michipicoten First Nation*. Academic Press.

Gray, J., & Beresford, Q. (2008). A 'formidable challenge': Australia's quest for equity in Indigenous education. *Australian Journal of Education, 52*(2), 197–223. doi:10.1177/000494410805200207

Gray, J., & Rose, W. (2011). Cultural adaptation for therapy with American Indians and Alaska Natives. *Journal of Multicultural Counseling and Development, 40*(2), 82–92. doi:10.1002/j.2161-1912.2012.00008.x

Gray, M., Coates, J., & Hetherington, T. (2007). Hearing indigenous voices in mainstream social work. *The Journal of Contemporary Social Services, 88*(1), 55–67. doi:10.1606/1044-3894.3592

Grayshield, L., Rutherford, J. J., Salazar, S. B., Mihecoby, A. L., & Luna, L. L. (2015). Understanding and healing historical trauma: The perspectives of Native American elders. *Journal of Mental Health Counseling, 37*(4), 295–307. doi:10.17744/mehc.37.4.02

Green, E., & Norberg, M. (2018). Traditional Landholding Certificates in Zambia: Preventing or Reinforcing Commodification and Inequality? *Journal of Southern African Studies, 44*(4), 613–628. doi:10.1080/03057070.2018.1461490

Grimshaw, P. (2017). *A Gullah family: Ron and Natalie Daise*. Retrieved from https://grandstrandmag.com/feature/a_gullah_family_ron_and_natalie_daise

Gryczynski, J., & Johnson, J. (2011). Challenges in public health research with American Indians and other small ethnocultural minority populations. *Substance Use & Misuse, 46*(11), 1363–1371. doi:10.3109/10826084.2011.592427 PMID:21810071

Guest, G., Bunce, A., & Johnson, L. (2006). How many interviews are enough?: An Experiment with data saturation and variability. *Field Methods, 18*(1), 59–82. doi:10.1177/1525822X05279903

Guillory, R. M. (2009). American Indian/Alaska Native college student retention strategies. *Journal of Developmental Education, 33*(2), 12.

Guillory, R. M., & Wolverton, M. (2008). It's about family: Native American student ppersistence in higher education. *The Journal of Higher Education, 79*(1), 58–84. doi:10.1353/jhe.2008.0001

Guthrie, J. T., McRae, A., Coddington, C. S., Klauda, S. L., Wigfield, A., & Barbosa, P. (2009b). *Reading Motivation Scale* [Database record]. Retrieved from PsycTESTS. doi:10.1037/t23360-000

Guthrie, J. T., & Klauda, S. L. (2014). Effects of classroom practices on reading comprehension, engagement, and motivations for adolescents. *Reading Research Quarterly, 49*(4), 387–416. doi:10.1002/rrq.81 PMID:25506087

Guthrie, J. T., Klauda, S. L., & Ho, A. N. (2013). Modeling the relationships among reading instruction, motivation, engagement, and achievement for adolescents. *Reading Research Quarterly, 48*(1), 9–26. doi:10.1002/rrq.035 PMID:26412903

Guthrie, J. T., McRae, A., Coddington, C. S., Klauda, S. L., Wigfield, A., & Barbosa, P. (2009a). Impacts of comprehensive reading instruction on diverse outcomes of low- and high-achieving readers. *Journal of Learning Disabilities, 42*(3), 195–214. doi:10.1177/0022219408331039 PMID:19264929

Hadley, M. L. (2001). Introduction: Multifaith reflection on criminal justice. In M. L. Hadley (Ed.), *The spiritual roots of restorative justice* (pp. 1–29). State University of New York Press.

Hallgrimsson, T. (2006). Access and finding aids. In *Web Archiving* (pp. 131–151). Springer. doi:10.1007/978-3-540-46332-0_6

Hall, M., Murombedzi, J., Nkonkomalimba, M., Sambo, P., & Sommerville, M. (2017). *Zambia customary land documentation tenure assessment.* USAID Tenure and Global Climate Change Programme.

Hall, R. (2011). Land grabbing in Southern Africa: The many faces of the investor rush. *Review of African Political Economy, 38*(128), 193–214. doi:10.1080/03056244.2011.582753

Hanstad, T., Nielsen, R., & Brown, J. (2004). *Land and livelihoods. Making land rights real for India's rural poor.* LSP Working Paper No. 12. FAO.

Harmon, A. (2010, April 10). Indian tribe wins fight to limit research of its DNA. *The New York Times*. https://www.nytimes.com/2010/04/22/us/22dna.html

Harris, D. M. (2012). Leveraging change via competition: The promise and limitations of Race to the Top. *JEP: eJournal of Education Policy*, 1-7.

Hau'ofa, E. (2005). The ocean in us. In A. Hooper (Ed.), *Culture and Sustainable Development in the Pacific* (pp. 32–43). ANU Press.

Hazen, D. (2012, October 26). *Rupert Ross* [Video]. YouTube.

heartspeak. (2013, November 12). *Community healing programs with Rupert Ross Trailer* [Video]. YouTube.

Heim, O. (2018). How (not) to globalize Oceania: Ecology and politics in contemporary Pacific island performance arts. *Commonwealth Essays and Studies, 41*(1), 131–145. doi:10.4000/ces.402

Herlihy, J. (2011). Reflections on social engineering and settler-American literature. *European Journal of American Studies, 6*(1), 6–1. doi:10.4000/ejas.8874

Hero, R. E., & Tolbert, C. J. (1996). A racial/ethnic diversity interpretation of politics and policy in the states of the US. *American Journal of Political Science, 40*(3), 851–871. doi:10.2307/2111798

Herre, R. (2013). *Fast Track Agribusiness: Expansion, Land Grabs and the Role of European Private and Public Financing in Zambia: A Right to Food Perspective*. FIAN FoodFirst Informations- & Aktions-Netzwerk.

Hill, D. L. (2006). Sense of belonging as connectedness, American Indian worldview, and mental health. *Psychiatric Nursing, 20*(5), 210–216. doi:10.1016/j.apnu.2006.04.003 PMID:17010824

Hill, D. V., Lenard, M. A., & Page, L. C. (2016). *The impact of Achieve3000 on elementary literacy outcomes: Evidence from a two-year randomized control trial*. Society for Research on Educational Effectiveness.

Hodge, D., & Limb, G. (2011). Spiritual assessment and Native Americans: Establishing the social validity of a complementary set of assessment tools. *Social Work, 56*(3), 213–223. doi:10.1093w/56.3.213 PMID:21848086

Hodge, F. S., Fredericks, L., & Rodriguez, B. (1996). American Indian women's talking circle: A cervical cancer screening and prevention project. *Cancer: Interdisciplinary International Journal of the American Cancer Society, 78*(7), 1592–1597. doi:10.1002/(SICI)1097-0142(19961001)78:7<1592::AID-CNCR39>3.0.CO;2-T PMID:8839577

Honig, L., & Mulenga, B. P. (2015). *The status of customary land and the future of smallholder farmers under the current land administration system in Zambia* (No. 1093-2016-87977). Academic Press.

Horn, K. (2016). *A report on the relationship between restorative justice and Indigenous legal traditions in Canada*. Canada Department of Justice. https://www.justice.gc.ca/eng/rp-pr/jr/rjilt-jrtja/rjilt-jrtja.pdf

Horton, S. (2006). Social capital, government policy and public value: Implications for archive service delivery. *Aslib Proceedings, 58*(6), 502–512. doi:10.1108/00012530610713588

Horwitz, T. (2014). Hundreds of women and children were coming towards us, and getting on their knees for mercy. *Smithsonian, 14*, 50–57.

Hoskins, K. (2015). Researching female professors: The difficulties of representation, positionality and power in feminist research. *Gender and Education, 27*(4), 393-411. Doi:.2015.1021301 doi:10.1080/09540253

Hsu, H. L. (2012). Guåhan (Guam), literary emergence, and the American Pacific in *Homebase* and *from unincorporated territory*. *American Literary History, 24*(2), 281–307. doi:10.1093/alh/ajs021

Huang, S.-H. (2012). A mixed-methods study of the effectiveness of the accelerated reader program on middle school students' reading achievement and motivation. *Reading Horizons, 51*(3), 229–246.

Huculak, B. (2001). Epilogue: Justice as hope. In M. L. Hadley (Ed.), *The spiritual roots of restorative justice* (pp. 217–223). State University of New York Press.

Huni Kuin, M. (2017). *Interview with the authors. With the participation of Teresa Di Somma.* Universidade Federal do Acre.

IMBD. (2019). *Gullah Gullah island.* Retrieved from https://www.imdb.com/title/tt0177444/

Indaba Agricultural Policy Research Institute (IAPRI). (2015). *Rural Agricultural Livelihoods Survey Report*. IAPRI.

Iris. (2010). The page transformed: A conversation with Craig Santos Perez. *Lanternreview*, 2. Retrieved from http://www.lanternreview.com/blog/2010/03/12/the-page-transformed-a-conversation-with-craig-santos-perez/

Irwin, R. L., & Springgay, S. (2008). *A/r/tography as practice-based research. Being with A/r/tography*. Sense Publishers.

Iyer, D. (2017). The role of government in expediting land expropriation: Reshaping the future of land reform. *Journal of Public Administration*, *52*(3), 508–519.

Jackson, A. P., Smith, S. A., & Hill, C. L. (2003). Academic persistence among Native America college students. *Journal of College Student Development*, *44*(4), 548–565. doi:10.1353/csd.2003.0039

Jacob, M. (2012). We wanted those people to see that Indians aren't stupid: Identity, Representation, and resistance in the cultural tourism of the Wapato Indian Club. *American Indian Quarterly*, *36*(4), 465–478. doi:10.5250/amerindiquar.36.4.0465

Jacobs, M. (2013). Remembering the forgotten child: The American Indian child welfare crisis of the 1960s and 1970s. *American Indian Quarterly*, *37*(1-2), 136–159. doi:10.1353/aiq.2013.0014

Jain, N., Chileshe, R., Muwowo, F., & Lupiya, M. (2016). Perceptions of customary land tenure security in western province of Zambia. *International Journal of Social Science Studies*, *4*(2), 78. doi:10.11114/ijsss.v4i2.1264

Jalata, A. (2016). The impact of colonial terrorism on indigenous Americans. In *Phases of Terrorism in the Age of Globalization* (pp. 49–71). Palgrave Macmillan. doi:10.1057/9781137552341_4

James, A., & Renville, T. (2012). Ohiyesa's path: Reclaiming native education. *Reclaiming Children and Youth*, *21*, 27–30.

Jena, M. (2017). *One Earth: Why the world needs Indigenous communities to steward their lands*. Inter Press Service News Agency. Retrieved from http://www.ipsnews.net/2017/08/one-earth-world-needs-indigenous-communities-steward-lands/

Jervis, L. L., Beals, J., Croy, C. D., Klein, S. A., Manson, S. M., & Team, A. S. (2006). Historical consciousness among two American Indian tribes. *The American Behavioral Scientist*, *50*(4), 526–549. doi:10.1177/0002764206294053

Jili, N., & Masuku, M. M. (2017). Access to land and women's participation in small-scale farming at uMlalazi local municipality. *Journal of Public Administration*, *52*(3), 548–561.

Johns Hopkins Center for American Indian Health. (2020, November 21). *Oren Lyons: Indigenous lessons for the world: Native American Heritage Month lecture* [Video]. YouTube.

Johnson, G. M. (2009). Instructionism and constructivism: Reconciling two very good ideas. *International Journal of Special Education*, *24*(3), 90–98.

Johnston-Goodstar, K., & VeLure Roholt, R. (2017). "Our kids aren't dropping out; They're being pushed out": Native American students and racial microaggressions in schools. *Journal of Ethnic & Cultural Diversity in Social Work*, *26*(1-2), 30–47. doi:10.1080/15313204.2016.1263818

Jordan, K. (2013). Incorporation and colonization: PostColumbian Iroquois satellite communities and processes of indigenous autonomy. *American Anthropologist*, *115*(1), 29–43. doi:10.1111/j.1548-1433.2012.01533.x

Jung, C. G. (1936). *The concept of the collective unconscious. Collected Works*, *9*(1), 42.

Kabinga, M. (2019). Mining developments and land acquisition processes in Zambia. *ASC-TUFS Working Papers 2019 Challenges of Development and Natural Resource Governance in Africa*, 167-182.

Kane, M. B. (1970). *Minorities in textbooks: A study of their treatment in social studies texts*. Quadrangle Books.

Kanu, Y. (2006). Getting them through the college pipeline: Critical elements of instruction influencing school success among Native Canadian high school students. *Journal of Advanced Academics*, *18*(1), 116–145. doi:10.4219/jaa-2006-348

Karlsen, S., & Nazroo, J. Y. (2002). Relation between racial discrimination, social class, and health among ethnic minority groups. *American Journal of Public Health*, *92*(4), 624–631. doi:10.2105/AJPH.92.4.624 PMID:11919063

Katungula, D., Kumwenda, M., Ncube, N., & Chilanga, M. (2019). Innovative Customary Land Governance in Zambia: Experiences, Lessons Learned and Emerging Impacts. *African Journal on Land Policy and Geospatial Sciences*, *3*, 105–115.

Katz, R. V., Kegeles, S. S., Kressin, N. R., Green, B. L., James, S. A., Wang, M. Q., Russell, S. L., & Claudio, C. (2008). Awareness of the Tuskegee Syphilis Study and the US presidential apology and their influence on minority participation in biomedical research. *American Journal of Public Health*, *98*(6), 1137–1142. doi:10.2105/AJPH.2006.100131 PMID:17901437

Kenyon, D., & Hanson, J. (2012). Incorporating traditional culture into positive youth development programs with American Indian/Alaska Native youth. *Child Development Perspectives*, *6*(3), 272–279. doi:10.1111/j.1750-8606.2011.00227.x

Keohane, S. K. (2006). *The reservation boarding school system in the United States, 1870-1928*. Retrieved from http://www.twofrog.com/rezsch.html#excerpt

Keown, M. (2007). *Pacific islands writing: The postcolonial literatures of Aotearoa/New Zealand and Oceania*. Oxford University Press.

Kepe, T. (2004). Land restitution and biodiversity conservation in South Africa: the case of Mkambati, Eastern Cape Province. *Canadian Journal of African Studies/La Revue Canadienne des Études Africaines*, *38*(3), 688-704.

Kesselring, R. (2018). At an extractive pace: Conflicting temporalities in a resettlement process in Solwezi, Zambia. *The Extractive Industries and Society*, *5*(2), 237–244. doi:10.1016/j.exis.2018.02.008

Kessinger, T. A. (2011). Efforts toward educational reform in the United States since 1958. *American Educational History Journal*, *38*(2), 263–276.

King, T. (2003). *The truth about stories: A native narrative*. The House of Anansi Press.

King, U. (1997). Spirituality. In J. Hinnells (Ed.), *A new handbook of living religions* (pp. 667–691). Blackwell Publishers.

Klest, B., Freyd, J., & Foynes, M. (2013). Trauma exposure and posttraumatic symptoms in Hawaii: Gender, ethnicity, and social context. *Psychological Trauma: Theory, Research, Practice, and Policy*, *5*(5), 409–416. doi:10.1037/a0029336 PMID:24660048

Knight, R. S. (2010). Statutory recognition of customary land rights in Africa: An investigation into best practices for lawmaking and implementation. *FAO Legislative Study*, 105.

Kovach, M. (2009). *Indigenous methodologies: Characteristics, conversations, and contexts*. University of Toronto Press.

Krezmien, M. P., Leone, P. E., & Achilles, G. M. (2006). Suspension, race, and disability: Analysis of statewide practices and reporting. *Journal of Emotional and Behavioral Disorders*, *14*(4), 217–226. doi:10.1177/10634266060140040501

Kristianto, B. (2013). The notion of the body and the path to healing. *The International Journal of Religion and Spirituality in Society*, *2*(3), 41–53. doi:10.18848/2154-8633/CGP/v02i03/51006

Krüger, R., Cundill, G., & Thondhlana, G. (2016). A case study of the opportunities and trade-offs associated with deproclamation of a protected area following a land claim in South Africa. *Local Environment*, *21*(9), 1047–1062. doi:10.1080/13549839.2015.1065804

Kumari, S. (2019). Sukru Jani: A legendary protagonist in Gopinath Mohanty's Paraja. *International Journal of English, Language, &. Humanities (Washington)*, *7*(12).

Kumar, R. (2018). Gopinath Mohanty's Paraja. *Studies in Humanities and Social Sciences*, *24*(2), 1–17.

Ladson-Billings, G. (2006). From the achievement gap to the education debt: Understanding achievement in US schools. *Educational Researcher, 35*(7), 3–12. doi:10.3102/0013189X035007003

Lai, P. (2011). Discontiguous States of America: The paradox of unincorporation in Craig Santos Perez's poetics of Chamorro Guam. *Journal of Transnational American Studies, 3*(2), 1–28.

Lajimodiere, D. (2011). Ogimah Ikwe: Native women and their path to leadership. *Wicazo Sa Review, 26*(2), 57–82. doi:10.1353/wic.2011.0011

Lajimodiere, D. (2012). A healing journey. *Wicazo Sa Review, 27*(2), 5–19. doi:10.5749/wicazosareview.27.2.0005

Lam, A. (2018). Enchantment. In A. Smith & S. O'Connor (Eds.), *Hearth: A global conversation on community, identity, and place* (pp. 31–47). Milkweed Editions.

Lambert, J. E., Holzer, J., & Hasbun, A. (2014). Association between parents' PTSD severity and children's psychological distress: A meta-analysis. *Journal of Traumatic Stress, 27*(1), 9–17. doi:10.1002/jts.21891 PMID:24464491

Lane, D., & Simmons, J. (2011). American Indian youth substance abuse: Community- driven interventions. *The Mount Sinai Journal of Medicine, New York, 78*(3), 362–372. doi:10.1002/msj.20262 PMID:21598263

LaRocque, E. (2011). *When the other is me: Native resistance discourse, 1850-1990.* University of Manitoba Press.

Lasalita-Zapico, F., Martin, T. T., Pena, R. J., & Gonzales, J. (2008). Farming and seed conservation practices of rice farmers in the marginal uplands of Lake Sebu, South Cotabato, Philippines. *Philippine Journal of Crop Science, 16*(1), 7–11.

Lavallée, L. (2007). Physical activity and healing through the medicine wheel. *Pimatisiwin, 5*(1), 127–153.

Laverick, D. M. (2014). Supporting striving readers through technology-based instruction. *Reading Improvement, 51*(1), 11–19.

Lawrence, J. (2000). The Indian health service and the sterilization of Native American women. *American Indian Quarterly, 24*(3), 400–419. doi:10.1353/aiq.2000.0008 PMID:17089462

Le Roux, C. S. (2017). Exploring rigour in autoethnographic research. *International Journal of Social Research Methodology, 20*(2), 195–207. doi:10.1080/13645579.2016.1140965

Lea, A. M. (1836). *Notes on the Wisconsin Territory; particularly with reference to the Iowa District or Black Hawk Purchase*. H.S. Tanner.

Leavy, P. (2017). *Research design: Quantitative, qualitative, mixed methods, arts-based, and community based participatory research approaches*. Guilford.

Lecher, H. E. (2006). Small scale academic web archiving: DACHS. In *Web Archiving* (pp. 213–225). Springer. doi:10.1007/978-3-540-46332-0_10

Leeson, B. (2018, November 5). Author details dark history of Chapleau's residential schools. *The Timmins Daily Press.* https://www.timminspress.com/news/local-news/author-details-dark-history-of-chapleaus-residential-schools

Lewis, H. S., & McLester, L. G. (Eds.). (2005). *Oneida Lives: Long-Lost Voices of the Wisconsin Oneidas.* University of Nebraska Press.

Library of Congress. (2010). *Ring shout.* Retrieved from https://www.loc.gov/item/webcast-5109

Liem, R. (2007). Silencing historical trauma: The politics and psychology of memory and Voice. *Peace and Conflict, 13*(2), 153–174. doi:10.1080/10781910701271200

Lihoma, P. (2008). Situation of archives in Africa: The case of national archives of Malawi. *African Research & Documentation*, (106), 3.

Lima, E. (2011). *Parque ecológico de Plácido de Castro vira motel a céu aberto.* Blog do radialista Edizio Lima. https://bit.ly/2U2jggi

Lim, C. C., & Bendle, L. J. (2012). Arts tourism in Seoul: Tourist-orientated performing arts as a sustainable niche market. *Journal of Sustainable Tourism, 20*(5), 667–682. doi:10.1080/09669582.2011.636817

Lippert, C., & Engel, J. (2014, April 14). The Great Lakes: An Ojibwe perspective. *The Decolonial Atlas.* https://decolonialatlas.wordpress.com/2015/04/14/the-great-lakes-in-ojibwe-v2/

Little, C. A., McCoach, D. B., & Reis, S. M. (2014). Effects of differentiated reading instruction on student achievement in middle school. *Journal of Advanced Academics, 25*(4), 384–402. doi:10.1177/1932202X14549250

Loomba, A. (2015). *Colonialism/Postcolonialism* (3rd ed.). Routledge. doi:10.4324/9781315751245

Lopez, F. A., Heilig, J. V., & Schram, J. (2013). A story within a story: Culturally responsive schooling and American Indian and Alaska Native achievement in the National Indian Education Study. *American Journal of Education, 119*(4), 513–538. doi:10.1086/670965

Louick, R., Leider, C. M., Daley, S. G., Proctor, C. P., & Gardner, G. L. (2016). Motivation for reading among struggling middle school readers: A mixed methods study. *Learning and Individual Differences, 49*, 260–269. doi:10.1016/j.lindif.2016.06.027

Lucena, G. X. D., & Barros, J. M. (2014). Memórias e Interações Midiatizadas: O Acre Existe? In *Anais do XII Congresso da Asociación Latinoamericana de Investigadores de las Ciencias de la Comunicación.* PUCP.

Luna, W. F., Malvezzi, C., Teixeira, K. C., Almeida, D. T., & Bezerra, V. P. (2020). Identity, care and rights: The experience of Talking Circles about the health of Indigenous People. *Revista Brasileira de Educação Médica, 44*(2), e067. doi:10.1590/1981-5271v44.2-20190309.ing

Lund, C., & Rachman, N. F. (2016). Occupied! property, citizenship and peasant movements in Rural Java. *Development and Change, 47*(6), 1316–1337. doi:10.1111/dech.12263

Lusaka Times. (2020). *The newly constructed Multi Facility Economic Zone in Central Province belongs to Chibombo District – Wina.* https://www.lusakatimes.com/2020/07/19/the-newly-constructed-multi-facility-economic-zone-in-central-province-belongs-to-chibombo-district-wina/

Lyons, O. (Ed.). (1992). *Exiled in the land of the free: Democracy, Indian nations, and the US Constitution.* Clear Light Pub.

Lyons, O. (Ed.). (1992). *Exiled in the land of the free: democracy, Indian nations, and the US Constitution.* Clear Light Publishers.

Lysenko, L. V., & Abrami, P. C. (2014). Promoting reading comprehension with the use of technology. *Computers & Education, 75*, 162–172. doi:10.1016/j.compedu.2014.01.010

Machado, A. (2015). *Prefeito autoriza ocupação do Parque Ecológico de Plácido por indígenas.* Amazônia: Notícia e informação.

Mackey, V. (2000). Holistic restorative justice: A response to McCold. *Contemporary Justice Review, 3*(4), 451–458.

Magbanua, F. S., Fontanilla, A. M., Ong, P. S., & Hernandez, M. B. M. (2017). 25 years (1988-2012) of freshwater research in the Philippines: What has been done and what to do next? *Philippine Journal of Systematic Biology, 11*(1).

Maidabino, A. A. (2010). The availability, organization, and use of archival records: A Study of Public Archives Agencies in the Northwestern States of Nigeria. *Library Philosophy and Practice*, 1.

Malik, S. (2020). Land alienation and the politics of tribal exploitation in Odisha. In *Land alienation and politics of tribal exploitation in India*. Springer. doi:10.1007/978-981-15-5382-0_4

Manuel, V. (2016). *Underlying causes, consequences and possible solutions to land tenure insecurity of indigenous peoples and local communities in Southern Chile: The case of the MapucheHuilliche Indigenous communities in the Coastal Range Rainforests of MaruLahual* [Unpublished PhD thesis]. Universidad Austral de Chile/TechnischeUniversitat Dortmund.

Manyabula, M. (2009). Public service reform, accountability and records management: A case study of Tanzania. *ESARBICA Journal*, *28*(1), 28. doi:10.4314/esarjo.v28i1.44395

Marowa, I. (2015). Archives as Extended Memory of Communities: The Case of Dandawa Chiefdom in Hurungwe District, Zimbabwe. *ESARBICA Journal*, *34*, 104.

Marr, C. J. (n.d.). *Assimilation through education: Boarding schools in the northwest.* Retrieved from https://content.lib.washington.edu/aipnw/marr.html

Martinez, D. (2018). *Documents of American Indian removal*. ABC-CLIO.

Mays, V., Gallardo, M., Shorter-Gooden, K., Robinson-Zanartu, C., Smith, M., McClure, F., Puri, S., Methot, L., & Ahhaitty, G. (2009). Expanding the circle: Decreasing American Indian mental health disparities through culturally competent teaching about American Indian mental health. *American Indian Culture and Research Journal*, *33*(3), 61–83. doi:10.17953/aicr.33.3.b27481242q461u25 PMID:25284917

McAuslan, P. (2007). *Improving Tenure Security for the Poor in Africa—Synthesis Paper: Deliberations of the Legal Empowerment Workshop—Sub-Saharan Africa*. LEP Working Paper No. 8. FAO.

McCabe, G. (2007). The healing path: A culture and community-derived indigenous therapy model. *Psychotherapy (Chicago, Ill.)*, *44*(2), 148–160. doi:10.1037/0033-3204.44.2.148 PMID:22122207

McCabe, G. (2008). Mind, body, emotions and spirit: Reaching to the ancestors for healing. *Counselling Psychology Quarterly*, *21*(2), 143–152. doi:10.1080/09515070802066847

Mccallin, B. E. M. (2018). Integrating customary tenure into formal systems (No. 129135). The World Bank.

McKenna, R. T. (2017). *American imperial pastoral: The architecture of US colonialism in the Philippines*. University of Chicago Press. doi:10.7208/chicago/9780226417936.001.0001

Mello, M. M., & Wolf, L. E. (2010). The Havasupai Indian tribe case—Lessons for research involving stored biologic samples. *The New England Journal of Medicine*, *363*(3), 204–207. doi:10.1056/NEJMp1005203 PMID:20538622

Melton, A. P. (1995). Indigenous justice systems: Tribal society is a way of life. *Judicature*, *79*, 126–133.

Menne-Haritz, A. (2001). Access—The reformulation of an archival paradigm. *Archival Science*, *1*(1), 57–82. doi:10.1007/BF02435639

Menzies, P. (2007). Understanding Aboriginal intergeneration trauma from a social work perspective. *The Canadian Journal of Native Studies*, *27*(2), 367.

Meriam, L., & Work, H. (1928). The problem of Indian administration. Report of a survey made at the request of the Honorable Hubert Work, Secretary of the Interior, and submitted to him, February 21, 1928 (No. 17). John Hopkins Press.

MetaMetrics. (2016). *Lexile infographic*. https://lexile.com/about-lexile/lexile-overview/lexile-infographic/

MetaMetrics. (2017). *Matching Lexile measures to grade ranges.* https://lexile.com/educators/measuring-growth-with-lexile/lexile-measures-grade-equivalents/

Meyer, J. (2002). It is a gift from the Creator to keep us in harmony: Original (verses alternative) dispute resolution on the Navajo Nation. *International Journal of Public Administration, 25*(11), 1379–1401. doi:10.1081/PAD-120013351

Miller, R. J. (2011). American Indians, the doctrine of discovery, and manifest destiny. *Wyoming Law Review, 11*, 329.

Ministério da Saúde. (n.d.). *Sistema Único de Saúde (SUS): Estrutura, princípios e como funciona.* Ministério da Saúde.

Ministry of Law. (2007). *The Constitution of India, 1950.* Retrieved from http://legislative.gov.in/sites/default/files/19_The%20Constitution%20%28ST%29%20Order%201950.pdf

Mishra, P., & Koehler, M. J. (2006). Technological pedagogical content knowledge: A framework for integrating technology in teacher knowledge. *Teachers College Record, 108*(6), 1017–1054. doi:10.1111/j.1467-9620.2006.00684.x

Mkuwira, R. M. (2015). Preservation of documentary heritage in Malawi. *Journal of the South African Society of Archivists, 48*, 55–65.

Mnjama, N. (2009, July). Archival programming in the digital era: The challenge for ESARBICA archivists. In *XXth Bi-Annual East and Southern Africa Regional Branch of the International Council on Archives (ESARBICA) General Conference, Documentary Heritage Management in the Digital Age: Beauty and the Beast, Namibia, National Archives of Namibia, Windhoek July* (pp. 1-3). Academic Press.

Mohanty, G. (1987). *Paraja* (B. K. Das, Trans.). Oxford University Press.

Momartin, S., Silove, D., Manicavasagar, V., & Steel, Z. (2003). Dimensions of trauma associated with posttraumatic stress disorder (PTSD) caseness, severity and functional impairment: A study of Bosnian refugees resettled in Australia. *Social Science & Medicine, 57*(5), 775–781. doi:10.1016/S0277-9536(02)00452-5 PMID:12850105

Momartin, S., Silove, D., Manicavasagar, V., & Steel, Z. (2004). Comorbidity of PTSD and depression: Associations with trauma exposure, symptom severity and functional impairment in Bosnian refugees resettled in Australia. *Journal of Affective Disorders, 80*(2), 231–238. doi:10.1016/S0165-0327(03)00131-9 PMID:15207936

Mongibello, A. (2014). Tracking the land/memory: Healing and reterritorializations in Jeannette Armstrong's breath tracks. In *Indigenous perspectives of North America: A collection of studies.* Cambridge Scholars Publishing.

Monkman, L. (2017, March 25). Historical ban on potlatch ceremony has lingering effects for Indigenous women, author says. *CBC.* https://www.cbc.ca/news/indigenous/historical-ban-spirituality-felt-indigenous-women-today-1.4036528

Mora, M. (2012). Tune and textile: interrelatedness in the music and weaving arts of the T'boli, Philippines. *Humanities Diliman: A Philippine Journal of Humanities, 9*(2).

Morales, L. (2007). *A Navajo student feels the tug of home.* Retrieved from http://www.npr.org/templates/story/story.php?storyId=6845552

Moravec, M. (2017). Feminist research practices and digital archives. *Australian Feminist Studies, 32*(91-92), 186–201. doi:10.1080/08164649.2017.1357006

Morgan, R., & Freeman, L. (2013). The healing of our people: Substance abuse and historical trauma. *Substance Use & Misuse, 44*(1), 84–98. doi:10.1080/10826080802525678 PMID:19137484

Morton, A. (2019). *Michipicoten First Nation elder interviews.* Bluestone Research.

Moustakas, C. (1956). True experience and the self. In C. Moustakas (Ed.), *The self: Explorations in personal growth* (pp. 3–14). Harper.

MoustakasC. (1990). *Heuristic research: Design, methodology, and applications*. SAGE.

MoustakasC. (1994). *Phenomenological research methods*. SAGE.

Moyo, S. (2007). Land in the political economy of African development: Alternative strategies for reform. *Africa Development. Afrique et Developpement*, *32*(4), 1–37.

Mullany, B., Barlow, A., Goklish, N., Larzelere-Hinton, F., Cwik, M., Craig, M., & Walkup, J. T. (2009). Toward understanding suicide among youths: Results from the White Mountain Apache tribally mandated suicide surveillance system, 2001-2006. *American Journal of Public Health*, *99*(10), 1840–1848. doi:10.2105/AJPH.2008.154880 PMID:19696377

Munge, E., Rotich, D. C., & Wamukoya, J. (2014). A situational analysis of information management in selected government ministries in the context of Kenya Vision 2030. *African Journal of Library Archives and Information Science*, *24*(1), 15–26.

Munshifwa, E. (2018, March). *Customary land governance in Zambia: Inertia, confusion, and corruption* [Paper Presentation]. World Bank 2018 Conference on Land and Poverty, Washington, DC.

Munshifwa, E. K., Chileshe, R. A., & Jain, N. (2020). Evolution of customary land tenure institutions in Zambia: The Case of Lufwanyama District in the Copperbelt Province. *Agrarian South - the Journal of Political Economy*, *9*(2), 117–143.

Mushinge, A., & Mwando, S. (2016). Implications of pro-market land policies on customary land users in Zambia: A case of large-scale land investments in Kaindu chiefdom, Mumbwa district. *International Journal of Social Science Studies*, *4*(8), 9. doi:10.11114/ijsss.v4i8.1585

Mushinge, A., Simposya, A. M., & Chowa, S. (2020). Threats of statutory tenure on customary land in Zambia: Evidence from Chamuka Chiefdom in Chisamba District. *African Journal on Land Policy and Geospatial Sciences*, *3*(1), 41–52.

Mwansa, S., Shaikh, J., & Mubanga, P. (2020). Special Economic Zones: An evaluation of Lusaka South-Multi Facility Economic Zone. *Journal of Social and Political Sciences*, *3*(2), 523–539. doi:10.31014/aior.1991.03.02.188

Myhra, L. (2011). It runs in the family: Intergenerational transmission of historical trauma among urban American Indians and Alaska natives in culturally specific sobriety maintenance programs. *American Indian and Alaska Native Mental Health Research Journal*, *18*(2), 17–40. doi:10.5820/aian.1802.2011.17 PMID:22302280

Na'puti, T. R., & Bevacqua, M. L. (2015). Militarization and resistance from Guåhan: Protecting and defending Pågat. *American Quarterly*, *67*(3), 837–858.

Nam, Y., Roehrig, G., Kern, A., & Reynolds, B. (2013). Perceptions and practices of culturally relevant science teaching in American Indian classrooms. *International Journal of Science and Mathematics Education*, *11*(1), 143–167. doi:10.100710763-012-9372-x

National Center for Education Statistics. (2011). *Trends in high school drop out and completion rates in the United States, 1972-2009*. Author.

National Center for Education Statistics. (2012). National Indian Education Study 2011. *National Assessment of Educational Progress*, *2012*, 1–64.

National Center for Education Statistics. (2014). *The condition of education 2014*. https://files.eric.ed.gov/fulltext/ED545122.pdf

National Center for Education Statistics. (2015). *NAEP 2015 mathematics & reading at grade 12*. https://www.nationsreportcard.gov/reading_math_g12_2015/#reading

National Center for Education Statistics. (2016a). *The condition of education 2016*. https://nces.ed.gov/pubs2016/2016144_ataglance.pdf

National Center for Education Statistics. (2016b). *Trends in high school dropout and completion rates in the United States: 2013*. https://nces.ed.gov/pubs2016/2016117rev.pdf

National Geographic. (2014). *Being Gullah or Geechee, once looked down upon, now a treasured heritage*. Retrieved from https://news.nationalgeographic.com/news/2014/10/141017-gullah-geechee-heritage-corridor-lowcountry-coast-sea-islands-sweetgrass/

National Public Radio. (2000). *Porgy and Bess*. Retrieved from https://www.npr.org/2000/10/08/1112186/porgy-and-bess

National Public Radio. (2012). *When did kumbaya become such a bad thing?* Retrieved from https://www.npr.org/2012/01/13/145059502/when-did-kumbaya-become-such-a-bad-thing

National Public Radio. (2017). *Ranky Tanky builds on the music and culture of slave descendants*. Retrieved from https://www.npr.org/2019/07/26/745583378/ranky-tanky-builds-on-the-music-and-culture-of-slave-descendants

Native American Languages Act, S.2167, 101st Cong. (1990). https://www.congress.gov/bill/101st-congress/senate-bill/2167

Native American Rights Fund. (2016, October 12). *About peacemaking - Robert Yazzie* [Video]. YouTube.

Nazroo, J. Y. (2003). The structuring of ethnic inequalities in health: Economic position, racial discrimination, and racism. *American Journal of Public Health*, *93*(2), 277–284. doi:10.2105/AJPH.93.2.277 PMID:12554585

Ndenje-Sichalwe, E., & Ngulube, P. (2009). Records management and access to information: Key to fostering accountability, good governance and protection of human rights in Tanzania. *ESARBICA Journal*, *28*(1), 28. doi:10.4314/esarjo.v28i1.44394

Nebelkopf, E., King, J., Wright, S., Schweigman, K., Lucero, E., Habte-Michael, T., ... Cervantes, T. (2011). Growing roots: Native American evidenced-based practices. *Journal of Psychoactive Drugs*, *43*, 263–268. doi:10.1080/02791072.2011.628909 PMID:22400455

Negi, R. (2014). 'Solwezi Mabanga': Ambivalent developments on Zambia's new mining frontier. *Journal of Southern African Studies*, *40*(5), 999–1013. doi:10.1080/03057070.2014.946215

Netshakhuma, N. S. (2018). Assessing the appraisal, disposal and transfer of records from 1994 to 2014: The case of Mpumalanga provincial government in South Africa. *Mousaion*, *36*(2), 1–20.

Netshakhuma, S. N. (2017). The role of archives on the incorporation of the former Kangwane homeland into Mpumalanga province. *Africanus*, *47*(2), 1–16.

Newton, X. A. (2016). Striking a balance: A mixed-methods approach to impact-oriented evaluation. *Studies in Educational Evaluation*, *51*, 96–107. doi:10.1016/j.stueduc.2016.10.005

Ngoepe, M., & Makhubela, S. (2015). Justice delayed is justice denied. *Records Management Journal*, *25*(3), 288–305. doi:10.1108/RMJ-06-2015-0023

Ngulube, P. (2009). Preserving South Africa's paper trail and making records available for present and future generations. *ESARBICA Journal*, *26*, 45–69.

Nguni, C. (2020). Chibombo economic zone shaping up. *Zambia Daily Mail*. http://www.daily-mail.co.zm/chibombo-economic-zone-shaping-up/

Nicolaidis, C., & Raymaker, D. M. (2015). Community based participatory research with communities defined by race, ethnicity, and disability: Translating theory to practice. In *The SAGE handbook of action research* (pp. 167–178). SAGE. doi:10.4135/9781473921290.n17

Ningewance Nadeau, P., & Valentine, J. R. (2013). *Western Ojibwe dictionary*. [Software].

Nolasco, R. M. (n.d.). *Proto-Austronesian transitivity revisited: Reviewing the Philippine evidence*. http://citeseerx.ist.psu.edu/viewdoc/download?doi=10.1.1.557.5948&rep=rep1&type=pdf

Nolte, K. (2014). Large-scale agricultural investments under poor land governance in Zambia. *Land Use Policy*, *38*, 698–706. doi:10.1016/j.landusepol.2014.01.014

Norman, T. S. J., & Dakshinamurthy, V. (2004). *A case study of Paliyar Tribe of Sirumalai Hills*. The Gandhigram Rural Institute.

Novins, D., Boyd, M., Brotherton, D., Fickenscher, A., Moore, L., & Spicer, P. (2012). Walking on: Celebrating the journeys of Native American adolescents with substance use problems on the winding road to healing. *Journal of Psychoactive Drugs*, *44*(2), 153–159. doi:10.1080/02791072.2012.684628 PMID:22880543

Nsibirwa, Z., Hoskins, R., & Stilwell, C. (2014). Building the South African nation through legal deposit: The impact of legislation on preservation of digital materials. *African Journal of Library Archives and Information Science*, *24*(1), 53–65.

Nugent, T. (2003, January 25). Tribal colleges a study in success. *Canku Ota, 79*, Article 6. Retrieved from http://www.turtletrack.org/Issues03/Co01252003/CO_01252003_New.htm

O'Leary, A. O., & Romero, A. J. (2010). *Chicano/o students' engagement with Arizona's "anti-ethnic studies" Bill 1108: Civic engagement, ethnic identity and well-being*. http://arizona.openrepository.com/arizona/bitstream/10150/219215/1/MASWP35.pdf

O'Loughlin, M. (2009). A psychoanalytic exploration of collective trauma among Indigenous Australians and a suggestion for intervention. *Australasian Psychiatry*, *17*(1, suppl), S33–S36. doi:10.1080/10398560902948746 PMID:19579103

Obidzinski, K., Takahashi, I., Dermawan, A., Komarudin, H., & Andrianto, A. (2013). Can large scale land acquisition for agro-development in Indonesia be managed sustainably? *Land Use Policy*, *30*(1), 952–965. doi:10.1016/j.landusepol.2012.06.018

Object. (n.d.). In *Merriam-Webster Dictionary*. www.merriam-webster.com/dictionary/object

Ochiai, A. (2001). The Port Royal Experiment revisited: Northern visions of Reconstruction and the land question. *The New England Quarterly*, *74*(1), 94–117. doi:10.2307/3185461

Office of Minority Health. (2018, March 28). *Profile: American Indian/Alaska Native*. https://minorityhealth.hhs.gov/omh/browse.aspx?lvl=3&lvlid=62

Ogbu, J. U. (1990). Minority education in comparative perspective. *The Journal of Negro Education*, *59*(1), 45–57. doi:10.2307/2295291

Ogunwole, S., Drewery, M., & Rios-Vargas, M. (2012). *The population With a bachelor's degree or higher by race and Hispanic origin: 2006-2010*. American Community Survey Briefs. https://www.census.gov/prod/2012pubs/acsbr10-19.pdf

Omar, H. (2013). *The development of sustainable cultural heritage tourism in Malaysia: Implication for planning and management*. Retrieved from http://etd.uum.edu.my/3595/

Ostler, J. (2016). 'Just and lawful war' as genocidal war in the (United States) Northwest Ordinance and Northwest Territory, 1787-1832. *Journal of Genocide Research, 18*(1), 1–20. doi:10.1080/14623528.2016.1120460

Oweghoro, B. M. (2015). Health Records Retention and Disposal in Nigerian Hospitals: Survey of Policies, Practices and Procedures. *African Journal of Library Archives and Information Science*, *25*(1).

Pacheco, C. M., Daley, S. M., Brown, T., Filippi, M., Greiner, K. A., & Daley, C. M. (2013). Moving forward: Breaking the cycle of Mistrust between American Indians and researchers. *American Journal of Public Health*, *103*(12), 2152–2159. doi:10.2105/AJPH.2013.301480 PMID:24134368

Papanek, J. L. (Ed.). (1994). *Cycles of life*. Time-Life Inc.

Papa, R. D., & Briones, J. C. (2014). Climate and human-induced changes to lake ecosystems: What we can learn from monitoring zooplankton ecology. *Journal of Environmental Science and Management*, *17*(1).

Paterno, M. P., & Oshima, N. M. (2001). *Dreamweavers*. Bookmark.

PattonM. J. (2002). *Qualitative research & evaluation methods*. SAGE.

Pearce, D., & Atkinson, G. (n.d.). *The concept of sustainable development: An evaluation of its usefulness ten years after Brundtland*. Retrieved from https://pdfs.semanticscholar.org/a986/23c43d6de44735ec6232b1fa208ec7281d50.pdf

Peek, M. (2013). Kinship flows in Brandy Nālani McDougall's *The Salt-Wind/Ka Makani Pa'akai. Feminist Review*, *103*, 80–98.

Pember, M. A. (2008). *Tribal colleges stay true to mission*. Retrieved from http://diverseeducation.com/article/11509/tribal-colleges-stay-true-to-mission.html

Pereira, L. (2011). *Eco Parque Municipal do Seringueiro: Ecologia do abandono*. Luiz Pereira Fala.

Pereira, R. (2018). Assessing the implementation of the National Archives and Records Services Act at Eduardo Mondlane University in Mozambique. *ESARBICA Journal*, *37*, 221–244.

Perez, C. S. (2015). *The poetics of mapping diaspora, navigating culture, and being from (Part 1)*. Doveglion Press. Retrieved July 20, 2019, from http://www.doveglion.com/page/2/?s=Craig+Santos+Perez%3A+The+Poetics+of+Mapping+Diaspora%2C+Navigating+Culture%2C+and+Being+From+&submit=Search...#038;submit=Search

Perez, C. S. (2019). Poet to poet interview: Rajiv Mohabir and Craig Santos Perez. *Kenyon Review*. Retrieved from https://www.kenyonreview.org/2019/02/poet-to-poet-interview-rajiv-mohabir-and-craig-santos-perez/

Perez, C. S. (2008). *From unincorporated territory* [Hacha]. Kaneohe, HI: Tin Fish Press.

Perez, C. S. (2015). Transterritorial currents and the imperial terripelago. *American Quarterly*, *67*(3), 619–624.

Perna, L. W. (2000). Differences in the decision to attend college among African Americans, Hispanics, and Whites. *The Journal of Higher Education*, *71*(2), 117–141. doi:10.2307/2649245

Pienaar, J. M. (2015). Land reform embedded in the constitution: Legal contextualisation. *Scriptura*, *114*, 1–20. doi:10.7833/114-0-1116

Pihama, L., Smith, L. T., Evans-Campbell, T., Kohu-Morgan, H., Cameron, N., Mataki, T., Te Nana, R., Skipper, H., & Southey, K. (2017). Investigating Māori approaches to trauma-informed care. *Journal of Indigenous Wellbeing: Te Mauri-Pimatisiwin*, *2*(3), 18–31.

Place, F., & Otsuka, K. (2002). Land tenure systems and their impacts on agricultural investments and productivity in Uganda. *The Journal of Development Studies*, *38*(6), 105–128. doi:10.1080/00220380412331322601

Plácido de Castro. (n.d.). Histórico. *Prefeitura de Plácido de Castro.*

PleasantD. (n.d.). *David Pleasant.* Retrieved from http://www.davidpleasant1.com/

Polkinghorne, D. E. (1988). *Narrative knowing and the human sciences.* SUNY Press.

Porras, R. E., & Buot, I. E. (2016). Profiling Lake Sebu and the indigenous community in the vicinity. *Journal of Wetlands Biodiversity, 6*, 85–96.

Powers, M. (1932). The Indian as peacemaker. Fleming H. Revell Company.

Pranis, K., Stuart, B., & Wedge, M. (2003). *Peacemaking circles: From crime to community.* Living Justice Press.

Pugliese, J. (2007). Geocorpographies of torture. *Australian Critical Race and Whiteness Studies Association Journal, 3*(1), 1–18.

Pugliese, J. (2015). Geopolitics of Aboriginal sovereignty: Colonial law as 'a species of excess of its own authority', Aboriginal passport ceremonies and asylum seekers. *Law Text Culture, 19*, 84–115.

Quijada Cerecer, P. D. (2013). The policing of Native bodies and minds: Perspectives on schooling from American Indian youth. *American Journal of Education, 119*(4), 591–616. doi:10.1086/670967

Quinn, A. (2007). Reflections on intergenerational trauma: Healing as a critical intervention. *First Peoples Child & Family Review, 3*(4), 72–82. doi:10.7202/1069377ar

Quizon, C. (2019). The weaver's house: Ethnography, translation, and video in the highlands of Mindanao. *Visual Anthropology Review, 35*(2), 148–161. doi:10.1111/var.12189

Raphael, B., Swan, P., & Martinek, N. (1998). Intergenerational aspects of trauma for Australian Aboriginal people. International handbook of multigenerational legacies of trauma, 327-339.

Ratner, C. (1999). Three approaches to cultural psychology; A critique. *Cultural Dynamics, 11*(1), 7–31. doi:10.1177/092137409901100102

Ratner, C. (2006). Contextualism and Positivism in Cross-Cultural psychology. In G. Zheng, K. Leung, & J. Adair (Eds.), *Perspective and progress in contemporary cross-cultural Psychology* (pp. 35–48). Light Industry Press.

Ratner, C. (2007). A macro cultural-psychological theory of emotions. In P. Schultz & R. Pekrun (Eds.), *Emotions in Education* (pp. 85–100). Academic Press. doi:10.1016/B978-012372545-5/50007-1

Ratner, C. (2008). Methodological individuism and holism. In L. Given (Ed.), *SAGE encyclopedia of qualitative research methods.* SAGE.

Ratner, C. (2009). The cultural psychology of oppression and liberation. *Journal of Social Distress and the Homeless, 18*(3-4), 213–268. doi:10.1179/105307809805365190

Ratner, C. (2011). Macro Cultural Psychology, The psychology of oppression, and cultural-psychological enrichment. In P. Portes & S. Salas (Eds.), *Vygotsky in 21st century: Advances in cultural historical theory and praxis with non-dominant communities.* Peter Lang.

Ratner, C., & Hui, L. (2003). Theoretical and methodological problems in cross-cultural psychology. *Journal for the Theory of Social Behaviour, 33*(1), 67–94. doi:10.1111/1468-5914.00206

Recht, J. (2009). Hearing indigenous voices, protecting indigenous knowledge. *International Journal of Cultural Property, 16*(3), 233–254. doi:10.1017/S0940739109990166

Reed, D. V. (2016, October 26). *Society for the preservation of spirituals.* Retrieved from https://www.scencyclopedia.org/sce/entries/society-for-the-preservation-of-spirituals/

Reed, D. K., Sorrells, A. M., Cole, H. A., & Takakawa, N. N. (2013). The ecological and population validity of reading interventions for adolescents: Can effectiveness be generalized? *Learning Disability Quarterly, 36*(3), 131–144. doi:10.1177/0731948712451976

Reha, B. (2007). *Tribal colleges offer specialized education.* Retrieved from https://minnesota.publicradio.org/display/web/2006/12/01/tribalcolleges/

Reid, L. (2019). The reconstruction of a dual pronoun to Proto Malayo-Polynesian. In B. Evans (Ed.), *Discovering history through language: Papers in honour of Malcolm Ross* (pp. 461–477). Pacific Linguistics.

Reyes, N., & Shotton, H. (2019). *Association for the study of higher education. Retrieved from Southwest Native American Relief Council.* History & Culture.

Richardson, J. W., & McLeod, S. (2011). Technology leadership in Native American schools. *Journal of Research in Rural Education, 26*(7), 1–14.

Richardson, T. A. (2015). Indigenous methodologies and educational research for meaningful change: Parsing postpositivist philosophy of science and mixed methods in collaborative research settings. *Journal of American Indian Education, 54*(1), 33–62.

Rigal, L. (2009). Watershed days on the Treaty Line, 1836-1839. *The Iowa Review*, 202-223.

Riley, G. (1977). Images of the frontierswoman: Iowa as a case study. *The Western Historical Quarterly, 8*(2), 189–202. doi:10.2307/967250

Riley, G. (1988). *The female frontier: A comparative view of women on the prairie and the plains*. University Press of Kansas.

Riley, G. (1992). *A place to grow: Women in the American West.* Harlan Davidson.

Robbins, J. A., & Dewar, J. (2011). Traditional Indigenous approaches to healing and the modern welfare of traditional knowledge, spirituality and lands: A critical reflection on practices and policies taken from the Canadian Indigenous example. *International Indigenous Policy Journal,* 2(4). Advance online publication. doi:10.18584/iipj.2011.2.4.2

Roman, L. G., Gobbi, R. D. P., Beaudry, J. S., & Blackbridge, P. (2020). Rippling excesses: A/r/tography becoming dis/a/r/tography. *International Journal of Art, 16*(1), 63–82. doi:10.1386/eta_00017_1

Romero, C. (2002). Envisioning a" network of tribal coalitions": Leslie Marmon Silko's Almanac of the dead. *American Indian Quarterly, 26*(4), 623–640. doi:10.1353/aiq.2004.0008

Ross, R. (1996). *Returning to the teachings: Exploring Aboriginal justice*. Penguin Canada.

Rowe, J. C. (2015). Transpacific studies and the cultures of US imperialism. In Y. Shu & D. E. Pease (Eds.), *American studies as transnational practice: Turning toward the transpacific* (pp. 259–275). Hanover, NH: Dartmouth College Press.

Rowland-Klein, D., & Dunlop, R. (1998). The transmission of trauma across generations: Identification with parental trauma in children of Holocaust survivors. *The Australian and New Zealand Journal of Psychiatry, 32*(3), 358–369. doi:10.3109/00048679809065528 PMID:9672725

Roy Burman, B. K. (1960). Basic concepts of tribal welfare and tribal integration. In L. P. Vidyarthi (Ed.), *Indian anthropology in action*. Ranchi University.

Ruffo, A. G. (2009). Exposing the poison, staunching the wound: Applying Aboriginal healing theory to literary analysis. *The Canadian Journal of Native Studies*, *29*(1/2), 91–110.

Russell, L. (2005). Indigenous knowledge and archives: Accessing hidden history and understandings. *Australian Academic and Research Libraries*, *36*(2), 161–171. doi:10.1080/00048623.2005.10721256

Russell, L. R., & Cuevas, J. (2014). Designing customizable reading modules for a high school literature classroom. *TechTrends*, *58*(5), 71–80. doi:10.100711528-014-0788-8

Sameroff, A. (2010). A unified theory of development: A dialectic integration of nature and nurture. *Child Development*, *81*(1), 6–22. doi:10.1111/j.1467-8624.2009.01378.x PMID:20331651

Sarche, M., & Whitesell, N. (2012). Child development research in North American native communities: Looking back and moving forward: Introduction. *Child Development Perspectives*, *6*(1), 42–48. doi:10.1111/j.1750-8606.2011.00218.x

Sarmiento, B. S. (2013, Mar. 10). A paradise lost. Lake Sebu, South Cotabato. *Mindanews*.

Sawchuck, C. N., Roy-Byrne, P., Goldberg, J., Manson, S., Noonan, C., Beals, J., & Buchwald, D. (2005). The relationship between post- traumatic stress disorder, depression, and cardiovascular disease in an American Indian tribe. *Psychological Medicine*, *35*(12), 1785–1794. doi:10.1017/S0033291705005751 PMID:16300692

Schcolnik, M., Kol, S., & Abarbanel, J. (2006). Constructivism in theory and in practice. *English Teaching Forum*, *44*(4), 12-20.

Schraufnagel, T. J., Wagner, A. W., Miranda, J., & Roy-Byrne, P. P. (2006). Treating minority patients with depression and anxiety: What does the evidence tell us? *General Hospital Psychiatry*, *28*(1), 27–36. doi:10.1016/j.genhosppsych.2005.07.002 PMID:16377362

Schuman, H., Schwartz, B., & d'Arcy, H. (2005). Elite revisionists and popular beliefs: Christopher Columbus, hero or villain? *Public Opinion Quarterly*, *69*(1), 2–29. doi:10.1093/poq/nfi001

Schure, M., Odden, M., & Goins, T. (2013). The association of resilience with mental and physical health among older American Indians: The native elder care study. *American Indian and Alaska Native Mental Health Research*, *20*(2), 27–41. doi:10.5820/aian.2002.2013.27 PMID:23824641

Segaetsho, T., & Mnjama, N. (2012). Preservation of library materials at the University of Botswana Library. *Journal of the South African Society of Archivists*, *45*, 68–84.

Senado Federal. (2009). *O tratado de limites Brasil-Peru*. Senado Federal, Conselho Editorial.

Sered, D. (2019). *Until we Reckon: Violence, mass incarceration, and a road to repair*. The New Press.

Siachitema, B. (2016). *Protecting Rural Zambian Communities from Displacement Resulting from Land-Based Investment*. https://www.southernafricalitigationcentre.org/wp-content/uploads/2017/08/GOAL-16-Book-Siachitema.pdf

Silove, D., Austin, P., & Steel, Z. (2007). No refuge from terror: The impact of detention on the mental health of trauma-affected refugees seeking asylum in Australia. *Transcultural Psychiatry*, *44*(3), 359–393. doi:10.1177/1363461507081637 PMID:17938152

Silva, F. B., Souza, J. A., & Messina, M. (2017). Contentious narratives in Amazonian cities along the Brazil–Bolivia border: Memories and resentments turned heroic and glorious. *Bitácora Arquitectura*, (36), 130–137. doi:10.22201/fa.14058901p.2017.36.62277

Simard, E. (2020). Critical Indigenous ways of knowing: Research, narratives, and self-actualisation. *International Journal of Critical Indigenous Studies*, *13*(2), 135–153. https://ijcis.qut.edu.au/article/view/1636/1002

Sinclair, R. (2004). Aboriginal social work education in Canada: Decolonizing pedagogy for the seventh generation. *First Peoples Child & Family Review, 1*(1), 49–62. doi:10.7202/1069584ar

Sitko, N. J., & Jayne, T. S. (2014). Structural transformation or elite land capture? The growth of "emergent" farmers in Zambia. *Food Policy, 48*, 194–202. doi:10.1016/j.foodpol.2014.05.006

Skelcher, B. (2003). Apartheid and the removal of black spots from Lake Bhangazi in KwaZulu-Natal, South Africa. *Journal of Black Studies, 33*(6), 761–783. doi:10.1177/0021934703033006003

Slivka, K. (2011). Art, craft, and assimilation: Curriculum for Native students during the boarding school era. *Studies in Art Education: A Journal of Issues and Research, 52*(3), 225-242.

Smith, A., & O'Connor, S. (Eds.). (2018). *Hearth: A global conversation on community, identity, and place*. Milkweed Editions.

Smith, L. T. (2013). *Decolonizing methodologies: Research and indigenous peoples*. Zed Books.

South Africa National Parks. (2019). *Annual report 2018/19*. Author.

South, T. (2019). Marine corps plan to relocate from Okinawa to Guam needs a review, Commandant says. *Marine Corps Times*, 3. Retrieved from https://www.marinecorpstimes.com/news/your-marine-corps/2019/05/03/marine-corps-relocation-from-okinawa-to-guam-worthy-of-review-commandant-says/

Souza, J. A. (2020). Os Huni Kuin e a luta contra o colonialismo de Estado na fronteira acreana. *Muiraquitã, 9*(1).

Souza, J. A., & Messina, M. (2018). Narrativas contenciosas na fronteira das Amazônias Boliviana e Brasileira. *Revista Igarapé, 5*(2), 332–349.

Specht, J. (n.d.). *Indian genealogical records volume 1: Lake Nipigon, Michipicoten, Grand Portage, Wikwemikong*. Academic Press.

Springgay, S., Irwin, R. L., & Wilson, S. (2005). A/r/tography as living inquiry through art and text. *Qualitative Inquiry, 11*(6), 897–912. doi:10.1177/1077800405280696

St. Germaine, R. (1995). *Drop-out rates among American Indian and Alaska native students: Beyond cultural discounted*. Academic Press.

Starna, W. (2008). Retrospecting the origins of the league of the Iroquois. *Proceedings of the American Philosophical Society, 152*, 279–321. PMID:19831230

State Historical Society of Iowa. (1970). *Studies in Iowa History: Iowa: The home for immigrants*. State Historical Society of Iowa.

Steel, Z., Silove, D., Phan, T., & Bauman, A. (2002). Long-term effect of psychological trauma on the mental health of Vietnamese refugees resettled in Australia: A population-based study. *Lancet, 360*(9339), 1056–1062. doi:10.1016/S0140-6736(02)11142-1 PMID:12383986

Steiner, C. E. (2015). A sea of warriors: Performing an identity of resilience and empowerment in the face of climate change in the Pacific. *The Contemporary Pacific, 27*(1), 147–180.

Stewart, T., Throne, R., & Evans, L. (2020). A critical review of gender parity and voice dispossession among executive women in higher education leadership. In G. Berg & L. Venis (Eds.), *Accessibility and diversity in the 21st century university*. IGI Global. doi:10.4018/978-1-7998-2783-2.ch005

Stillwell, R., & Sable, J. (2013). *Public school graduates and dropouts from the common core of data: School year 2009-10: First look (Provisional data).* https://nces.ed.gov/pubsearch

Strand, J. A., & Peacock, T. D. (2003). Nurturing resilience and schools success in American Indian and Alaska Native students. *The International Child and Youth Care Network.* Retrieved from http://www.cyc-net.org/cyc-online/cycol-1203-resilience.html

Strong, P. T., & Van Winkle, B. (1996). "Indian Blood": Reflections on the Reckoning and Refiguring of Native North American Identity. *Cultural Anthropology, 6*(4), 547–557. doi:10.1525/can.1996.11.4.02a00050

Stumbling-Riddle, G., & Romans, J. (2012). Resilience among urban American Indian adolescents: Exploration into the role of culture, self-esteem, subjective well- being, and social support. *American Indian and Alaska Native Mental Health Research, 19*(2), 1–19. doi:10.5820/aian.1902.2012.1 PMID:22875470

Sundararaju, V. (2018). Neelakurinji: Blue bloom in a blue moon. *Down To Earth.* Retrieved from https://www.downtoearth.org.in/blog/environment/neelakurinji-blue-bloom-in-a-blue-moon-61295

Sundqvist, A. (2017). Archival mediation: Studying users' interaction with access systems. In A. J. Gilliland, S. McKemmish, & J. A. Lau (Eds.), *Research in the archival Multiverse.* Monash University.

Swisher, K. G., & Tippeconic, J. W., III. (Eds.). (1999). *Next Steps, Research and Practice to Advance Indian Education.* Charleston, WV: ERIC.

Szasz, M. C. (2005). "I knew how to be moderate. And I knew how to obey": The commonality of American Indian boarding school experiences, 1750s-1920s. *American Indian Culture and Research Journal, 29*(4), 75–94. doi:10.17953/aicr.29.4.b2220582h05507u2

Tafoya, T., & Kouris, N. (2003). Dancing the circle: Native American concepts of healing. *Modern psychology and ancient wisdom: Psychological healing practices from the world's religious traditions*, 125-146.

Tambs, L. A. (1966). Rubber, rebels, and Rio Branco: The contest for the acre. *The Hispanic American Historical Review, 46*(3), 254–273. doi:10.1215/00182168-46.3.254

Tann, S., Yabiku, S., Okamoto, S., & Yanow, J. (2007). Triadd: The risk for alcohol abuse, depression, and diabetes multimorbidity in the American Indian and Alaska Native population. *American Indian and Alaska Native Mental Health Research, 14*(1), 1–23. doi:10.5820/aian.1401.2007.5 PMID:17602410

Tavuyanago, B. (2017). Our fathers and grandfathers were born here..." Shangaan eviction experiences from the Gonarezhou National Park, 1957-1968. *Historia (Wiesbaden, Germany), 62*(2), 46–67.

Teicher, S. A. (2006). *Nurturing Native Americans on campus.* Retrieved from https://www.csmonitor.com/2006/0222/p14s01-legn.html

Teuton, S. K. (2008). *Red Land, Red Power.* Duke University Press.

Thebe, T. P. (2016). Community participation: Reality and rhetoric in the development and implementation of the Integrated Development Plan (IDP) within municipalities of South Africa. *Journal of Public Administration, 51*(4), 712–723.

TheDRCA2. (2015, May 1). *Kay pranis: Using peacemaking circles in juvenile court, 4/22/2015* [Video]. YouTube.

Thompson, M. (2001). *Charles Lummis: Native American Rights Crusader.* Retrieved from http://www.charleslummis.com/Native Americanrights.htm

Thornton, R. (2003). Repatriation as healing the wounds of the trauma of history: Cases of Native Americans in the United States of America. In *The dead and their possessions* (pp. 35–42). Routledge.

Thrane, L., Whitbeck, L., Hoyt, D., & Shelley, M. (2004). Comparing three measures of depressive symptoms among American Indian adolescents. *American Indian and Alaska Native Mental Health Research, 11*(3), 20–43. doi:10.5820/aian.1103.2004.20 PMID:15536587

Throne, R. (2018a). The letter: Fidelity in researcher positionality to exhume dispossessed voices for Leavy's concept of coherence in feminist narrative research. *Gender and Women's Studies, 2*(1). Retrieved from http://riverapublications.com/journal/gender-womens-studies

Throne, R. (2019). Autoethnography and heuristic inquiry for doctoral-level researchers: Emerging research and opportunities. Hershey, PA: IGI Global.

Throne, R. (2012). Positionality. In *Practitioner research in doctoral education* (pp. 55–77). Kendall Hunt.

Throne, R. (2018b). Hermeneutic archival research & artistic license: Exhuming dispossessed Sauk voices through creative non-fiction. In *14th Annual International Congress of Qualitative Inquiry*. University of Illinois.

Throne, R. (2020). Dispossession of land cultures: Women and property tenure among Lowcountry heirs in the Gullah Geechee Corridor. In U. Onyebadi (Ed.), *Multidisciplinary issues surrounding African Diasporas* (pp. 152–174). IGI Global. doi:10.4018/978-1-5225-5079-2.ch007

Thurston, A. (2015). Access to reliable public records as evidence for freedom of information in Commonwealth Africa. *The Round Table, 104*(6), 703–713. doi:10.1080/00358533.2015.1112095

Thurston, E. (1909). *Castes and tribes of southern India* (Vol. 3). Government Press.

Tian, W., Zhou, Z., Ma, X., Heerink, N., van Ierland, E., van den Berg, M., & Shi, X. (2013). Land tenure security and land investments in Northwest China. *China Agricultural Economic Review, 5*(2), 281–307. doi:10.1108/17561371311331133

Tierney, W. G. (1992). An anthropological analysis of student participation in college. *The Journal of Higher Education, 63*(6), 603–618. doi:10.2307/1982046

Torpy, S. J. (2000). Native American women and coerced sterilization: On the Trail of Tears in the 1970s. *American Indian Culture and Research Journal, 24*(2), 1–22. doi:10.17953/aicr.24.2.7646013460646042

Toulmin, C. (2009). Securing land and property rights in sub-Saharan Africa: The role of local institutions. *Land Use Policy, 26*(1), 10–19. doi:10.1016/j.landusepol.2008.07.006

Trafzer, C. E., Keller, J. A., & Sisquoc, L. (Eds.). (2006). *Boarding school blues: Revisiting American Indian educational experience*. University of Nebraska Press.

Trembinski, D. (2011). Comparing premodern melancholy/mania and modern trauma: An argument in favor of historical experiences of trauma. *History of Psychology, 14*(1), 80–99. doi:10.1037/a0020430 PMID:21688753

Triandis, H. C., Malpass, R. S., & Davidson, A. R. (1973). Psychology and culture. *Annual Review of Psychology, 24*(1), 355–378. doi:10.1146/annurev.ps.24.020173.002035

Trimble, J., & Clearing-Sky, M. (2009). An historical profile of American Indians and Alaska Natives in psychology. *Cultural Diversity & Ethnic Minority Psychology, 15*(4), 338–351. doi:10.1037/a0015112 PMID:19916669

Truth and Reconciliation Commission of Canada. (2015, December). *Honouring the truth, reconciling for the future: Summary of the final report of the Truth and Reconciliation Commission of Canada.* http://www.trc.ca/assets/pdf/Executive_Summary_English_Web.pdf

Truth and Reconciliation Commission. (2015). *Honouring the truth, reconciling for the future.* Summary of the final report of the Truth and Reconciliation Commission of Canada.

Turgut, G. (2012). A case study on use of one-to-one laptops in English as second language classrooms. *Turkish Online Journal of Qualitative Inquiry*, *3*(4), 32–51.

Turner, S., & Pope, M. (2009). North America's native peoples: A social justice and trauma counseling approach. *Journal of Multicultural Counseling and Development*, *37*(4), 194–205. doi:10.1002/j.2161-1912.2009.tb00102.x

U.S. Senate. (1969). *Indian education: A national tragedy—A national challenge*. Special Subcommittee on Indian Education of the Committee on Labor and Public Welfare, Senate Report No. 91-501. Washington, DC: U.S. Government Printing Office.

UNHABITAT. (2017). *Monitoring tenure security, data collection questionnaire modules and manual: Cameroon, Nigeria and Kenya*. GLII Working Paper No. 6 /2017.

United Nations Development Programme. (2003). *Country level impact assessment: The Philippines*. http://web.undp.org/evaluation/documents/CLIA-Philippines.pdf

University of California Television (UCTV). (2008, January 31). *Reconciling love: Archbishop Desmond Tutu* [Video]. YouTube.

Unrau, N. J., & Quirk, M. (2014). Reading motivation and reading engagement: Clarifying commingled conceptions. *Reading Psychology*, *35*(3), 260–284. doi:10.1080/02702711.2012.684426

Ursano, R. J., Grieger, T. A., & McCarroll, J. E. (1996). *Prevention of posttraumatic stress: Consultation, training, and early treatment*. Guilford Press.

Uslu Ustten, A., & Pilav, A. (2014). A research on high school students' reading interests and habits. *Journal of Theory and Practice in Education*, *10*(4), 764–782.

Valiandes, S. (2015). Evaluating the impact of differentiated instruction on literacy and reading in mixed ability classrooms: Quality and equity dimensions of education effectiveness. *Studies in Educational Evaluation*, *45*, 17–26. doi:10.1016/j.stueduc.2015.02.005

Van Dalsen, A. (2017). *Land reform: Presidential policy statements on expropriation without compensation*. https://hsf.org.za/resource-centre/hsf-briefs/landreform-presidential-policy-statement

Van Dijk, T. A. (2000). New(s) racism: A discourse analytical approach. *Ethnic Minorities and the Media*, *37*, 33–49.

Vansina, J. M. (1985). *Oral tradition as history*. University of Wisconsin Press.

Verbos, A. K., Gladstone, J. S., & Kennedy, D. M. (2011). Native American values and management education: Envisioning an inclusive virtuous circle. *Journal of Management Education*, *35*(1), 10–26. doi:10.1177/1052562910384364

Vizenor, G. (2008). *Survivance: Narratives of native presence*. Lincoln, NE: University of Nebraska Press.

Vygotsky, L. (1978). *Mind in society*. Harvard University Press.

Waldram, J. (2013). Healing history? Aboriginal healing, historical trauma, and personal Responsibility. *Transcultural Psychiatry*, *0*, 1–17. PMID:23788570

Wallace, M. (2019). *Timeless traditions: Council circles in a modern world*. Washington State University. http://hdl.handle.net/2376/14211

Wallace, J. M., Goodkind, S., Wallace, C. M., & Bachman, J. G. (2008). Racial, ethnic, and gender differences in school discipline among US high school students: 1991-2005. *Negro Educational Review*, *59*(1-2), 47. PMID:19430541

Walls, M., & Whitbeck, L. (2013). The intergenerational effects of relocation policies on ingenious families. *Journal of Family Issues, 33*(9), 1272–1293. doi:10.1177/0192513X12447178 PMID:23024447

Wamukoya, M. J. (2015). Reflections on African archives: Their role in meeting societal needs in the 21st century. *Journal of the South African Society of Archivists, 48*, 14–20.

Wanberg, K. (2013). Pedagogy against the state: The ban on ethnic studies in Arizona. *Journal of Pedagogy, 4*(1), 15–35. doi:10.2478/jped-2013-0002

Wang, H., Riedinger, J., & Jin, S. (2015). Land documents, tenure security and land rental development: Panel evidence from China. *China Economic Review, 36*, 220–235. doi:10.1016/j.chieco.2015.09.005

Ward, A. (2013). Understanding postcolonial traumas. *Journal of Theoretical and Philosophical Psychology, 33*(3), 170–184. doi:10.1037/a0033576

Watts, J. (2003). *Native American students.* Retrieved from http://www.montana.edu/teachlearn/Papers/Native%20 American.pdf

Watts, V. (2013). Indigenous place-thought and agency amongst humans and non humans (First Woman and Sky Woman go on a European world tour!). *Decolonization, 2*(1). https://jps.library.utoronto.ca/index.php/des/article/download/19145/16234/

Weaver, H. N. (1998). Indigenous people in a multicultural society: Unique issues for human services. *Social Work, 43*(3), 203–211. doi:10.1093w/43.3.203 PMID:9597944

Weaver, H. N. (2001). Indigenous identity. *American Indian Quarterly, 25*(2), 240–256. doi:10.1353/aiq.2001.0030

Weaver, H. N., & Brave Heart, M. (1999). Examining two facets of American Indian identity: Exposure to other cultures and the influence of historical trauma. *Journal of Human Behavior in the Social Environment, 2*(1-2), 19–33. doi:10.1300/J137v02n01_03

Weiner, E. (2017). How geography shapes our identity. *Transcending Borders.* Retrieved from https://trend.pewtrusts.org/en/archive/trend-summer-2016/foreword-how-geography-shapes-our-identity

Whitbeck, L. (2006). Some guiding assumptions and a theoretical model for developing culturally specific preventions with Native American people. *Journal of Community Psychology, 34*(2), 183–192. doi:10.1002/jcop.20094

Whitbeck, L., Adams, G., Hoyt, D., & Chen, X. (2004). Conceptualizing and measuring historical trauma among American Indian people. *American Journal of Community Psychology, 33*(3-4), 119–130. doi:10.1023/B:AJCP.0000027000.77357.31 PMID:15212173

Whitbeck, L., McMorris, B., Hoyt, D., Stubben, J., & LaFromboise, T. (2002). Perceived discrimination. Traditional practices, and depressive symptoms among American Indians in the upper Midwest. *Journal of Health and Social Behavior, 43*(4), 400–418. doi:10.2307/3090234 PMID:12664673

Whitbeck, L., Walls, M., Johnson, K., Morriseau, A., & McDougall, C. (2009). Depressed affect and historical loss among north American indigenous adolescents. *American Indian and Alaska Native Mental Health Research, 16*(3), 16–41. doi:10.5820/aian.1603.2009.16 PMID:20052631

White Shield, R. (2009). Identifying and understanding indigenous cultural and spiritual strengths in the higher education experiences of indigenous women. *Wicazo Sa Review, 24*(1), 147–163. doi:10.1353/wic.0.0022

Whitinui, P. (2013). Indigenous autoethnography: Exploring, engaging, and experiencing "Self" as a Native method of inquiry. *Journal of Contemporary Ethnography*, 1–32.

WhyteK. P. (2017). What do Indigenous knowledges do for Indigenous Peoples? Retrieved from https://ssrn.com/abstract=2612715

Wigfield, A., & Guthrie, J. T. (2008). *Reading instrument index.* http://www.corilearning.com/measures/REI.pdf

Wigfield, A., & Guthrie, J. T. (1997). Relations of children's motivation for reading to the amount and breadth of their reading. *Journal of Educational Psychology, 89*(3), 420–432. doi:10.1037/0022-0663.89.3.420

Wigfield, A., Guthrie, J. T., Perencevich, K. C., Taboada, A., Klauda, S. L., McRae, A., & Barbosa, P. (2008). Role of reading engagement in mediating effects of reading comprehension instruction on reading outcomes. *Psychology in the Schools, 45*(5), 432–445. doi:10.1002/pits.20307

Wilbur, J. R., Wilbur, M., Garrett, M. T., & Yuhas, M. (2001). Talking circles: Listen, or your tongue will make you deaf. *Journal for Specialists in Group Work, 26*(4), 368–384. doi:10.1080/01933920108413785

Wilder, L., Jackson, A., & Smith, T. (2001). Secondary transition of multicultural learners: Lessons from the Navajo Native American Experience. *Preventing School Failure, 45*(3), 119–124. doi:10.1080/10459880109603326

Williams, K., & Brant, S. (2019). Good words, good food, good mind. *Journal of Agriculture, Food Systems, and Community Development, 9*(B), 1-14.

Williams, R. B. (2007). Tribal colleges: The model for cultural- and Community-based Education Reform. *Diversity.* Retrieved from http://www.diverseeducation.com/artman/publish/article_10287.shtml

Williams, L., Wilson, A., & Thorpe, K. (2006). Identity and access to government records: Empowering the community. *Archives and Manuscripts, 34*(1), 8.

Wilson, S. (2001). What is an Indigenous research methodology? *Canadian Journal of Native Education, 25*(2), 175–179.

Wilson, S. (2008). *Research is ceremony. In Indigenous research methods.* Fernwood.

Wily, L. A. (2010, April). Whose land are you giving away, Mr. President. Proc. of the Annual World Bank Land Policy & Administration Conference.

Wily, L. A. (2011). 'The law is to blame': The vulnerable status of common property rights in sub-Saharan Africa. *Development and Change, 42*(3), 733–757. doi:10.1111/j.1467-7660.2011.01712.x

Winters, A., & America, N. (2014). Using Talking Circles in the classroom. *Heartland Community College*, 1-8.

Wollants, G. (2012). *Gestalt therapy: Therapy of the situation. Sage (Atlanta, Ga.).*

Wood, S., Carbone, K., Cifor, M., Gilliland, A., & Punzalan, R. (2014). Mobilizing records: Re-framing archival description to support human rights. *Archival Science, 14*(3-4), 397–419. doi:10.100710502-014-9233-1

Woodward, V. S. (2013). "I guess they didn't want us asking too many questions": Reading American empire in Guam. *The Contemporary Pacific, 25*(1), 67–91.

World Bank Group. (2018). *Cultural heritage, sustainable tourism and urban regeneration: Capturing lessons and experience from Japan with a focus on Kyoto.* Retrieved from https://documents.worldbank.org/curated/en/938741531140109250/pdf/128058-WP-Kyoto-CHSTUR-postTDD-final-PUBLIC.pdf

Wright, S., Nebelkopf, E., King, J., Maas, M., Patel, C., & Samuel, S. (2011). Holistic system of care: Evidence of effectiveness. *Substance Use & Misuse, 46*(11), 1420–1430. doi:10.3109/10826084.2011.592438 PMID:21810076

Writer, J. H. (2008). Unmasking, exposing, and confronting: Critical race theory, tribal critical race theory and multicultural education. *International Journal of Multicultural Education, 10*(2), 1–15.

Yamut, V. T. (2008). Ritual dances of the T'Boli. *Journal of Higher Education Research, 5*(2).

Yehuda, R., Daskalakis, N., Bierer, L., Bader, H., Klengel, T., Holsboer, F., & Binder, F. (2015). Holocaust exposure induced intergenerational effects on FKBP5 methylation. *Biological Psychiatry*. Advance online publication. doi:10.1016/j.biopsych.2015.08.005 PMID:26410355

Yehuda, R., Halligan, S. L., & Bierer, L. M. (2001). Relationship of parental trauma exposure and PTSD to PTSD, depressive and anxiety disorders in offspring. *Journal of Psychiatric Research, 35*(5), 261–270. doi:10.1016/S0022-3956(01)00032-2 PMID:11591428

Young, R. S., Joe, J. R., Hassin, J., & St. Clair, D. (2001). Addressing psychosocial issues and problems of co-morbidity for Native American clients with substance abuse problems: A conference proceedings. *American Indian and Alaska Native Mental Health Research, 10*(2), 1–7. doi:10.5820/aian.1002.2001.ed PMID:11698986

Zaid, Y., & Abioye, A. (2010). Museums, libraries and archives: Collaborating for the preservation of heritage materials in Nigeria. *African Research & Documentation*, 59–70.

Zapf, H. (2008). Literary ecology and the ethics of texts. *New Literary History, 39*(4), 847–868. doi:10.1353/nlh.0.0066

Zapico, F., Aguilar, C. H., Eroy, M., Marie, J. R., Barbosa, D. S., & Banisil, S. R. (2014). Morpho-agronomic variability and gxe interactions of manila hemp (musa textilis l. Née) genotypes grown in varying agro-ecozones in Southern Mindanao, Philippines. *International Journal of Agronomy and Agricultural Research, 4*(2), 12–20.

Zeng, D. Z. (2016). *Multi-Facility Economic Zones in Zambia: Progress, challenges and possible interventions*. Centre of Structural Economics Perking University.

Zhou, Y., Ma, X., Ji, D., Heerink, N., Shi, X., & Liu, H. (2018). Does property rights integrity improve tenure security? Evidence from China's forest reform. *Sustainability, 10*(6), 1956. doi:10.3390u10061956

Zorc, R. D. (1986). The genetic relationships of Philippine languages. In *FOCAL II: Papers from the Fourth International Conference on Austronesian Linguistics* (pp. 147-173). Canberra: Department of Linguistics, Research School of Pacific Studies, Australian National University.

About the Contributors

Robin Throne, PhD, is a research methodologist and dissertation supervisor for the University of the Cumberlands. Her research agenda continues to consider doctoral researcher positionality and agency, and voice and land dispossession from various social justice research approaches. She is the author of *Autoethnography and Heuristic Inquiry for Doctoral-Level Researchers: Emerging Research and Opportunities* (IGI Global, 2019), editor of *Practice-Based and Practice-Led Research for Dissertation Development* (IGI Global, 2021), and a non-indigenous researcher/member of the Gullah Geechee Cultural Heritage Corridor Commission Research Consortium.

* * *

John-Paul Chalykoff, Instructor, American Indian & Indigenous Studies / Linguistics and Germanic, Slavic, Asian & African Languages, is a graduate of Algoma University / Shingwauk Kinoomaage Gamig in Sault Ste Marie, Ontario, where he completed a Bachelor of Arts in Anishinaabemowin. He went on to complete a Bachelor of Education from Lakehead University in Thunder Bay, Ontario, with qualifications to teach Native Studies and History. He completed additional qualifications to teach Ojibwe and French as Second Languages. In addition to being an Ontario Certified Teacher in Good Standing through the Ontario College of Teachers, he holds a Master of Education from Lakehead University. His academic interests are Ojibwe / Anishinaabe language revitalization, second language teaching / acquisition, Anishinaabe history / history of the Great Lakes region, Indigenous Studies, and finding ways to combine music, language, and education. One of his main focuses while working on his Master of Education was writing new and original Ojibwe children songs. Chalykoff is Ojibwe / Anishinaabe from Michipicoten First Nation, and French Canadian.

Roy Alexander Chileshe is an Associate Professor at the Copperbelt University in Zambia. He is a former Dean of the School of the Built Environment. His key research interest is land tenure and livelihoods. He has published in a number of renowned journals.

Delmo Dulay is a T'boli. He is currently pursuing his MA in Anthropology degree in Ateneo de Davao University. Mr. Dulay is a school teacher whose advocacy is the promotion and preservation of their culture. He desires to continue the legacy of his late grandmother who is considered as a national artist of the country.

Emmanuel Villoria Hernani is the current Chair of the Research Ethics Committee of Cebu Normal University. He is an associate professor of the said university teaching in the undergraduate and graduate studies. He has been in countless academic in the Philippines and abroad as a presenter and participants on topics related to gestalt therapy, psycho-legal issues and mental wellness and wellbeing.

Ma Rosita Ampoyas Hernani is the current chair of the Kinesthetics Department of Cebu Normal University. As a researcher, physical education and dance advocate, she has been into countless academic conferences in the Philippines and abroad.

Niraj Jain is a Senior lecturer of land economy at the Copperbelt University in Zambia. His research interests are mainly inclined towards land tenure security with emphasis on customary land holding. He has published in a number of renowned journals.

Kirsten Koenig, PhD, is an outpatient therapist for Western Montana Mental Health Center.

Jacob Lauritzen is a high school teacher and an adjunct English professor in rural Arizona.

Marcello Messina is a Sicilian composer and academic based in João Pessoa, Paraíba, Brazil. He holds a PhD in composition from the University of Leeds (UK), and is currently Professor Visitante Estrangeiro at the Universidade Federal da Paraíba. He has been recipient of the Endeavour Research Fellowship at Macquarie University, Sydney, Australia, and of the PNPD/Capes post-doctoral bursary at the Universidade Federal do Acre, Brazil.

Ephraim Kabunda Munshifwa is an Associate Professor and Dean of the School of the Built Environment at the Copperbelt University in Zambia. His research focus is on the application of institutional economics to land and real estate, particularly to land and property rights, formal and informal real estate markets and land policy and governance.

Anthony Mushinge is a Lecturer at Department of Real Estate Studies, Copperbelt University since 2012. He has practised with G.S. Chiyanda Property Consultants (Pty) Ltd., D.W. Zyambo and Associates and Anderson, and Anderson International Property Consultants as a private real estate consultant. Anthony is a licenced valuation surveyor and member of Surveyors Institute of Zambia. His research interest is customary and statutory land governance, environmental management, and corruption in the land sector. He has published various papers in real estate related issues.

Elizabeth Peralez, PhD, is an Associate Professor at Colorado Technical University. She earned her Ph.D. in Education from Capella University. Her research centered on the resiliency of Native American students earning a degree at a tribal college in New Mexico. As a Native American scholar, she continues researching Native American education. Dr. Peralez has a Masters Certificate in College Teaching and has been teaching at CTU since July of 2000 and is currently teaching doctoral education courses. She considers it a privilege to teach. She has presented at the IT Summit, an executive technology conference, on the value of employees with doctoral degrees. She is a native of Colorado a member of the Piro-Manso-Tiwa Tribe from Pueblo de Las Cruces in New Mexico.

Thomas James Reed is a member of the Oneida Nation, an adjunct professor in American Indian Studies at California State University of Long Beach, and is a PhD student at the University of San Diego studying Leadership and Organizational Consulting.

Melanie Shaw has spent the past decade teaching and serving as an administrator in online higher education settings. She is the Assistant Dean, Dissertation Faculty in the School of Education at Northcentral University. She also serves as an adjunct faculty at several institutions and facilitates webinars for the Online Learning Consortium. In addition to her teaching roles, she trains faculty to develop and deliver courses online, conducts research on topics related to nontraditional education, and is involved in strategic leadership relative to the vision for online education. Melanie received a Ph.D. in Education with a specialization in Curriculum and Teaching from Northcentral University, a master's degree in Education Administration from Grand Canyon University, and a second master's degree in School Counseling for the University of West Alabama. She received her bachelor's degree in Liberal Studies and Music from Excelsior College. She holds teaching certificates in online teaching, elementary education, and guidance counseling.

Paul Shaw grew up in Millville, New Jersey. He earned a Bachelor of Science degree in music and American history from Excelsior College. He also earned a Professional Certification in jazz arranging from the Berklee School of Music. He earned a Master's of Music from New York University and is currently pursuing a Doctorate of Philosophy from Union Institute & University. Paul retired from the United States Air Force after serving a 20 year career as a musician. From 2013-2016, Paul served at the Air Force Academy as an Academy Military Trainer. He also served as Assistant Director of the Cadet Drum and Bugle Corps, Director of the Cadet Jazz Band, and as commissioning education faculty. Paul has written music and lyrics for over 60 songs and has authored two drum instruction books. He is married to Dr. Melanie Shaw and has two adult children, Carly and Rebekah.

Jairo Souza is a Lecturer in English at the Federal University of Acre.

Anna Erzsebet Szucs is a PhD candidate at the Foreign Languages and Literature Department of National Sun Yat-sen University, Taiwan. She received her Masters double degree in Communication and Hungarian Literature at University of Szeged in her home country, Hungary. Her research focuses on contemporary indigenous literature. While working on her dissertation, Szucs is a part-time lecturer in two prominent Taiwanese universities.

T. Anantha Vijayah is an assistant professor and teaches the English language and literature. His research and teaching interests include postcolonial literature, indigenous literature, and culture studies.

Index

O

P

Q

R

S

T

U

V

W

Z